MODERN BRAZIL

Manchete from Pictorial
Brasília

MODERN BRAZIL
New Patterns and Development

Edited by John Saunders

UNIVERSITY OF FLORIDA PRESS
Gainesville / 1971

A University of Florida Press Book

The type for the text of this book
is ten-point Janson. Initials are
Delphian and the chapter heads are
Bembo number 405.

*This book is dedicated
to the memory of*

*Hélcio Martins
Arthur Neiva
Anisio Teixeira
and
Arthur Weiss*

*each of whom in his own way
helped build Modern Brazil*

Introduction

Brazil ranks among the few nations of the world which have the potential for the achievement of major power status within the next century. In the contemporary world the basic requirements for such status are a large national territory, a large population, and high levels of technology and industrial production, whose concomitant is the consumption of massive amounts of energy. Brazil presently meets two of these three basic requirements.

Brazil's territory comprises about one-half of the entire South American continent, exceeds in size the continental United States less Alaska, and is only somewhat smaller than Europe including the European portion of the Soviet Union. Its rapidly growing population ranks among the largest in the world, being smaller only than those of China, India, the United States, Russia, Pakistan, and Japan. Brazil's population is larger than that of any African, Latin American, or European nation, excluding Russia.

It is in the areas of technology and industrial and agricultural development that Brazil lags behind the leading powers, and it is in these areas that the task of reaching and overtaking them will be the most arduous. Yet, rapid advances are being made. Industrial production since the Second World War has grown many-fold. Brazil has become, since that time, self-sufficient in virtually every category of manufacturing and industrial products. Substantial new sources of energy, particularly hydroelectric, have been created, and industrial production is now a major sector of the economy. It is, indeed, no longer accurate to speak of Brazil, as a whole, as an underdeveloped country. The southern states, in particular, have achieved levels of development that require more careful characterization, while the northeastern states unquestionably deserve that designation.

It is not, however, solely in the urban-industrial area that national development is reflected. Gains have been made in education and in agriculture, and the interior spaces are beginning to fill up as a consequence of an expanding road network, particularly stretching out in every direction from the new capital city. The bases of social mobility have been transformed by social change so as to conform more closely to the requirements of an industrialized and urban society. Societal patterns are being transformed; the organization of rural life and agriculture changed; legal, educational, and other institutions developed; and the arts and literature are acquiring new prominence not only within the nation but internationally.

Consequently, even though the industrial and technological levels of Brazil still compare unfavorably with those of fully modernized industrial countries, significant changes are occurring in Brazilian society which are raising those levels, fostering development in general, and transforming Brazil into a modern nation.

In the following pages, a distinguished group of scholars from both Brazil and the United States explores these and other aspects of the emergence of Brazil as a modern nation and analyzes the physical and demographic bases upon which it must depend.

July, 1970   JOHN SAUNDERS

Contents

Chapter 1

The Modernization of Brazilian Society

John Saunders

ODERNIZATION in the context of this chapter means the transformation of an underdeveloped society into one which shares certain common basic characteristics with the developed nations of the world.* It refers to extensive social change which cuts across the entire fabric of society and which proceeds in a given direction. It involves far-reaching modifications in social institutions, and a contemporary urban rather than a traditional rural way of life. The development of economic, educational, and political institutions (in the broad sense of this term) is at the roots of this transformation. Changes in these institutions in turn affect the other major social institutions, the family and religion. Thus the entire social structure and culture are transformed over a period of time. Two processes are among the principal effects and, simultaneously, are causes of these changes. These are social differentiation and cultural integration.

Modernization produces an increasingly more complex society. The development of societal structures necessary for the provision of the multitude of services, and the attainment of new and expanded goals which permit high levels of living for the population as a whole, and the development and application of sophisticated industrial, educational, bureaucratic, and organizational technologies inevitably imply an increasing division of labor and accentuated social differentiation.

The cultural integration of the population as a whole into more universal national patterns develops concurrently, as means of transportation are expanded, as the geographical mobility of the population increases, as the influence of more numerous and larger urban centers reaches out into rural

* Grateful acknowledgment is made to the U.S. Office of Education for a faculty research grant awarded through the Center for Latin American Studies of the University of Florida, which made possible the research on which this study is based.

1

areas, as literacy rates increase, as mass communications of all kinds become more widely diffused and find national audiences, as political parties expand from their local and regional spheres of influence and become national in character—as, in essence, a common national life is formed into which an ever-increasing share of the population is drawn, reducing the acute differences among members of the society that were the result of geographic and social isolation, sharp rural-urban, educational and regional differences, widespread status differentials, and highly unequal access to the means of upward social mobility.

Modernization, furthermore, has a regenerative quality in that in an increasingly differentiating and expanding society new positions carrying relatively high status are constantly being created. Occupants of these positions frequently must be recruited from a lower social stratum and, through what might be termed a process of social promotion, in that statuses are achieved rather than ascribed, come to occupy higher status positions. Upward social mobility and especially a growing middle class that recruits its members from the lower classes are characteristic of modernizing societies.

The foregoing gives some idea of the changes involved in the transformation of society here referred to as "modernization." Let us now examine underdeveloped societies from the standpoint of an ideal type to which Brazil conforms increasingly less with the passage of time.

The one unifying common denominator of most underdeveloped societies is the concentration of land ownership.[1] This more than any other factor is responsible for the concentration of power in the hands of a small land-owning or land-based elite. Such a system of social organization in turn produces conditions which seriously retard modernization.

Economically the concentration of land ownership results in an extremely low average productivity among the members of the population as a whole, even though productivity in given areas of economic activity may be fairly high and even though productivity as measured by units of land, for example, may be high. Since the agriculture engaged in is labor-intensive and of a low technical order and since labor is abundant and cheap, investment by landowners in agricultural producers' goods and other forms of capital investment is limited, for it often offers no apparent economic gain. Average productivity is low, average incomes are low, the capacity to save is low, and capital is scarce.[2] The elite sees little reason for investing its

1. There are, of course, exceptions to this generalization, notably certain areas of Africa where a pastoral economy prevails. Nevertheless, much of Africa in which white agricultural colonization occurred, such as the Union of South Africa, Kenya, etc., is noted for the high degree of concentration of land ownership.

2. Nurkse expands this point into an economic model consisting of two vicious circles. Cf. *Problems of Capital Investment in Underdeveloped Areas* (New York: Oxford University Press, 1962), chapter 1.

savings in agriculture, and national markets are not favorable for large-scale industrial or manufacturing enterprises, because of low per capita incomes. Consequently, the elite invests these savings abroad, thus contributing to the development of nations other than its own. Frequently agricultural wages are spent in their entirety before they have been earned. This restricts commercial activities and also contributes to a low investment incentive. Land ownership per se becomes a highly valued means to legitimize wealth and status earned in commerce or industry. The economic exploitation of land frequently is a secondary consideration, at best.

On the sociological side of this coin, a society organized in this manner awards a low status and prestige ranking to any occupation involving manual work or commercial activity of a lower order. Thus, entrepreneurship tends to be stifled. Furthermore, the low social valuation of manual labor in turn results in a reluctance to invest in industrial apprenticeship and other training programs which might serve to create an efficient industrial labor force. Achievement of high social status is difficult, since most important statuses are in one way or another ascribed, or the roles to which they correspond restricted, by members of the elite to fulfillment by persons of their own social class.[3]

Specialization and the division of labor as compared with developed societies is embryonic, as are other forms of social differentiation, especially those associated with some of the principal social institutions, notably educational, governmental, and, of course, economic.

Major decisions become concentrated in the hands of a self-seeking elite. This elite defines its own best interests as residing either in the status quo or, at best, in a high degree of control over social change. Its actions, instead of stimulating change, tend to intensify existing social inequalities, thus producing tensions which pave the way for the adoption of drastic measures for achieving modernization.[4]

EDUCATION

Education probably is the social institution most basic to modernization, a point which needs no elaboration. Brazil has made impressive gains in this area, particularly in secondary and higher education, which impart the skills which are most relevant to modernization. The years since 1940 have

3. This general topic is discussed through the prism of Parson's pattern-variables in Bert F. Hoselitz, *Sociological Aspects of Economic Growth* (Free Press, 1960), pp. 30–60, passim.
4. Hoselitz, p. 44. For a more extensive discussion of these and other points in relation to the modernization of Latin America as a whole, see John V. D. Saunders, *Social Factors in Latin American Modernization*, Vanderbilt University, Graduate Center for Latin American Studies, Occasional Paper no. 5 (Nashville, 1965).

witnessed far-reaching changes in the extent to which secondary and higher education are available to the population.[5]

The Historical Perspective

During the colonial and early republican periods an educational system appropriate to an elitist, static society was developed. The cornerstone of the implicit educational policy instituted by the Empire and continued by the early Republicans was denial of access to the higher educational levels to members of the lower social classes. This was accomplished by the development of a dual educational system, particularly at the secondary level. One-half, the vocational secondary school, was oriented toward the so-called popular masses and the provision of minimal educational and artisanship skills. The other half, the academic secondary school, which granted access to the faculties of higher learning, was oriented toward the training of an elite whose major function was the maintenance of the existing social order and the preparation of individuals to assume the higher-ranking positions in the social structure. Access to academic secondary schools and, hence, to higher education was denied the less-privileged classes by the simple expedient of withholding public support to secondary schools, so that, in 1929, 96.4 per cent of all secondary schools in Brazil were private institutions charging tuition.[6] Higher education was, therefore, restricted almost exclusively to the elite.

Beginning particularly in the 1920's the state-supported educational systems, both primary and vocational (especially normal schools), were captured by a developing middle class. The normal school, intended as a vocational secondary school to prepare girls as primary teachers, had already become a prestigious training ground for the daughters of middle-class families. Public primary schools, at first intended to provide a minimum educational foundation for the masses, became transformed by the social and educational aspirations of the middle class into selective schools, whose aim was the preparation of the student for entrance exams into secondary academic institutions and, eventually, into institutions of higher learning. The rapid growth of the middle class created enormous pressures for the expansion of academic secondary institutions. Although the number of public secondary schools increased, these pressures were met mainly by the proliferation of private institutions, the bulk of which were run as profit-

5. This section has been adapted, in part, from John V. D. Saunders, "Education and Modernization in Brazil" in *The Shaping of Modern Brazil*, ed. Eric N. Baklanoff (Baton Rouge: Louisiana State University Press, 1969), pp. 109–41.

6. Departamento Nacional de Estatística, Ministério de Trabalho, Indústria e Comércio, *Estatística Intellectual do Brasil, 1927*, vol. 1 (Rio: Tipografia do Departamento Nacional de Estatística, 1951), p. 27.

making enterprises, offering, at a price the new middle class could afford to pay, academic instruction preparatory for university entrance examinations. In 1962 nearly two-thirds of secondary students were enrolled in private schools.[7]

Accessibility and Expansion

At least since the 1930's, secondary enrollments have increased at a rate well in excess of that of the population. This trend was especially accentuated from 1950 to 1964. During those years secondary enrollments rose by 251 per cent while the population grew by 54 per cent. Furthermore, as secondary education expands, so does the middle class, its prime beneficiary and principal source of support. This expansion in turn creates a further demand and resource base, producing a rapid cumulative effect. One reason why this cumulative effect is possible is the private character of most secondary schools, which are, therefore, directly dependent on that portion of the population that is most willing and able to contribute to their maintenance and has the most to gain by so doing. Thus the nation has, in effect, depended on the comparatively affluent classes to finance much of secondary education out of their own pockets while concentrating public funds in primary and higher education.

In spite of rapid enrollment gains, it is evident that this situation represents a severe limitation with regard to accessibility. In effect, secondary education is largely accessible only to those who can afford to pay the cost of privately supported instruction, while large numbers of students from the economically less-advantaged classes compete among themselves, and with children from more affluent homes as well, for the limited number of seats in the public secondary schools. As the society modernizes, it will depend increasingly on the skills and training received in the secondary schools, which are prerequisites to the development of the myriad of technical, secretarial, industrial, commercial, and other skills upon which it must count for the performance of services essential to the functioning of the overall structure. The limited accessibility of secondary education will need to be broadened for the modernization of Brazil to continue at an even pace.

Modern Versus Traditional Courses

Even though the catalog of ills that afflict Brazilian higher education is extensive, it is having a considerable impact on the society and its moderniza-

7. Instituto Brasileiro de Geografia e Estatística (IBGE), *Anuário Estatístico do Brasil, 1962* (Rio: Conselho Nacional de Estatística, 1962), p. 293. Future references to these volumes will be given as *Anuário, 19___.* The year of publication is the same as the date of the yearbook in every instance.

tion. Engineers, physicians, economists, and the rest are being graduated at an accelerated rate. Between 1940 and 1963 the number of graduates leaving institutions of higher learning increased from approximately 4,223 to 19,687, a gain of 366 per cent.[8] The number of students pursuing degrees in engineering, economic sciences, and the several disciplines included under phi-

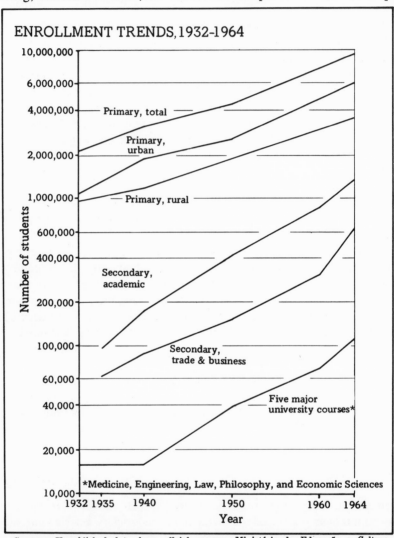

SOURCE: Unpublished data from official sources, Ministério da Educação e Cultura, Serviço Estatístico.

Figure 1. Enrollment Trends in Higher Education, 1932–1964

8. *Anuário, 1954*, p. 392; *1965*, p. 440.

losophy and science and letters, has risen sharply since 1932 (fig. 1). Law and medicine, the traditional studies of the upper class, have lost the undisputed supremacy they once possessed, and philosophy and science and letters, which in 1932 had a negligible enrollment, in 1964 enrolled more students than faculties of law. The big enrollment gains were made in those faculties which represent new approaches and are, to some extent, educational innovations. Furthermore, it was the specialized, nontraditional branches of engineering such as chemical, mechanical, and electrical rather than civil engineering that were responsible for virtually all of the enrollment increase in that field. Overall, enrollments in the five principal branches of higher learning increased by 608 per cent between 1940 and 1964.[9]

TABLE 1

ENROLLMENTS IN HIGHER EDUCATION BY FIELDS
OF STUDY AND PERCENT CHANGE, 1960–1964

Course of Study	Enrollment		Percent Change	Index Numbers
	1960	1964		
All courses	93,202	142,386	52.8	100.0
Philosophy; science & letters	20,418	32,396	58.7	111.2
Law	23,293	30,974	33.0	62.5
Engineering	10,821	20,701	91.3	172.9
Economics	7,934	14,360	81.0	153.4
Medicine	10,316	14,183	37.5	71.0
Dentistry	5,591	5,946	6.3	11.9
Agronomy	1,936	3,878	100.3	190.0
Social services	1,289	2,834	119.9	227.1
Administration	904	2,558	183.0	346.6
Architecture	1,589	2,448	54.1	102.5
Pharmacy	1,841	2,320	26.0	49.2
Art	2,813	2,219	— 26.8	— 50.8
Veterinary medicine	802	1,516	89.0	168.6
Nursing	1,624	911	— 78.3	—148.3
Others	2,031	5,142*	151.2	286.4

SOURCE: Serviço de Estatística da Educação e Cultura, *Sinopse Estatística do Ensino Superior, 1964* (Rio: Ministério da Educação e Cultura, 1965), p. ix (unnumbered).

* This datum appears as 5,102 in the source.

In the brief period from 1950 to 1964, enrollments in higher education expanded by more than one-half. The most rapid gains were made in engineering, economics, agronomy, social services, administration, and veterinary medicine (table 1). It is not supposed, however, that the shift (in the relative number of students enrolled) from traditional to modern courses is altogether a reflection of the changing values and career orientations of Brazilian youth. Rather, it is a consequence of a more rapid expansion in the

9. Data from official sources in the Ministério da Educação e Cultura, Serviço de Estatística, made available through the courtesy of Dr. Anisio Teixeira.

number of openings in higher learning among modern than among traditional courses, representing a choice forced upon students by those persons who are responsible for the planning of higher education. Medicine, for instance, attracted, in 1964, 22,151 candidates for admission to 3,036 openings, a ratio of 7.3 candidates per opening. During the same year 34 per cent of all applicants for admission to institutions of higher learning sought admission to law and medicine.[10] An applicant who is unsuccessful in gaining admission to one course of study frequently will take the exams for another the following year.

If we group philosophy, science and letters, law, civil engineering, and dentistry in the traditional category and non-civil engineering, economics, agronomy, social work, administration, and architecture in the modern category, the following shifts in the percentage of students enrolled in each group can be discerned between 1953 and 1964—a drop from 83.4 per cent to 67.9 per cent of the enrollment for traditional courses and an increase of 16.2 to 32.1 per cent of the enrollment for modern courses.[11] Yet, if we examine the choice of course as expressed by applications to take the entrance examinations for the several courses, we find 80 per cent of the applicants seeking admission to traditional courses of study and only 20 per cent attempting to gain admission to modern courses. There is, however, a notable exception to this generalization: specialized engineering (as opposed to civil) attracted, in 1964, 22,539 candidates for 5,318 openings, a ratio of 4.2 to 1,[12] a higher ratio by far than that for any other course of study except medicine. Applicants in specialized engineering outnumbered those in civil engineering by more than 10 to 1. The increasing demand for graduates in these fields and the high salaries being paid them are sufficient to override, for many applicants, the pressures favoring traditional career choices, a pattern that is likely to become more accentuated with the passage of time, as specialization, the division of labor, and industrial production increase.

THE RURAL-URBAN TRANSITION

The transition from a rural and agricultural society to one that is based on an urban and industrial foundation finds its most obvious and visible expression in the growth and multiplication of cities and in differential rates of growth over time between the urban and rural populations, favoring the former. The multiple sociological and economic implications of this transi-

---

10. Serviço Estatístico da Educação e Cultura, *Sinopse Estatística do Ensino Superior, 1964* (Rio: Ministério da Educação e Cultura, 1965), pp. 1–2.

11. *Sinopse Estatística, 1964*, p. xiii (unnumbered). These courses enroll over 90 per cent of university students.

12. *Sinopse Estatística, 1964*, pp. 1–2.

tion can best be evaluated against a background of knowledge of the degree, extent, and distribution of this pervading change in the residential composition of a nation's population.

Historical Trends in Regional Growth

Seven censuses spanning eighty-eight years have been taken in Brazil. The first, taken in 1872, when Brazil conformed, in many aspects, to the ideal type of a rural paternalistic and patriarchal society, yielded a count of some 10 million inhabitants. The last census, taken in 1970, enumerated a population of 92 million, a ninefold increase in the short span of time between them (fig. 2). Although all of Brazil's regions shared to a degree in the rapid growth of the national population, important shifts occurred in the distribution of the population by regions as a consequence of different growth rates among them.

The older, northeastern region of first occupancy and colonization, which inherited and sustained, through time, traditional patterns of agriculture, man-land relations, and the social organization instituted and developed during the Colonial period, resisted change and innovation to a greater extent than did the eastern and particularly southern regions, which experienced a more rapid rate of development, population growth, and urbanization. The southern region, principal destination of European immigration, outstripped the others at first in agricultural production and then in industrial development. Thus, its population, which was, in 1872, one-third that of the older eastern region and one-half that of the traditional northeastern region, was, in 1960, more than one and one-half times larger than that of the northeast and slightly exceeded that of the east. The northern, largely Amazonian, region, relying almost exclusively on a primitive agricultural economy consisting largely of gathering rather than cultivation, has likewise been overtaken, particularly since 1940, both in population and development by the west-central region, which is developing as the location of the new capital of Brasília and as a source of foodstuffs, notably beef, for the large urban populations of the adjacent southern and eastern regions.

The consequent shifts in the distribution of the regional populations in relation to the national population can be observed in figure 3. The south, which in 1872 contained only 16 per cent of the total population, increased its share to 35 per cent of the total in 1960, equalling the eastern region, which was proportionately three times larger in 1872, and surpassing by a considerable margin the northeast, which was proportionately twice as large in 1872. Of Brazil's five census regions, only the south consistently increased its share of the total during the period in question.

The relative disadvantage of the northeast is the result not only of slower growth rates but also of a decline in its rate of growth. It was the only region to experience a drop in its annual rate of increase between 1940 and 1960.

The growth rates for the south exceeded those of the other regions from 1940 to 1960, with the exception of the west-central region, which had the advantage of a small numerical base at the beginning of the period (1,258,679 inhabitants) so that the addition of small numbers produced large proportional gains. The probable continuation of present trends will result in the southern states completely overshadowing the remaining units of the

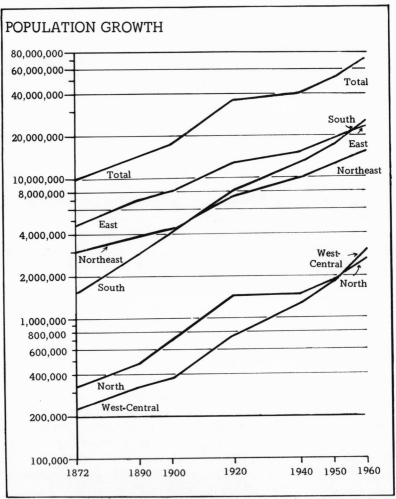

SOURCE: Instituto Brasileiro de Geografia e Estatística, *Anuário Estatístico do Brasil, 1964* (Rio: Conselho Nacional de Estatística, 1964), p. 30.

Figure 2. Population Growth by Regions, 1872–1960

republic not only in industrial output (heavy machinery, automotives, appliances, etc.), as at present, but also in numbers.

The Rural-Urban Growth Differential

Growth rates of the urban population substantially exceeded those of the rural population between 1940 and 1960. Furthermore, urban growth rates have increased very substantially while rural growth rates have experienced

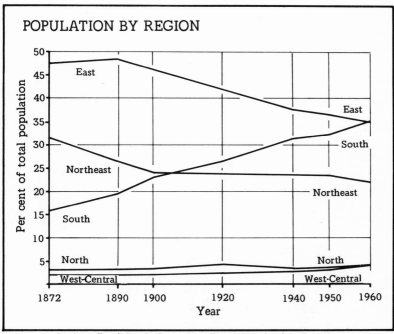

SOURCE: Instituto Brasileiro de Geografia e Estatística, *Anuário Estatístico do Brasil, 1964* (Rio: Conselho Nacional de Estatística, 1964), p. 30.

Figure 3. Per Cent of the Total Population in the Several Regions for Census Years 1872–1960

smaller increases or reductions. The national urban growth rate increased from 39 per 1,000 for 1940–1950 to 54 per 1,000 for 1950–1960. But the rural growth rate remained constant during both periods at only 16 (fig. 4). The east shows this same pattern although its rates of increase are somewhat lower.

The northeast, a chronically depressed region, has suffered a substantial rural exodus, reducing its rural growth rate. It was the only region to be so affected. The other regions showed gains between the two decades in both urban and rural rates of population increase although the gains in urban rates greatly exceeded those of the rural population. The extraordinary growth rate of the west-central region for 1950–1960 is largely due to a small base onto which was added the population of the newly created national capital.

The considerable differentials between the rates of increase of the urban and rural populations can best be observed with the aid of index numbers. During the 1950–1960 decade the national urban growth rate index (the nation = 100) stood at 180, while the rural index was only 53 and the urban rate was 3.4 times the rural rate. The greatest differentials so calculated oc-

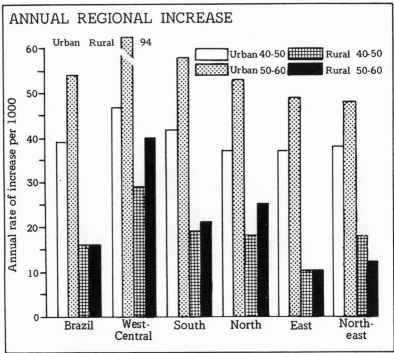

SOURCE: Instituto Brasileiro de Geografia e Estatística, *Anuário Estatístico do Brasil, 1963* (Rio: Conselho Nacional de Estatística, 1963), p. 32.

Figure 4. Annual Rates of Increase for the Nation and Its Regions, by Residence, 1940–1950 and 1950–1960

curred in the older northeastern and eastern regions. For all of the regions, the urban rates were at least twice as large as the rural ones. The regions that exceeded the national overall growth rates (north, south, and west-central) had the lowest differentials in urban-rural growth rates, all under 3; while the two regions with total rates of increase smaller than the national figure (northwest and east) had the highest differentials, both bordering on 5. This was principally because rural growth rates in the regions with low overall rates were relatively much lower than in regions with somewhat higher overall rates. Thus, it seems probable at this level of analysis that exceptionally heavy out-migration from rural areas is responsible for these very large differentials in the northeastern region, as well as for lower urban and overall rates, since there is no reason to assume significant differences in the rates of natural increase of the rural population of the several regions.

A concomitant of these trends is the proportion of the total increase in inhabitants which occurred in urban areas. Thus, although in both 1950 and 1960 the urban population was well under one-half of the total population, the increase in its numbers accounted for more than one-half of the overall increase.

The Urban Population's Increasing Share of the Total

The Brazilian census definition of "urban" is based, as is the case in several other Latin American censuses, on the administrative function of the locality. Thus, the population of the national capital, of capitals of states and territories, and of county and district seats are all included in the urban population regardless of size. Many of these localities are exceedingly small, so that the effect is to inflate the urban population through the inclusion, by definition, of inhabitants of localities that should more properly be considered as rural.

In order to alleviate this problem, the "urban population" has been defined in this paper as consisting of the residents of localities of 2,000 or more inhabitants and the figures arrived at by summation of the appropriate census data. A comparison of the figures thus obtained with the population classed as "urban" by the census reveals a numerical "inflation" of some 10 to 15 per cent in the census definition or a relative difference of approximately 5 percentage points.[13]

According to this criterion, the percentage of Brazil's population that is urban increased from 31 in 1950 to 40 in 1960, reflecting a rate of increase of 78 per cent for the decade (table 2). The east and south were by far the most urban regions, and the west-central, for reasons already noted, increased its urban population by the spectacular figure of 189 per cent.[14]

The Growth of Middle-Sized Cities

These data, however, merely reflect trends in total numbers. By breaking

13. IBGE, *VII Recenseamento Geral do Brasil, 1960. Sinopse Preliminar do Censo Demográfico* (Rio: Serviço Nacional de Recenseamento, 1961, 1962 [the several state volumes]), table 1.

14. *Sinopse Preliminar*, table 1.

down the urban population into size categories, trends in the distribution of the urban population among localities of different sizes may also be discerned. The west-central and northern regions, which contained 8 per cent of the national population in 1960 and a small urban population, have been excluded from this analysis (table 3).

TABLE 2

PER CENT OF THE POPULATION LIVING IN PLACES OF
2,000 OR MORE INHABITANTS, 1950 AND 1960, AND
PERCENT CHANGE, BY REGIONS, 1950–1960

Region	Per Cent of Total		Percent Change
	1950	1960	
Nation	31	40	78
North	25	33	83
Northeast	21	29	75
East	34	43	69
South	32	47	83
West-central	15	25	189

SOURCE: Instituto Brasileiro de Geografia e Estatística, *VII Recenseamento Geral do Brasil, 1960. Sinopse Preliminar do Censo Demográfico* (Rio: Serviço Nacional de Recenseamento, 1961, 1962 [the several state volumes]), passim.

TABLE 3

GROWTH OF URBAN CENTERS, 1950–1960, ACCORDING TO
THE SIZE OF THE CENTER IN 1950, FOR THE NATION
AND MAJOR REGIONS

Region and Size Category	Percent Change	Region and Size Category	Percent Change
Nation	63	East	55
2,000–4,999	54	2,000–4,999	48
5,000–9,999	69	5,000–9,999	69
10,000–49,999	85	10,000–49,999	89
50,000–99,999	73	50,000–99,999	77
100,000–249,999	66	100,000–249,999	40
250,000+	48	250,000+	39
Northeast	58	South	71
2,000–4,999	47	2,000–4,999	62
5,000–9,999	60	5,000–9,999	74
10,000–49,999	61	10,000–49,999	86
50,000–99,999	61	50,000–99,999	80
100,000–249,999	73	100,000–249,999	81
250,000+	54	250,000+	58

SOURCE: Instituto Brasileiro de Geografia e Estatística, *VII Recenseamento Geral do Brasil, 1960. Sinopse Preliminar do Censo Demográfico* (Rio: Serviço Nacional de Recenseamento, 1961, 1962 [the several state volumes]), passim.

Between 1950 and 1960 it was the middle-sized cities, from 5,000 to 100,000 inhabitants, that increased the most rapidly. This pattern was especially pronounced in the eastern region. In each of the three major regions the smallest increases occurred in the population of cities under 5,000 and 250,000 and over in 1950.

Certain centers defined here as "urban" increased their populations between 1950 and 1960 by 75 per cent or more, well in excess of the national rate, and are termed rapid-growth urban centers. Nearly one-third of all urban centers in existence in 1950 fell into this category, and nearly all were in the middle-sized range. Together they were responsible for nearly two-thirds of the total urban increase and doubled their population 1.2 times (table 4).

TABLE 4

RAPID-GROWTH URBAN CENTERS, RELATIVE AND ABSOLUTE NUMBERS AND
PERCENT GROWTH OF THEIR POPULATION, BY REGIONS AND
SELECTED STATES, 1950–1960

Region and State	All Urban Centers Number*	Rapid-Growth Urban Centers**			
		Number	Per Cent	Percent Increase in Popul.	Per Cent of Total Urban Increase
Nation	1,164	349	29	120	38
North	35	13	37	113	23
Northeast	257	45	17	126	22
East	423	108	25	114	44
Espírito Santo	17	10	58	178	51
South	409	160	39	122	40
Paraná	52	27	51	128	63
Santa Catarina	33	17	51	122	57
West-central	40	23	57	138	57
Mato Grosso	15	8	53	99	57
Goiás	25	15	60	172	57

SOURCE: Instituto Brasileiro de Geografia e Estatística, *VII Recenseamento Geral do Brasil, 1960. Sinopse Preliminar do Censo Demográfico* (Rio: Serviço National de Recenseamento, 1961, 1962 [the several state volumes]), passim.
* Places of 2,000 or more inhabitants in 1950.
** Seventy-five percent or more increase, 1950–1960.

Not surprisingly, the most rapidly urbanizing regions, the south and west-central, also had high proportions of rapid-growth centers. In the eastern states of Espírito Santo and the southern states of Paraná and Santa Catarina, and in the two states comprising the west-central region, more than half of the urban centers were rapid-growth centers, and they accounted for more than half of the urban population increase.

The Decline in Urban Primacy

Urban primacy, or the degree of concentration of the urban or the total population in the largest city or cities, has been noted as being characteristic of many rapidly urbanizing less-developed nations. This condition is accompanied by a substantial difference in the sizes of the largest and second-largest cities. The data for Brazil show an overall decline in the size difference between first- and second-rank cities of the several states, and also in the percentage of the urban population of the states that resides in the first- and second-rank cities (table 5).

This trend toward a decreasing concentration of the urban population is reflected in the trend in the proportion of the urban population living in small, middle-sized, and large cities (fig. 5). From 1940 to 1960 there was a consistent decline in the percentage of the urban population living in cities of 100,000 or more and in cities under 10,000, while cities of 10,000 to 100,000 inhabitants steadily increased their share of the total.

TABLE 5

URBAN PRIMACY. POPULATION OF THE FIRST- AND SECOND-RANK CITIES OF THE SEVERAL STATES, BY REGION, 1950 AND 1960

Region	Population of First-Rank Cities ÷ Population of Second-Rank Cities		Per Cent of Urban Population in First- and Second-Rank Cities	
	1950	1960	1950	1960
Nation	7.3	6.3	43	39
North	11.7	14.4	81	74
Northeast	5.7	4.7	52	48
East	6.3	4.7	30	27
South	7.5	8.1	46	40
West-central	1.7	2.1	43	38

SOURCE: Instituto Brasileiro de Geografia e Estatística, *VII Recenseamento Geral do Brasil. Sinopse Preliminar do Censo Demográfico* (Rio: Serviço Nacional de Recenseamento, 1961, 1962 [the several state volumes]), table 3.

Only the northeastern region offered a minor exception to this rule in that large cities retained their proportion of the total.

Urbanization and Modernization

Brazil is urbanizing at an accelerating rate. Rather than being concentrated in a small number of large cities, the resultant growth of the urban population is being felt to a greater extent in middle-sized cities. The rural population, on the other hand, has had much lower growth rates, so that urban growth has been, to a substantial degree, the result of net rural out-migration.

A rapid rural-urban transition is a characteristic of the process of modernization. It may reflect the shift from an agricultural to an industrial base, effect a reorientation in ways of life, attitudes, and values, and is a valuable adaptive mechanism. On the other hand, it may also be the result of serious discontinuities between the urban and rural sectors of the economy. Greatly limited employment opportunities in agriculture and other rural enterprises; rising expectations of the rural populace, which have no chance of being realized within the context of existing patterns of man-land relations; and the promise, frequently unfulfilled, of higher incomes and better educational

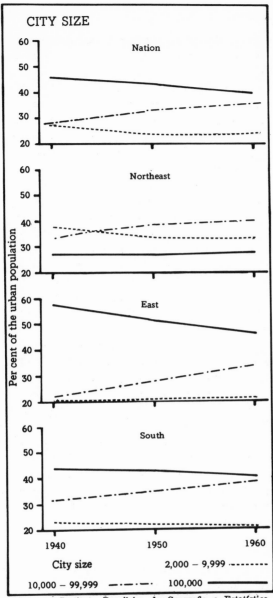

Figure 5. Per Cent of Urban Population in Cities of Stated Size Categories, for the Nation and Its Major Regions, 1940, 1950, and 1960

opportunities and health services in the cities can stimulate rural-urban migration, which simply represents the transfer of a social pathology from a rural to an urban environment.

The extent to which this massive displacement of the rural population represents a desirable adaptation to a modernizing process of rural-urban transition or merely reflects serious maladjustments in rural life, matched by the inability of urban occupations to absorb the flood of rural migrants, is difficult to evaluate. That the latter is true for a percentage of the migrants is attested by the growth of Rio's *favelas*, Bahia's *mocambos*, Recife's *alagados*, and so on. Unemployment and underemployment have probably increased in several of Brazil's major cities. Because of the high visibility of the "marginal" populations in these urban centers, they have attracted wide attention. Yet these migrants to large cities, mainly located in Brazil's underdeveloped regions, do not represent a majority of the total number. The growth of urban centers having fewer than 100,000 inhabitants was responsible for approximately one-half of the total increase in the urban population. Furthermore, approximately one-half of the total increase took place in Brazil's most developed region, the south, and in its most rapidly developing region, the west-central.

The southern region, in particular, has demonstrated its ability to profitably absorb great numbers of migrants originating both from internal migration and immigration. The west-central region has grown rapidly, attracting migrants not only to the recently built new capital of Brasília but also to an expanding agricultural economy that supplies eastern and especially São Paulo markets. The urban industrial expansion in the southern region, and most notably São Paulo, has been great. The rapid development of the western agricultural frontier of the state of Paraná was in large measure responsible for the accelerated growth of the larger urban centers in that area, such as Londrina, and the appearance of a considerable number of new urban centers in 1960. It is most likely that a large percentage of the growth of cities does in fact reflect modernizing forces.

AGRICULTURE

Resistance to the modernization of Brazilian agriculture is probably greater than that to any other segment of the economy or society. Patterns of man-land relations remained essentially the same between 1950 and 1960, and there is no reason to believe that significant changes have occurred since 1960. There were during the fifties some reductions in the per cent of land under cultivation held in large holdings, of land in farms held in large holdings and of farms of large size, accompanied by corresponding relative increases in the smaller size categories (fig. 6). But, barring large-scale agrarian reform programs, substantial changes in existing patterns of man-land relations are not to be expected, and the potential for modernization which such a change in rural social organization could create will remain unrealized.

In other respects, however, notably the use of tractors, considerable gains were made (table 6). Between 1950 and 1960 the number of tractors in Brazil increased by 658 per cent and the ratio of tractors to agricultural

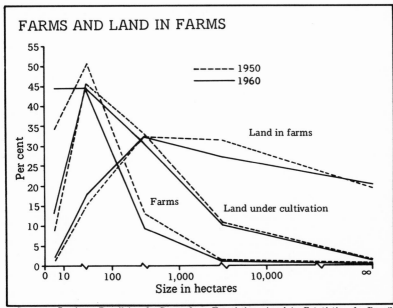

FARMS AND LAND IN FARMS

SOURCE: Instituto Brasileiro de Geografia e Estatística, *Anuário Estatístico do Brasil, 1964* (Rio: Conselho Nacional de Estatística, 1964), pp. 66–67.

Figure 6. Per Cent of Farms and of Land in Farms and of Land under Cultivation, in Given Size Categories, 1950 and 1960

workers increased fivefold. These implements were, however, heavily concentrated in the southern region, where, in 1960, 80 per cent of the tractors in use were to be found; more than two-fifths of all the tractors in use were located in the state of São Paulo.

Dual Technology

A number of factors in addition to these related to patterns of man-land relations serve to inhibit, although not prohibit, the modernization of Brazilian agricultural practices.[15] Foremost among these are the consequences

15. See T. Lynn Smith, *Brazil, People and Institutions,* rev. ed. (Baton Rouge: Louisiana State University Press, 1963), chapters 13 and 14, for a discussion of pertinent aspects of man-land relations.

of a dual technology in the agricultural sector, especially noticeable in southern Brazil, and of high prices for modern agricultural inputs, in combination with low prices for many agricultural products.[16]

Both advanced agricultural technology and traditional labor-intensive agricultural practices are to be found in many regions of Brazil. Production practices used by traditional farmers result in a situation of efficient allocation of the production factors involved (given their technological level), so that no increases in yields can be obtained through a more efficient allocation of these factors of production. Production can only be substan-

TABLE 6

NUMBER OF TRACTORS, RELATIVE AND ABSOLUTE, PERCENT CHANGE
AND NUMBER OF TRACTORS PER 10,000 AGRICULTURAL WORKERS
BY REGION AND SELECTED STATES, 1950–1960

Region	Number of Tractors		Per Cent of Total		Percent Change	Tractors per 10,000 Agricultural Workers	
	1950	1960	1950	1960	1950–1960	1950	1960
Nation	8,372	63,493	100.0	100.0	658	8	41
North	61	266	0.7	0.4	351	2	5
Northeast	324	2,318	3.9	3.6	615	1	5
East	1,463	7,785	17.5	12.2	432	4	17
Minas Gerais	763	5,024	9.1	7.9	559	4	24
South	6,385	50,821	76.3	80.0	696	18	105
São Paulo	3,819	28,101	47.0	43.9	636	25	167
Paraná	280	4,996	3.3	7.8	1,684	6	39
S. Catarina	41	1,049	0.5	1.7	2,459	1	17
R. G. do Sul	2,245	16,675	26.8	26.1	643	21	131
West-central	139	2,303	1.7	3.6	1,557	4	34

SOURCE: Instituto Brasileiro de Geografia e Estatística, *Anuário Estatístico do Brasil, 1963* (Rio: Conselho Nacional de Estatística, 1963), p. 58.

tially increased by shifting cultivation to new areas of fertile soil which render high yields through the use of traditional production factors.

The shift to modern agricultural practices and inputs is inhibited by the high cost of the latter relative to the price of the product and to alternative behaviors. Thus, for instance, the cost in Brazil of 100 pounds of phosphate fertilizer was 4.93 times that obtainable for 100 pounds of rice. The same ratio in the United States for the same period (1960–1961) was 1.13. Likewise, a medium-sized tractor cost the equivalent, in Brazil, of 150 monthly minimum wages, while in the United States the cost was that of 15 monthly minimum wages. Thus, the Brazilian farmer had to make a saving in labor (considering this factor alone) 10 times greater than his United States counterpart in order to be compensated for the cost of the machine. This has

16. The analysis that follows is largely derived from Ruy Miller Paiva, "Possibilities of Modernizing Brazilian Agriculture," mimeographed (lecture delivered at the University of Florida, October 1965).

been further aggravated in recent years by inflationary pressures which have brought about more rapid increases in the cost of modern inputs than in prices obtained by farmers for their products. Under these conditions the cost per unit of many agricultural products is at least as high when they are cultivated with modern as when they are cultivated with traditional methods.

Modern methods become economically feasible under special circumstances, such as when the crop or livestock cannot be produced except by

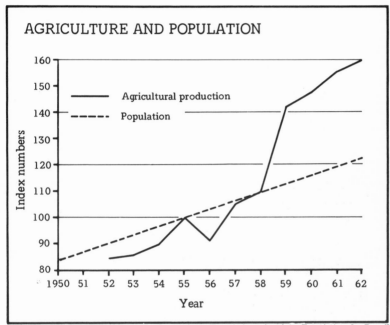

SOURCE: Instituto Brasileiro de Geografia e Estatística, *Anuário Estatístico do Brasil, 1963* (Rio: Conselho Nacional de Estatística, 1963), p. 58.

Figure 7. Agricultural Production and Population, Index Numbers 1950–1962 (1955 = 100)

the application of modern inputs and large urban markets demand those products and pay high prices for them; or, when production by traditional methods of cultivation is insufficient to satisfy the demand for a product, resulting in a rise in prices which makes the use of modern inputs feasible, providing incentives for modernization. This situation is likely to persist until industry becomes more efficient and able to offer modern inputs at relatively lower prices.

In spite of the various factors which militate against the modernization of Brazilian agriculture, food production has increased more rapidly than the population, and the proportion of the labor force employed in agriculture has decreased, while other sectors of the economy have claimed larger shares of the available manpower (figs. 7 and 8). In addition, food consumption has risen at a rate in excess of that of the growth of the population.[17] An examination of the percent change in different occupational

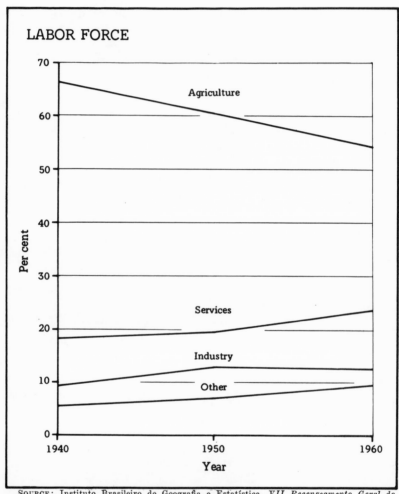

SOURCE: Instituto Brasileiro de Geografia e Estatística, *VII Recenseamento Geral do Brasil. Resultados Preliminares*, Série Especial 2 (Rio: Serviço National de Recenseamento, 1965): 3.

Figure 8. Per Cent of Labor Force Employed in Agriculture, Services and Industry, 1940, 1950, 1960

17. See "Indices Econômicos Nacionais," *Conjuntura Econômica* 20, no. 1 (Janeiro 1966): 89.

categories from 1940–1960 underscores the rapid shift from rural to urban employment. While, during that period, the percent increase in the labor force employed in agriculture, fishing, and forestry was 18.2, increases in the labor force engaged in urban occupations ranged from 82 to 198.8 per cent, or from 4 to 10 times more (table 7).

TABLE 7

PERCENT CHANGE IN THE NUMBER OF PERSONS IN THE LABOR FORCE
BY OCCUPATIONAL CATEGORY, 1940–1960

Occupational Category	Percent Change 1940–1960[d]
TOTAL[a]	53.5
Agriculture, fishing, forestry	18.2
Extractive industries	46.8
Manufacturing and processing[b]	82.0
Construction	198.8
Wholesale and retail trade[c]	102.9
Transportation, communication, warehousing	117.7
Services	90.1
Other	163.8

SOURCE: Instituto Brasileiro de Geografia e Estatística, *Anuário Estatístico do Brasil, 1965* (Rio: Conselho Nacional de Estatística, 1965), p. 35.

a. The inactive population was subtracted from the total in order to provide an approximation of the labor force concept. Population, ten years old and over.
b. "Indústrias de transformação."
c. "Comércio de mercadorias."
d. Based on a 1.27 percent sample of census schedules.

TRANSPORTATION AND COMMUNICATION

The great expansion of generally available means of mass communications has created, for the first time in Brazil, audiences which approach a national scale. The transistor radio, in Brazil as elsewhere, has become a common possession of urban populations and has penetrated into many rural areas as well. The small cost of these receivers has placed them within reach of many, if not most, minimum-wage earners and, of course, within reach of the more affluent income earners as well. Between 1950 and 1964 the ratio of radio receivers to total population dropped from 1 receiver per 20 inhabitants to 1 receiver per 10 inhabitants and presently is no doubt even smaller.[18] Television sets, although still largely concentrated in the principal cities of the southern region, numbered 2,300,000 in 1964.[19] The number of radio stations has increased at an extremely rapid rate (fig. 9) and now exceeds 1,000, which blanket virtually the entire population. In 1963 the cir-

18. *United Nations Statistical Yearbook, 1965* (New York: United Nations, 1966), p. 733.
19. *United Nations Statistical Yearbook, 1965*, p. 733.

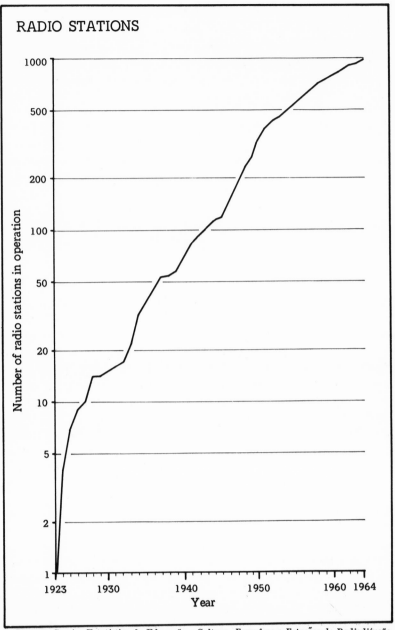

RADIO STATIONS

SOURCE: Serviço Estatístico da Educação e Cultura, *Emprêsas e Estações de Radiodifusão e Radiotelevisão em 31/XII/64* (Rio: Ministério da Educação e Cultura, 1965), passim.

Figure 9. Number of Radio Stations in Operation, 1923–1964

culation of periodical publications, other than newspapers, most of which were published on a monthly, bi-monthly, or weekly basis, was 15,631,548, or approximately 1 issue per 5 inhabitants, and 4,010 books were published.[20]

One of the most impressive developments in recent years has been the enormous growth of passenger bus traffic. The completion of many paved highways has contributed to low-cost modern bus transportation which joins the nation in an extensive network over which 811 interstate bus lines operated in 1963. From 1953 to 1964 the number of miles of highway increased by 61 per cent.[21] Large bus terminals constructed in major cities have been outgrown by the unexpectedly rapid increase in passenger traffic. The cost of tickets is such as to place bus travel generally within the means of much of the population, so that domestic servants in Rio and São Paulo can spend their vacations visiting their families in northeastern Brazil, making the trip by bus.

The personal automobile is becoming a symbol of middle-class rather than upper-class status and is taken for granted much as are refrigerators and television sets. The number of passenger vehicles, largely manufactured in Brazil, increased from 360,715 in 1953 to 894,846 in 1962, and production exceeded 200,000 units in 1966,[22] representing an increase in the number of passenger vehicles per 100 population of from 6.3 to 11.9. The personal mobility which this has conferred has not only crowded the highways and aggravated rush-hour traffic congestion, but has also, in conjunction with a greatly expanded road system, brought all of Brazil within reach of the personal experience of middle-class Brazilians and made auto touring a major form of recreation.

These developments in transportation and communication are breaking down the geographical and psychological isolation of many years and enabling Brazilians to view their nation as an interdependent unity to an extent that has not been possible in the past. A truly national political party now seems possible, as does the development of a national public opinion and consensus.

DIFFERENTIAL MODERNIZATION

The several regions and states of Brazil have modernized at different rates. The southern region, and within it the state of São Paulo, has modernized far more rapidly than the remainder of the nation. This has been reflected in long-run gains in practically every significant economic and social index. It is not inappropriate to speak of southern Brazil as a developed if not modernized area, although this process has not proceeded as far as in North

20. *Anuário, 1965*, pp. 452, 458.
21. *Anuário, 1965*, pp. 246, 253; *1954*, p. 181.
22. *Anuário, 1954*, p. 182; *1965*, p. 252.

America or Western Europe. It contained, in 1960, 35 per cent of the population. At the other extreme is the northeastern region, one of the less developed areas of the world, which in 1960 was the residence of 22.1 per cent of all Brazilians. The eastern region, also with 35 per cent of Brazil's inhabitants, occupies an intermediate position closer to that of the south than of the northeast. Only 8 per cent of the population lives in the very large and sparsely inhabited northern and west-central regions.

This section is mainly concerned with a comparison between the northeastern and southern regions. The northeastern region has been recognized as Brazil's major problem area for some decades. It is the region which most closely fits the model of underdevelopment presented above. This has not always been the case. During most of the nineteenth century, the northeast was as fully developed, by the standards of those times, as was the south. During the present century, especially, the south began to develop rapidly and outdistance the northeast. This development is a corollary of the transition from the traditional to the modern and from rural to urban economic and social patterns. The major thrust of the forces producing this change has been felt in the southern region. The influence of these changes has spread from an epicenter in São Paulo, south to the states of Paraná and Rio Grande do Sul, especially, and north notably into Minas Gerais.

This rapid impulse toward modernization bypassed the northeastern region almost entirely. Consequently, it is now difficult to find an index of development which, when used to compare the two regions, shows the northeast in a favorable light. A series of such indices is presented in table 8. With only one exception, the various educational, demographic, and economic indices presented reveal considerable disparities between the two regions, favoring the south. It would be possible to greatly extend this list by citing per capita income figures, industrial production, mortality from infections and contagious diseases, sanitation, literacy, and so on. A reflection of the differential modernization of the two regions, and especially of the notable development of the southern region, is the increasing share of the total population which has become concentrated in the south since the first census was taken in 1872, in spite of rates of natural increase of the population which were probably as high if not higher in the northeast. Southern industry, which now produces a great number of "made in Brazil" industrial goods, from transistor radios to automobiles and large-tonnage ocean-going ships, has created, directly and indirectly, the economic differentials which spell opportunities for many hundreds of thousands of internal migrants in search of a better life.

However, it should be noted that the northeast is not a problem because of its underdevelopment per se. It is the differential between it and the rest of the nation, particularly the south, which has created a problem, for the

TABLE 8

THE NATION, SOUTH, AND NORTHEAST
COMPARED, SELECTED FIGURES

	Nation	South	Northeast	Index Numbers (South = 100)	
				Nation	Northeast
Per capita expenditure on education (*cruzeiros*)[1]	433	722	85	60	12
School (over) enrollment factor, first grade[2]	355	312	433	114	139
Percent increase in secondary school enrollment, 1950–1960[3]	111.2	112.2	139.8	99	125
Per cent of children 7–11 years old attending school, 1960[4]					
Urban population	81.0	83.4	78.5	97	94
Rural population	51.4	64.6	37.3	80	58
Per cent of primary school enrollment enrolled in first grade[5]	52.2	42.9	66.7	122	155
Per cent of the population 10–19 years old attending secondary schools, 1960[6]	7.5	10.5	3.9	71	37
Percent increase in the population, 1950–1960[7]					
Total	36.6	46.4	25.5	79	55
Urban	70.3	77.3	61.2	91	79
Rural	17.5	24.1	11.3	73	47
Infant mortality rate[8]					
Recife (1948–1950)			243.6		283
São Paulo (município) (1946–1948)		86.1			
Tractors per 10,000 agricultural workers, 1960[9]	41	105	5	39	5
Per cent of the labor force, 1960, engaged in[10]					
agriculture, fishing, forestry		44.6	65.9		148
manufacturing and processing		13.2	6.0		45
construction		3.8	1.8		47
transportation and communication		5.6	2.9		52
Per cent of land in farms in holdings of 10,000 or more hectares, 1960[11]	19.9	5.8	8.8	343	152

1. Instituto Brasileiro de Geografia e Estatística, *Anuário, 1961, 1965*, pp. 383 and 32–33, respectively.
2. *Anuário, 1964*, pp. 339–40.
3. Instituto Brasileiro de Geografia e Estatística, *Censo Demográfico* (1960), passim; *Anuário, 1956*, p. 41.
4. Instituto Nacional de Estudos Pedagógicos, *Censo Escolar do Brasil, Resultados Preliminares* (Rio: IBGE, Comissão Central do Censo Escolar, 1965), table 1.
5. *Anuário, 1964*, p. 339.
6. *Censo Demográfico* (1960), passim; *Anuário, 1956*, p. 81. Enrollment data from sources in Ministério da Educação e Cultura, Serviço Estatístico, courtesy of Anisio Teixeira.
7. *Anuário, 1962*, pp. 26–27.
8. *Anuário, 1960*, p. 28.
9. *Anuário, 1963*, p. 58.
10. *Censo Demográfico* (1960), pp. 16, 24, 32.
11. *Anuário, 1964*, pp. 65–66.

same reason that families with incomes of less than $3,000 in the United States are considered poor. It is not the actual level of incomes or development which is significant, but rather the internal disparities within the nation. The northeast is a problem area because its population has become an economic burden and a potential political threat for the remainder of the nation. Its low level of development has become intolerable, and its population is developing aspirations related to education, housing, income, and so on which it feels cannot be realized. The consequent feeling of deprivation is perceived as a threat by ruling and policy-making groups. Development programs such as that of SUDENE, the Northeastern Development Superintendency, will have to contribute not only to the development of the region, but to a rate of development that substantially exceeds that of the south if its efforts are to be truly successful.

Chapter 2

Brazil's Half-Continent

Donald R. Dyer

IT IS INTERESTING to note that Brazil's half-continent strikingly reflects the shape of the continent of South America itself, being broad in the north and tapering to the south, resulting in great expanses of tropical land and a small amount of extra-tropical territory. Called nation-continent and giant state by Deffontaines, Brazil is one of the five largest countries in the world in area and eighth in population.[1] Its large size (about 3,270,000 square miles of land) allows considerable variety of land forms, climates, and other natural conditions.[2] It is three times the size of Argentina and covers almost half of the continent, the state of São Paulo alone being approximately the size of Great Britain or Wyoming. And it is the world's largest tropical country of predominantly white population.

In Geologic Time

Being of such large size, Brazil's half-continent has undergone significant modifications in geologic time, resulting in a variety of relief regions (fig. 1). Key to its development are two relatively stable massive blocks of plateaus, the large complex of plateaus in the east and the Guianan plateau in the north. From a chain of ancient islands in Precambrian time that stretched from Guiana through Brazil on far to the south, continental land masses of considerable size were uplifted near the close of the Cambrian period, but seas still covered large areas presently in the lower Amazon corridor, the São Francisco basin of eastern Brazil, and the Paraguayan basin (including the Pantanal region), with seas extending far to the west. Following further uplift during the Devonian period—toward the end of

1. Pierre Deffontaines, *Geografia Humana do Brasil* (Rio: Conselho Nacional de Geografia, 1940; reprinted in *Revista Brasileira de Geografia*, Ano 1).
2. Aroldo de Azevedo, ed., *Brasil: A Terra e O Homen*, vol. 1: *As Bases Físicas* (São Paulo: Companhia Editora Nacional, 1964).

29

the Paleozoic era, lagoons and swamps were formed along the southeastern coast of Brazil and scattered coal beds developed—the sea disappeared from the São Francisco basin but still covered a strip in the lower Amazon corridor.

The middle geological periods were characterized by extensive sedimentation, and marine incursions were limited to the extreme western part of

BRAZIL: RELIEF REGIONS

Figure 1. Brazil Relief Regions

the Amazônia and to regions neighboring the present coastline. Extensive lava flows alternated with sandy sediments during the Triassic period, covering the southern part of Brazil and adjacent areas of the Paraná region. Toward the end of the Cretaceous period, Andean folding began and continued into the Tertiary, or Cenozoic, era. Although the rise of the tremendous Andes from the western ocean occurred outside Brazil, their uplift to great heights has resulted in deposition of great quantities of sediments as rivers flow eastward to the Atlantic.

Recent geological periods have consisted of modification of land forms from prior periods through processes of erosion and deposition, with occasional foldings and faultings. Principally, relatively low plateaus and restricted areas of mountains have been rounded by erosion and low-lying areas built up by sediments, while ocean currents and winds sculpture the coasts.

Having been above the sea level for such a long part of geologic time, Brazil exposes large expanses of ancient crystalline rocks, with large occurrences of iron ore in places. Intense foldings and faultings have brought about increased hardness of rocks, and veins have cut through in places, depositing diamonds and a variety of semiprecious stones, as well as gold.

CURVES AND WRINKLES

The shape and surface of Brazil may be described as predominantly curves and wrinkles. The coastline curves gently throughout most of its extent of about 4,600 miles, and gently rolling uplands are the typical relief. The sharpest turn of the coast occurs at Cabo Frio, where the predominantly north-south trend turns sharply east-west, putting the coast at Rio de Janeiro in a position of facing south toward the Atlantic Ocean.

Approaching Brazil from the Atlantic along the central or southern coasts would give one the impression of a mountainous country, and some mountains do exist, but the dominant relief of Brazil's wrinkles is that of modest topography. There are no alpine-type mountains, no high-altitude glaciation, and no recent volcanic features with their sharp characteristics. Brazil is dominated by massive blocks of medium-altitude to low plateaus. Nearly 60 per cent of the country lies between 200- and 900-meters (about 650–3,000 feet) elevation, and less than 3 per cent rises above 3,000 feet, with the highest being under 10,000 feet.

Most of the 40 per cent of Brazil's territory that lies below 650-feet elevation is located in interior plains, particularly the Amazon lowland and the Pantanal of the Paraguay River system. Coastal lowlands are very narrow and are discontinuous. Although the Amazon system drains more than one-half of the country, some of the headwater areas of its tributaries, especially in its southern sector, extend above the 650-feet line. Its lowland forms a grandiose amphitheater locked between the Guianan and Brazilian plateaus and extending westward toward the interior arc of the Andes. Its gently undulating surface is interrupted in places by low, sandy tablelands that are situated at varying distances from the wide zones of inundations. On the western edge of the Brazilian shield is the Pantanal, which measures about

300 miles in length with an average width of nearly 150 miles and which is almost completely surrounded by higher land, thereby giving the lowland the nature of labyrinthine drainage with widespread inundations and difficult outlet through the Paraguay River to the south. The coastal lowland belt extends all the way from Amapá on the French Guianan border to Rio Grande do Sul on the Uruguayan border but is not continuous. Neither is it composed exclusively of coastal plains, since many sections consist of low tablelands or coastal terraces.

The most common type of surface in the Brazilian plateaus' shelf is the crystalline *planalto*, which either occurs as a dome or back of the hard-rock shelf or as rejuvenated ridges that correspond to the edge of the *planalto* or to a zone of tectonic faulting. These are ancient crystalline areas reduced through ages of weathering and erosion, whose summits now rarely exceed 4,000–6,000 feet, with occasional rejuvenated mountains reaching 9,000 feet. In general, these plateaus are highest on their eastern margins, where steep escarpments drop to the sea or coastal lowlands, and decline toward the west. They expose the oldest rocks of the continent—Archean metamorphosed igneous rocks, chiefly granites and gneisses—which occur on the eastern margin from Bahia to São Paulo and Paraná, in central Goiás, the northeast, and along the Uruguayan frontier.

Sedimentary and basaltic plateaus cover considerable areas of the Brazilian and Guianan plateaus. These include the sedimentary-basaltic plateau of the Paraná-Uruguay basin, where sandy sedimentary deposits are interrelated with lava flows, and elevations are generally between 1,000–3,000 feet; the extensive tablelands (650–2,000 feet) of Maranhão and Piauí in the north, where sedimentary and basaltic deposits occur; isolated sedimentary plateaus in the northeast with elevations to 3,000 feet; and extensive plateaus between 1,600 and 3,000 feet in the central and central-western regions. Sedimentary plateaus also occur in northern Brazil on the borders with Venezuela and the Guianas, with sedimentary formations resting on the ancient crystalline shield. Elevations in the Guianan plateau are typically low, though the highest tableland extends to almost 10,000 feet.

In sum, the surface features are dominated by extensive areas of low, rolling plateaus which exhibit a few abrupt mountains, particularly on the margins overlooking the Atlantic along the central part of the coastline, and which merge with the great Amazon lowland to the northwest.

NATURAL REGIONAL VARIETIES

Brazil's half-continental size provides conditions (one of which was presented above—namely, relief of the land) that can lead to the selection of a number of kinds of regions. When one considers, as well, the multiple climates and vegetation associations or other physical features, regional divisions of the national territory proliferate.[3] Moreover, the degree of generalization—whether by group of states or by fractions of states—determines the number of divisions into which the country may be partitioned. Also, it should be noted that most regions are not bounded sharply, but rather form transitional boundaries with adjoining regions.

In spite of its great size, Brazil is overwhelmingly a tropical country. The southern tropic line passes just south of Rio de Janeiro and through São Paulo to the southern tip of Mato Grosso, placing only 7 per cent of the country outside the tropics. However, this exclusively latitudinal concept of tropicality should be modified, so that upland areas inside the tropic line be considered as subtropical, with the result that parts of the Brazilian highlands in São Paulo and Minas Gerais, states not typically tropical because of their elevation, are considered subtropical. Consequently, Brazil exhibits two regions that are not tropical (fig. 2). These account for about 12 per cent of the country's area, though about one-third of the nation's population lives in such subtropical regions.

Tropical climates in Brazil show considerable variety—from wet to semiarid. The wettest, that which is popularly considered typical tropical, occurs in the upper Amazon basin, with continuously high temperatures and quite high rainfall regularly distributed through the year. A humid tropical type, with considerable rainfall though less than the wet tropical and with a definite drier season, extends through the middle and lower Amazon regions and also occupies a narrow belt along the Atlantic coast from the bulge to just south of the tropic line. Most of the Brazilian plateaus and part of the Guianan plateau are covered by a tropical climate with definite seasonal variations in rainfall, being wettest in the warmer season; temperatures may be modified by altitude but are still predominantly warm to hot. A surprising tropical type is the semiarid region of the northeastern interior, where not only is average rainfall low but variations from year to year are great.

Vegetation associations reflect regional differences in climate and conditions of relief and soils.[4] Typically, dense broadleaf forests occupy the Amazon basin, covering about 40 per cent of the nation's territory and being one of the most extensive forest areas in the world. Tropical broadleaf forests also occupy the humid Atlantic coastal slopes and the most humid parts of the Brazilian plateaus, especially the river valleys in the central parts and on the south, though the growth is not as exuberant as in the Amazon region. Another forested region is the southern plateau, where the Arau-

3. *Paisagens do Brasil*, 2d. ed. (Rio: Conselho Nacional de Geografia, 1962), pp. 97–106.
4. Alceu Magnanini, "Aspectos Fitogeográficos do Brasil," *Revista Brasileira de Geografia* 23, no. 4 (Outubro–Dezembro 1961): 681–90.

caria forest, dominated by pines, covers large expanses. Most of the seasonal tropical areas of the Brazilian plateaus are covered by *cerrado*, which consists chiefly of close-growing short trees, bushes, and tough grasses. The semiarid northeast and adjacent areas covered by a seasonal tropical climate have *caatinga* vegetation, a stunted and rather sparse forest whose trees lose their leaves in the dry season, and cactus occurring in many places. *Cam-*

Figure 2. Brazil Climatic Regions

pos, extensive grasslands, cover the extreme southern margin of the country in Rio Grande do Sul, parts of the southern plateau, as well as scattered areas in the Amazon basin, and particularly the eastern half of Marajó Island at the mouth of the Amazon.

Taking into account several factors, six large regions of Brazil are recognized and are described individually in the following sections. Although major consideration is given to such physical factors as relief, climate, and vegetation, human and economic geography also play an important part in delimiting the geographic regions, which are the Atlantic coastal zones, the south, northeastern interior, central-west, upper Amazon, and lower Amazon (fig. 3).

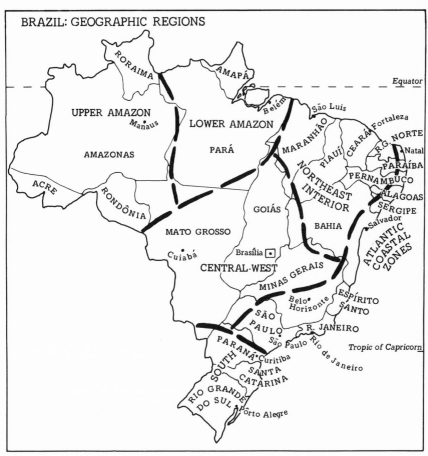

Figure 3. Brazil Geographic Regions

ATLANTIC COASTAL ZONES

In broadest terms, Brazil can be divided into "two Brazils" on the basis of human densities, namely, (1) a relatively wide eastern belt extending from the Uruguayan border to the mouth of the Amazon, though narrowing in the north and reaching inland as far as Brasília and southern Goiás, and (2) the human "desert" of the Amazon basin, the central-western plateaus, and part of the northeast. Densities are high in Atlantic Brazil and extremely low in the *sertão*, the backlands of the interior.

The Atlantic coastal zones region, as considered here, extends from the northeastern coastal plain to the coastal and plateau sections of São Paulo. Its average width in the northeast is about 50 miles and broadens to more than 200 miles in its southern part (fig. 3). It should be noted that this region covers considerably more than the narrow coastal plain. Its western margin corresponds most closely to the edge of dense settlement, which, by relationship to man's adjustment to natural resources, corresponds more or less to physical conditions of relief, climate, vegetation, and soils. More than one-half of Brazil's population lives in this region.

The coast itself between the northeastern bulge and the border of the São Paulo and Paraná states presents three distinct types. In the northern section as far south as Bahia, the continental shelf is narrow (less than fifteen miles wide); the shoreline itself has few indentations; long coral-line and sandstone reefs extend as far south as the mouth of the São Francisco River; and the littoral zone consists of a slightly elevated coastal plain, with low marine terraces separated by small river valleys that form tablelands and hills whose elevations rarely exceed 500 feet. Elevations increase toward the interior as the escarpment of the old northeastern plateau is reached.

The climate of the northeastern coastal belt may be described as pseudo-tropical, in view of the fact that most of the year's rainfall is concentrated in the fall and winter (which has still a warm average of nearly 75 degrees in the coolest month) due to the action of the Atlantic polar front that moves northward into the normally dry air masses over the northeast. Along the coast rainfall averages between about 55 inches at Natal to about 95 inches at Barreiros near Recife and 45 inches at Aracajú, with half of the year being dry. The wetter parts of the region give rise to a humid tropical broadleaf forest, but most of the northeastern coastal belt is characterized by a less dense forest that reflects the seasonal rainfall and areas of relatively porous soils. Much of the forest has been cleared for agriculture, especially along the river plains, where sugarcane generally occupies the best soils. Most of the population of the small northeastern states lives in the *mata* (forest) belt, with its density becoming less into the *agreste* (rural zone of somewhat barren soils) toward the west. Considering the traditional plantation-agriculture system with its large labor demand, however, the states, though small in area, have large populations. The eastern parts of Rio Grande do Norte, Paraíba, Pernambuco, Alagoas, and Sergipe total more than 7,000,000 inhabitants.

The Atlantic coastal zone between Bahia de Todos os Santos (Salvador) and Cabo São Tomé, northeast of Rio de Janeiro, is characterized by extensive sand bars, lagoons, and mangrove swamps. The escarpment of the Brazilian plateau is relatively distant from the shoreline, and low tablelands and hills are less continuous than in the northeastern type. The large bay of Todos os Santos forms a large indentation in the coastline, with good anchorage. Several large rivers, such as the Contas, Pardo, Jequitinhonha, and Doce, reach for considerable distances back into the plateau. The Doce, in particular, provides the best access to the interior through a breach in the *serras* (mountains) that rise above the general level of the plateau near the eastern margin of the Brazilian shield. The highest of these rejuvenated mountains rises to almost 9,500 feet at Bandeira Peak within 75 miles of the coast, on the border of Espírito Santo and Minas Gerais states. The somewhat rugged eastern margin slowly gives way to the rolling interior plateau.

Climatic conditions of the middle Atlantic zone exhibit rainfall fairly well distributed through the year though with an obvious summer maximum, and average totals range from about 80 inches in the Bahian coastal zone to 40 inches in Espírito Santo, with a general pattern of decrease toward the interior. Tropical forests are best developed in the hot, humid section of Bahia, with lighter forests appearing toward the interior. Extensive areas of cacao production have been concentrated along the hot, humid lowlands of Bahia, south of Todos os Santos Bay. Population density in the middle Atlantic zone is less than in the northeastern coastal zone, chiefly because of more rugged relief and denser forests. Petroleum deposits exist and are being exploited in the Recôncavo basin around Todos os Santos Bay.

The southern section of the Atlantic coastal zones region presents a precipitous front to the ocean, with steep escarpments rising to nearly 2,000 feet in several places and with excellent harbors, such as Guanabara Bay at Rio de Janeiro, being formed. Strong folding and faulting parallel to the coastline back behind Rio de Janeiro resulted in the formation of the Paraíba do Sul corridor and the high Mantiqueira range on the Minas Gerais border. Except for the Paraíba River, the drainage system is one of headwaters near the Atlantic escarpment and rivers flowing westward to the Paraná River in the interior. This situation has led to the development of hydroelectric power along the westward-flowing rivers by turning headwaters of the Tietê River eastward across the escarpment between São Paulo and Santos.

Tropical climate with fairly heavy rainfall concentrated in the summer but with some precipitation in winter follows the coast southward on past Rio de Janeiro and even for some distance beyond the tropic line. Back into the mountains and on the plateau, however, temperatures decline to average minimums below 64 degrees, such as at São Paulo City (58 degrees average in July), and a pattern of summer rains and winter drought prevails. Dense tropical forests cover the Atlantic slopes and extend somewhat back toward the interior, where lighter tropical forest takes over. Much of the plateau, however, has been cleared for agriculture and stock raising in São Paulo state and in southern Minas Gerais, where coffee, cotton, sugarcane, citrus, and a variety of other crops are produced, especially on *terra roxa* (rich purple soil) land. Valuable deposits of iron and other ores, as well as gold, diamonds, and a variety of semi-precious stones, are found in this section of the ancient crystalline plateau, particularly in Minas Gerais. A combination of good agricultural land, minerals, and power for industrialization have provided background for rapid economic development.

THE SOUTH

Brazil's south occupies a relatively narrow corridor about 350 miles wide between the Atlantic Ocean and the Uruguay and Paraná rivers, with frontiers with Uruguay, Argentina, and Paraguay. Although situated far from most parts of the country, it is located relatively close to the economic heart of Brazil, which is the São Paulo-Rio de Janeiro-Minas Gerais heartland. Its distinctiveness as a region stems largely from its subtropical features. Although occupying only about 7 per cent of the national territory, it counts about 17 per cent of the nation's population, which in itself would make it much larger than most Latin American nations.

The southern region's dominant cohesiveness is tied to the structure of the southern plateau, whose landscapes are derived from the Mesozoic (middle-aged) sedimentary Paraná basin. Although similar features appear in the northern part of the basin, where the Paraná River has its headwaters and flows southwestward through the interior, the southern section east of the Paraná and Uruguay rivers is distinctive in its extensive basaltic lava flows in the midst of sandstone sedimentary layers. This large plateau of medium elevations (generally between 1,000–3,000 feet) rests upon the old Brazilian shield, whose hard-rock crystalline forms are exposed along the eastern margin near or at the Atlantic coast. Elevations decline somewhat toward the south and toward the west, with a representative vertical profile across the state of Paraná showing well-marked steps in the structure and surface from about 3,000-feet elevation on the eastern edge (except for the highest peaks) to below 1,000 feet at the Paraná River (fig. 4). The sharp rise behind the scanty coastal lowland to the Serra do Mar, with peaks as high as 6,500 feet, is followed by a rolling upland tilted toward the west.[5] Low, eastward-facing escarpments on the plateau give rise to a trapezoidal stream pattern, with the major streams superimposed on the westward-tilting structure and with tributaries joining at more or less right angles with the main stream as a result of the *cuestas*, which represent hard, upturned edges. A

5. *Grande Região Sul: Tomo I* (Rio: Conselho Nacional de Geografia, 1963).

succession of plateaus gradually loses altitude toward the west, and numerous rapids and falls occur as rivers pass over resistant layers.

The steep Serra do Mar confronts the coastline as far south as Santa Catarina, where Atlantic drainage has been particularly active and has cut back the wall and produced deep notches into the crystalline basement and even into part of the sedimentary plateau, forming deep valleys. Consequently, the scanty coastal lowlands interspersed with hills are somewhat broader. The plateau again comes close to the sea in the northeastern part of Rio Grande do Sul only to drop away as the low crystalline shield in the extreme south appears. The easternmost of the basaltic lands is called the Serra Geral, appearing close to the coast in northeastern Rio Grande do Sul and farther inland in Santa Catarina and Paraná. A wide belt of coastal sand bars, lagoons, and tidal marshes form a long string along the coast to Rio Grande do Sul, obstructing the river mouths.

The subtropical south experiences precipitation that is abundant (rang-

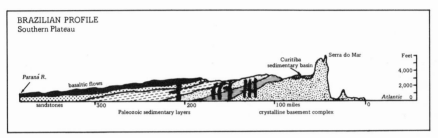

Figure 4. Brazilian Profile Southern Plateau

ing from more than 40 to nearly 100 inches annually) and well distributed throughout the year. The higher elevations receive the most precipitation, with the extreme south consequently receiving the lower amounts. Fall and winter are the wettest seasons, as polar Atlantic air masses bring low temperatures, drizzly rains, freezes, and snowfalls to the highest levels, with the most frequent snows occurring along the Santa Catarina-Rio Grande do Sul border near the eastern edge of the plateau and with an average of more than 25 days of freezing temperatures each year. Tropical Atlantic air masses also reach as far south as Santa Catarina, causing heavy rainfall especially on the Serra do Mar in summer. The greatest heating in the region occurs along the Paraná River fringe in the interior from continental air masses that prevail in summer. Except for the highest elevations, summers are hot and winters mild.

The subtropical south possessed an original vegetation cover divided between treeless savanna on the smoothly undulating topography of the extreme south and forests, predominantly the araucaria (often called Paraná pine) forests which cover a large part of the higher surfaces. Large expanses of araucarias, with their unusual flat crowns and flat branches with scalelike leaves, are concentrated in Paraná and Santa Catarina and extend into northern Rio Grande do Sul and into the southern part of São Paulo. Their distribution is tied to climate, which in turn is conditioned by relief and elevation, ranging from about 1,500 feet in northern Rio Grande do Sul to about 2,500 feet in northern Paraná. They do not cover the plateaus completely, but avoid the large river valleys and give way to broadleaf forests on diabase basalt dikes and sills. However, they are disseminated over a great variety of soils from the poorest to the richest, with preference for silicic clays, and groups of araucarias mottle expanses of savanna, especially in the Lajes region in southeastern Santa Catarina. There is an old saying that "the pine does not want to see the sea," and they generally are at least ten to twenty-five miles from the coast. Generally associated with the pine forest is the *erva-mate* (*Ilex paraguariensis*), a holly-like species used as a tea and called "Paraguay tea" by some. It grows as a smaller tree amidst the tall pines.

Broadleaf forests mixed with some araucarias generally occupy richer soils and the valleys, as well as slopes of the Serra Geral; and a tropical type of perennial broadleaf forest covers the seaward slopes of the Serra do Mar. Treeless savannas occur in some relatively small sections of the plateau, cover almost all of the extreme south, and spread into Uruguay. Much of the western part of Rio Grande do Sul lies below 650-feet elevation, namely, the central and southern parts. A wide depression with nearly smooth topography separates the sandstone-basaltic plateau from the roughly undulating crystalline plateau of the extreme south, whose highest levels do not reach more than 1,600 feet above sea level. The extreme south is sometimes called *gaúcho* (cowboy) prairie because of the large expanses of grass that are used for livestock grazing.

In addition to the extensive grasslands used for pasture in the south, other resources include the araucaria forests that provide the principal source of pine lumber for building purposes and some for the pulp and paper industry. *Erva-mate* provides the basis for a small gathering industry. The best soils are used for cultivation, but the coffee industry only extends as far southward into the northern part of Paraná state as the perennial danger of freezes will permit. Medium- to low-grade deposits of coal are found in the coastal plain of Santa Catarina and in the central lowland of Rio Grande do Sul. Water power resources are abundant as a result of the numerous falls and rapids of the westward-flowing rivers and of the Paraná River itself.

NORTHEASTERN INTERIOR

From a strict point of view of natural regions, the narrow coastal belt of the northeast of Brazil is more similar to coastal zones farther south along the Atlantic coast than it is to the interior. Landscapes, vegetation, soils, and human occupancy of the humid coastal lowlands were described in a previous section on Atlantic coastal zones. It should be noted, however, that the coastal belt, not only because of its geographic position, but also because of its economic and other ties with the interior, could have been included in a separate region called simply "the northeast." Nevertheless, the interior of the northeast is a distinctive geographic division and is so treated here.

As distinguished from the slightly elevated coastal plain, with its low terraces, small tablelands, and hills between small valleys, the northeastern interior consists essentially of old worn-down plateaus with some exposures of the ancient crystalline basement, particularly in the east, where elevations are higher (to more than 3,500 feet). The Borborema plateau is the largest and most characteristic elevation in the northeast and occupies an area of about 150 by 200 miles between the Atlantic coastal belt and the extensive, parched surfaces of the *sertão*. It has essentially a radial shape due to erosional rounding of the old massif since its initial uplifting. In general in the northeast, land slopes somewhat gently from the coast to the interior with a few high platforms and some mountain "islands" that show sheer profiles. In its southern part, the northeastern interior includes the wide corridor of the São Francisco River valley that runs parallel to the Atlantic shoreline for several hundred miles before cutting around the northern end of the Diamantina plateau toward the ocean.

The most important natural element of the northeastern interior is the climate, whose trademark is the occurrence of a rigorous dry season every year and whose duration averages eight months, from March or April to October or November. The short rainy period in summer (called "winter" by local inhabitants) is followed by a long dry period, which is often prolonged to calamitous proportions of general drought. Rain falls irregularly on the *sertão* in any lapse of years, irregularly in a season, and even irregularly over the surface itself. The typical regime in the core areas consists of sporadic thunderstorms between October and December, steady but not heavy rains from February to April, and dryness for the remainder of the year. The inner core area, which extends from the northern coast of Rio Grande do Norte and forms an arc around to the big bend of the São Francisco River in the interiors of Bahia and Pernambuco, has an average annual rainfall of only 20 inches, varying from year to year by average extremes as low as 16 and as high as 26 inches. The driest areas are in the *sertão* of Paraíba (only 11 inches) and in the São Francisco valley between the border of Alagoas and Juazeiro-Petrolina, where average annual temperature is a high 79°F. It should be pointed out that the dry season is regular but drought is not. However, droughts are too frequent to be unexpected, with periods ranging from a one- to four-year duration; the longest recent period of drought was 1941–1944. In contrast to the extreme northeastern coast, coastal zones farther west are more humid, with averages increasing from about 55 inches annually at Fortaleza to 80 inches at São Luis, toward the Amazonian region.

The semiarid climate of most of the northeastern interior gives rise to drought-tolerant vegetation. Irregularity of rainfall, high average temperatures, and shallow soils are responsible for the *caatinga*, whose trees, with accentuated and thorny branches, lose their leaves in the dry season, and there are large numbers of cactus and other xerophytes. The characteristically short trees and bushes with few branches and small leaves cover vast areas, a hostile picture of vegetation that reflects the curse of drought. The higher plateaus, as well as the coastal plains in the northern part of Piauí and parts of Maranhão are covered by *cerrado*, which typically has close-growing short trees, bushes, and tough grasses, though there are significant expanses of predominantly coarse grassland with scattered or grouped trees. Great numbers of palms are characteristic of the more humid soils, especially in Piauí and Maranhão, and in general signal the transition zone between the semiarid northeast and the Amazon forests.

The fundamental problem of the northeastern interior is water. Throughout most of the region, rivers are temporary, running and even overflowing during the short rainy season and drying up completely for a large part of the year. The Parnaíba River, which forms the axis of the sedimentary basin in the western part of the region as well as the heart of Piauí, has perennial tributaries from the west and temporary ones from the east. In the eastern part, the only perennial river of the backlands is the São Francisco, which has headwaters in the highlands of the Atlantic coastal zone of Minas Gerais, but has to reduce its volume considerably in the dry season upon entering the semiarid zone, commonly dropping between ten and twenty-five feet between February and September. It has to drop over Paulo Afonso Falls before emerging onto the Atlantic coastal plain between Alagoas and Sergipe states, and there are four other important cascade areas, but the river is navigable in its middle course for 850 miles between Juazeiro and Pirapora.

The area occupied by the states of Piauí and Maranhão in the northwestern part of the region under consideration has somewhat distinctive characteristics and may be considered a separate region (called *meio norte*, i.e., middle-north, by some) or at least a *sub*-region.[6] It is derived basically from a large sedimentary basin which has given rise to plateaus and tablelands in the interior that present abrupt cliffs to a large lowland in the north. It is more humid than the remainder of the northeast, with abundant summer

6. *Grandes Regiões Meio-Norte e Nordeste* (Rio: Conselho Nacional de Geografia, 1962).

rains being absorbed in the soil to form a water table for perennial rivers. The Amazon forest in the west gives way to a transition forest dominated by *babaçú* oil palm in Maranhão and to *babaçú* forests mixed with *carnauba* wax palm in the Parnaíba valley of Piauí. Rice culture is significant in the wet lowlands of Maranhão.

The problem of water in the northeastern interior involves continual concern for water supplies, and hundreds of small dams have been built, along with a multitude of water holes, cisterns, and wells. Temporary streams, which are so numerous, are useless for navigation or for hydroelectric power development. In terms of natural resources, the palm forests contain *babaçú*, whose oil is used for soap, and *carnauba*, whose wax is used for candles, varnish, and other purposes. Other plants of the *caatinga* and *cerrado* are useful for such products as leather tanning extract and essential oils. Livestock raising on relatively poor pastures is the basis for the economy of the interior, though agriculture is practiced, wherever possible, on soils with adequate water supply.

The human element in the resource picture of the northeast has had to adapt to the difficult conditions of the natural environment, particularly to the problem of water. When drought besets the region for long periods, hardships are extreme and human resources are often forced to migrate to the cities of the northeast coast or to other parts of Brazil. Some of the migrants return to the land when the rains return, a kind of transhumance, whereas others never return. Total population of the *Polígono das Secas* (Polygon of Droughts) is about 15 million.

CENTRAL-WEST

The central-west region consists chiefly of the states of Goiás and Mato Grosso, but is considered here to include also the western parts of São Paulo, Minas Gerais, and Bahia (fig. 3). In some ways, this might be called the Wild West of Brazil, involving frontier development and the dominance of livestock raising. It is a huge region, accounting for almost one-fourth of the national territory; in fact, Mato Grosso alone is as large as Peru (third largest country in South America in área) and is larger than the southeastern part of the United States.

The central location of this region gives it boundaries with all of the other regions, and, as such, this region exhibits transitional zones on its margins. Moreover, its position as water-divide among Brazil's major river systems contributes to such traditional margins, with elements of the dry northeastern interior, of the subtropical southern plateau, and of the rolling interior section of the Atlantic coastal zone in central São Paulo and Minas Gerais, as well as the wet Amazon lowland, crowding in. Nevertheless, the central-west has distinctiveness.

The dominant landscape of the central-west is not that of vast expanses of perfectly flat land, as often has been generalized, though the region is predominantly one of simple structure whose eroded forms lie generally between 1,200- and 3,000-feet elevation. More or less typical of the region is the Anápolis plateau west of Brasília, which has an open landscape on a very gently undulating upland with low, sparse vegetation and with trees limited almost entirely to the river valleys. Elevations extend to 3,500 feet, and it is interesting to note that the upland around Brasília gives rise to three major river systems—Paraná to the south, São Francisco to the northeast, and Tocantins to the north. The highest parts are modeled on the crystalline basement rocks, with the crystalline plateau descending northward into central and northern Goiás to elevations of 1,000–2,000 feet above sea level.

Tabular land forms dominate in the northern part of Mato Grosso, whose sandy upland forms the water-divide between the Amazon and Paraguay systems, ranging generally between 1,200 and 2,500 feet. The higher mesas with their sand-covered platforms lack water on their surfaces, but streams form at their bases, giving rise to headwaters. The southern part of Mato Grosso is more undulating and generally not as high, with less sandy soils. A rather strange contrast in the region is the scarcity of water at the surface in spite of numerous large rivers cutting through the region. Two unusual hydrographic features in the central-west are Bananal Island in the Araguaia River, the largest river island in the world (nearly 200 miles in length), and the vast Pantanal (nearly the size of Ohio), the seasonally flooded flat plain east of the Paraguay River.

The central-west's tropical position, combined with its low to moderate uplands, gives rise to tropical and subtropical climates, with emphasis on the former.[7] Temperatures by and large are not excessively high or low. The hottest area is the Pantanal near the Paraguay River, where average annual temperatures are about 80°F. and hot summers are the result of low pressure areas of the interior of the continent. The widest range in average temperatures from summer to winter is about 15° (between 64–79°) in southern Mato Grosso, where winter freezes are felt. The higher elevations in the eastern part of the region also experience frosts and are described as subtropical. A fundamental element of the climate, of greater variation than average seasonal temperatures, is the daily range of temperature. For example, the average daily range in winter (July) at Cuiabá, capital of Mato Grosso, is more than 40°—from about 55° before dawn to 95° in the afternoon's heat. This means hot days and cool nights, with dry air in the winter.

The typical rainfall. pattern is that of a five-to-seven-month rainy season from October or November to March or April, which corresponds to the hotter period and leads to considerable evaporation and high humidity, fol-

7. *Grande Região Centro-Oeste* (Rio: Conselho Nacional de Geografia, 1960).

lowed by a long dry season. Total precipitation is more than 40 inches everywhere and reaches to 80 inches in the northern parts. The rivers follow the regime of rains, whose seasonality is not conducive to ideal navigational conditions.

Variations in topography influence vegetation formations, and vegetation is the most complex of natural features in the central-west. In spite of rather high total rainfall (to 80 inches), vegetation is relatively sparse, chiefly as a result of the long rainy season and shorter dry season. Other contributing factors are the widespread poor, porous, sandy soils and the heavy winds. Large amounts of subsurface water and permanent streams give rise to forests in the wetter areas. Vegetation is more dense on slopes, and forests occur on areas of undulating relief not underlain by sandy formations. Mato Grosso, meaning literally "thick forest," is poorly named, since forests cover only one-third of its area.

The most extensive and most characteristic vegetation associated with the central-west is the *cerrado*, consisting of relatively close-growing trees of 25–35 feet height, bushes, and coarse grass. Adaptations to the dry season include gnarled trunks and branches, thick bark, deep roots, large and tough leaves, and falling leaves. The monotonous physiognomy of the nearly flat uplands covered with dull green or light gray vegetation (depending on the season) as far as the eye can see is interrupted by tropical forests in valleys or on humid soils, generally as a gallery, or fringing forest. Throughout the central-west are large amounts of grass which have been burned for generations to provide new growth of pasture grasses. Scattered through the large expanses of *cerrado* are smaller areas of *campo limpo*, a grassland sometimes of tall tuft grasses and in other places a prairie land of close-growing grasses, occurring generally in areas of gently undulating relief on water-divides. The luxurious, humid, dense, intensely green equatorial forest, with its characteristic rubber trees (*Hevea braziliensis*), Brazil-nut (*Bertholetia excelsa*), and ipecac (a creeping plant), covers the northern and northwestern parts of Mato Grosso on upper Amazon tributaries.

Human resources of the central-west are widely scattered and total only about four million in this vast territory. The sparseness of population largely reflects the dominant cattle economy, which depends upon unimproved grasslands of limited carrying capacity. The method of frontier farming has been largely cut and burn, although in some older areas where the soil is rich, corn, rice, beans, and cassava are major crops. Some coffee is grown in southern Goiás and southern Mato Grosso. Forest resources exploited are rubber, ipecac, and hard woods. Minerals of importance are quartz crystals and diamonds; some gold, iron ore, and manganese are mined. A recent but still largely undetermined resource is the new capital of Brasília, whose presence affects the development of other resources of the region.

UPPER AMAZON

Partly because of its tremendous extent, but essentially because of regional differences, Brazil's Amazônia is divided here into two regions. Upper Amazon corresponds to the states Amazonas and Acre and the territories of Rondônia (in the south) and Roraima (in the north); whereas, the lower Amazon region encompasses the state of Pará and the territory of Amapá (fig. 3). The former measures more than 800,000 square miles, one-fourth of Brazil's territory. Its population of about one million, however, represents only slightly more than 1 per cent of the nation's inhabitants.

The upper Amazon region is an extensive lowland plain or low plateau between the Brazilian and Guianan shields, though it is not monotonously identical all over the basin. Its shape is asymmetrical, the southern flank being twice as wide as the northern section, with correspondingly long tributaries. Three kinds of zones can be recognized; namely, (1) the hard-rock crystalline flanks sloping gently up to the Brazilian highland on the south and to the Guianan highland to the north, (2) the *terra firme*, or elevated sedimentary formations above the flood plain, and (3) the flood plain itself—sometimes distinguished as *várzea*, which is flooded only during the rainy season, and as *igapó*, which is flooded most of the year.

Statistics of the Amazon River, the river-sea, are sensational. The tremendous volume of water discharged into the Atlantic, coming not only from abundant rainfall over vast areas of the basin but also from snowclad Andes outside Brazil's territory, staggers the imagination. The average width of the main stream is nearly three miles and extends without considerable flooding to a width of twelve miles at its junction with the Xingú in its lower course. The mighty force of the stream has cut down deeply (to 200 feet at Óbidos, for example), which, considering that the elevation of the river upon entering Brazil from Peru is only 200 feet above sea level, is phenomenal. On the average, the rise and fall of the waters during the year is about 30 feet near Manaus. Great meanders characterize the Amazon, and the regularly flooded plain extends to more than thirty miles wide in places.

The *várzea* flood plain commonly is several miles wide along the Amazon and of lesser width along major tributaries, but it is not as large percentagewise as one might imagine, since seasonally flooded plains cover a relatively small part of the entire Amazon region (fig. 5).[8] However, there are located the best, silty soils of the region for agricultural use, being dedicated to such subsistence crops as rice and beans and to such commercial crops as jute fiber. The idea that the presence of a luxuriant forest throughout the region is an index to good soils is extremely deceiving, because trees can live well on water and very poor soils. Older soils on the higher lands of *terra firme*

8. *Grande Região Norte* (Rio: Conselho Nacional de Geografia, 1959).

are by and large poor, being acid, badly leached, and poor in important mineral elements, such as phosphorous, potassium, and nitrogen.

The Amazonian climate is a victim of exaggerated ideas, whereas a fair description would be that it is hot without being torrid, quite humid, and somewhat enervating without being essentially unhealthy, though one might argue that some unhealthful conditions are related to climatic conditions. Throughout the region, average annual temperatures range from 80° at Manaus to 75° in Rondônia in the southern part of the region, with a range

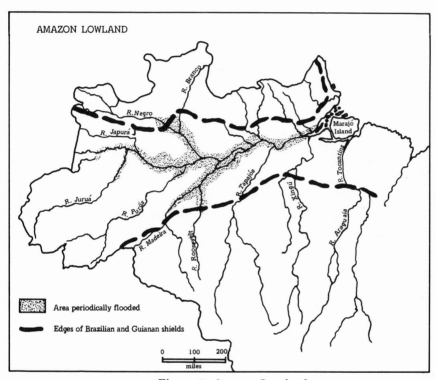

AMAZON LOWLAND

Area periodically flooded

Edges of Brazilian and Guianan shields

0   100   200
miles

Figure 5. Amazon Lowland

of only a few degrees between summer and winter. Daily contrasts of temperature are much greater than seasonal ones, particularly in places of high humidity, which includes most of the region with percentages usually above 80 per cent; the "sensible" temperatures (i.e., the degree to which one senses the temperature) are strong. Local terminology refers to the rainy season as winter because the sensible temperatures are low at that time. Record temperatures as low as 45° have been recorded in the southwest, in Acre state, as a result of occasional cold waves from the south.

The "typical" tropical climate (continuously hot and wet, with at least

2 inches of rain falling each month) occurs only in a zone in the upper Amazon region west of Manaus and within four degrees of the equator. The wettest area along the western margin receives about 135 inches annually. The amount of precipitation decreases toward the eastern edge of the region to about 65 inches annually. The number of days in which rain occurs varies greatly, from 259 days in the northwest to 100 days in the extreme north of the Rio Branco valley in a rain-shadow location behind mountains. In the parts of the region farthest from the equator, both north and south, seasons alternate from wet to dry, depending upon the sun's position and atmospheric pressure. Such alternation provides the great river system with a constant supply all year.[9] In general, the northern tributaries are at their highest in March and April and the southern upper tributaries in December to March; consequently, the lower course generally reaches its maximum in May.

Except in the extreme north of the Rio Branco plains and in the upland of Rondônia near the southern margin, the upper Amazon region is covered by evergreen tropical forests which are dense, rich in species, and greatly stratified by several vertical layers of differing characteristics. Variations in topographical conditions lead to variety in vegetation formations. On the nonflooded higher lands of *terra firme* is the best-developed multi-story forest with the tallest trees, such as groupings of the majestic Brazil-nut tree, reaching to more than 150 feet in height. Marshy forests occupy the continuously wet lands, while periodically flooded areas bordering the streams carry a forest that is rich in species, with a few exuberant individuals, such as the rubber tree, which sometimes reaches 125-feet heights, though trees in general are shorter than on *terra firme*. Throughout the forest of the Amazon are valuable trees that provide oils, waxes, fibers, medicines, and lumber, but a major problem is confronted in trying to get the products out.

LOWER AMAZON

The lower Amazon region exhibits some characteristics that are common to the upper Amazon, though its geographical position results in a certain distinctiveness. The factor of greater accessibility accounts in large part for a considerably larger population (approaching two million) in a smaller area. The vast majority of the inhabitants live in the port city of Belém and in the adjacent northeastern corner of Pará state.

A dominant feature of the lower Amazon region is the mouth of the giant river with its vast discharge of water and sediments. The delta cannot be described as "typical," because the coast has characteristics of drowning. The river has built at its mouth a large archipelago with numerous channels in the great gulf. The largest island, Marajó, is nearly 200 miles long and

9. Lucio de Castro Soares, *Amazônia* (Rio: Conselho Nacional de Geografia, 1963).

more than 100 miles wide and separates the main (northern) channel from the southern arm, which is the Pará River that empties into the ocean past Belém to the east of Marajó. Continual sedimentation at the southwestern edge of Marajó has forced most of the discharge of the Amazon into the northern channel, though the main navigation channel is from Belém around the southern end of the island to the main river. Highest elevations on Marajó Island reach to 65 feet above sea level, and the eastern half is an extensive grassland where large herds of cattle graze.

The coastline of Amapá (west of the Amazon) and of Pará (east of the Amazon) is indented by numerous estuaries and is covered by extensive mangrove swamps. Low cliffs (to a maximum of about 60 feet) occur, and low natural terraces rise gently toward the interior, reaching to levels of 300 feet in places. The higher soils are red and yellow sands, sandy clays that have been subjected to the process of laterization in many places, with its resulting crust of iron and aluminum oxides. Parallel to the Amapá coast is a relatively wide belt of *campo cerrado*, a curiously open landscape in a wet tropical lowland. Otherwise, dense evergreen tropical forests cover the lower Amazon region, except for agricultural clearings. Cultivation is localized, particularly in the northeastern part of Pará, where the main crops are rice, cassava, and black pepper.

The entire coastal belt receives more than 80 inches of rainfall each year, and the wettest zone is along the Amapá coast, with averages to 125 inches. Although still humid, areas farther from the coast toward the south and west experience as little as 65 inches annually, with seasonal though not pronounced variations of wet and less wet. Temperatures are continuously high; average monthly temperatures at Belém, for example, range between 77–79°F., whereas daily variations are about 17°—a strong contrast to the 2° monthly range. Belém experiences an average of 250 days with some rainfall each year. With some justification has the night been called by some the "winter" of the tropics.

LIVING SPACE

Brazil's half-continent provides a tremendous expanse of living space for natural vegetation, crops, animals, and man himself. Although essentially tropical by nature, it exhibits considerable variety in physical features and resources and supports a large population at various levels of living. Not only do the diverse landscapes of Brazil hold great charm in themselves, but the combinations of natural and human characteristics that are typical of the different regions of the country attract one's attention.[10] Although the

10. Instituto Brasileiro de Geografia e Estatística, *Tipos e Aspectos do Brasil* (excerpts from *Revista Brasileira de Geografia*), 7th. ed. (Rio: Conselho Nacional de Geografia, 1963).

traditional intimate relationships between man and the land still exist in many parts of Brazil, people are crowding more and more into cities and, most particularly, into the largest cities. A fundamental question still left unanswered is how the vast expanses of territory largely unoccupied by man can be brought into a condition of effective living space for the nation's inhabitants.

Chapter 3

The People of Brazil and Their
Characteristics

T. Lynn Smith

HANKS TO the 1940, 1950, and 1960 censuses and the increased
"know-how" in the field of demography, the verified facts and
tested hypotheses about Brazil's people are increasing rapidly. In
this chapter an attempt is made to summarize briefly some of the more important facts about the number, distribution, characteristics, vital processes,
and growth of the population in Brazil.[1]

NUMBER AND DISTRIBUTION

The latest official census taken as of September 1, 1960, placed the total
population of Brazil at 70,967,185. Lest some may be of the opinion that
little or no credence may be given to this figure, it should be indicated that
Brazil's recent censuses were either done under the competent guidance of
Professor Giorgio Mortara or were taken by those strongly influenced by
him. This authority has calculated that the percentage of omissions in 1940
was only 1.7, which compares not too unfavorably with an index of 1.4
per cent for the corresponding census of the United States. Since 1960 the
excess of births over deaths in Brazil has made for a very rapid increase in
population; so it may be estimated conservatively that in 1970 there were
at least 95,000,000 persons in the republic.

In evaluating these figures it may be helpful to consider that Brazil contains approximately 2.4 per cent of the population of the world, 50 per cent

1. A large share of the materials presented here was taken from the author's earlier
studies *Brazil: People and Institutions*, 3rd ed. (Baton Rouge: Louisiana State University
Press, 1963); and "The Growth of Population in Central and South America" in U.S.
House of Representatives, Committee on the Judiciary, Subcommittee No. 1, *Study of
Population and Immigration Problems, Western Hemisphere (II)* (Washington: U.S.
Government Printing Office, 1963), pp. 125–84.

of the people of South America, and about 35 per cent of all the inhabitants of the extensive area known as Latin America. It is also of interest to know that Brazil's population in 1960 was about 39 per cent as large as that of the United States. About 17.5 per cent of all the inhabitants of the New World are Brazilians.

Even though it contains more than one-third of the population of Latin America, Brazil's boundaries encircle more than 41 per cent of the total land area south of the Rio Grande, so the average density of population is considerably less than that in some other parts of Latin America. Thus the number of persons per square mile was only 21.6 in 1960, which is practically the same as the 20.7 average for the South American continent, but somewhat greater than the specific figures for some other countries, such as 18.5 for Argentina, 20 for Peru, and 20.5 for Venezuela. It was much less than the 46 persons per square mile of national territory in Mexico, the 154 in Cuba, and the 302 in El Salvador.

The striking thing about the distribution of population in Brazil is the degree to which it is concentrated within a few hundred miles of the seacoast (fig. 1).

From the mouth of the Amazon to the Uruguayan border there are only a few coastal stretches that are not rather densely populated. Most of the large cities lie directly upon the seaside or only a short distance inland, and the narrow coastal band is also the home of the bulk of the rural population. On the other hand, except in the southern portions of the country where the twentieth century has seen the population surging to the interior in a tremendous burst of colonizing activity, there are only a few scattered localities in which the fingers of dense settlement have pushed inland to any great extent. Exceptions to this rule are penetrations along the Paranaguá River, which forms the boundary between the states of Maranhão and Piauí, the band of densely settled territory extending into southern Ceará from Paraíba, the fairly well-populated stretch of territory along the railway that runs from Salvador to Joazeiro in the state of Bahia, and another in the southern part of that state. By far the greatest penetration of settlement into the interior is the one which has pushed up into central Goiás along the highway to Brasília and the railway which has been extended from São Paulo through the Triangulo of Minas Gerais to the thriving little city of Anápolis.

Throughout a large portion of all Brazilian territory, the density of population is very low. However, only a small part of it is entirely unoccupied, for even in the vast interior, one occasionally will find a small village; a cattle *fazenda*; a post for dispensing supplies to and assembling the products of those who gather rubber and other things the forest has to offer; and, at widely separated intervals, a town or city of considerable importance. But the distances between each of these are enormous, and most of the interior can hardly be thought of as territory that has been settled. The great expanses of central Brazil are practically devoid of inhabitants.

The center of population in 1960 fell far to the south of the center of national territory, being located in the east south-central portion of the

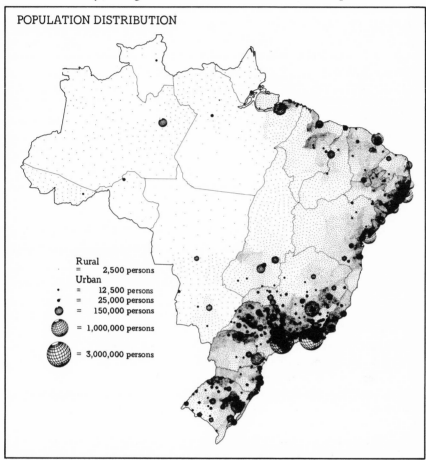

POPULATION DISTRIBUTION

Rural
= 2,500 persons
Urban
• = 12,500 persons
⚬ = 25,000 persons
◉ = 150,000 persons
= 1,000,000 persons
= 3,000,000 persons

Figure 1. Population Distribution

state of Minas Gerais, not far from its capital, Belo Horizonte, and almost due north of Rio de Janeiro. Furthermore, between 1920 and 1960 the center of population moved a short distance to the south in a slightly easterly direction.

COMPOSITION OF POPULATION

There are few places in the world in which the racial makeup of the population is more involved and complex than it is in Brazil. All the principal varieties of mankind, all the basic stocks into which the human race may be divided—red, white, black, and yellow—have entered into the composition of the population of this great half-continent. For some reason, the impression has been widely diffused abroad that the Negro races are the ones that have contributed most heavily to the formation of the Brazilian people. The present writer believes such a thesis to be absolutely untenable. Certainly the Caucasian races have contributed more heavily than the Negro to the genes of Brazil's population as presently constituted, and probably the importance of the black races has been no greater than that of the aboriginal Indians. During the twentieth century the injection of several hundred thousand Japanese into São Paulo and the adjacent states, where they are multiplying at a very rapid rate, added the last of the great types of mankind to the Brazilian color scheme.

Racial Elements

In the 1950 census the population of Brazil was classified according to color into the following groups:

Color	Number	Per Cent
White	32,027,661	61.7
Black	5,692,657	11.0
Yellow	329,082	0.6
Brown	13,786,742	26.5
Undeclared	108,255	0.2

Although the writer thinks there is little doubt that the Caucasian races have contributed most to the biological makeup of the Brazilian population, he believes these figures should be viewed with a degree of caution. In the first place, the category of whites must be thought of as designating those who are white or whitish, and it should be realized that a considerable number of those who were placed in this category have a substantial strain of Indian heritage. Furthermore, the admixtures from Negroid sources, although probably of less importance than from the Indian, are by no means lacking entirely in a substantial part of those who are classified as whites. The number of persons classed as blacks, or Negroes, certainly is the absolute minimum, and any change whatsoever in the criteria used probably would have increased this number. It is unfortunate that the single category of *pardo*, or brown, was used to designate the mixtures of two fundamentally different types, the crosses of whites and Negroes and also those of whites and Indians, as well as the Indians themselves. As it stands, the two mixed groups are probably represented in about the same proportions, although, as indicated above, many who might be placed in this mixed category are included with the whites. *Cafusos*, who spring from the Negro-Indian cross, although not entirely lacking, are too few to make any substantial difference in the total figures.

The data from the 1950 census also offer an opportunity of observing how the proportions of the different races vary from one part of the country to another. These data have been mapped in figure 2. This illustration

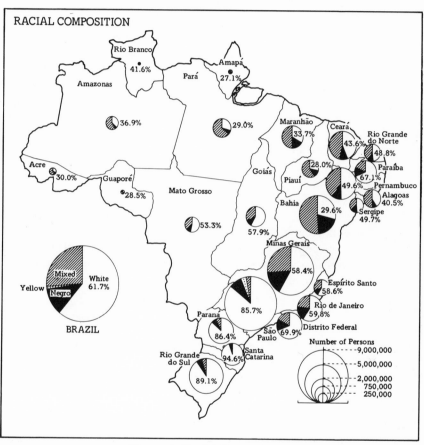

Figure 2. Racial Composition

has the advantage of showing the relative importance of the total population of each state at the same time that it reveals how the inhabitants of each are distributed among the several color categories. It deserves careful study by anyone who has an interest in the fundamental types of mankind as they are represented in the population of Brazil.

Lest some may think that the writer tends to overstress the importance of the white element in Brazil, attention should be directed to the southern part of the country. Note especially that São Paulo, the most populous state in Brazil, Rio Grande do Sul, which ranks fourth in population, Santa Catarina, and Paraná contain very small proportions of Negroes and mixed bloods. In all of these the descendants of recent immigrants from Europe constitute the bulk of the inhabitants. The high proportions of whites in Minas Gerais, the Distrito Federal (now the state of Guanabara), the state of Rio de Janeiro, and in Espírito Santo also should be taken into account.

The concentrations of the Negroid elements deserve comment. The data in figure 2 bear out the general impression that, from the racial standpoint, Bahia is the darkest spot on the map of Brazil. Not only are the absolute number and relative importance of Negroes large in the state, but the mixed category in Bahia undoubtedly consists largely of mulattoes. Other states in which the majority of the population that has been placed in the mixed category consists of the white-Negro crosses are Rio de Janeiro, Sergipe, Alagoas, Pernambuco, Paraíba, and Maranhão; the Distrito Federal also belongs with the group.

Indians and their crosses with whites make up the principal colored strain in the populations of such states as Amazonas and Pará and are to be reckoned with also in Mato Grosso, Goiás, Piauí, Ceará, and Rio Grande do Norte. As a matter of fact, throughout the inland, or *sertão,* and portions of the entire northeast, the Indian strain is important; but of course the more densely populated, sugar-growing, coastal districts, in which the Negroes and mulattoes constitute the lion's share of the population, tip the balance greatly in favor of the black element in all of the states from Bahia to Paraíba.

National Origins

Brazil is outstanding among the nations of the world, and even among those of the Western Hemisphere, in the extent to which large numbers of immigrants from various countries have been incorporated into the population. Following are a few general and basic facts about the foreign-born population, their origins, and their distribution.

In 1920, 1,565,961 persons, or about 1 out of every 20 persons living in Brazil (5.2 per cent), had come from another country. Of these, the largest contingent, 558,405, or 35.7 per cent, was from Italy; with Portugal (27.7 per cent), Spain (14 per cent), Germany (3.4 per cent), and Turkey (3.2 per cent) following in the order named. Uruguay, Poland, Russia, Japan, Austria, Argentina, Paraguay, and France, also in the order of their importance, were the other countries which had contributed 10,000 or more persons to help swell the population of South America's largest country. Most of these immigrants were located in a few of the southern states, 52.4 per cent of them being in São Paulo, 15.1 per cent in the Distrito Federal, 9.7 in

Rio Grande do Sul, 5.5 in Minas Gerais, 4 in Paraná, 3.4 in Rio de Janeiro, and 2 in Santa Catarina. On a relative basis, the foreign-born were most important in the Distrito Federal, where they constituted 20.8 per cent of the inhabitants; then followed São Paulo (18.2 per cent), Mato Grosso (10.4 per cent), Paraná (9.2 per cent), and Rio Grande do Sul (7.1 per cent).

Immigration to Brazil, which was very high from 1887 to 1897 and from 1912 to 1914, never regained its former importance after the close of World War I, although it was fairly large between 1920 and 1930. As a result, the total number of foreign-born in the population has been falling steadily since 1920. By 1950 it was only 1,224,184, or 2.3 per cent of the national population. Of these foreign-born, the largest number, 336,826, or 27.5 per cent, were natives of Portugal; and the second largest contingent, 242,337, or 19.8 per cent, was from Italy. The other six countries which had contributed most to the foreign-born population of Brazil (and the number of persons from each) are as follows: Spain, 131,608, or 10.8 per cent; Japan, 129,192, or 10.6 per cent; Germany, 65,184, or 5.4 per cent; Poland, about 48,806, or 4 per cent; and Syria and Lebanon, 44,718, or 3.7 per cent. Persons originating in these eight countries made up 82 per cent of all the foreign-born in Brazil.

By 1950 the immigrant population of Brazil was even more highly concentrated in a few sections of the country than it was in 1920. Thus, at the time of the mid-century enumeration, São Paulo alone contained 693,321 foreign-born persons, or 56.6 per cent of all those in Brazil. The Distrito Federal was the home of an additional 210,454 (17.2 per cent). Therefore the two together had almost three-fourths of all those who were born elsewhere than in Brazil. In 1920 they contained two-thirds of Brazil's foreigners. The four other states containing the largest contingents of the foreign-born in 1950, with the corresponding numbers and percentages, are as follows: Rio Grande do Sul, 78,134, or 6.4 per cent; Paraná, 76,502, or 6.3 per cent; Rio de Janeiro, 38,395, or 3.1 per cent; and Minas Gerais, 32,896, or 2.7 per cent. Together, these five states and the Distrito Federal had 92.3 per cent of the entire foreign-born population. As these figures suggest, by 1950 the relative importance of those born in other countries had decreased greatly in comparison with the situation in 1920. By 1950 in the Distrito Federal the foreign-born made up only 9 per cent of the population, and in São Paulo only 7.6 per cent. Elsewhere, of course, the proportions of the immigrants were much smaller, the largest being 3.6 per cent in Paraná, 1.9 per cent in Rio Grande do Sul, and 1.7 per cent in the state of Rio de Janeiro. Although Minas Gerais ranks with these in having 30,000 or more of the foreign-born within its limits, the immigrants are engulfed completely in the state's teeming millions and make up less than 1 per cent of the population.

Residence

Quantitatively and qualitatively Brazil's population was for centuries among the most rural in the world. No other fact is of greater importance than this for one who would understand Brazil and the Brazilians. In the words of Dr. F. J. Oliveira Vianna, the great sociologist and culture historian:

From the first days of our history we have been an agricultural and pastoral people. . . . Urbanism is a modern element in our social evolution. All of our history is that of an agricultural people, is the history of a society of farmers and herdsmen. In the country our race was formed and in it were molded the intimate forces of our civilization. The dynamism of our history in the colonial period came from the countryside. The admirable stability of our society in the Imperial period was based in the country.[2]

The quantitative aspects of the subject are made abundantly clear from the data gathered in the 1940 census. According to the criteria employed, 68 per cent of the population was classified as rural and the remainder as urban. However, these criteria provided that the inhabitants of every seat of a *município* and those of many district seats, regardless of the number of inhabitants, were to be placed in the urban category, so that this group actually embraced the residents of several thousand very small villages and hamlets, including one in the far-away part of Mato Grosso which had a population of only 61. Brazil's towns and cities of 5,000 or more inhabitants numbered only 319, and only 27 of them had as many as 40,000 residents. Were criteria similar to those used in the United States census employed, the percentage of the population in the urban category probably would have been between 20 and 25.

From the qualitative standpoint, also, the population of Brazil has been extremely rural. With its people spread throughout an enormous territory, with relatively few important focal points of urban and industrial cultural influences, with a high proportion of the population engaged directly in agricultural and collecting activities, and with the systems of communication and transportation still in a rudimentary form, it should be evident that the degree of rurality in Brazil is very high. The inhabitant of the average little town or village in Brazil is conditioned to a far greater extent by cultural influences arising from the surrounding rural environment, and less by those emanating from large urban centers, than is the resident of a center of equal size in the United States or Western Europe. It still will be many decades before good roads, automobiles, electricity, telephones, radios, tele-

2. Instituto Brasileiro de Geografia e Estatística, "O Povo Brasileiro e sua Evolução," *Recenseamento do Brasil, 1920*, vol. 1 (Rio: Tipografia de Estatística, 1922): 281.

vision sets, newspapers, and the many other commodities which have come to be considered as necessities in the average rural community in the United States are found to any considerable extent in the rural districts of Brazil. In the meantime, the footpath, trail, or stream, the canoe, pack animal, riding horse, and oxcart, the homemade candle and lamp, and communication by word of mouth remain the basic elements in the rural scheme of living in Brazil. There is no reason for doubting that, while Brazilian cities have moved ahead in the stream of modern progress, her rural districts have continued decade after decade with little or no visible change. Cultural lag has been tremendous. Whereas in the United States social changes since 1920 have tended to eliminate the differences between the ways of living in rural and urban districts, in Brazil the same forces have tended to accentuate even more the differences between the two.

Since 1950, however, drastic changes have taken place in the rural-urban distribution of Brazil's inhabitants. An exodus of tremendous proportions has transplanted millions of persons, primarily those of humble origins and low socioeconomic status, uprooting them from the rural districts and putting them down in teeming cities and towns and the miserable "suburbs" which encircle them. The present writer's own estimates indicate that the overwhelming rush of population from the open country to cities and towns between 1950 and 1960 involved about 7,000,000 persons; that is, about 1 out of every 10 persons enumerated in the 1960 census personally had migrated from a rural area to an urban center during the preceding ten years. As large as are this number and proportion, they must be strictly in accord with the expectations on the part of anyone who has been in a position to observe the mushrooming of existing cities and towns, the sudden appearance of great sprawling slums in the zones surrounding all the principal metropolitan centers, and the emergence and growth of hundreds of additional urban places. See table 1.

Age Distribution

Few features of Brazil's population are of greater significance than the manner in which it is distributed according to age. As is true in any country in which the birth rate is very high, the population of Brazil is highly concentrated in the tender years of life (fig. 3). Thus, according to the 1940 and 1950 censuses, in Brazil 40 per cent of the population is less than 15 years of age, whereas in the United States in 1950 the corresponding percentage was only 25. On the other hand, elderly folk in Brazil are much less important, relatively, than they are in countries such as the United States, France, Great Britain, Germany, and Australia, where the birth rate is lower and the expectation of life greater. The specific type of age profile that is characteristic of Brazil and other Latin American countries affects every aspect of institutional life, but is particularly significant in the economic and educational spheres. As compared with his fellows in North America or Western Europe, the average Brazilian in the productive years of life has more mouths to feed. Therefore, he must either produce more goods and services, or he, his children, and his parents who have passed the productive ages must get along on a much lower per capita consumption. Such an age distribution also favors a situation in which thousands of youngsters, many of them hardly more than babes in arms, are thrust out into the world to make their own way.

If one considers persons of less than 15 years of age and those 65 years and over as dependents, while those 15 to 65 are classed as producers, an interesting and significant ratio of dependents to producers can be computed. On this basis, in 1950 there were in Brazil 80 dependents for every

TABLE 1

NUMBERS OF TOWNS AND CITIES IN BRAZIL ACCORDING TO THE
SIZES OF THEIR POPULATIONS, 1940, 1950, AND 1960

Number of Inhabitants	Number of Places		
	1940	1950	1960
TOTAL	900	1,174	1,799
More than 3,000,000	0	0	2
2,000,000 to 3,000,000	0	2	0
1,000,000 to 2,000,000	2	0	0
500,000 to 1,000,000	0	1	4
250,000 to 500,000	3	3	4
100,000 to 250,000	5	8	21
50,000 to 100,000	12	19	42
25,000 to 50,000	18	44	80
10,000 to 25,000	125	145	252
5,000 to 10,000	177	258	378
2,000 to 5,000	558	694	1,016

SOURCE: Instituto Brasileiro de Geografia e Estatística, *VII Recenseamento Geral do Brasil, 1960. Sinopse Preliminar do Censo Demográfico* (Rio: Serviço Nacional de Recenseamento, 1962), passim.

100 producers, whereas in the United States the corresponding ratio was only 54.

Similarly, the nature of the age distribution of Brazil's population means that the proportions of those who should be attending primary and secondary schools are inordinately high. This greatly magnifies the nation's problem of keeping the solemn pledge it made in signing the Charter of Punta del Este, popularly known as the Alliance for Progress, whereby it made the commitment to provide before 1970 access to a minimum of six years of elementary schooling for every child of appropriate age throughout its immense territory.

It also is important to indicate that the chances are slight that any substantial modification in the basic features of Brazil's age distribution will take place within the next few decades. Immigration and emigration could swell to many times their present levels without producing any readily observable effects upon the proportions of the very young, those in the productive ages, and those who have lived for more than sixty-five years; and the effects of the now rapidly falling death rate are spread over all of the age groups. Therefore, any substantial changes in the proportions of the population in the various age groups must result primarily from a sudden, drastic fall in the birth rate. Such a significant trend may develop within the next quarter of a century, as the population becomes primarily urban and as a knowledge of modern birth control techniques are made available to

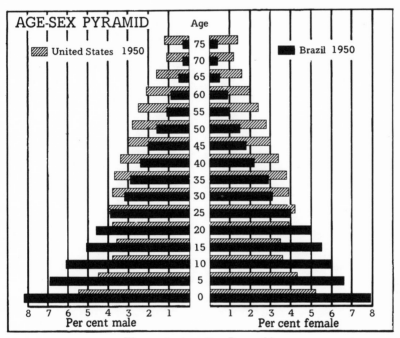

Figure 3. Age-Sex Pyramid

the masses, and, if so, it is not impossible that we shall see in Brazil another example of the sudden drop in fertility rivaling that which took place in the United States between 1900 and 1930 and that in Japan after 1947.

If such a large and rapid fall in the birth rate should materialize, the time would come when there would be in Brazil more persons aged 15 to 20 than those under 5, for example, and a considerable number of other closely related shifts in the relative importance of the age groups in the lower part of the age-sex pyramid would occur. A radical trend of this nature could produce, as it did in the United States in 1930, a situation in which the pop-

ulation was highly concentrated in the economically and biologically productive ages. But, we must hasten to add that the commencement of the
required abrupt decline in the birth rate is not yet observable and that it
appears to be at least another decade or so away. Moreover, even after it
gets well started, a quarter of a century may be required for its effects upon
the age distribution to become pronounced. Finally, a fall drastic enough to
bring about any very substantial changes in the relative importance of the
very young, those between 15 and 65, and the aged, may not take place at all.

As generally is the case, there is a marked contrast between the age dis-
tributions of the urban and rural segments of Brazil's population. This may
be illustrated with data which show the percentage classified as urban for

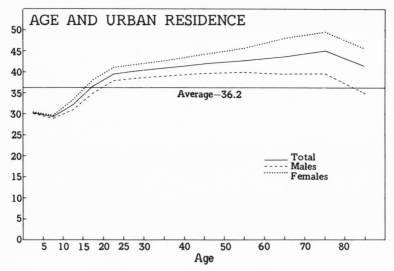

Figure 4. Age and Urban Residence

each of the age groups used in the official tabulations (fig. 4). One should
note especially the high degree to which those who are very young are
concentrated in the rural population and the large proportions of those in
the biologically and economically productive ages in the cities and towns.
Moreover, even though persons who have passed their sixty-fifth birthdays
are conspicuous by their relative scarcity in Brazil, the tiny segment of the
population that is made up of such persons is concentrated to a considerable
degree in the nation's urban centers.

Marital Status

Although the people of Brazil do not shun formal marriage ties to the same
extent as those of Colombia, Venezuela, and some of the other Latin Amer-

ican countries, legal mating is still far less prevalent among them than it is in most European countries, in the United States and Canada, or in Japan. At all ages, the percentages of Brazilians, male and female, who are living in the marital state (including common-law as well as legal and religious marriages) are comparatively low by the standards prevailing in the United States and Western Europe, although they are high in comparison with those in other Latin American countries, such as Venezuela (figs. 5 and 6). The fact that the curves representing the percentages of single persons in the population drop more precipitously in Brazil than in the United States indicates that the age of marriage in the former is somewhat higher than it

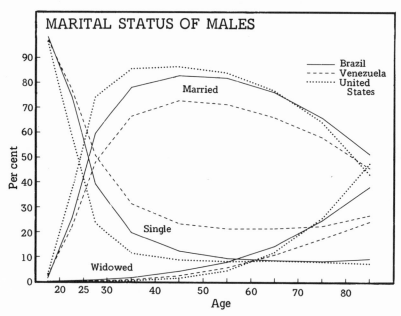

Figure 5. Marital Status of Males

is in the latter. The differences between the same curves at the more advanced ages indicate that the Brazilian woman is almost twice as likely to live out her entire life without contracting matrimony as is her sister in the United States. No such differential prevails between the male populations of the two countries. These sex differences may be due in part to the fact that the higher death rates in Brazil give the old bachelors greater opportunities for marrying widows than are present in the United States. Such a hypothesis receives some support from the nature of the differences in the curves representing the percentages of widows in the populations. But the greater relative importance of immigrants, among whom the men greatly outnumber the women, in the United States could also have an important bearing on the difference.

Higher death rates among all age groups in Brazil and Peru than in the United States are responsible for the fact that the curves representing the widowed rise more rapidly in those Latin American countries than in our own. This, in turn, creates more opportunities for widowers to remarry; so the differences between the male populations of the two countries are far less than those between the female populations.

In Brazil, by the time the female population reaches age sixty-one, the number of widows exactly equals the number of married women. This situation does not prevail in the United States until the sixty-eighth year of

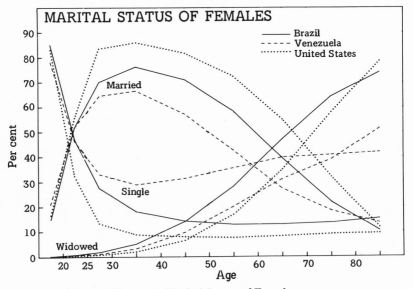

Figure 6. Marital Status of Females

age. The chances are equal that the Brazilian woman who lives to be 67 years of age will be a widow, while in the United States the corresponding age is 74. The basic fact which deserves emphasis is that the population of Brazil contains high proportions of single and widowed persons and relatively low proportions of those living in the married state.

THE VITAL PROCESSES

The rate of reproduction and the mortality rate, or expectation of life, are the two most important items in national accounting. Unfortunately it will be some time before either of them in Brazil can be accurately gauged, but even so it is essential that the present state of affairs be known.

The Birth Rate

Only recently has it been possible to determine much about the birth rate in Brazil, except the fact that it was very high. As yet, the registration of births is quite inadequately organized, so that the number of births recorded in the civil registers is much lower than the number of baptisms reported annually by the Catholic Church. Working with the data on baptisms and other materials, the present writer had reached the conclusion that the birth rate per 1,000 inhabitants of Brazil in 1940 must have been 40 or above. Subsequently, Professor Giorgio Mortara, after a most careful study of the thoroughgoing materials pertaining to human fertility which were collected in the 1940 census, concluded that the birth rate in Brazil was at least 42, being highest in the state of Santa Catarina at 45.5 per 1,000 inhabitants and lowest in the state of São Paulo at 37.8. Presently it seems certain that the true rate is at least 43.

Another simple index of the rapidity with which a given population is reproducing is obtained by determining the number of children under 5 per 100 women aged 15 to 44, inclusive. Computations based on the 1950 census data support the conclusion that the birth rate in Brazil is very high. Thus in 1950 there were approximately 65 children under 5 for each 100 women in the childbearing ages as specified above. Comparable indices for a few other countries at about the same time are as follows: Venezuela, 71; Chile, 57; Mexico, 63; Ecuador, 71; France, 28; Australia, 40; and the United States, 42.

Since Brazil's high rate of reproduction is unequaled in most parts of the world, it means that most of the factors which have reduced the fertility of western populations during the last century are still inoperative in this great South American country. However, even with crude devices, it is possible to demonstrate that there is a tremendous rural/urban differential, which leads to the belief that, as Brazil now urbanizes and industrializes, the birth rates there may soon fall precipitously just as they did in Europe and North America.

The Death Rate

The registers of vital statistics in Brazil must be greatly improved before it will be possible to determine with any degree of accuracy the death rate or expectation of life for the country as a whole. That the mortality rate is very high is evident from a few soundings that have been made here and there and from the nature of the age-sex pyramid, but just how high will not be known for some time to come. The best estimate that I have been able to make would place the death rate in Brazil at about 15 per 1,000 population, a figure half again as high as that prevailing in the United States. Even this allows for the drastic reduction which seems to have taken place since 1950.

Even with the inadequate data, it is evident that the preventable and transmissible diseases continue to take a frightful toll of life throughout Brazilian territory. Tuberculosis, influenza and pneumonia, and syphilis are among the greatest killers (see table 2).

Infant Mortality

Any figures on infant mortality in Brazil can be little more than considered guesses. Since this particular index, one of the most sensitive measures of the well-being of a people or a society, is secured by relating the number of infants who die in the course of a given year to the number of live births occurring during that year, the present deficiencies in the registries of births

TABLE 2

SELECTED CAUSES OF DEATH IN THE CITY OF RIO DE JANEIRO AND THE
MUNICÍPIO OF SÃO PAULO, 1954–1956*

Causes of Death	Number of Deaths per 100,000 Population	
	Rio de Janeiro	São Paulo
Diphtheria	2.7	2.2
Dysenteries	5.3	9.8
Ailments of the circulatory system	240.5	203.7
Ailments of the digestive system	171.0	155.5
Ailments of the genitourinary system	24.5	18.8
Ailments of the respiratory system	84.3	69.2
Typhoid fever	2.8	0.4
Malaria	0.2	0.4
Malignant neoplasms	96.9	111.9
Syphilis	13.9	8.7
Tuberculosis	93.6	36.7

*Compiled and computed from data in Instituto Brasileiro de Geografia e Estatística, *Anuário Estatístico do Brasil, 1960* (Rio: Conselho Nacional de Estatística, 1960), p. 27.

make it impossible for anyone to make the necessary calculations. However, among the rates that are reported for the period 1956–1958 are the following ones for the *municípios* containing some of the nation's principal cities: Natal, 431; Maceió, 415; Recife, 233; São Luis, 203; Salvador (Bahia), 166; Belém, 153; Curitiba, 139; Manaus, 131; Porto Alegre, 124; Rio de Janeiro, 111; Belo Horizonte, 98; and São Paulo, 77. Most of these figures are highly suspect, and the deficiencies of the data are such that some of them may even be too high. For comparative purposes, by 1940 the infant mortality rate in the United States had been reduced to 47, and for the three years 1956–1958 it averaged only 26.5.

GROWTH OF POPULATION

As has been indicated above, the latest census enumeration placed the population of Brazil at 70,967,185 as of September 1, 1960. This figure represented an increase of more than 19 million (37 per cent) over the population in 1950, a truly phenomenal rise, and it played a major role in bringing about the now rather widely known fact that in the second half of the twentieth century the population of the twenty Latin American countries are in the forefront of the huge upsurge of world population that is taking place. Over the seventy-year period 1890 to 1960 the annual rate of Brazil's population increase was high, and between 1950 and 1960 it was 3.1 per cent, an amazing figure. In this connection it is well to have in mind the fact that prior to 1950 an annual rate of growth of more than 3 per cent had never been experienced by the population of any large segment of the earth's surface, with the single exception of the United States between 1800 and 1860.

TABLE 3

GROWTH OF POPULATION IN BRAZIL, 1808–1960*

Year	Population	Year	Population
1808	2,419,406	1900	17,318,556
1823	3,960,866	1920	30,635,605
1830	5,340,000	1940	41,565,083
1854	7,677,800	1950	51,944,397
1872	9,930,478	1960	70,967,185
1890	14,333,915	1970	95,000,000**

    * Instituto Brasileiro de Geografia e Estatística, *Recenseamento do Brazil, 1920,* vol. 1 (Rio: Tipografia de Estatística, 1922): 403–21; and Instituto Brasileiro de Geografia e Estatística, *VII Recenseamento Geral do Brasil, 1960. Sinopse Preliminar do Censo Demográfico* (Rio: Serviço Nacional de Recenseamento, 1962), pp. 2–3.
    ** Author's estimate.

Prior to the 1940 census, counts of Brazil's inhabitants left a great deal to be desired, although the censuses from 1890 on were much better than the crude enumerations which took place during the period in which Brazil was an empire. It is probably impossible to take under consideration data on the long-time growth of population in the half-continent that are any more reliable than those assembled in table 3.

Regional Differences

The rapidity with which the population has increased during recent decades varies greatly from one section of Brazil to another. In order to supply the basic data necessary to bring out clearly the principal features of this, table 4 and figure 7 were prepared. Observation of them emphasizes the fact that the great increases of population, on the relative basis as well as on the absolute, have taken place in the southern part of the country. In terms of total numbers, the increase from 1940 to 1960 of almost 6 million in the popula-

TABLE 4

ABSOLUTE AND RELATIVE INCREASES OF POPULATION IN THE VARIOUS
BRAZILIAN STATES, 1940–1950 AND 1950–1960*

Country	Number of Inhabitants			Increase 1940–50		Increase 1950–60	
	1940	1950	1960	Number	Per Cent	Number	Per Cent
Brazil	41,236,315	51,944,397	70,967,185	10,708,082	26	19,022,788	37
North:							
Acre[1]	79,768	114,755	160,208	34,987	44	45,453	40
Amazonas[2]	438,008	532,215	750,704	94,207	22	218,489	41
Pará[3]	944,644	1,160,750	1,619,824	216,106	23	459,074	40
Northeast:							
Maranhão	1,235,169	1,583,248	2,492,139	348,079	28	908,891	57
Piauí	817,601	1,045,696	1,263,368	228,095	28	217,672	21
Ceará	2,091,032	2,695,450	3,337,856	604,418	29	642,406	24
Rio Grande do Norte	768,018	967,921	1,157,258	199,903	26	189,337	20
Paraíba	1,422,282	1,713,259	2,018,023	290,977	20	304,764	18
Pernambuco	2,688,240	3,395,185	4,136,900	706,945	26	741,715	22
Alagoas[1]	951,300	1,093,137	1,271,062	141,837	15	177,925	16
Fernando do Noronha[1]	0	581	1,389	581	—	808	139
East:							
Sergipe	542,326	644,361	760,273	102,035	19	115,912	18
Bahia	3,918,112	4,834,575	5,990,605	916,463	23	1,156,030	24
Minas Gerais	6,736,416	7,717,792	9,798,880	981,376	15	2,081,088	27
Serra dos Aimores[4]	66,994	160,072	384,297	93,078	166	224,225	140
Espírito Santo	750,107	861,562	1,188,665	111,455	15	327,103	38
Rio de Janeiro	1,847,857	2,297,194	3,402,728	449,337	24	1,105,534	48
Guanabara	1,764,141	2,377,451	3,307,163	613,310	35	929,712	39
South:							
São Paulo	7,180,316	9,134,423	12,974,699	1,954,107	27	3,840,276	42
Paraná	1,236,276	2,115,547	4,277,763	879,271	71	2,162,216	102
Santa Catarina	1,178,340	1,560,502	2,146,909	382,162	32	586,407	38
Rio Grande do Sul	3,320,689	4,164,821	5,448,823	844,132	25	1,284,002	21
West-central:							
Mato Grosso[5]	432,265	558,979	981,045	126,714	29	422,066	76
Goiás[6]	826,414	1,214,921	2,096,604	388,507	47	881,683	73

* Compiled and computed from data in Instituto Brasileiro de Geografia e Estatística, *VII Recenseamento do Brasil, 1960. Sinopse Preliminar do Censo Demográfico* (Rio: Serviço Nacional de Recenseamento, 1962), pp. 2–3.

1. Territory.
2. Data for Amazonas include those for the territory of Rio Branco, which was separated from it subsequent to the 1940 census.
3. Data for Pará include those for the territory of Amapá, which was separated from it subsequent to the 1940 census.
4. Area in dispute between the states of Espírito Santo and Minas Gerais.
5. Data for Mato Grosso include those for the territory of Rondônia, which was separated from it subsequent to the 1940 census.
6. The 1960 data for Goiás include the 141,742 residents of the new Federal District (Brasília), created after 1950 from territory formerly constituting a part of Goiás.

tion of São Paulo is by far the largest gain, although the addition of more than 3 million persons to the population of Paraná and another 3 million to that of Minas Gerais must be thought of as major developments.

On a relative basis, the increase between 1950 and 1960 of 102 per cent in the population of Paraná is indicative of the tremendous development going on in that highly important state, especially since it came on the heels

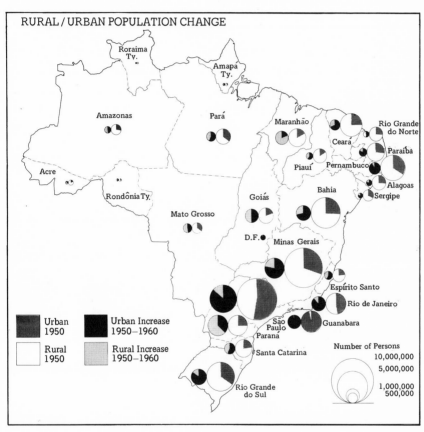

Figure 7. Rural / Urban Population Change

of a 71 percent increase during the preceding decade. Substantial influxes of migrants into the southern parts of Mato Grosso and Goiás also helped greatly to produce very high percentage increases of population in those two large and sparsely inhabited units of the Brazilian confederation. In the latter, of course, the mushrooming of the "free" suburbs of Brasília, that is the workers' districts just outside the new Federal District, and other developments drawing people to south and central Goiás which resulted from the building of the new capital, had much to do with the rapid rate of population growth. Moreover, it is interesting to note that between 1950 and 1960, Maranhão in the far north, the westernmost state in the northeastern region, experienced a 57 percent increase in population.

Finally, it is important to stress a fact clearly demonstrated by a study of figure 7. This is the one mentioned above, which indicates that the great bulk of Brazil's recent population growth has taken place in its cities and towns and relatively little of it either in the established rural settlements or on the frontier. Northern Paraná and north-central Maranhão are, of course, important exceptions to this generalization. But, in Brazil as a whole, between 1950 and 1960 the urban population experienced an increase of 13,208,000, or 70 per cent, whereas the numerically much larger rural population mounted by only 5,815,000, or 18 per cent. Based upon the data presented here, and others available to the present writer, one is on safe grounds in generalizing that the only parts of Brazil's immense territory in which recently and currently there are any substantial efforts going on to bring new zones into agricultural production are the following: the northern part of Paraná; the north-central section of Maranhão; the portions of Goiás which are in fairly close proximity to Brasília; the valley of the Rio Doce and the section to the north of it in Minas Gerais; and the extreme northwestern part of São Paulo.

As a result of the recent rapid urbanization of Brazil, by 1960, 45 per cent of the population was classified in the urban category, a rise from only 36 per cent in 1950. This produced an increase of over 13,200,000 (or 70 per cent) in the urban population, during the decade involved, compared with one of only 5,800,000 (18 per cent) in the rural population. In 1960, of course, the new state of Guanabara, or the old Distrito Federal—which consists largely of the city of Rio de Janeiro—was 93 percent urban. Moreover, Brazil's most populous state, São Paulo, was 63 percent urban at that time, as was the new Distrito Federal, in which Brasília is located. Furthermore, even by 1960 the growth of the suburbs of Rio de Janeiro, which are located in the adjacent state of the same name, had proceeded to the extent that the state of Rio de Janeiro had 61 per cent of its people classified as urban. In addition, two of the other most populous states in Brazil, Rio Grande do Sul and Pernambuco, had 45 per cent of their inhabitants in the urban category by 1960, with the trends progressing in a manner which makes it fairly certain that by 1970 each of these states will have substantially more urban than rural residents. Indeed, before 1970 arrives, Brazil almost certainly will have become a country in which the urban population outnumbers the rural.

Chapter 4

The Changing Role of Education
in Brazilian Society

Anisio S. Teixeira

O NE CANNOT analyze education in Brazil without keeping in mind its relationship to Brazilian society and culture. To deal with it as if it were a simple service rendered to society, such as electricity or water, whose quality and distribution it would be proper to examine and evaluate, would not only be useless but would tell us nothing about the nature of that which is distributed or how it is distributed. The quality, content, and distribution of education are determined by social and cultural conditions and reveal means for achieving and preserving objectives and values which are not always explicitly stated but which are important and cherished in the existing social organization.

We shall keep in mind this organic relationship between education and society as we examine education in Brazilian society.

BRAZILIAN SOCIETY

The seeds of Brazilian society were broadcast on the new soil of America during the full flowering of the Renaissance and Reformation. But we must remember that at that time Brazil and all of what is now called Latin America constituted lands and peoples to be conquered for Catholic culture within the Counter-Reformation movement, whose spirit, spread by the means of the Company of Jesus, would dominate the evolution of the nascent societies.

The paradox of Brazilian society—new in its territory and its geography but old in its organization, for that organization was intentionally restorative of ideals and aspirations already undergoing revolutionary change in Europe—prevented the experience of discovery and colonization from being spontaneous and from evolving the creative attitudes that generally accompany the development of something that is new and open.

71

Brazil's distance from the metropolis and the great expanse of Brazil's geographic space gave the country, it is true, a certain freedom; but, because of the dominance of the spirit of restoration and counter-reformation, the situation of the colony reflected the social phase of the Middle Ages rather than that of the Renaissance and Reformation, which were already transforming Europe.

The Middle Ages were sustained on the bases of a feudal structure with regard to the land and of a co-operative structure with regard to urban labor. Political organization was based, essentially, on the establishment of the repressive power necessary for the imposition of a rigid and uniform order and for defense against internal and external enemies. The Portuguese empire adopted this policy in its relations with its American colony. Its work consisted of building administrative cities and fortresses for territorial defense and of maintaining a bureaucracy for the collection of tribute and the control of foreign commerce. Within Brazilian territory, life was organized on the medieval basis of territorial fiefdoms and an incipient urban guild system. The Portuguese were to organize the servitude of the Indian. But, since the latter proved excessively anarchic and gained the support of the Jesuits in their resistance against serfdom, the importation of Africans as slaves became necessary. Thus we regressed to pre-medieval forms and social life became archaic, resting upon territorial feudalism and slavery.

In urban centers, except for the oppressors and the oppressed, there was only a handful of *free* men—organized in guilds more of beneficence than defense or living as single individuals. The resemblance was not to medieval Europe but to ancient Rome. Only the patriarchal family, a basic form of power, subordinated to the distant and invisible force of the empire, deserved to be called an institution. The very bureaucracy was only *fiscal* or military. The church carried out the catechism of the Indians and organized the spiritual theocratic regime of the civil society. In this context of a millenial age, the new phenomena were the tropics, the Indian, and the Negro. The distinguishing characteristics of the nation come from the intermixture of these three original factors with Roman Catholicism, feudalism, and imperial organization of power.

In the beginning no notion of individualism or self-government, except in the form of the patriarchal family, reached these South American shores. Portuguese municipalism itself, with its "chambers," was no more than a mechanism of *acquiescence* and obedience to an all-powerful central government. Under these circumstances, no institution existed in Brazilian life which could develop a sense of responsibility; there developed, instead, a sense of discretionary command wielded by the authorities and a sense of obedience, dependence, and passivity on the part of the subjects or the subjected, with the inevitable corollary involving the resistance of the repressed and the arbitrariness of the oppressor. Life was organized according to these elementary forces, having as tools a neolithic technology received from the Indians and the Negroes, to which were added the wheel, the candle, and the iron of the Portuguese—a superimposition of the iron age upon the age of stone. With these elements, we reached the beginning of the nineteenth century, when the Portuguese empire, already in decadence, allowed its colony independence under the command of a Portuguese prince regent.

Brazilian society, thus, was founded on the patriarchal family, slavery, and the latifundia, whose characteristics are immobility, limitation of opportunities, and supremacy of the private order. Everything indicated that this society would terminate its natural evolution by constituting itself a hereditary, aristocratic society, with the development of a sense of responsibility, of *noblesse oblige*, in the dominant group. However, this did not take place. Our nobility came to be one of titles and privileges conceded for life, without rights to succession. This served to inhibit the development of any sense of *noblesse oblige* that constitutes the positive aspect of an aristocracy.

To me this fact is significant and indicative of the substantial insecurity that the dominant class was never able to overcome, being, as it was, the holder of powers always *granted* but never *conquered*. Portuguese colonialism never admitted the transitory nature of its domination. The colonies were the provinces of the empire, and the empire was the metropolis whose power was exercised fully as much in the metropolis itself as in the territory of its colonies. It should be noted that later European empires were different. England, France, Holland, and even Belgium were imperial nations that, while maintaining their colonies, saw their metropolitan societies undergo great political transformations. When the colonies were emancipated, the metropolitan nations themselves, whose social and political organizations were much more advanced than that of the colonies, provided models for them to follow. The Portuguese colony was, on the contrary, an extension to a distant territory of the immobility of the metropolis, of Portugal itself.

The Permanence of the Colonial Structure in Brazilian Society

Education in the colonial period necessarily reflected the organization of a society simultaneously dominating and dominated, for, just as Brazil suffered the oppression of the metropolis, not being allowed the printing press or higher education, it was itself a society of masters and slaves. The distance from the metropolis provided the masters with a freedom that bordered on absolute power. In this society only priests and public servants, defined broadly to include persons in the service of the church and the crown, required a formal education, and for this the colony and the metropolis were associated in the provision of an apparently adequate supply of personnel.

The schools of the Jesuits and of the other religious orders provided, in the colony, an education to be completed later with courses taken in the metropolis. The other educational needs of the colony were met with the arrival of Portuguese already educated in their home country. The important positions in the two hierarchies—the ecclesiastic and the bureaucratic—generally speaking were the privilege of the Portuguese. In this sense the society was one with that of the metropolis. Within the rigid limits of these confines, there moved a colonial sub-society made up of patriarchal masters with ample powers, which were more limited by the conflict with the Jesuits, defenders of the Indian population, than by the metropolis itself, whose collection of taxes and tribute allied it with the exploitive spirit of the masters.

All education was reduced to the training of the clergy and those lettered men that the colonial society might necessitate, while higher education, denied to the colony, was entrusted to the metropolitan universities, where, without exception, the Jesuits dominated.

The schools of the Company of Jesus were scattered throughout the entire colony; for a long period, they constituted the only formal education which existed. The Jesuits, however, soon came into conflict with the colonizers, due to their defense of the Indians, and devoted themselves primarily to the task of catechizing and to training the clergy. Nevertheless, despite their conflict with the colonizing classes, who also were all Catholics, we owe to the Jesuits the spread of Catholicism among the indigenous population and its diffusion throughout Brazilian society.

Until 1759 all the formal education in the nation consisted of this education in the catechism and the training of clergy, as well as a few of the lay population that would go on to the metropolis to obtain a higher education in order to pursue lay careers in law, administration, or medicine. To meet the needs for skilled laborers, the artisans were educated through apprenticeships in the trades, which were organized in groups that vaguely resembled the guilds of the Middle Ages. Thus the organization, content, and distribution of education were adapted to the theocratic and artisan society of the period, dominated by the predominantly Jesuit clergy.

In 1759 the Jesuits were expulsed. In the reconstruction period that followed, a secular or public education was initiated. In this way the nation lost the more severely theocratic aspects of the first two centuries, and the struggle for the political supremacy of the state began. The royal school replaced the Jesuit college; it had broader objectives than the formation of the clergy. In the metropolis the reform of the university and of the college of the nobles completed the new educational system, which emphasized civil society and its integration with the state under the command of the enlightened despotism of the period.

During this entire colonial period, formal education in the nation was Portuguese education itself, which was common to the metropolis and the colony, with modifications introduced into the system by local conditions and by the mixed ethnic composition of the colonial society.

Education had been a task for the church and not for the state; in the colonization of Brazil the church made itself a formative force of the society and was much more influential and powerful than the state. Only with Pombal did the latter achieve more independence in its quest for spiritual influence.

Let us not forget that the local society was merely a producer of export goods, with all commerce reduced to an exchange with foreign areas. The life of the country was limited to a narrow adaptation to the environment and to a subsistence and barter economy.

The control of colonization was exercised from abroad and was limited to achieving efficiency in the shipments made to the metropolis. Local authority was allowed a considerable margin of freedom in the management of purely domestic affairs. Thus the conflict with the church and, above all, with the Jesuits was more visible than that with the officials of the crown, except when the latter sporadically supported Jesuit policies. The oppressive power of the slavocratic order was mitigated only by the influence of religion, which soon, however, accepted Negro slavery and limited itself to opposing the enslavement of the Indians, whom it had taken under its protection.

In these distant parts of the empire the white master enjoyed ample freedom to implant an internal social order based on the complete submission of the directly oppressed groups of slaves and servants and of the indirectly subjugated group made up of the few free men of the lower classes.

This fact produced a division of society into strata that resembled castes more than classes, thus suggesting an oriental rather than occidental model in its organization. The needs for education in such a society were limited to those of the masters and of the higher ranks of officials allied with them, including, after the expulsion of the Jesuits, the clergy. It was, fundamentally, an education for conformity and the maintenance of the status quo.

These circumstances must be kept in mind in order to understand the absence in colonial society of any substantial libertarian strain and such a society's conformity with the existent kind of social organization. Essentially, colonial society was more conservative than that of the metropolis, a fact verified by its resistance to the reforms, more apparent than real, of Pombal.

With the move of the Portuguese royal family to Brazil in 1808, the process was initiated which resulted in independence under a constitutional monarch. Through it, the nation got some education for independence. First, Brazil became the metropolis, with the presence of the court in Rio de Janeiro for more than twelve years; later, it had a semi-independent status under a prince regent; and, finally, independence was declared by the prince regent himself. Brazil became a colony by virtue of conquest from abroad; the decision for its independence was made by a Portuguese prince. In this way, the nation "continued" Portugal in its own territory. A constitutional monarchy, apparently liberal from some points of view, was established in the colony. But independence and a constitution were *granted* the country from above, and a national court was established to govern the young nation.

The political life of the nation began in a succession of incidents which originated in disagreements between the newly designated members of the dominant class. In 1831 the emperor was forced to abdicate, leaving as emperor his five-year-old son. There was a succession of four regencies from 1831 until 1840, when, at the age of fourteen, Dom Pedro II was proclaimed emperor. He governed the nation until 1889, when the republic was proclaimed.

It would be difficult to imagine a more gradual progression toward independence, self-government, a constitutional system, and representative democracy. All of this must be learned, however, by experience and not by concession, toleration, or permission of those who govern. The emperor made all these concessions, but he reserved for himself the *moderative power*, a kind of paternal power over the nation, that perhaps maintained the country's stability but kept it from coming of age. The empire was a dramatization of the liberal and constitutional system. In the nation slavery and the fundamental dualism between the elite and the masses continued. No structural changes occurred. A paternalistic and enlightened monarch presided with magnanimity over the liberal and democratic skit.

During this whole period, education reflected the dominant culture of the society, which was divided between the conservatism of customs and the liberalism of empty gestures, between a reactionary and oppressive social structure and an intellectual, formal superstructure of constitutionalism and freedom. Let us analyze briefly the organization, content, and distribution of this education.

THE NATIONAL EDUCATIONAL SYSTEM
DURING THE MONARCHY

During colonial times, with the movement of the royal family to Brazil, a royal library, a royal press, a museum of natural history, botanical gardens, a school of fine arts, and military and medical schools were established. Elementary and secondary instruction continued in the royal schools and in those of the religious orders.

After independence, higher education was expanded by the establishment of two law schools. This completed Brazil's system, previously united with that of Portugal, where Brazilians had had to go for university study.

Education, formerly entrusted almost exclusively to the church, began, with Pombal's reforms, to be organized and maintained by the state, i.e., by an absolute monarchy. With independence it became a constitutional monarchy; but the constitution was an imperial grant. Brazilian society had no native movements. It was shifted from subordination to the hierarchy of the church to subordination to the hierarchy of the crown. The state prescribed an education judged to be more suited to the preservation of the dominant hierarchy than to that of the society. At that time the school system lacked a single germ of autonomy or independent growth. It was, in this phase of Portuguese enlightenment, a result of the imposition of a secular order to oppose the once exclusive domination by the theocratic order. This organization of education from the outside in, having as its objective the training of a special group of functionaries and of the dominant elite, left its imprint on the entire subsequent evolution of Brazilian education.

Brazilian national character has been molded far more by the education received in the home than by that secured in the school. The latter dispensed a "specialized" education, essentially vocational, for the lettered, the functionaries, the higher-level professionals, and the administrators. The "educated" person generally became a specialist, a holder of special privileges trained for the performance of certain functions and, due to the classical and universalistic nature of the instruction received, became alienated from his own country and his local conditions. The intellectuals themselves, who somehow began to be trained in the law schools, were nourished on European ideas and, when they dealt with local issues or passions, betrayed their alienation from their environment by struggling for the acceptance of ideas without realizing that these can only be implemented by means of institutions. The democratic idea, for example, apparently became dominant. But it never was truly institutionalized in the local community, reaching only the stage of proclamation by law and of the formal organization of the central government. For the same reasons, the law came to be considered as something absolute. Instead of being a plan of action and organization to be implemented (and accompanied by the difficulties arising from the natural changes it would bring about in existing habits and customs), the law was viewed as a magic act that would transform everything of its own accord.

Thus this duality between the educational system and the nation perpetuated the situation of the colonial regime. It conferred upon the state, or the national political power, the characteristics formerly possessed by the foreign political power. The most profound phenomenon of the Brazilian situation is that of a people subjected to governments, first foreign and then national, which act with reference to a foreign political framework that is not integrated into the intimate context of the society. Paradoxically, and largely because of the great geographic space in which it acted, this society felt free to preserve the elemental and ancient structures of the patriarchal family and the great landed estate, both based on ingrained habits and customs which the forms of government were unable to affect. These authoritarian structures facilitated the development of oligarchies, whose members were the de facto rulers of the nation and had an understanding with the high echelons of the elite who governed officially. Since only the members of the elite received formal education, to become educated was a process by which one left the general and common society and was admitted into the privileged special society which ruled the nation.

In accordance with the dominant ideas of liberal constitutional monarchy, when (following independence) the society was organized, the education of the Brazilian people was entrusted to the provinces; the elite system was left under the custodianship of the central power, evidently in order to preserve its former character. This decentralization provided for by the *Ato Adicional* of 1834 gave to the provinces the responsibility for "popular" education, and the primary school, as it was conceived in the nineteenth century, was instituted. It was supplemented by the normal school for the training of primary school teachers and by vocational education, consisting of household skills for women and trades for men. This new system of education was created by the provinces (now the states).

The other system (composed of the preparatory courses of the academic high schools and those of college level) was preserved, as stated above, under the control of the central power. It carried on the preparation of the elite in official or private, religious or secular schools.

The duality of formal education reflected the duality of Brazilian society: the provincial (later the state) system of primary and vocational schools was for the "people," or "the less favored classes"; the system of secondary and higher education was for the "elite." The two systems were independent; there was no interchange between the two. Inasmuch as society continued to be slavocratic, the "people" were the free men. The slaves were the floor of the society and did not constitute a class. Hence, the "popular" system essentially was transformed into the system for the emergent middle class. Small and modest, it had to be content with the few schools in existence, upon which it could confer in some fashion the prestige of middle-class schools. The provinces created normal schools (the first ones in 1835 and 1836) for the preparation of primary school teachers. These schools, primarily for females, developed into institutions for girls which paralleled the *ginásios, liceus,* or *ateneus* for the boys in the elite-oriented system.

In this way the state systems, which were created in a spirit of social discrimination against the lower classes, redeemed themselves by enrolling middle- and even upper-class girls.

In 1889, when the monarchy ended, Brazilian education was composed of the elite system under federal control, consisting of secondary-level academies and colleges of medicine, law, engineering, and agronomy; of the provincial system of primary schools offering from six to eight years of elementary and complementary training; and of vocational schools at the intermediate level, among which the normal schools stood out since they were, in fact, academies for girls.

Formal education had been intended for the few, but the few had increased. It now included women (who lacked opportunity in the elite system except for the rare secondary schools operated by the religious orders), and it conferred social prestige on the provincial system purposely created for the "common people." Only vocational schools for boys seeking to become artisans preserved their "popular" character and failed to develop into socially prestigious schools. The normal schools and the vocational schools for girls began to be frequented by middle-class students and came to achieve considerable social prestige. Primary schools also became schools for those of middle-class status. The schools maintained by the provinces were predominantly public.

The federally controlled system for the elite, on the contrary, was predominantly private. The national government maintained only one public secondary school in the capital, in addition to the professional, higher education, schools in Recife, Bahia, São Paulo, and Rio de Janeiro. Private boarding schools, some directed by educators who were quite similar to certain headmasters of English schools, prepared the sons of upper-class parents for entrance into the colleges and professional schools. The few public preparatory schools offered meager opportunities to students of slight means, while the more affluent students had plenty of educational opportunities assured by the private academies.

Both systems, provincial and national, were for the few, thus helping maintain the status quo in a society made up of slaves, an embryonic middle class, and a dominant oligarchy.

ABOLITION, THE REPUBLIC, AND THE EFFECT ON EDUCATION

Following the abolition of slavery in 1888, Brazilian society experienced its first great structural change. The northern rural patriarchate entered upon a period of decadence. The influx of European immigrants into the south introduced a new element with which it would overcome the crisis and at long last become the first example in contemporary Brazilian society to experience the process of intense social change. The empire disintegrated as a consequence of the abolition of slavery; and, in an essentially bloodless and peaceful movement, the republic was proclaimed by the military.

After an initial stage in which the military replaced the monarchy, the republic was consolidated under the dominant influence of the oligarchies of two states, São Paulo and Minas Gerais, which alternated between themselves the presidency of the republic. Until about 1920 the old elite maintained the nation in relative stability with a regime of limited democracy and with direct elections so skillfully manipulated that they actually constituted indirect elections. The nation recovered from the shock of abolition and maintained the latifundia with the plantation system in São Paulo, now served by European immigrants. It also preserved the old structure on the *fazendas* of Minas Gerais, those of the entire north, and even those of Rio Grande do Sul. The country continued to be one of lordly landowners, with the process of urbanization still in its beginnings and that of industrialization hardly begun.

Until the First World War, Brazilian society, although no longer slave-holding, remained colonial economically, exporting raw materials and agricultural products and buying manufactured and consumer goods. Its commerce was dominated by foreign firms. The members of its dominant landholding class divided their activities between the government, the liberal professions, and leisurely visits to Europe.

The war destroyed this equilibrium, speeded up the process of urbanization, produced a beginning of industrialization, and gave impetus to the development of the middle class. Capitalism definitively was substituted for mercantilism; and, in the normal course of events, it would have destroyed the latifundia and created a competitive modern society. But this was not the case. The landholding class furnished the model for the industrialization movement, which derived from the latifundia not only its social prestige but its methods of concession and monopoly as well. The great rural patriarchal families became the great industrial families, and the old social structure took on new rigor, especially as long as coffee, sugar, and cocoa constituted an appreciable portion of national wealth and were dominant products in foreign commerce. Hence the latifundium was the model for the industrialization of this apparently renovated, but actually stationary, society; the education of the elite became the model for a somewhat modified type of education for social ascension that did little to transform the aristocratic and conservative structure of the society.

For this it was sufficient to keep education scarce and to preserve its previous "encyclopedic" or ornamental character. It was an education for "culture" and did not become an education with a scientific and technological basis for efficiency and work. Despite brilliant and eloquent exhortations, the republic was not able to enlarge educational opportunities appreciably. Following the First World War, education was extremely deficient with respect to primary and secondary schooling and the duality of systems. It offered few means for rising in the social scale. The system was adequate for the social stagnation essential for the maintenance of existing privileges.

The federal government continued to maintain one secondary academy and a handful of institutions of higher learning, which, being free of cost to the students, represented its total contribution to democratic participation in the system for preparation of the elite. Since admission to these institutions was highly selective, the students of slight means who gained admission to them possessed the personal qualities necessary for integration into the dominant class even though they did not then belong to it. Most of the students were recruited from private schools catering to the children of affluent families. In this manner, higher learning, although free, was in effect limited to members of the upper class. In addition, schools were located in only a few of the capitals of the country. So tranquil was the situation that the public academies, *ginásios* or *colégios* that prepared students for admission to institutions of higher learning consisted of just one in the federal capital and one in each of the capitals of the more important states. The demand for entrance to them was not great. Some of these schools appeared to be practically abandoned, and the states showed little concern about their development.

The other system now received the attention of the state governments. It was organized for the purpose of providing a watered-down education to children of persons of intermediate status, which did not prepare students for admission to institutions of higher learning. It was entirely free and consisted of primary schools, normal schools for the preparation of primary school teachers, vocational schools for girls, and other vocational schools for men. Since it did not prepare students for higher education and, therefore, did not threaten the dominant class, it was a kind of education that could be developed by a paternalistic government preoccupied with maintaining the supposed practical or utilitarian nature of a curriculum which prevented the schools from supplying any disturbing intellectual or cultural stimulation that might arouse the ambitions of the students. The aristocratic nature of Brazilian society thus defended itself against the possibility that a modest educational expansion might lead to social transformations. The federal government itself maintained several public establishments which engaged in this emasculated teaching, even though such was not one of its direct attributions, while at the same time it limited the opportunities for higher education so as to defend the dominant class that feared to see its numbers enlarged. Higher education did not rely solely upon restricted enrollments in order to serve the dominant oligarchy. Its intellectualist and universalist curriculum also betrayed the purpose of serving only the affluent classes.

Even though the institutions of higher learning were professional schools, their curricula avoided instruction in applied knowledge or science and were restricted to programs of a general and encyclopedic nature—in law, in medicine, and even in engineering. The first of these institutions were of "juridical and social sciences" and were the best Brazilian schools of general instruction. The medical schools gave academic instruction in the biological field; engineering schools trained mathematicians and general engineers. Even though these were professional schools, they gave the nation a general academic culture, producing the men of letters, the politicians, and the administrators of the nineteenth and early part of the twentieth centuries.

Thus the duality of the educational system was not a simple division of labor between the states and the nation, for the national government provided some education at the intermediate level and the states supplied some academic instruction at the secondary and higher levels. The duality reflected the real organization of Brazilian society. It supplies one of the richest proofs of the thesis that education is not an abstract problem but a concrete expression of manifest purpose. Its distribution, quantity, quality, and content are determined by the structure and organization of society. The brilliant theoretical arguments developed in Brazil in favor of "humanistic" and against "practical" education, in support of intellectual and in opposition to vocational utilitarian training, were mere rationalizations. They enveloped with rhetoric the conservative goals of a society subtly divided into a leisure elite and the masses.

In spite of these explicit or implicit purposes, after the republic was established, the nation expanded and this dual structure began to be undermined. A middle class emerged and used, in order to ascend, the state-supported systems of education (public primary and secondary schools and modest free public establishments of higher academic learning). The ways in which the emerging middle class took possession of the state systems and eventually forced the expansion of federal academic instruction, thus unifying the two systems, is highly enlightening with respect to the nature of the relationships between society and education, even when the society is a closed one such as that of Brazil. This transformation took place between the world wars.

THE DISINTEGRATION OF THE DUAL
EDUCATIONAL SYSTEM

In the 1920's the educational system of the country was practically stagnant. It consisted of primary education for a small proportion of the school population, intermediate vocational training maintained by the states, and federal academic instruction at the secondary and higher levels designed for the elite and undergoing a very modest expansion through the development of private institutions. The vocational and normal schools for girls were well accepted, but the vocational schools for boys were disdained, suffering from the stigma attached to manual work.

The state system was predominantly for the middle classes, with even the primary schools having a socially selective enrollment, not only because they were few, but because of the cost of clothing, books, and so on, which excluded students in poor circumstances. Moreover, the philosophy was adopted that the basic function of the primary school was to prepare students for entrance to secondary schools, and the objective of a common education for all virtually disappeared. By means of rigorous examinations, a considerable fraction of the students was eliminated, and the schools were reserved for the few who were to *continue* their education. This distortion of the primary school was not difficult, given the ancient traditional pattern of measuring its efficiency by the performance of the "prepared" student, which meant the student who managed to be passed in the last year.

There are no analyses of that period that reveal an awareness of this distortion of the primary school, but there must have been dissatisfaction with the way in which it functioned. Indeed, there arose in São Paulo, the most economically developed state, the idea of reforming primary education so as to extend it to all. The reform consisted in reducing the primary course, normally of six-years duration, to two years. This was a tacit recognition that the existing schools were excessively ambitious to be able to serve the people and were in reality serving only the emerging middle class. Resistance to the idea of the two-year primary school was not lacking, but opposition finally was overcome and four-year primary schools were accepted for the cities and three-year schools for rural areas.

This shortened primary instruction, which before had been, together with complementary education, of eight-years duration, was not sufficient for the middle class, and its members turned to intermediate schooling. In reality, with the shortening of primary education, Brazilian society had, in a sense, organized an educational system for each class: the primary for the lower classes, the intermediate state system for the middle class, and the academic secondary and higher systems for the elite. It became necessary to maintain the barriers between the three systems with which the status quo of the social hierarchy would also be maintained. These barriers were selective examinations for admission to the academic secondary course; prohibitions against transferring from the intermediate vocational courses to the secondary academic course; and the termination of vocational instruction at the intermediate level, which eliminated the possibility of preparation for higher education. In this spirit, around 1930 the federal government undertook a reform of secondary academic instruction. It set the age for entrance at eleven years, on condition of passing a rigidly selective admission examination. This requirement was independent of primary schooling. In order to accentuate the independence of the academic secondary school from primary instruction, the federal school system preserved the four-year primary school terminating at age eleven. Since the federal government had no responsibility for primary instruction, it could do this without concern for the repercussion of its actions on the state system. Let us recall that its educational system, intended for the elite, was independent of the state system. The initiation of the secondary academic course at eleven years of age (upon passing an entrance examination) was intended for students of the affluent classes. They prepared themselves for the examination by taking preparatory courses in private schools or by studying with private tutors in their homes.

Actually, the federal system of secondary education was private rather than public although, as a public concession of the federal government, it was declared to be equal to the one model publicly supported secondary institution. In this way, federal legislation ignored the state public educational systems, which still retained, legally, an educational dualism, even though this already was being undermined by the expansion of the middle class.

Nevertheless, one of the consequences of the new reform of academic secondary education by the federal government, which prescribed that it begin at age eleven, was the establishment of a bridge between the four-year state primary school and the elite system of academic secondary education. Since an academic education carried the greatest social prestige, the new middle class sought to benefit by it. Therefore, the four-year primary school did not become a school for the masses as intended by São Paulo's reformers, but, like its predecessor, it became an institution for preparing students to pass examinations for admission to the secondary schools.

Secondary academic schools remained few in number, almost all of them privately supported and relatively expensive, for they were intended for the children of the members of affluent classes. There was a manifest need for the expansion of low-cost private secondary schools or, barring this, of publicly supported secondary schools. Since the latter was not among the objectives, stated or unstated, of the government, the only way out was the improvisation of private secondary academic schools, by making it easier to establish their "equivalency" with the federally supported model, the Colégio Dom Pedro II.

This model high school, maintained to serve the elite members of society, had a curriculum appropriate to its nonexpansion. This included the study of Latin, two foreign languages, physical and social sciences, history, and geography, for a total of from twelve to fifteen subjects. Its expansion was practically impossible. Only in great centers could the necessary faculty be assembled and even there recruitment was difficult.

But, under pressures from the rising middle class, even these factors could not impede expansion. Teachers and schools were improvised; all of the precepts of an academic, encyclopedic type of instruction for the elite were broken; and the middle class was given instruction, with enrollment rising from 30,000 students in 1930 to 48,000 in 1940. The expansion continued until it reached 406,920 in 1950 and 868,178 in 1960. Thus, between 1930 and 1960, enrollments in the secondary academic schools increased almost thirtyfold.

The facts merit a careful analysis, for they illustrate very clearly the first vigorous, although disordered, reaction of Brazilian society against patterns of school organization as imposed by the elite.

As indicated above, the Brazilian school system was intended to meet the educational needs of society without altering its social structure, or to limit the distribution of each type of education to the minimum needs of each class. This organization was not original but, rather, it imitated European models. The new fact in Brazilian society was that the new middle class, lacking middle-class traditions of the European type, aspired to the status of the elite, from which it inherited prejudices against the masses. It first sought for exclusiveness on the part of the free state-supported primary and secondary schools, and then it attempted to find ways of gaining access to the institutions of higher learning reserved for the elite. The reduction of the primary schools to four years in urban centers, and three years in rural areas, which in no way prepared students for admission to other educational levels, accelerated the pressure for change and hastened a fusion of the systems. The lack, in Brazilian society, of real cultural traditions that impeded the breaking of established patterns in each type of class-oriented education, contributed to this. Europe maintained multiphased educational systems, but each system had its own standards and offered opportunity for the continuation of education to higher levels, even though the differentiation between the several branches was maintained and safeguarded. In Brazil, however, the distinction between the several systems of education was principally that of the social destinations of the students. There were no corresponding differences in philosophy and methods of instruction, except in the content of the curriculum, which accentuated the discriminatory nature of the system.

Brazil's real educational tradition was that of educating the members of a small elite class, and all education confers privileges. Hence, there was resistance to any education designed to prepare the student for any social status other than a privileged one. The real criterion for selecting those to be trained was not the merits of the students but simply their social condition. However, since the appraisal of merit itself is highly dependent on social condition, modern educational systems were able to establish a certain equilibrium between the two. But in Brazil the lack of any reasonableness in the criteria for selection and the lack of alternatives for the unsuccessful eventually produced social pressure to search for ways to bypass the standards and to make the existing instruction more generally available. This bypassing of the standards was made more acceptable because the general

TABLE 1

POPULATION AND ENROLLMENTS, 1930–1960

	Population and Enrollment 000's			
	1930	1940	1950	1960
Total population	33,568*	41,236	51,944	70,967
Urban population	9,735*	12,866	18,782	31,990
Rural population	23,833*	28,370	33,162	38,977
Enrollment in primary schools	2,085	3,068	4,352	7,141
Enrollment in vocational secondary schools	41	75	134	309
Enrollment in academic secondary schools	48	170	406	868
Enrollment in institutions of higher learning	14	19	50	93

SOURCE: Specially compiled by the Ministério da Educação e Cultura, Serviço Estatístico.
* Estimates

intellectualist type of education required only the professor and the book. It was thought that it was possible to improvise both. The fact that neither students nor their families understood this type of education produced great complacency with regard to its effectiveness.

The final consequences were highly paradoxical. Because the country insisted upon an intellectualist education for the dominant classes, this prestigious type of education was anxiously sought. It was expanded in disorder and, as a result, lost its possible desirable characteristics. The improvisation involved in this mushroom growth led the other kinds of intermediate education (vocational middle schools) to try to make their courses equivalent to the academic ones or in effect to become preparatory schools, and their efforts met with success.

Primary schools, on the other hand, with their reduced terms, lost sight of their basic objectives and became places in which to train for passing the examinations for gaining entrance to the secondary schools. Since 1950 all of this has resulted in the fact that the triple system of education, one for each class, has been transformed into a single one having the objective of providing access to higher education and training for the liberal professions. The number of students entering primary schools is reduced until only one-fifth finish the course and can seek admission to secondary schools. At the secondary level, the group gaining admission suffers additional large reductions, and only a small percentage of students finish this level of instruction. These are judged to have the right of admission to institutions of higher learning. But there is still a barrier: the vestibular or university entrance examination. Only one-half of the secondary-school graduates are able to pass it. This final group of survivors, super-selected more by arbitrary examination. Only one-half of the secondary-school graduates are able to enjoy the privileges of the socially elite. The entire system functions in order to produce a small privileged class of university graduates distributed among the liberal professions and governmental service. Only recently have commerce and industry begun to employ any of them.

INADEQUATE EXPANSION AND
CONSEQUENT DISORGANIZATION
OF THE SCHOOL SYSTEM

Let us consider the expansion that resulted in the fusion, now underway, of the three school systems into a single and continuous one from the primary school to the university. Table 1, with data for the three decades between 1930 and 1960, shows that expansion was general but that the truly explosive growth was in academic secondary education. This reflects the strong social pressure for greater educational opportunity.

The expansion in all levels and branches of education was that of the organization and content as they were during the 1930's. This growth disorganized the entire school system, but most affected were the academic high schools, because their nature was such that, strictly speaking, they could not be expanded. In fact, their schooling was intended for the elite. The organization and curriculum of these schools could not be extended indiscriminately, not only because of a lack of teachers, but also because such training was inappropriate for any students except those of a certain social class who, because of their habits, tastes, and attitudes, aspired to an encyclopedic type of learning. Its indiscriminate expansion meant either the preservation of its efficiency and the training of many more persons with this type of education than the society could absorb or use or, should improvisations take place, the disorganization of the structure, methods, and curriculum of this special type of school.

The second of these possibilities took place, leading to the burgeoning and complete deterioration of the academic secondary schools and a change in the character of the vocational high schools. The two were thrown together confusedly into a single and absorbing search for some vague kind of instruction that would prepare students for admission to institutions of higher learning.

Naturally, once this disorganization in the school system was complete, with the curriculum and methods of the schools no longer in touch with reality, the entire system came to function on the basis of a set of unyielding, sacred formalities. This formalism assumed the most extreme forms, capable of astonishing an observer unacquainted with the facts, being entirely indifferent to the bureaucracy that had been created for the purpose of maintaining in it at least a semblance of efficient teaching. Education became a processualistic problem, resembling the phenomena of juridical relations in which merit can be examined only in extreme cases of fraud or crime.

Similar conditions have occurred in certain periods of decadence of educational institutions as, for example, that at the end of the eighteenth century in Europe; but, in such cases, periods of stagnation were followed by changes and radical reforms. The singularity of the Brazilian situation is that the phenomenon of the supremacy of the formalistic over the meritorious took place during a period of dynamic and vigorous social change and during the consequent educational expansion under the impulse of new forces which struggled against the immobility of the formal structure of education.

Let us recognize that the period was characterized by an intense criticism of the inadequacy of the resultant system. This debate, which was especially intense after the Second World War, was a unique effort of introspection and of searching for an education adequate to new social conditions. Finally, in 1960, a new educational act, the Law of Directives and Bases of Education, was approved. It cannot be said that this law has overcome the distortions and contradictions of the situation. The divided state of society was reflected in the law. The way for the anarchic expansion of schools through private initiative was left open, but reforms of organization and content were made. The most significant modification was a decentralization of the system. The law conferred upon the states the power to organize their respective educational systems, this time to include all levels, and thus gave rise to a process of experimentation and emulation among them. Efficacious results are to be expected from this, for, at least, the previous sterilizing and ineffectual uniformity were abandoned. This reform movement deserves a closer examination.

THE LAW ESTABLISHING DIRECTIVES AND
BASES FOR EDUCATION

The development of the Brazilian educational system, as we have tried to demonstrate, shows that in a changing society education becomes a process of social promotion by which educated people come to enjoy higher status and to occupy more advantageous social positions. With the appearance of the middle class and its rapid growth, that class seized control of the educational system and developed it as best it could, thereby violating the aristocratic standards which formerly had been established for it by a small upper class. From the historical point of view, the great defect of this development was that a real tradition of universal and compulsory education for all, a change characteristic of the nineteenth century and of the democratic and industrial revolution, was not instituted.

We observed that in what now are the most highly developed countries of Europe and America the establishment of such a tradition constituted the great educational effort of the nineteenth century. This was followed, in the twentieth, by the expansion of the concept of universal education to include the secondary level, the development of secondary schools for all, and a consequent modification of their structure.

In Brazil we had, during the 1920's, with the reform of primary education in São Paulo, a realistic vision of education for all; but we reduced it to a four-year course in schools operating only half a day, thus making the training so limited that the primary school was inadequate to meet the needs of a society which already was undergoing a process of economic and social transformation. The primary school functioned merely as a preparatory school for those going on to high school. Even in 1965 these schools enrolled only 66 per cent of the children of primary school age, and of these less than 20 per cent completed the four-year course.

Four years of primary schooling is adequate only if properly organized secondary education is available to all. Hence the fact that students who complete primary school in Brazil seek secondary education. They come predominantly from the middle class.

The children of the working classes remain without schooling in rural areas, and even among certain industrial groups (road and construction workers) in urban areas. In other fields, especially manufacturing, once a minimum of education in primary school has been obtained, it can be supplemented by on-the-job training, which became possible as a result of the advances of mechanization. Generally, though, minimum primary schooling does not mean the completion of four years of study, and the working classes are recruited from among those with no schooling and those who failed to complete the work. Thus the primary school became a selective school. As indicated below, only about one-fifth of those entering primary school complete the four years of work.

In the same way the intermediate vocational and academic schools eliminate large portions of their students; and, finally, the university entrance examination completes the selection process. A small elite finally obtains admission to the institutions of higher learning, where there are few failures.

Data for 1960 are as follows:

A.	School-age population	100.00 per cent
B.	Entering primary school	60.00 per cent
C.	Completing primary school (20 per cent of B)	12.00 per cent
D.	Entering first three-year secondary school cycle (50 per cent of C)	6.00 per cent
E.	Completing first secondary school cycle (46 per cent of D)	2.76 per cent
F.	Completing second three-year secondary cycle (30 per cent of D)	1.80 per cent
G.	Entering institutions of higher learning (12 per cent of D)	0.72 per cent
H.	Completing institutions of higher learning (30 per cent of F)	0.54 per cent

These computations illustrate the eliminatory nature of the school system. For the many diversified services and occupations of a modern society, the nation has to depend upon those failed or eliminated by this selective educational system.

Because of the inefficiency and part-time operation of the schools, from the primary level to the university, their eliminatory nature is the only way to make them functional to a certain extent. As in colonial days, education continues to be for the few, even though the numbers enrolled have increased.

The new Law of Directives and Bases allows for some modification of this situation, but it also permits the system to continue unchanged. Let us examine in detail, however, the small new perspectives that are open and also the inadequacies of the law.

The law *permits* but does not require the increase of primary schooling to six years of study. It does not prohibit the two-shift school, which perforce is a part-time school. It *penalizes* the students who complete six years of primary school (with the loss of one year of study), for it allows them to enter the second year of the intermediate school by passing an entrance examination, whereas youths who have completed only four years of primary schooling may, by passing the entrance examination, begin the first year of secondary schooling. It does not provide that students completing the primary course could enter the intermediate schools, but specifies that admission to the latter should be by examination. The secondary schools can continue to consider themselves as selective and primarily preparatory for higher education. As a result, primary education is not stimulated to perfect itself.

Primary education might be improved if there were competency and training of primary school teachers. The law did not alter the previous situation. It maintained the previous requirement that teachers in rural schools should have four years of study above the four years of primary schooling and that those in urban schools should have an additional three years of schooling. It did *permit* the raising of these standards by one additional year, an opportunity already used by Rio Grande do Sul and Brasília.

The law maintained the equality between secondary vocational and normal courses (for the preparation of primary school teachers) and the academic courses, and it prescribed that the respective curricula consist of a core curriculum required by the federal government, two subjects to be determined by the state government, and two electives from other courses to be offered by the school. This contrasts with the previous situation, in which the secondary academic school had a uniform encyclopedic curriculum including Latin, two foreign languages, and twelve other subjects. The chaotic expansion of these schools had made the curriculum practically impossible, and the legislators had the good sense to reduce it.

Except for these modest changes, the schools continue to operate on a part-time basis, having two or three shifts (one at night) and having instructional activities reduced in practice to exposition.

The law says nothing specific about the preparation of teachers for these new secondary schools. This training continues to be entrusted to the faculties of philosophy; in order to meet the needs of schools situated in areas not served by faculties of philosophy, the rule of certification to teach based on "sufficiency" examinations prevails.

In certain ways the law was more generous with regard to higher education, opening opportunities for its transformation and progressive enlargement. However, it submitted all proposed changes to approval by the Federal Council of Education, intending in this manner to limit the powers conceded.

If this Law of Directives and Bases were considered a kind of educational constitution, it would be possible for the Federal Council of Education, to whom its enforcement is entrusted, to provide leadership for the conduct of the educational progress of the nation through a broad interpretation of its text. But this is not happening, and Congress continues to legislate on problems of concern to the universities or the school and to inhibit their autonomous, organic growth.

The most important parts of the law are those establishing the bases for the financing of education and, to a certain extent, institutionalizing educational planning. The funds for education were set at a minimum of 12 per cent of the federal income from taxes and 20 per cent of such incomes of the states and the county-like *municípios*.[1] The power to develop educational plans in the respective areas was delegated to the Federal Council of Education and to the state educational councils. The federal resources are distributed in three equal funds for primary education, secondary schooling, and institutions of higher learning. This represents some increase in the portion of primary schooling that is regulated by the federal government.

No analysis of the law would be complete, however, which omitted the question of private schooling and the means through which the law proposed to deal with it.

There have been three diverse orientations with regard to private education, i.e., that education not controlled by the state. The first is that education is a problem for the church. We should not forget, however, that in the period in which the system was dominant, the church was in effect a public institution and exercised functions equivalent to those of the state. The second is that education is unrestricted and that the families will constitute and maintain private schools for the education of their children by means of the church or through private educators. The third is that private education is unrestricted and maintained with the resources of the families themselves, but that the results will only be validated by the state when confirmed by a system of public examinations.

In colonial days until the period of Pombal, Brazil entrusted education to the church. After Pombal, education by the state was instituted, but with the church united to the state and thus a participant in public education, a situation which lasted throughout the empire. In the republic, with the separation of church and state, instruction by church or private schools was validated by public examinations. The pressure of social forces striving for the expansion of academic instruction produced the idea of private education through *concession* by the state. Such instruction then came to be regulated by and dependent upon the *authorization* of the state, and the *equivalency* to a state or public model was established. At the time this was considered a great imposition on the good and prestigious private schools, which reluctantly accepted this yoke from the state. This created a kind of state monopoly of education. The success of the measure was attained thanks to the advantage offered of awarding validity and official sanction to the results of instruction, an advantage that the makeshift and ineffectual schools also received. For the best schools, the system was frankly oppressive and inhibitive of progress. It was the salvation, however, of the bad schools.

This system, developed and nurtured during the dictatorship, as a result

1. These provisions were revoked by the new "granted" constitution, as was also the provision of special funds for the three levels of schools.

of the regime's demagogic submission to the social pressures of the rising new middle class, was defended during the debate over the Law of Directives and Bases as assuring "freedom of teaching." Teaching would be "free" if, even though a state monopoly, it was "ceded" to private persons, and would be "statist" if maintained and directed by public officials. Although elaborate rationalizations were developed with regard to this singular thesis, the reasons for its success are not very edifying. The interests that cloaked themselves in this strange version of "freedom of teaching" were those of the second-rate private schools, unable to serve the affluent class (whose members were financially able to underwrite high standards of education for their children), and those of the church-maintained schools, which in a poor society, due to the need to collect fees, would become schools for the rich.

Because the church was undergoing a period of renewal and expansion and wished to serve all of society, the system of "public concession" of teaching and the consequent public subsidy was in its interests. The combination of these vested interests caused the Law of Directives and Bases to remove all measures favoring instruction maintained and administered by the state and to consider absolutely identical the results obtained through "private" and "public" instruction, for both were subject to public legislation and were considered mutually equivalent. In this manner, the way to the disordered expansion of teaching was kept open, and the maintenance of high standards became extremely difficult, while the use of public funds for the maintenance of "private" schools was made easier. This measure is the consequence of a strange alliance between reactionary thinking and educational demagoguery. It serves, in the first instance, as a protective shield against the fear of a possibly progressive attitude of public authority; and, in the second, as a support for the well-intentioned but dangerous pretentions of those who wish to capitalize on the public's desire for education by offering it in any fashion, whether effective or not.

CONCLUSION

We must not conclude our analysis without indicating, though briefly, the vigor and sacrifice represented by the educational efforts of Brazilian society. The school system includes nursery schools and kindergartens; primary schools for eleven million children (in 1967) between the ages of seven and fourteen; secondary vocational and academic schools for more than two and one-half million adolescents; and institutions of higher learning for over 200,000 students. There also are some institutions for the physically handicapped and the mentally deficient. Elementary school teachers number about 350,000, of whom over 100,000 work in rural areas. There are around 130,000 teachers in the secondary schools and some 36,000 in institutions of higher learning.

In Brazil as a whole, 66.2 per cent of children seven to eleven years old attend primary schools, the percentage being 81.5 in urban areas and 51.5 in the rural. In the age groups twelve through fourteen, 66.5 per cent of the children are enrolled in school, the percentages being 81 in the urban, 51.4 in the rural areas.

Sixteen per cent of adolescents twelve to eighteen years old attend secondary schools, the percentage for the first, four-year cycle, or *ginásio*, being 12.23 and that for the second, three-year cycle, or *colégio*, being 3.77. Table 2 reflects the growth of the school system from 1950 to 1967.

Although the rate of population growth is an astounding 3.1 per cent per annum, the rate of increase in school enrollment is considerably higher. It is true that the number of adult illiterates in rural areas is still very high, but Brazil, being a Catholic nation, has a long tradition of oral culture, and there have been no studies to determine with exactitude the effect of the

TABLE 2

GROWTH OF SCHOOL ENROLLMENTS, 1950–1967

Year	Primary	Secondary	Higher
1950	4,352,000	540,000	49,700
1960	7,141,000	1,177,000	93,000
1967	11,000,000	2,700,000	214,000

SOURCE: Specially compiled by the Ministério da Educação e Cultura, Serviço Estatístico.

diffusion of culture by means of the radio (transistors) in countries long habituated to an oral culture. Perhaps the transistor radio may substitute partially for reading, if not for writing, in liberating the unlettered man from full dependency on others. The truth is that the nation is developing more rapidly than its poor and deficient educational diet will allow. Mass media of communication, the mobility of the population by means of newly available transportation (above all, the automobile, the motor truck, and the airplane), and the diffusion of the machine and of machine technology, all of which may be used even by the unlettered, compel us to examine anew certain problems of cultural diffusion. In the nineteenth century, reading and writing were the only means for the diffusion of culture, and the very rudimentary technology depended mainly on the capacity and training of the operator. Today, many machines can be operated by those with minimal training and necessitate little instruction of an intellectual nature.

A culture capable of creating new technologies and of building the machines of contemporary technology is that which nations must possess in order to be autonomous and independent. The culture required for the *use* of existing technology is infinitely simpler. It would seem that Brazil is acquiring the latter in spite of the poor quality of its schools. Those who observe the country are impressed with the capacity of the Brazilian workman despite his limited or complete lack of formal schooling—the deficiencies of education and cultivated intelligence are more visible with regard to services than with regard to the mechanical tasks of machine operation or execution of planned manual work.

It is clear that these are characteristics of peripheral nations, a euphemism we use to designate their colonial levels. The quality of present-day formal education must be far superior to that of the nineteenth century if a nation is to master effectively contemporary technology and to use and develop the complex and varied world of scientific knowledge which such technology involves. However, this scientific culture is new even among the developed nations. The formal education which Brazil possesses and is implementing inadequately is not, as yet, this scientific culture. Rather, it is still the old intellectualist and informative culture of the nineteenth century, although it is transmitted with less efficacy now than it was then.

What I am here daring to suggest is that perhaps this informative and illustrative culture no longer is as important as it was in the nineteenth century and that for this reason the nation can survive and develop in spite of the poor quality of the schools that transmit this type of culture.

Without these explanatory comments, this entire severe essay on education in Brazil would seem to be in contradiction with the vigor of urban development in Brazil, and it would appear out of line with the extraordinary contributions in art, architecture, literature, and journalism, with the high standards of its medicine, with the modest but genuine spurt in the development of scientists, with an incipient but real industrial development, and with the energy and dynamism of a population which migrates to the cities and to the more advanced areas of the nation.

This does not obviate the need for a solid and efficient system of formal education and for a profound transformation of higher education, tasks which must be carried out regardless of the difficulties compounded by the demographic explosion, the migratory explosion, and the explosion of aspirations. It seems, however, that the nation, its hopes awakened and in spite of the dangers of our times, has sufficient energy and, aided by the diffusion of culture through oral and audiovisual means, will develop the creative power to guide its development, if its financial problems can be solved. This development seems inevitable in spite of the poverty and distortions of the formal instruments of written culture which the nation seeks anxiously, but in a tumultuous and disorderly manner. In modern times, formal education has always lagged behind the knowledge available in society. Brazil is one of the examples of this lag. It is reasonable to believe that this malady, grave as it is, may not be beyond repair.

Chapter 5

The Political and Legal Framework
of Brazilian Life

Anyda Marchant

ODERN BRAZIL's political life began in 1808, when the royal family of Portugal, driven from Lisbon by Napoleon's Marshal Junot, fled across the Atlantic to Rio de Janeiro. Thus, by an accident of history, the course of Brazilian development was set entirely outside the pattern established in the dependencies of the Spanish empire. The Portuguese court remained in Brazil until 1821. During those years Brazil acquired the habit of metropolitan life, at least in the capital, and those Brazilians whose social and economic status made them part of that life became accustomed to the idea of political power and independence. The attitude of the prince regent himself did much to promote this growth of independence, for with his Brazilian subjects he was more at ease and less fearful of intrigue and assassination than he had been in Portugal. This fact gave a certain advantage to the Brazilians at his court in dealing with the arrogance and political possessiveness of his Portuguese retinue, determined to maintain its domination over these semibarbarians in a savage new world. In 1816, Maria I of Portugal, who had been insane for many years, died in Rio. The prince regent became Dom João VI and as such lived another five years in Brazil before Napoleon's final defeat and other events in Europe required him reluctantly to leave his easy, subtropical court for the more rigorous political climate of the Old World.

During his stay Brazil was politically an anomaly. It was no longer merely a colony since it was the seat of the imperial government. The oriental seclusion of its former life was shattered by this sudden intrusion from abroad. Dom João, so given to hesitation and a love for the familiar, nevertheless, was a surprising innovator, establishing a printing press, a botanical garden, and a conservatory of music.

In departing for Lisbon, he left his son Pedro as regent for Brazil. It was inevitable that on his departure a violent conflict should ensue at any attempt to thrust the Brazilians once more into complete political and economic dependence on the mother country. The *émigrés* returning to Lisbon lost no time in reasserting their supremacy. In 1821 a constituent assembly was convoked in Lisbon to prepare a new constitution for the empire, and on April 15 and 16 elections were held throughout Brazil for the seventy deputies to be sent to join the Portuguese representatives. But the Brazilians on arrival in Lisbon were not welcomed as equals, and the contemptuous treatment they received at the hands of the Portuguese underlined the significance of various administrative changes made in the course of that year: the placing of all the provincial governments directly under the authorities in Lisbon, withdrawing them from the control of the central government in Rio; the merging of the Brazilian army with the Portuguese; and the abolition of all the law courts, the Treasury Department, the Commerce Commission, and other administrative organs created in Brazil by Dom João during his sojourn. The crowning blow was the order to Prince Pedro to give over his government in Rio to a commission directly responsible to the Lisbon Assembly and to return to Lisbon "to complete his education."

The prince, under the influence of José Bonifácio de Andrada e Silva (the grand master of Brazilian freemasonry and the greatest of the three remarkable Andrada brothers), decided to remain in Brazil. He was of a violent and ungovernable temperament, but intelligence and courage were also his. He had grown up in Brazil and had no strong attachment to Portugal or the Portuguese. He sent the Portuguese troops home from Rio in 1822; appointed a new ministry headed by José Bonifácio; made a triumphal procession through the province of Minas Gerais; on June 2, 1822, convoked a Brazilian constituent assembly at Rio; on August 6, 1822, issued a manifesto that demanded for Brazil not absolute independence, but political equality with Portugal. Shortly after this last event, while he was in the province of São Paulo, using his personal magnetism to win popular adherence to his government, word was received from Lisbon of the actual text of the humiliating decrees of the Portuguese Assembly, which returned Brazil to the status of colony. On the banks of the Ipiranga where the dispatches reached him, the prince, with dramatic gestures, proclaimed the independence of Brazil.

Pedro, in spite of his unstable and autocratic nature, possessed remarkable political acumen. Soon after his declaration of Brazilian independence, he summoned a constituent assembly, which, however, wrangled so violently over side issues that in November of 1823 he angrily dissolved it. In its place he appointed ten men to prepare a constitution, which he proclaimed in force on March 25, 1824.

The charter was a remarkably liberal and modern one for a prince who was the product of a most absolutist regime and a haphazard education. It declared, "The Empire of Brazil is a political association of all Brazilian citizens. They form a free and independent nation, which does not admit any tie of union or federation with any other nation that may affect its independence." It established a national assembly in which senators were selected for life by the emperor from three lists of nominees, and deputies were chosen for a four-year term by indirect election. The assembly had full legislative powers, voted the budget, and levied taxes. The distinguishing feature of the emperor's relationship to the assembly was the so-called moderative power. Thus, besides possessing the power to sanction or veto bills, to appoint and dismiss the ministry at will, and to dissolve the assembly, the emperor was a moderator "to watch incessantly over the maintenance of the independence, equilibrium, and harmony of the rest of the political powers." The principal weakness of the Constitution of 1824 was the attempt to impose a highly centralized form of government on so vast a country with such strongly marked regional differences. Greater autonomy was therefore given to the provinces by the Additional Act of 1834.

Pedro's behavior, however liberal might have been his political thought, was thoroughly arbitrary. Having provided for a government by the representatives of the people, he proceeded to quarrel constantly with them, ranging the senators on his side and ignoring the parliamentary majority. In 1831 he was forced to abdicate; he left Brazil to attempt to establish his daughter Maria on the throne of Portugal. He left his five-year-old son in Brazil to reign as Pedro II, during whose minority the country was governed by four regencies: two three-men regencies from 1831 to 1835; the regency of Padre Antônio Diogo Feijó from 1835 to 1837; and the regency of Pedro de Araújo Lima, the marquis of Olinda, from 1837 to 1840. Feijó was strong-willed and fertile in ideas of what the new country needed—the abolition of the slave trade, new codes of law—but his very determination resulted in the collapse of his regency. He was succeeded by the more politic Araújo Lima, who turned over the political administration of the country to Bernardo Pereira de Vasconcellos, who, aided by the later duke of Caxias, brought most of the turbulence in the provinces under control. As a final effort in the pacification of the country, the young Pedro was proclaimed emperor on July 23, 1840, at the age of fourteen, and crowned a year later.

The empire of Pedro II was an entirely Brazilian phenomenon. The emperor himself was the key to it. Deprived of his parents in early childhood, he was carefully and peculiarly educated for the task ahead of him. Under staid, conscientious governesses and tutors, he absorbed the habit of thinking of himself as the mainstay of this great new incoherent empire, still largely wilderness, with a half-servile population. The lack of stability of the Bragança, the violent and erratic temperament of Pedro I, the want of decision of João VI, the mental confusion of various others of his relatives—all were remote from this judicious, fair-minded, studious prince with rigorous ideas concerning his duties as preceptor of the new and inexperienced people. Two qualities are habitually associated with Dom Pedro II: he was magnanimous and democratic. Both descriptions are justly applied to him, but they need amplification. His magnanimity was that of a wise father who had no doubts about the rightness of his views concerning the needs and conduct of his children. He was democratic in the sense that, as a reflection of the training he had absorbed, he believed in the abstract principle of the equality and fraternity of man, and he tried to put it into practice within certain clearly defined limits. For example, he fostered scientific research, artistic creations, and general intelligence by active and personal aid to poor boys who displayed aptitude for such things but possessed no resources and no families capable of developing it. Nevertheless, this attribute of his never was carried so far as in any manner to attack the conservative society that was the base of his throne.

Dom Pedro's great strength lay in the stability of his character and of his political point of view. His belief was sincere and strong in the necessity for public morality and the responsibility of public men for their actions while in office. He looked upon himself as the principal public servant of Brazil, and the standards he maintained for himself he imposed on the men who served him. The very rigor of his demands produced a large number of conscientious ministers and encouraged the idea that mercenary considerations were beneath their notice. Dom Pedro also gained much strength from his careful avoidance of favoritism. As was natural, when he first came to the throne, various political groups sought to gain power through personal influence. But the young emperor had grown up an orphan in comparative loneliness. His one close boyhood friend, the Viscount Bom Retiro, preserved his friendship by carefully avoiding the temptations of a political career as Pedro's favorite. Dom Pedro, therefore, when confronted with difficult alternatives in the choice or dismissal of ministers, knew how to act with complete and pointed indifference to any personal considerations. Especially among a people as sensitive and as conscious of personal relationships as the Brazilians, this indifference was a powerful disciplinary weapon.

In nothing were his personal attributes more clearly illustrated than in the two constants of his reign: his use of the moderating power in relation to the cabinet and assembly, and his role as chief of a slavocratic empire. Underlying the situation was the social and economic pattern of the country. Brazil in the nineteenth century was a predominantly agricultural land dependent on servile labor, with its wealth in the two great crops of sugar and coffee. The bulk of the population was divided between, on the one hand, the great families with infinite ramifications, whose power and wealth were almost entirely in land and slaves, and, on the other, their dependents and slaves. The landowning class was the only group that could exercise political power and be the source of public opinion.

In this context, Dom Pedro's empire was a showpiece, a transplantation to the wilds of the New World of the English parliamentary system, one of the most sophisticated phenomena of the Old. There was no reality in the new setting. Two parties—the conservative and the liberal—had crystallized out of the welter of opposing forces that had created such turbulence early in his reign. Theoretically speaking, the conservatives favored a strong central government, a powerful emperor, and no change in the social and economic conditions of the country; whereas the liberals preferred a stronger legislature, more autonomy for the provincial governments, and the adoption of modern ideas in social and economic matters. But these two major parties had no real division of interest on vital issues. Conservatives and liberals alike were landowners or the sons of landowners, with the point of view and habits of slaveholders and planters, although individuals among them might have ideas in opposition to those of the majority. Politics, therefore, in Dom Pedro's empire, was an absorbing pastime for those members of the ruling class who found such an occupation a relief from the monotony of life on the great *fazendas*—an elaborate game, in which the prize was the holding of office as one of the emperor's ministers. The emperor himself, to some extent conscious of the fact, did not encourage the growth of real political power in any man, especially one who in any way represented interests not entirely identical with his own. He had a convenient way of checking such a growth, by "banishing a man to Siberia," as Nabuco de Araújo said—that is, naming him a senator, with lifelong tenure but no further political importance. Dom Pedro conscientiously eschewed any display of political preference; yet through the years his basic sympathies appeared as inevitably conservative.

In his use of the moderating power in relation to these circumstances, Dom Pedro was scrupulous in observing the letter of the constitution. He had inherited an empire that had escaped fragmentation (perhaps more by good fortune than anything else) but that still suffered from the turbulence of local politics in the provinces. Early in his reign he found himself confronted with an effort by both political parties to make the cabinet responsible to the assembly—in other words, to remove it from his control. His quick political sense made him realize the threat to his predominance as the executive; by his refusal to be intimidated by belligerent ministers, he soon made plain that ministers held office at his pleasure and that he would choose them outside the majority in the assembly, if he saw fit to do so.

All the major events of Dom Pedro's reign are an exemplification of his sense of the prerogatives of the executive and of the way in which he governed a slavocratic society. Underlying his liberal, well-tempered point of view concerning the improvement of his Brazil and his Brazilians, for whom his feeling was real and constant, and his genuine dislike of slavery and all the evils of a slave regime, was the realization that his throne and the social structure of the country were dependent entirely upon the slaveholding class. The slaveowner on his plantation, surrounded by numerous less well-endowed relatives and crowds of slaves, spending half his time in the pleasures of the court and later abroad, was the economic basis of the Brazilian empire. Dom Pedro acknowledged the fact in many significant ways, while at the same time attempting to give an air of modernity and enlightenment to his court. The result was an essential oddity that set it off from any similar society, that made it unmistakably Brazilian. The characteristics of a landholding aristocracy were present—in this case, Portuguese descent and the ownership of large plantations—and were necessary for a position of social and political importance. Trade or mechanical skill of any kind was not acceptable as a background. In a gesture of deprecation of the undemocratic, Old World phenomenon of a nobility, titles were granted for services granted Brazil only for the lifetime of the titleholder. Under this guise of reward for merit, however, lay the fundamental fact that Dom Pedro's peers were overwhelmingly the large landowners, men of substance, slaveowners. Thus, when the principal banker of his empire, Irinêo Evangelista de Souza, the builder of Brazil's first railroad, was made Baron Mauá, several viscounts were created whose chief contribution was the fact that they were powerful men in their local communities. When Mauá was made viscount for his enterprise in laying the first submarine cable to connect Europe and South America, the emperor created several marquises from among the landowners.

The major events of a political nature in Dom Pedro's reign were the long struggles over the electoral system, the attempt at the abolition of slavery, and the Paraguayan War. Under the Imperial Constitution, the legislature was indirectly elected by a small proportion of the population, the landholding ruling class, which meant that power lay in the hands of those who controlled local affairs in the provinces. The emperor was forced to approve this state of things, for the loyalty of the *fazendeiro* class meant not only a conservative and stable government in Rio but also good order and civil quiet in the provinces. So, though in principle he approved the reforms suggested in the electoral system that culminated in the Saraiva Law of 1881, he continued to use his power as moderator to dominate the composition of the Chamber of Deputies and to determine the length and effectiveness of any of his ministers' political lives. Any disturbance of the status quo meant to the emperor a serious threat to order and stable government, and nothing was more abhorrent to his just, conservative, magnanimous nature than riot and civil commotion.

The Paraguayan War, arising in 1865 from the troubles between the fanatical dictator of Paraguay and the other three powers of the River Plate region, searched out the weakness of the emperor's regime. It highlighted the restless and essentially lawless spirit of the southernmost province, Rio Grande do Sul, never so obedient to the power of the central government as its northern neighbors. It demonstrated the growing breach between the emperor's personal government and the rising power of elements outside the traditional imperial pattern—the businessmen and industrialists increasing under the shift of the economic development of the country from the slow-moving, sugar-growing north to the ebullient and enterprising coffee-growing province of São Paulo. It emphasized the problem of the increasing numbers of emancipated slaves, since so many of them fought as substitutes for white men in this unpopular military campaign. It was also the most serious mistake of his reign, for in this matter his personal pride triumphed over his usually astute perception of the temper of the country. It seemed to him a shameful thing that Brazil, smarting already from her diplomatic difficulties with the British government over the slavetrade, should be proved incapable of achieving a decisive military victory over so small a neighbor. But it was in the end a war of attrition against a fanatical, savage enemy, able to use every device of the jungle to defeat the efforts of an organized military force. The Brazilians tired of the profitless struggle, but the emperor insisted on its prosecution until the Paraguayan dictator was killed in the jungle by a Brazilian sergeant. The result of this expensive obstinacy was serious financial embarrassment for the Brazilian treasury and the largest measure of personal unpopularity that Dom Pedro had ever experienced.

It was, however, the slavery question that not only lent the distinctive color to the reign but served as the obvious cause of its collapse. The problem of slaveholding was in reality an outward sign of the more fundamental conflict between the decaying economic structure of the northern provinces of Bahia and Pernambuco and the vigorous, modern coffee-growers' wealth of São Paulo. As a matter of principle, also, slavery was an anomaly in a country governed by an emperor renowned for his liberal and humanitarian views. Some of the most ardent supporters of the abolition movement came from the traditional slaveholding and slave-importing north. The fact that the emperor, however cautiously, lent his support to these ideas and that these egalitarian principles of his also led him away from a complete acquiescence in the ultramontane policies of the church, bore exactly the result that the emperor himself had always anticipated—the withdrawal of the support of the ruling elements in his government and the collapse of his dynasty.

The men who took over the government on the emperor's abdication in 1889 were interested in political action, restless with the changes taking place in the economy of the country, aware of the unreality of the political maneuvers of the court and the administration, and impatient of the personal power of the emperor. Their republic was in equal parts romantic and practical. It was practical in that it represented a seizure of power by men who had learned, as the result of the Paraguayan War, to place greater emphasis on the military, which Dom Pedro had always tended to deprecate. It was romantic in that it contained many men who had grown up imbued with the principles of liberalism, the adherents of Auguste Comte's "positivism," with a touching faith in the regeneration of man through rational principles.

The provisional government, set up by a military clique under the leadership of Marshal Manuel Deodoro da Fonseca, was to last for five years. The government's first decree provided for an interim federal republic, in which the old provincial assemblies were dissolved and wider powers granted to the legislature of the new states. Church and state were separated. Immigration was encouraged by making naturalization easier.

The constitution[1] of the new republic was adopted in 1891, the draft having been prepared by a committee of five under the chairmanship of Ruy Barbosa. It created a federal republic of twenty states and a federal district, in general imitation of the Constitution of the United States. It was a learned and carefully prepared document but it could not ensure the operation in Brazil of a truly representative and democratic government, for Brazil, merely by changing from an empire to a republic, had not solved the problems that had hampered its social and economic progress during the greater part of the century. The electorate was a mere handful of property-holding male citizens over the age of 21 who could read and write. To some Brazilians contemporary with these events, the change seemed one very much for the worse. In place of a wise, experienced, altruistic emperor whose main endeavor was to mitigate the evils of the Brazilian economy, there was a group of men, chiefly military in viewpoint and training, full of personal ambition, and, under the best circumstances, completely inexperienced in dealing with the complexities of government in so large and heterogeneous a country. They tended, also, to favor their native provinces, a dangerous source of conflict since regional differences were strong. To many conservative Brazilians, it also appeared that their country was being engulfed by all the evils of separatism and factionalism, typical of Brazil's

1. Described more fully below in the section on constitutional law.

Spanish American neighbors, which their country had avoided through a combination of the political astuteness of Pedro I, the efforts of the regency, the devotion of Pedro II, and a large measure of good fortune.

The early days of the new republic were a struggle between the partisans of the military clique that had engineered the overthrow of the empire and those who insisted that the civilian tradition of the empire should continue. This conflict has, in fact, persisted to the present day. The army, conscious of its power and proud of its part in establishing the republic, has maintained a permanent influence in the selection of the federal executive. The early republic also confirmed the shift in political as well as economic dominance from Bahia and Pernambuco to São Paulo, with increased jealousy and discontent among the political groups of the rest of the country.

Its first three civilian presidents (José Prudente de Moraes Barros, 1894–1898; Manuel Ferraz de Campos Salles, 1898–1902; and Francisco de Paula Rodrigues Alves, 1902–1906) were Paulistas. Thereafter, until the accession to power of Getúlio Vargas in 1930, it became traditional for the states of São Paulo and Minas Gerais to alternate in the presidency, with two exceptions: the Rio Grandense Marshal Hermes da Fonseca (1910–1914), and Epitácio Pessoa, from Paraíba do Norte (1919–1922).

The question of regionalism and its influence in Brazilian national politics is one that goes back to the very beginning of independent Brazil. There have always been three major focuses of political importance: the old, Portuguese-dominated north (Bahia and Pernambuco); the more vigorous center, made up of Minas Gerais, São Paulo's most Brazilian offspring, and São Paulo itself, so open to foreign influence because it had received the most foreign immigration; and Rio Grande do Sul, half-Brazilian, half-Platine frontier with the Spanish American lands to the south. Even during the reign of Dom João, the southernmost portion of the country was troublesome to the central government. The importance to Brazil of events in the Plate was chiefly the effect upon the *gaúchos* in Rio Grande do Sul of all the ferment over the independence of Uruguay. A mere international boundary could not separate the interests of the people who inhabited the region. There was, in fact, greater disparity between the *gaúchos* and their fellow Brazilians of the north than there was between them and the Uruguayans. Rio Grande do Sul was a country of great open plains and cool winters, sparsely populated by a vigorous people, good horsemen, good marksmen, touchy in matters that they believed involved their honor. Life on the cattle ranches was often violent. Raiding across the border was a common occurrence. Families were divided, not by the boundary, but by feuds that were deadly and recurrent. They were not a people easily obedient to a distant, unsympathetic central government, and the ideas of independence and republicanism that flourished in the River Plate region were attractive to them, so attractive, in fact, that for ten years (1835–1845) they waged war with the empire (the Guerra dos Farrapos, a nickname referring to the cowboy's fringed chaps characteristically worn by the gaúchos). Dom Pedro II, always sensitive to anything that affected his personal power, had been wary of the Rio Grandenses in his government. The troubles leading up to the Paraguayan War and the war itself emphasized the restless character of these southerners. Typically, in the seventies he relegated to the senate the most important gaúcho to serve in his government (briefly, as minister of the treasury) after the war—Gaspar Silveira Martins.

As has been indicated, by the end of the empire the shift in political dominance from north to south had established the predominance of São Paulo. The republic, in its first forty years, was to feel the effect of a further southern trend. One of the most potent figures of the early republic was Pinheiro Machado, who gained his political skill and power as boss of Rio Grande do Sul. In 1910 he maneuvered the election of Hermes da Fonseca as president. The battle was precipitated between the older elements embodied in Ruy Barbosa, the Bahian draftsman of the Constitution of 1891 and the champion of civilismo, and Pinheiro Machado, the forces he controlled, the army, and those who expected rich political rewards for loyal services rendered (a transference to national political life of the personal service and reward of the household of a local chieftain). Because of the dissension and chaos created by his vigorous if disruptive influence, he earned too much mistrust to succeed Hermes as president, and the election of 1914 went to Wenceslau Braz, once governor of Minas Gerais.

Throughout the forty years of the republic until 1930, there was no real improvement in the electoral system nor could there be much genuine enlargement of the representative character of the electorate, for the increase in population of the country was not accompanied by an equivalent raising of the educational level. The typical pattern of Brazilian government was still the oligarchy, though the character of that oligarchy might have changed.

There was enough change, however, in the country at large to allow some radical developments in the political scene. The Hermes administration had encouraged immigration and had brought in great numbers of European laborers, especially to the coffee fazendas of São Paulo. At the same time, industrialization on a modest scale began to appear and, as an effect of World War I, began to create an urban proletariat. Brazilian finances, which had been a source of contention and complaint in the last years of the empire, continued so during the incumbency of Ruy Barbosa as minister of finance in the provisional government and in the Hermes administration. But no permanent solution for disorder in the national finances was reached, and, increasingly, the government had to resort to extraordinary measures.

More and more, in civil as well as financial affairs, the executive came to rule by decree instead of in harmony with the legislature. The effects in Brazil of worldwide depression only aggravated the situation, and Brazilians, as a whole, whether they enjoyed the suffrage or not, were restless and discontented with their government.

It was again a *gaúcho* from Rio Grande do Sul who took advantage of the situation. Getúlio Dornelles Vargas, an astute and vigorous campaigner in political as well as military matters, having seized power in 1930, had himself elected president and in 1934 promulgated a new constitution.

The essential feature of his regime from 1930 to 1945 was the centralization of all power in the hands of the executive. Elective and representative institutions were progressively eliminated, and their place was increasingly taken by administrative ministries, departments, councils, bureaus, and boards, all deriving their authority from him. State governors were replaced by his interventors, and the representative and administrative systems of the states were subordinated to the capital.

Vargas was aware of the chief weaknesses of Brazil—lack of education among the general mass of the people, an ill-distributed population, inadequate transportation and means of communication. He made use of these weaknesses to consolidate his own power by making a direct appeal to the illiterate and economically deprived. Much of what he did was thus self-serving, but several benefits accrued to the Brazilian masses, nevertheless. He was the first politician to address himself directly to the stratum of Brazilian society that had never been recognized as having a voice in government, especially to the urban workers, who, because of the accelerating pace of industrialization in the country, were growing in number and economic strength. To these, Vargas gave enough of a social program, including housing developments and at least a promise of more elementary schools and adult-education programs, to make this class his supporters. But the control of the labor unions, pension funds, unemployment relief payments, etc., all remained securely in his hands, not theirs.

To capital he made equivalent concessions. Whatever alarm big business felt about favors bestowed on workingmen was largely allayed by expedient disregard of the labor laws, by the maintenance of order and security, and the prohibition of strikes. His government spent large sums in leading an official expansion into the western frontier, but at no time was there any sign of a concomitant agrarian reform that would modify the existing system of land tenure. Above all, the army received all he thought safe to let it have.

His administration was not efficient, and charges of corruption and graft were frequent, although public criticism was not permitted. The administrative agencies of the government were overburdened with an excessive and ill-trained personnel. But with the aid of a notably effective political police he manipulated both the men in his government and his critics outside in an unusually successful bid to remain in power.

In the end, however, his deviousness contributed to his downfall. The worldwide tensions generated by the events of the years of World War II proved too much for his regime; distrust of his real motives lost him the support of many Brazilians and compromised his prestige among the other countries of the Western Hemisphere. On May 28, 1945, under pressure to return to a more democratic form of government, he signed a decree providing for the holding of presidential and congressional elections on December 2, 1945. But this failed to reassure the army, whose traditional sense of its guardianship of constitutional authority had been heightened by service in the war in Europe as an ally of the United States and the other allied powers. The appointment of his younger brother, Benjamin Vargas, as federal police chief precipitated a crisis which resulted in the removal of Vargas from office on the night of October 29–30 by a coup d'etat carried out by General Góes Monteiro (the minister of war) and other army officers. José Linhares, the president of the Supreme Court of Brazil, became president ad interim of the republic on October 30, 1945.

In the campaign that led up to the elections of December 2, 1945, two of the candidates, General Eurico Gaspar Dutra and Brigadier Eduardo Gomes, were military men. A third, Yeddo Fiuza, supported by Luis Carlos Prestes, headed the Communist ticket. A fourth, Mario Telles, ran as the candidate of the Agrarian party. Only Prestes and his lieutenants, in support of Fiuza, made any appeal to the bulk of the population in urban centers. They did so by providing temporary schools where the illiterate might learn at least to sign their names in preparation for the elections. Gomes, the candidate of the National Democratic Union, appealed chiefly to educated people, on a lofty plane of nineteenth-century liberalism. But Dutra, the Social Democratic party candidate, inherited the Vargas machine, especially in the back country, and, after squelching the diehard Vargas supporters (the *Queremistas*), won decisively, with army and conservative support.

Dutra was inaugurated January 31, 1946. On February 5, 1946, the Constituent Assembly met for the first time to consider the draft of a new constitution. The text was approved by the Constituent Assembly on September 17 and was promulgated by the president on September 18, 1946. It provided for a federal, presidential form of government with a bicameral legislature. Its provisions are discussed at greater length below.

Dutra served out his term, providing the country with a conservative government, which, however, was unable to bring order out of the administrative chaos left by the Vargas regime or to satisfy the political and economic aspirations of the restless mass of the people suffering from the effects of postwar inflation, aggravated by the continuing rapid pace of industrialization and the consequent migration of population from the rural back country to the cities. On November 22, 1947, Brazil broke off diplomatic relations with the Soviet Union. The Brazilian Communist party was outlawed on January 7, 1948, which resulted in the unseating of one senator, Luis Prestes, and fourteen deputies, besides numerous members of several state legislatures. On January 22, 1948, the Social Democratic party signed an agreement with the two principal opposition parties, the National Democratic Union and the Republican party, promising joint support for Dutra.

In the elections held in 1950 Vargas was once more elected. He polled 49.3 per cent of the vote. In his second administration, however, he proved unable to regain the control he had exercised in the earlier years of his first administration or to retain the popularity he had enjoyed during the period he was out of office. His government continued the policy of nationalizing certain industries, principally the petroleum industry; adopted strict controls over the price of coffee; and attempted various other measures to control inflation and runaway prices. But lack of thoroughgoing enforcement of corrective legislation undid the benefits that might otherwise have accrued to the economy. In the latter part of June 1953, six of the seven civilian members of his cabinet resigned in protest over the economic difficulties created by the decline in exports, restrictions on the balance of payments, the consequent weakening of the cruzeiro, and the rise in the cost of living. Vargas also failed to reconcile the army and found himself in a confrontation with the army command brought about by a political crisis precipitated by an unsuccessful attempt to assassinate Carlos Lacerda, editor of a leading Rio de Janeiro paper, in which Vargas' son Lutero and members of his bodyguard were implicated. Faced with the demand to resign, he shot himself to death in his bedroom on August 24, 1954. A long letter, the authorship of which is suspect, found with his body stated his case against those elements in the ruling classes of the country which, he declared, had prevented him from leading all Brazilians to a more satisfactory level of well-being.

Vargas was temporarily succeeded by his vice-president, João Café Filho. In elections held on October 3, 1955, Juscelino Kubitschek de Oliveira, the candidate of the Labor party and the Social Democratic party, was elected president; João Melchior Marques Goulart was elected vice-president. On November 8, 1955, Café Filho took an indefinite leave of absence after a heart attack. The president of the Chamber of Deputies, Carlos Coimbra da Luz, became acting president of the republic, but he was deposed on November 11 by a coup d'etat led by the minister of war, General Teixeira Lott, when he supported an army officer who called for an uprising to prevent the inauguration of Kubitschek and Goulart the following January.

Also on November 11, Nereu Ramos, president of the senate, was elected acting president of the republic by the congress, to serve until the inauguration of Kubitschek on January 31, 1956.

Kubitschek, the grandson of an immigrant from Bohemia (his mother's father), had already served as governor of the state of Minas Gerais. Kubitschek is actually his mother's maiden name, which he uses in preference to his father's, Oliveira, which he considers too commonplace. His administration was chiefly notable for various ambitious economic development plans and for the creation of the new capital of Brazil. The question of a new capital for the country was one that had been debated often in the past, many Brazilians believing that the transfer of the seat of the federal government away from the coast and into the interior of the country would have a salutary effect not only on the economic development of Brazil but also on the social outlook of its people. During Dutra's administration, plans were announced for a new capital, and a law containing transitional constitutional provisions adopted by the Constituent Assembly called for the setting up of a commission to study the exact location. On September 20, 1956, Kubitschek signed a law authorizing the government to take preliminary steps to transfer the capital to a site located 600 miles northwest of Rio de Janeiro and more than 3,000 feet above sea level in the state of Goiás. Brasília, as it was christened, was built in four years by a force of 40,000 men working in shifts around the clock. The city, whose plan was the creation of Lúcio Costa and whose striking architecture that of Oscar Niemeyer, has been acclaimed as the greatest success in city-building anywhere in this century. It will eventually have a population of a half-million and be surrounded by satellite towns. The Brasília-Belém highway, in part carved through the Amazon jungle, was inaugurated on February 1, 1960. Eventually, rail communications will be added to the road and air networks already in existence. Brasília was inaugurated as the new capital on April 21, 1960. The former Federal District—the city of Rio de Janeiro, which had been the capital since 1763—became the twenty-first state of the union as the state of Guanabara.

Kubitschek's administration received widespread and severe criticism for its all-out effort to create Brasília, which, it was claimed, added greatly to the already formidable problems arising from the various development plans fostered by his government. This criticism came not only from those who objected to leaving the cosmopolitan splendors of Rio for a raw city in the backlands, but also from those who believed that he had done irreparable damage to the financial condition of the country through the enormous demands of the task of conquering the wilderness and transporting men and materials without adequate roads. The fact remains that Brasília has become the symbol of a new Brazil.

In anticipation of the expiration of Kubitschek's term of office, elections were held in October 1960. The successful candidate was Jânio Quadros, who had made a name for himself as the reform mayor of the city of São Paulo by pulling that city's finances out of the red and had shown some success as the governor of the state of São Paulo. His campaign, in which he was supported by the National Democratic Union and the Christian Democratic party, was based on his slogan of the new broom to sweep corruption and extravagance out of the government. Quadros was inaugurated January 31, 1961, the first president to be inaugurated in Brasília. João Goulart, who had served as vice-president with Kubitschek, was re-elected to that office. Seven months later Quadros suddenly resigned, declaring that he had been deliberately thwarted in his attempts at reform. A factor contributing to his resignation was the accusations made by Carlos Lacerda that he was about to seize dictatorial powers. Goulart was at the time on a visit to Peking, conferring with the leaders of the Chinese Communist government. Controversy arose, centering in the army, as to the legality of Goulart's right to succeed to the presidency. On September 2 and 3, 1961, before his return, the congress adopted constitutional amendments providing for a parliamentary system of government, under which the executive powers were to be exercised by the president and a council of ministers responsible to congress. The president of the council, nominated by the president of the republic and approved by congress, was to function as a prime minister. A plebiscite was also provided for, to be held nine months before the end of the unexpired presidential term, January 31, 1966, on whether or not a return to the presidential form of government should be made.

The presidency of the republic was offered to Goulart on these terms, which he accepted. He was received back in Brazil with some enthusiastic support, chiefly in the state of Rio Grande do Sul. In July 1962 Goulart and the leaders of congress agreed that the plebiscite would be held on April 3, 1963. However, in September 1962, Goulart and the prime minister, Brochado da Rocha, demanded that the plebiscite be held at the same time as the forthcoming congressional elections on October 7, 1962. The unrest in the country, created not only by the continuing and worsening economic crises but also by the instability of the government, produced a general strike. In face of this, the congress approved on September 14–15 a compromise bill providing for a plebiscite to be held on January 6, 1963. The congress also granted Goulart emergency powers to form a provisional government to act without congressional approval until the congressional elections were held on October 7, 1962. The new congress approved the provisional government in November 1962. The plebiscite was held on January 6, 1963, and a large majority voted for return to the presidential system. Goulart signed a bill to that effect on January 23, 1963.

Goulart's motives and political sympathies were increasingly suspect in the eyes of the more conservative elements of Brazilian society, especially the army command. Although a wealthy landowner in the state of Rio Grande do Sul, his political affiliations had always been with the left and he was known for his enthusiastic admiration for Juan Perón of Argentina. It was suspected that his insistence on a nonalignment policy for Brazil in international affairs involving the Russian and Chinese Communist governments and the extreme nationalism of his view were a cloak for his real intentions, which were to align Brazil with the radical left at home and abroad. These suspicions were reinforced by his support of his brother-in-law, Leonel da Moira Brizzola, governor of the state of Rio Grande do Sul, who did not disguise his own ideological views. Goulart set up the Commission for the Nationalization of Public Service Concessionaires on June 18, 1962. Agreements for the nationalization of public utilities companies representing foreign capital, with what was generally considered to be inadequate compensation, were reached during the first half of 1963. On March 22, 1963, in line with the Three-Year-Plan requirements announced on December 30, 1962, Goulart sent to the congress proposals calling for expropriation of certain "unexploited" lands and their redistribution to rural and other workers. The Chamber of Deputies on April 19 approved a plan to study the legislation and constitutional amendment necessary to achieve this purpose. New restrictions were placed on the remittance of profits abroad, Brazil's balance-of-payments position grew steadily worse, and the cruzeiro continued to lose purchasing power.

On April 1–2, 1964, the army once more acted to remove the president, on the basis of its self-appointed role as the guardian of constitutional authority. Goulart was accused by the army leaders of intending to turn the country over to the radical left, with himself as dictator. He fled to Uruguay, power was assumed by the armed forces, and sweeping arrests were made of Communists and those alleged to be their sympathizers. Congress elected General Humberto Castelo Branco, army chief of staff, president of the republic to complete the unexpired presidential term to January 31, 1966. Castelo Branco, a career soldier with forty-six years of service, including service in World War II as an officer in the Brazilian Expeditionary Force, was a native of the state of Ceará. He was known for his personal integrity, and in his initial statements on assuming office foreswore any intention of placing in power members of the extreme right.

On April 9, 1964, the ministers of war, navy, and air, as the Supreme Military Revolutionary Command, issued an "Institutional Act," which conferred extensive powers on the president and authorized the suspension of the political rights of individuals for ten years, "in the interests of peace and the national honor." This act was to remain in force until January 31, 1966. Within a week, 167 people had been deprived of the right to vote and to hold political office—including Goulart, Quadros, and Brizzola. For a while Castelo Branco resisted pressure from members of the extreme right to include Kubitschek, but the increasing probability that Kubitschek would be a popular candidate in the next elections finally provoked the inclusion of his name in the list of June 8, with a vague accusation of corruption in his administration which he vigorously denied. A final list, approved June 15, 1964, brought the purge to an end with a total of 337 names.

On July 22, 1964, the congress approved an extension of Castelo Branco's term of office from January 31, 1966, to March 15, 1967, with elections to be held in December 1966. Castelo Branco, who had no political background and no political aspirations, considered his to be a caretaker administration and himself a referee and moderator between opposing extremes. Thus he saw his duty to be that of providing an interregnum to allow the heated political atmosphere generated by Quadros' resignation and the subsequent stirring up of the radical left, with or without Goulart's active encouragement, to cool off. His own marked conservatism did not save him from attack, especially in regard to the postponement of the elections. Attack came from the spokesman for the extreme right, Carlos Lacerda, at the time, governor of the state of Guanabara, who announced his intention of running for president in the next campaign.

In October 1965 Juscelino Kubitschek returned to Brazil after sixteen months of voluntary exile in France, to be greeted enthusiastically at Galeão airport by a large crowd of supporters. During his absence elections had been held for governors in eleven states. The successful candidates in the two most important states, Israel Pinheiro in Minas Gerais and Francisco Negrão de Lima in Guanabara (who had been foreign minister in Kubitschek's administration), were members of Kubitschek's party. Their election so alarmed the army command that, in spite of some efforts on Castelo Branco's part to maintain at least an outward appearance of democratic process, he was forced on October 27 to issue a decree greatly increasing the authoritarian powers of the federal executive. Among the most important were those permitting the president to rescind electoral mandates, to suspend the political rights of persons unfavorable to the regime, and to assume direct control in states considered to be in the grip of "internal commotion." Also, all existing political parties were dissolved. Castelo Branco, however, also expressly excluded himself from re-election when his term of office expired in March 1967.

The severest and most outspoken critic of this decree—which was cast in the form of a "revolutionary" amendment to the constitution, was Carlos Lacerda, who as a consequence was officially denied access to the Rio broadcasting networks. A month later, in another decree, the ban on political parties was somewhat relaxed. The result was the formation of two parties, one in support of the government, which assumed the name of the National Renovating Alliance (ARENA), and the other described as a "tolerated opposition," which went by the title of the Brazilian Democratic Movement. In spite of efforts on the part of an obdurate group of military men, Castelo Branco, with the tacit support of the majority of the army command, permitted the seating, in December 1965, of the duly elected governors of Minas Gerais and Guanabara.

By April 1966 it had become increasingly apparent that Castelo Branco's most likely successor would be another army general, General Artur Costa e Silva, his minister of war. Popular election of the president having been eliminated, his election would require a majority vote of the four hundred nine members of the Chamber of Deputies and a two-thirds majority of the senate. Costa e Silva, a native of Rio Grande do Sul, was, in fact, duly elected on October 3, 1966, for a four-year term at a joint session of the congress which was boycotted by members of the opposition party. The only member of the opposition present, the minority leader Vieira de Melo, remained long enough to declare the indirect election of the president by the congress to be "a democratic fraud." In November the first congressional elections since 1964 were held. Of the twenty-two million registered voters in the country, nearly twenty million were estimated to have voted to maintain the regime in power. Castelo Branco, as he had previously announced he would do, retired to private life. He was killed in a plane collision on a flight to Fortaleza on July 18, 1967.

In December 1966 the draft of a new constitution was presented. Its most controversial provision was that establishing the election of the president by an electoral college. It was adopted on January 22, 1967, by an extraordinary session of the congress. A new press law was adopted at the same time which provided stiff penalties for reporting matters that the administration might consider damaging to the national security or the financial stability of the country.

Costa e Silva (after a preliminary visit to the United States) was inaugurated on March 15, 1967, in Brasília. Of the eighteen members of his new cabinet, half were military men. Nevertheless, he declared in his inaugural address that "social humanism" would be the foundation of his government. He also acknowledged that "there exists a profound cleavage of inequality in Brazilian society" and that he had "more than once the impression that, while we live in the same national space we do not live in the same social time."

His administration was at first marked by apathy among the majority of Brazilians. But although at first he provoked no general outspoken criticism, he also failed to achieve the popularity he openly sought. A random sampling of public opinion obtained by a poll conducted by government agents in the cities indicated that 45 per cent of those questioned considered his regime to be average and 32 per cent believed it good. The younger element of the population, however, represented by student protest, and the more radical members of the public, increased their opposition, and in June 1968, some ten thousand persons, including some teachers, members of religious orders, and members of the congress, paraded through the center of Rio demanding the resignation of Costa e Silva's government. The demonstration produced no serious incidents, partly because the administration ordered the police to remain in their barracks. Later demonstrations, however, provoked some violence. In July Jânio Quadros was detained briefly by the federal police in Santos for questioning as the result of criticism he had publicly made of the regime. By the end of 1968 it had become apparent that much middle-class sentiment was in sympathy with the students and the more outspoken critics of the administration. In the middle of December 1968, hundreds of persons were arrested, including some of the most prominent political and intellectual figures of Brazilian life, Kubitschek and Lacerda among them; army censorship was imposed on the press, the radio, and television. Congress was indefinitely recessed by the president, a move provoked by the refusal of the Chamber of Deputies to acquiesce in the disciplining of one of its members, Marcio Moreira Alves, for criticism of the armed forces made in an address delivered in the chamber on the preceding September 7.

In January 1969 Costa e Silva summarily dismissed three of the fifteen justices of the supreme court, provoking the resignation of the presiding justice, Antonio Gonçalves de Oliveira. The president's dismissal of these justices was the first instance in the twentieth century of interference by the executive with the supreme judiciary, which was traditionally considered to be aloof from politics. In February the central committee of the National Conference of Bishops, representing all the Roman Catholic prelates in Brazil, met in Rio and issued a declaration calling on the president to return democratic government to Brazil as soon as possible. Even these protests on the part of influential persons failed to sway the military regime. At the end of February Costa e Silva issued several new decrees, including the so-called Seventh Institutional Act, which barred interim federal, state, and municipal elections before the next general elections scheduled for the end of 1970. This meant that "interventors" appointed by the federal government would fill any vacancies created by death or resignation in the meantime.

In May 1969 Pedro Aleixo, the vice-president, in private life a professor of law with liberal tendencies, was secretly entrusted with the task of making a review of the constitution. He consistently advocated the reconvening of the congress, partially in order to prove some resistance to the pressures brought to bear on the president by political and private groups seeking legislation by decree to further their own interests. This slight advance towards a return to normal government was brought to an abrupt halt by the sudden illness of the president, who at the end of August suffered a cerebral hemorrhage. His official powers were immediately assumed by a triumvirate of military men—General Aurélio de Lyra Tavares, minister of war; Admiral Augusto Rademaker, minister of the navy; and Air Marshal Marcio de Souza e Mello, air force minister—thus nullifying the constitutional provision under which the vice-president would assume the duties of the president.

In September 1969 a bizarre note was added to the undercurrent of protest against the regime (which occasionally burst into the open, as during July) by the kidnapping by a group of radical anti-government sympathizers of the United States ambassador, C. Burke Elbrick, who was released unharmed when the administration agreed to the release of a number of political prisoners seized earlier by government agents. In October, General Emilio Garrastazú Médici, another native of Rio Grande do Sul and an old friend of Costa e Silva, was appointed president by the Armed Forces High Command. Médici, a former chief of the National Intelligence Service with some experience in the foreign service, was chosen over Major General Alfonso Albuquerque Lima (a native of the northeast of Brazil and minister of interior under Costa e Silva), who had been popularly regarded as the most likely candidate. It is obviously too soon at this writing to assess the impact of the new president on the course of political events in Brazil. However, the tensions within the group of military men who control the government of Brazil, which have persisted since the coup of 1964, causing on various occasions serious embarrassment to both Castelo Branco and Costa e Silva, will obviously not lessen, especially since many of the younger and more ambitious men are advocates of the unsuccessful candidate Albuquerque Lima.

A further comment may also be made concerning the support that the military regime has received over the last five years from civilian officials. It must be recognized that many economists and monetary experts, including the highly regarded minister of planning, Roberto Campos, believe that an authoritarian regime is necessary for the preservation of the Brazilian economy, the control of inflation, the effective administration of the tax-collection system, and the attraction of capital for the expansion of industrial and agrarian development. Also, in spite of the very slow pace of any real improvement for the majority of—and especially the rural—Brazilians in the educational system, in agricultural reform, and in public health facilities, the fact remains that enough general prosperity and improvement in the living standards of at least the urban substratum of Brazilian society has occurred to produce considerable popular apathy in regard to the form of government under which the country lives. How long this state of affairs will subsist only time will tell.

One final comment may be made concerning Brazil's relations with the world at large, especially as regards invitation and protection of foreign investment capital, since 1964. On the whole, the federal administration has maintained a middle course between extreme nationalism and indiscriminate dealings with foreign investors. In doing so, both Castelo Branco and Costa e Silva and their economic advisers have had to contend, especially as concerns Brazil's attitude towards the United States, with the more or less violent opposition of the radical left and the extreme right, both of whom tend to consider any expression of opinion, official or unofficial, on the part of United States citizens as an intrusion into Brazil's national affairs.

LAW

The following sections describe constitutional and administrative law; the judiciary; the civil, commercial, and criminal codes; procedural law; general legislation; and treaty law.

Constitutional Law

During its independent life, Brazil has had six constitutions: 1824, 1891, 1934, 1937, 1946, and 1967.

The Imperial Constitution of March 25, 1824, with the Additional Act of August 12, 1834, was in effect throughout the life of the empire. It declared Brazil to be a hereditary constitutional monarchy under the Bragança dynasty. In its bicameral legislature, senators were appointed for life and deputies were elected indirectly for four years. The country was divided into provinces, each with a president appointed by the emperor, and an advisory assembly, the members of which were elected indirectly for four years.

The position of the emperor was strong. He could veto acts of parliament; his ministers were responsible to him and not to the assembly. He appointed the members of his Council of State for life, and consulted them on the occasions of his using the moderative power. This latter attribute was undoubtedly the most important of the emperor's powers, for, as mentioned above, it enabled him to intervene with cause in any disturbance of government routine.

The constitution was otherwise a mixture of the liberal and the conservative. Roman Catholicism was established as the state religion. Freedom of the press, religious liberty (within certain practical restrictions), the inviolability of the home, equality before the law, property rights, public education, and freedom to trade were guaranteed.

The Additional Act of 1834 set up legislative assemblies in the provinces, its chief purpose being to increase the autonomy of the local governments, thus taking a step toward federation and away from too centralized a government.

The Republican Constitution of February 24, 1891.—The draftsmen of the first constitution of the republic, under the leadership of Ruy Barbosa, were considerably influenced by the old Imperial Constitution and the Constitution of the United States, as well as by the constitutions of France and the other republics of the Western Hemisphere. The new constitution set up a republic of twenty states and a federal district. In theory the federal principle had triumphed, for governmental powers were distributed between the national and the state governments.

Certain factors, however, must be borne in mind in this regard. The powers of the national government were those inherited from the imperial government and were not conferred on it by the states. This descent emphasizes an important element in the Brazilian historical scene: that the autonomy granted first the provinces and then the states was in reality a recognition of the actual power of local political groups rather than the exemplification of the principle of authority emanating from the people through local sovereignty to the national sovereignty. A legislature composed of a senate and chamber of deputies was to meet once a year in May and hold sessions for four months. Three senators were elected from each state and the Federal District, making sixty-three in all, for a nine-year term, one-third to be elected every three years. The deputies, in numbers determined on the basis of population, were elected for three-year terms. A president and vice-president were to be elected for four-year terms. The president's powers included the approval of acts of the congress and the appointment of ministers who were responsible to him and not to the congress. The states were left free to set up their own governments within the general principles of the constitution. They were granted great autonomy in levying taxes. A bill of rights was included.

The Constitution of July 16, 1934.—One of the outstanding features of the first Vargas constitution was its change from the old theory of drafting constitutions, which called for an expression of general principles, to the new fashion of a document that attempted to define in detail the powers and functions of the state. It also had the inherent weakness of attempting to bridge the gap caused by the perennial conflict between the trend toward centralization and the demand for greater autonomy in state government. It declared that all power emanates from the people and is exercised in their name. In addition to providing for a chamber of deputies and a senate, this long instrument contained a declaration of rights and guarantees, chapters on the economic and social order, the family, education, and national security. Because it neither clearly departed from the traditional pattern nor adopted the new, which in some respects it imitated, it was an unsatisfactory charter.

The Constitution of November 10, 1937.—This instrument spoke unmistakably of its times. Article 1 declared that Brazil was a republic, that political power emanated from the people and was exercised in their name and in the interest of their well-being, honor, independence, and prosperity. It preserved some aspects of the federal character of the republic but provided that the legislative power should be exercised by a national parliament with the cooperation of a national economic council. The parliament was composed of a chamber of deputies and a federal council. The deputies were indirectly elected by the municipal councilors of each *município* and ten citizens elected by direct suffrage at the same time the municipal council was elected. The Federal Council was composed of one representative elected by each state assembly and ten members appointed by the president of the republic. The governors of the states could veto the choice by the assemblies. The National Economic Council, the duties of which included the "promotion of the corporate organization of the National Economy," was made up of representatives of various branches of national production chosen from persons qualified by special ability, professional association, etc., with equal representation of employers and employees. The constitution also included elaborate chapters on the economic order, the family, education, national security, public employees, military forces, and defense of the state.

Throughout the period of its life, however, the 1937 Constitution remained in an anomalous status. Article 187 provided that it should be submitted to a national plebiscite in a form regulated by a decree of the president of the republic. Since President Vargas never signed such a decree and the constitution was never submitted to a plebiscite, its legality was questioned. It contained a provision which gave the president sweeping powers, permitting him considerable latitude in declaring a state of emergency to exist. It also was amended by numerous constitutional laws. One of these, dated November 17, 1945, finally abolished the National Security Tribunal, which, with jurisdiction to adjudge "crimes against the existence, security, and integrity of the state," was one of the features of the Vargas regime that did most to give it the character of a police state.

The Constitution of September 18, 1946.—This constitution, as originally promulgated during the Dutra administration, declared Brazil to be a federal, representative republic, with a president as executive, a bicameral legislature, and a judiciary composed of a federal supreme court and other federal courts. As has been related above, at the time of Quadros' resignation as president, the congress approved Amendment 4 to the constitution, which substituted a parliamentary form of government, with the executive power to be exercised by a president and a council of ministers responsible to the congress. The president of the council, appointed by the president of the republic with the approval of the congress, would act as prime minister. The referendum held on January 6, 1963, resulted in the abolition of this system (Amendment 6) and a return to the presidential form of government provided for in the constitution as originally promulgated.

The president of the republic was to be elected by popular vote and could not succeed himself. Originally the presidential term was five years, but this was shortened to four by an amendment adopted July 22, 1964 (Amendment 9). This amendment also declared that the president, the vice-president, and both houses of the congress were to be elected simultaneously. The union was comprised of the states, the Federal District (now Brasília), and the territories. The powers of the federal government were enumerated and included jurisdiction to legislate in the fields of civil, commercial, criminal, procedural, electoral, air, and labor law; on natural resources; and on foreign and interstate commerce. Grounds for federal intervention in state governments were enumerated. Each state was to be governed by the constitution and laws adopted by it, and all powers not expressly or impliedly forbidden to them by the federal constitution were reserved to them. State courts were provided for and their jurisdiction defined. A bill of rights was included in Articles 141–44. Like its predecessors, this constitution contained chapters dealing with the economic order (including labor relations and social welfare), the family, education, the armed forces, and public employees.

The constitution adopted on January 22, 1967, during the incumbency of Castelo Branco, to be effective on March 15, superseded the 1946 Constitution. In format it is very similar to its predecessor, but there are important differences in the allocation of powers. The present constitution declares Brazil to be a federal republic, changing the official name of the country from the United States of Brazil to Brazil. Most taxes, with the exception chiefly of taxes on real estate, are to be levied by the federal government and a share of the proceeds distributed to the states and municipalities. The president is to be elected by an electoral college made up of members of the federal congress and other persons elected by the state legislatures. Only the president may initiate legislation affecting the national security or public finances, and he has the power to suspend the political rights of individuals. His power to create legislation by decree is extensive. Military courts are given jurisdiction over civilians accused of crimes against the national security. The formation and dissolution of political parties is to be governed by federal law. Coalitions among political parties are prohibited.

This charter has been amended several times on the basis of political expediency. Some of these amendments have been referred to above. The more liberalizing amendments contemplated just prior to the incapacity of Costa e Silva referred to previously, which would have transformed the constitution, have apparently been abandoned under the present administration.

Administrative Law

One of Dom João's first acts on arrival in Brazil was to organize his cabinet on March 10, 1808, by appointing Fernando Jose de Portugal e Castro (later marquis of Aguiar), minister of the affairs of the realm; Rodrigo de Sousa Coutinho (first count of Linhares), minister of foreign affairs and war; and João Rodrigues de Sá e Menezes (later count of Anadia), minister of the navy and overseas possessions. As soon as the new cabinet took office, the following governmental bodies were created: the Council of State; the Supreme Military and Judicial Council; the General Police Intendancy; the Royal Exchequer; the Treasury Council; the mint; the Office of the Chief Magistrate; the royal printing press; various courts that are elsewhere described; and several other less important organs. This general pattern was not departed from under the Imperial Constitution. Under the republic, considerable efforts were made to modernize the governmental machinery of the country.

A detailed discussion of Brazilian legal thought on the subject is not appropriate here, but it may be noted that Brazil has clung more or less to the general principles of the interrelation of governmental powers expressed and developed in Great Britain and the United States. This has been the case in spite of the fact that important differences exist between the legal theses of governmental responsibility in the Brazilian judicial system, as a descendant of Roman law, and those of the common-law countries. In judicial thought Brazil has been considerably influenced by the doctrines of administrative law developed in France during the late nineteenth and the present centuries.

One characteristic feature of Brazilian public administration, chiefly the creation of the Vargas regime and developed under the economic pressure of rapid and uneven industrialization, has been the establishment and multiplication of specialized governmental agencies. Some of these have resulted from the expansion of the sphere of labor legislation to include welfare and old age services, such as social security bureaus, public housing agencies, hospitals, child care and public health posts. There are also many regulatory agencies governing the production, pricing, marketing, and export of specific commodities, including coffee, cacao, sugar and alcohol, mate, rice, tobacco, salt, meat, wheat, and pine lumber. The National Economic Council was established in 1949 under a provision of the constitution of 1946 and served as an advisory body to the president and congress. It was expressly abolished by the 1967 Constitution. There are numerous agencies concerned with the development of certain basic industries such as coal mining and steel and petroleum production, which have come into existence as a result of the various economic development plans adopted by the government. There are a number of agencies charged with the carrying out of certain portions of these development plans, such as that in charge of the rehabilitation of the northeastern part of the country, which suffers from periodic and disastrous droughts. A coordinating body, with a coordinator general, to integrate these various governmental development programs was created in 1963 (Decree 52256 of July 11). In 1964 the powers and functions of the Coordinator General were turned over to a minister of state extraordinary (Decree 53890 of April 20).

Also, both the federal and the state governments are principal shareholders in many mixed stock corporations for the development of certain industries, notably that involving the expansion of hydroelectric power. Petroleo Brasileiro, S.A. (PETROBRAS), a corporation controlled by the federal government, has a monopoly in the production of petroleum. The railroads have been largely nationalized. The further nationalization of the public utilities companies, including foreign-owned and operated electric power and telephone companies, was interrupted by the overthrow of the Goulart administration in 1963. The extent of governmental control and participation in the economic life of the country is so great that it makes a detailed account here impossible.

What are probably two of the most important pieces of regulatory legislation adopted recently are Law 4595 of December 31, 1964, and Law 4728 of July 14, 1965. The first of these revamped the governmental machinery to control the monetary and banking systems of the country. It abolished the Superintendency of Money and Credit (SUMOC) and its council. Instead, the National Monetary Council (Conselho Monetario Nacional) was created, and the Central Bank of Brazil was established, which has the power to issue paper money and coinage, to control all credit operations, including the investment of foreign capital in Brazil, and to supervise all banks and other financial institutions. The Central Bank of Brazil remains the fiscal agent for the National Treasury.

The second statute, Law 4728 of July 14, 1965, declares that the financial and capital markets of the country shall be regulated by the National Monetary Council and controlled by the Central Bank of Brazil. This, in effect, creates an agency to regulate the issuance and registration of stock and commercial paper by corporations, trading on the stock exchanges, and the operations of investment companies. It represents the first serious attempt to control speculation and fraud in stock market transactions.

The Castelo Branco and Costa e Silva administrations have gone forward with the program for agrarian reform. Law 4504 of November 30, 1964, creates an institute of agrarian reform and establishes a fund to carry out the institute's programs, to be financed by 3 per cent of the federal revenues, as well as by the issue of bonds. It also lays down procedures for expropriation of land purchase and colonization and grants tax benefits and special assistance to owners who undertake improvements approved by the institute.

The Judiciary and the Court System

During Brazil's earliest days as a colony, judicial functions were not clearly differentiated from the general administration of the municipal councils. The captain-general or governor, who were the king's representatives, exercised police authority, which he received from the *câmaras*, the local governing bodies. The ordinary judges were elected annually, like the aldermen, and in case of absence or other impediment, were substituted for by the senior aldermen. Otherwise, the usual Portuguese judicial officers were duplicated in Brazil, including the *juiz de fora*, who was usually a young man with a legal diploma fresh from a university in Portugal and whose functions were a mixture of civil and administrative jurisdiction, with police functions but no criminal jurisdiction.

The court of the *Relação do Brasil*, established in Bahia by an edict on March 7, 1609, was made up of ten judges called *desembargadores*, one of whom acted as chancellor. This court was suppressed once and revived (during the Dutch and Spanish interregnum). The court of the *Relação do Rio de Janeiro*, to which was attached a court of the *Mesa do Desembargo do Paço*, in imitation of the *Mesa* in Lisbon,[2] was created in 1751 and, by an *alvará* of May 10, 1808, was raised to the status of *Casa da Suplicação do Brasil*, that is, the supreme court. Its jurisdiction was wide, for the Portuguese medieval tradition of the interpenetration of judicial, administrative, and police functions was maintained.

The importance to Portugal of British aid was demonstrated shortly after Dom João's arrival in Rio, when the *Juiz Conservador da Nação Inglesa* was set up—a special court to hear causes involving Englishmen, which survived for many years, a monument to the ubiquitous British merchant.

2. The court of the *Mesa do Desembargo do Paço*, attached to the *Relação do Rio de Janeiro*, was suppressed by a law of September 28, 1828. Its functions had been to issue *alvarás* and *provisões*, such as bonds, pardons, commutations of minor penalties, and other summary matters involving small amounts, not important enough to be taken cognizance of by the metropolitan magistrates.

Under the constitution of the empire two types of judges were created: the judge learned in law (the *juiz de direito*) and the lay judge (the *juiz de facto*). The *juiz de direito* was appointed for life, was not removable, and constituted a court of first instance. The emperor could suspend him by complaint and proceedings before the *Relação* of the district. The courts of the *Relações* in Rio de Janeiro, Bahia, Pernambuco, and Maranhão were the courts of second and third instance. There were also justices of the peace, elected with the aldermen of their local districts.

The Imperial Constitution provided for a supreme court of justice, which was actually established by a law of September 18, 1828. It was composed of sixteen judges chosen by the emperor from the judges of the *Relações*, in order of seniority, and functioned under a president twice a week for a three-year term. It had powers of review and jurisdiction over the following: proceedings against ministers, judges of the higher courts, diplomats, and presidents of provinces; conflicts of jurisdiction; and habeas corpus proceedings in cases of persons illegally arrested by order of the president of a province, etc. Law 609 of August 19, 1851, gave it jurisdiction over proceedings against archbishops and bishops. The emperor could suspend the judges through the exercise of the moderative power, a means of controlling the court that was put in practice by Dom Pedro ii. A decree of June 9, 1850, provided courts of first, second, and third instance for each *comarca* (district) of the empire and required that the magistrate of these courts should rise from the first to the second after four years' service and then to the third after an additional three years' service.

Under the Republican Constitution of 1890, the courts were reorganized by Decree 848 of October 11, 1890, as follows:

The supreme court became the Federal Supreme Court, composed of fifteen judges, appointed by the president of the republic *ad referendum* to the federal senate. The federal judges who held office for life took cognizance of (1) causes in which one of the parties sued on or used as defense some provision of the federal constitution; (2) litigation between a state and citizens of another, or between citizens of various states, in the case of conflict of laws; (3) suits between foreign states and Brazilian citizens; (4) actions brought by aliens and based either on contracts with the federal government or on conventions or treaties between the republic and other nations; (5) questions of maritime law and navigation, whether ocean-going or on rivers and lakes; (6) questions of international law, whether civil or criminal; and (7) political crimes.

Besides the supreme court, the constitution provided for a system of lower federal courts. Each state, also, was free to organize its own judiciary. A series of decrees from 1890 to 1923 set up the courts for the Federal District.

The Constitution of 1934 described the federal judiciary as consisting of the supreme court, composed of eleven members (a number that might be raised to sixteen but that could not be reduced) who were appointed for life but who were compelled to retire at the age of seventy-five; federal courts; military courts; and electoral courts. A public ministry, the chief of which was the attorney general of the republic, appointed by the president with the approval of the senate, was created, as well as an accounts court. State courts remained a matter for state legislation.

The most important change in the 1937 Constitution was the suppression of the system of lower federal courts. Provision was made for a supreme court, state courts, courts for the Federal District and the territories, and military courts.

The 1946 Constitution did not restore the lower courts. It provided for a supreme court, a federal court of appeals, military courts, electoral courts, labor courts, state courts, and the public ministry.

The 1967 Constitution provides for a federal supreme court composed of sixteen justices, federal appellate courts, a federal district court to be located in the capital of each state and federal territory, and federal military, electoral, and labor courts. It also includes the general requirements that must govern the court system to be established by each state. Brazil has no system of administrative courts as such. There are numerous administrative bodies with the power to judge cases arising in their specialized field, but these are really administrative boards, whose decisions may be appealed to the regular courts. The most important of these are the arbitration boards[3] to decide disputes in labor questions,[4] certain treasury councils, the National Council of Education, the Maritime Administrative Court, etc.

Since the empire, Brazil has not had special courts to take cognizance of matters involving the responsibility of the government or governmental officials, known in France as the *jurisdiction contentieux-administrative* and commonly in the Spanish American republics as the *jurisdicción contencioso-administrativa*. Such matters in Brazil are considered by the regular courts.

The Civil Code

Brazil possesses, in its civil code, one of the monuments of legal thought in Latin America. It required, however, about a hundred years to achieve.

The law that prevailed in Brazil at the time of Independence was the compilation of statutes known as the *Ordenações Philippinas*. It was a hodge-

3. The Constitution of 1946 expressly stated that the labor courts were an integral part of the general judicial system.
4. Labor legislation and labor courts are not discussed here, as they are treated elsewhere in this volume.

podge of legislation, antiquated, undigested, reflecting the usages of Portugal, and wholly unsuited to the needs of the new empire in the Western Hemisphere.[5] The Imperial Constitution of 1828 promised a new civil code, but the drafting of such a statute was put aside in favor of the more urgently needed Criminal Code, Code of Criminal Procedure, and Commercial Code.

In 1851 Eusébio de Queiroz, then minister of justice and a man inclined to seek positive action in the solution of Brazil's problems, suggested the adoption of the *Digesto Português*, prepared by the Portuguese Corrêa Telles as an interim code, but the idea was spurned by the Brazilian bar. In 1855 the imperial government commissioned Augusto Teixeira de Freitas, Latin America's finest constructive jurist, to compile all the civil laws, which he did in three years under the title of *Consolidação das Leis Civis*, with annotations showing the source of each article. The *Consolidação* served Brazil as a civil code for many years. It was basically the old law contained in the *Ordenações*, amended by the statutes adopted in Brazil in the period intervening since the Independence. Subsequently, Teixeira de Freitas published an *Esboço* or sketch for a real civil code, but he died before he was able to prepare more than a few articles of the definitive work. However, he laid the foundations upon which his successors were to build. He had in mind the integration of the civil and commercial law, an idea persisting today with some reformers of Brazilian law. His work served as a model for the Argentine and Uruguayan civil codes, which in turn have served several of the other Latin American republics as models for their own.

It was followed in Brazil by two other attempts: one in 1872 by Nabuco de Araújo, who made few changes in the original draft; another in 1881 by Felício dos Santos, which was under consideration by the national parliament for several years. A parliamentary committee was set up in July 1889, just before the collapse of the empire, to draw up a code, but its work was interrupted by the advent of the republic.

Campos Sales, minister of justice under the provisional government, convinced of the need for the codification of the law, commissioned Coelho Rodrigues, a well-known law professor and writer, to prepare a draft, which was ready January 16, 1893, but was not finally adopted, although in 1895 the senate got as far as voting to adopt it in place of the draft by Felício de Santos. At last, in 1899, Epitácio Pessoa, the minister of justice, appointed Clovis Bevilaqua to prepare a code. Bevilaqua was an indefatigable worker with considerable acquaintance with contemporary judicial thought. He had been trained in the law faculty of Recife, at the time the most distinguished law school in Latin America. He had absorbed the work of Tobias

5. It must be borne in mind that Brazil, inheriting its judicial thought from Portugal, is a civil-law country and that its legal system is patterned after the Roman law rather than that of countries inheriting the English common law, such as the United States.

Barreto de Menezes, the popularizer in Brazil of modern theories in the reform of legal education and attempts at systematization and codification of law. The scheme of classification that he adopted for his code was in general that of the drafters of the German Civil Code. He divided the whole into three parts: (1) general principles for the interpretation of the remainder and the rules relative to conflict of laws; (2) persons, property, and the creation and extinction of rights; (3) the law of the family, of property, of obligations, and succession. In defending the system he adopted, Bevilaqua declared that, in considering man as the nucleus of society and man in the social group as taking precedence over the individual, he placed the law governing family relationship first. The laws governing property, obligations, and inheritance are thus seen as developing most naturally from the central idea of the individual and the family.

Bevilaqua's appointment, however, had not been popular. His ideas were novel, and his draft therefore encountered much criticism when, in November 1899, he submitted it to the president, who sent it on to the congress on November 17, 1900. Some of the most brilliant criticism was that by Ruy Barbosa, the principal draftsman of the constitution of the republic, who complained of its style and the youth of its author. The draft was approved by the Chamber of Deputies on April 8, 1902, but, as a result of the controversy aroused, enactment was suspended for fourteen years. It was finally approved by both houses and promulgated by the president on January 1, 1916, to go into effect on January 1, 1917.[6] It is a conservative document, but its virtues have frequently been enumerated: it is concise and still sufficiently general, flexible, comprehensive, and practical. It has been praised for its method, technical structure, clarity of judicial concepts, and liberal thought; its influence outside of Brazil has been great, especially in the rest of South America.

The most important amendment to the Civil Code to date has been the enactment of a new introductory law (Decree-Law 4657 of September 4, 1942). Speaking of the old law which it superseded, Bevilaqua defined its purpose thus: "It is not a component part of the Code. . . . Its provisions include material relative to public law, to hermeneutics, and to private international law." The most striking changes made by the new law are in Article 7, which provides for the nonrecognition of foreign divorces in Brazil, if the parties are Brazilian.[7] Article 10, in clarifying a much discussed point, provides for the application of the law of the domicile of the deceased in cases of inheritance of property, the former law having provided for the application of the law of the country of which the deceased was a national. Article 12 makes definite provision for exequatur and letters rogatory, another obscure question in the old law.

6. Law 3071 of January 1, 1916, corrected by Law 3725 of January 15, 1919.
7. The Brazilian Civil Code does not recognize absolute divorce.

Other recent legislation containing important amendments to the code includes Decree 4857 of November 9, 1939, governing the public registry of documents required by the code to be registered (birth certificates, titles to real property, etc.) and various other laws implementing rather than changing the text of the code, in conformity with contemporary needs.

Revision of the Civil Code has been under study for a number of years. In July 1963 the Committee on Revising the First Draft (*Anteprojeto*) of the Civil Code made its report to the minister of justice and interior. The text of the first draft was published in the official gazette on May 15, 1964, for the purpose of inviting learned comment.

Up to the present time, the subject of obligations has been covered in Book III of the Civil Code. There is now a move on foot for the adoption of a separate code of obligations. A first draft of a code of obligations was submitted to the minister of justice and interior on December 25, 1963, and the text was published in the official gazette on March 2, 1964.

The Commercial Code

Because of the importance of trade to Portugal and its chief overseas offspring, Brazil, it was natural that the drafting of a commercial code should be one of the first considerations of the transplanted government. Dom João was fortunate in having for his adviser in economic matters the astute and practical José da Silva Lisboa, Viscount Cairú, upon whose advice the ports of Brazil were opened on January 28, 1808, to direct trade with the outside world. Silva Lisboa stated, in his tract on trade regulations published in 1832 (*Regras da Praça ou Bases do Regulamento Comercial, Conforme os Novos Códigos de Comércio e a Legislação Pátria*): "When the commercial court [the Court of the Royal Board of Trade, Agriculture, Industry, and Navigation] was set up in 1809, I was commissioned to prepare a commercial code. This herculean task much exceeded my powers; it needed time, leisure, assistance, business experience, and youthful vigor, and I lacked all these." He limited himself, therefore, to making an outline of a provisional regimen for business affairs, which, if it did not actually lay the foundations for a code, provided useful ideas for such codification. On October 30, 1825, a law was passed requiring the observance in Brazil of the Portuguese law of August 18, 1769, which provided that the mercantile legislation of the civilized nations of Europe should have a persuasive effect in Portugal. The French Commercial Code of 1807 had great authority in Brazil under this legislation.

In August 1834, during the regency, a codifying committee headed by José Clemente Pereira presented a draft code modeled on the French Code of 1807, the Spanish Code of 1829, and the Portuguese Code of 1833. It was favorably received by a mixed committee of the chamber and senate in

1835, but was then laid aside. This delay greatly chagrined the merchant fraternity, whose affairs were much hampered by the confused state in which the mercantile legislation then was. A commission of ten merchants then offered a body of amendments to the draft. Widespread complaint, not only in Rio de Janeiro but in Bahia and Pernambuco, finally resulted in the appointment of a new committee. The drafts and the amendments, slowly making their way through the Chamber of Deputies and the senate, were at last approved and promulgated by the emperor on May 2, 1850, and published the following June 25. A committee, including three outstanding men, José Clemente Pereira, Nabuco de Araújo, and Baron Mauá, then drew up Regulamento 737 of November 25, 1850, to provide regulations and procedure for the code, one of the most useful and well-thought-out pieces of legislation ever adopted in Brazil.

The code was the first to appear in the Western Hemisphere, since the Haitian Code of 1826 was merely a reproduction of the French, and the Bolivian Code of 1834 a copy of the Spanish. The chief criticism made of it was that, because Brazil still lacked a civil code, it encroached, in an attempt to supply certain important deficiencies, on matters not properly within the scope of a commercial code.

During the period since its enactment, now nearly a hundred years ago, so many changes have taken place in the business world that the code has become outmoded and seriously inadequate. For example, railroads did not exist in Brazil in 1850, and maritime transport was carried on entirely by sailing vessels. The greatest development of credit operations and investment banking came, even in Europe and the United States, after the middle of the nineteenth century. The code had made no provision for modern commercial companies, especially *sociedades anônimas* (in general, the equivalent of corporations). Law 1083 of August 22, 1860 (with its regulatory Decree 2711 of December 15, 1860), created *sociedades anônimas;* further modifications were brought together in Decree 434 of July 4, 1891. Decree-Law 2627 of September 26, 1940, with subsequent amendments, completely revised this legislation. Cooperative companies were created by Law 1637 of January 5, 1907, and limited companies by Law 3708 of January 10, 1919.

These changes had the natural consequence of making the section of the code dealing with bankruptcy inadequate. The banking crisis of 1864 resulted in temporary emergency legislation on the subject, but permanent revision of the bankruptcy laws continued to be discussed throughout the remainder of the nineteenth century. Finally, Decree 917 of October 24, 1890, adopted the draft prepared by Carlos de Carvalho, one of Brazil's outstanding lawyers. It had serious weaknesses, however, which were vigorously protested against by the Commercial Association of São Paulo and other merchant groups. It was, therefore, replaced shortly thereafter by other legislation which, in turn, has been amended on various occasions.

On January 4, 1911, Law 2379 authorized the preparation of a new draft commercial code to replace the entire Code of 1850. It was originally entrusted to Herculiano Marco Inglez de Souza, a foremost legal authority, who presented his draft to the senate in 1912. It has been considered and discussed by various committees, but so far no definitive draft has been produced. The necessity of a complete modernization of the commercial law is obvious. As it now stands, the Commercial Code has been extensively modified since 1890 by an ever growing mass of supplementary laws concerning commercial companies, coastwise trade, negotiable instruments, corporations, cooperatives, bankruptcy, liability of common carriers by rail, trade marks and patents, and various other matters. The mere listing of such subjects indicates how completely the modern world has outgrown the scope of the old code.

The pressure of modern financial dealings, arising from the increasing industrialization of the country; the growing number of small investors in large undertakings; and the demand for more flexible methods of financing new enterprises are resulting in a number of developments in corporate law and practice that must in time be reflected in a new commercial code.

The Criminal Code

Article 179, no. 18, of the Imperial Constitution of 1824 provided for the immediate preparation of civil and criminal codes. The confused state of all the law applicable in Brazil at the time made new legislation imperative, but the restlessness caused by the upheavals during the sojourn of Dom João in Brazil and immediately following his return to Portugal prompted greater attention to the criminal code, which was adopted December 16, 1830. It was during its life considered to be one of the best of modern codes. The old Imperial Code was replaced in 1890 (Decree 847 of October 11) by the new Code of 1889, which abolished capital punishment except under military law in wartime.

The code now in force was adopted by Decree-Law 2848 of December 7, 1940. The main difference between it and its predecessors was the basic change in attitude toward crime and criminals which has come about as a result of modern sociological thought. The current school of criminal law stresses the idea of the criminal as a victim of maladjustment in society rather than the older concept of all crime as a breach of moral law. The new code is, therefore, better adapted to contemporary methods of crime control and the rehabilitation of the convicted criminal.

Civil and Commercial Procedure

During the empire, procedure in civil and commercial causes was governed by Book 3 of the *Ordenações Philippinas*. In 1850, Regulamento 737 of November 25, implementing the commercial code, provided rules for procedure in commercial suits. Decree 763 of September 19, 1890, of the new republican government ordered the application of the old *regulamento* except in certain cases in which the provisions of the *Ordenações* were not sufficient.

Procedure for the federal courts, under the new dual system of federal and state courts set up by the republican government, was provided for by Decree 848 of 1890. Subsequently, a *Consolidação de Leis da Justiça Federal* was prepared by José Higínio and published as Decree 3084 of 1898. The states, in the meantime, began to publish their own procedural codes, adapted in general from the old Regulamento 737. The state of São Paulo did not complete a code until it promulgated one in Law 2421 of January 14, 1930.

The majority of Brazilian lawyers, however, remained convinced that procedural law was a subject in which uniformity throughout the courts of the country should be established. This opinion, which prevailed in the Constitution of 1934, required the preparation of procedural codes within three months. No codes, however, were adopted until after the Constitution of 1937, which permitted concurrent power in the states to legislate in matters of procedure affected by local peculiarities.

The Federal Code of Civil Procedure was finally adopted by Decree-Law 1608 of September 18, 1939, to go into effect March 1, 1940. It has application throughout the union, except in the case of certain special topics such as labor laws or fiscal matters, bankruptcy, naturalization, etc., which are governed by special legislation.

A first draft (*Anteprojeto*) of a new code of civil procedure was presented to the minister of justice and interior on January 1, 1964. The text was published in the official gazette on April 8, 1964. There have been a few amendments since then.

Criminal Procedure

The second code adopted by independent Brazil was that of the Criminal Procedure of 1832. It did much not only to modernize procedure in criminal cases but also to protect the individual liberties set forth in the constitution. It provided that the accused be given a statement of the charge against him and the names of his accusers within twenty-four hours of his arrest. He was entitled to the services of a lawyer; secret interrogation was abolished; and the writ of habeas corpus was available to him in case of unlawful detention.[8]

8. This writ, borrowed from the Anglo-American common law, was used during the next hundred years to protect other rights than that of physical freedom. The Brazilian law did not provide any efficacious means of protecting the other liberties established

The 1832 Code also incorporated the jury, which, however, chiefly because of the difficulty of naturalizing in one legal system an institution entirely foreign to it, has not been extensively used in Brazil. The code now in effect is that adopted in Decree-Law 3693 of October 3, 1941. It preserves the jury system.

General Legislation

There is a large body of important Brazilian legislation that lies outside the major categories just outlined. Only a few topics may be mentioned here to indicate the scope of federal legislation touching on the political and economic life of the country.

The extent of legislation affecting the exploitation of natural resources and the major economic crops, the development of basic industries, the social and welfare systems, and the monetary and banking systems has already been indicated above. Legislation relating to mines and mining has been compiled into a Code of Mines (Decree-Law 1985 of January 29, 1940). Legislation governing civil air navigation and transport was first codified in Decree-Law 483 of June 8, 1938, which has been superseded by Decree-Law 32 of November 18, 1966. The use of water courses for agricultural and industrial purposes, such as the development of hydroelectric power, is regulated by the provisions of the Code of Waters (Decree 24643 of July 10, 1934). The exploitation of forests and woodlands is governed by the Forestry Code (Decree-Law 23793 of January 23, 1951). The fishing industry is governed by the Fisheries Code (Decree-Law 794 of October 19, 1938). The development of nuclear energy is under the control of a commission created by Law 4118 of August 27, 1962. The law of patents and trademarks is contained in the Industrial Property Code (Decree-Law 7903 of August 27, 1945). Copyright is governed by Decree 4790 of January 2, 1924, and by various treaties to which Brazil is a party.

The question of agrarian reform and the improvement of legislation affecting title to land is one that has figured prominently in the political developments of the last few years. Its importance is highlighted by the adoption by the president on February 26, 1969, of the Eighth Institutional Act Amending the Constitution, which provided new means for the expropriation of large estates for purposes of agrarian reform.

---

by the constitution, and therefore the courts continually enlarged the scope of this writ in an effort to supply the deficiency. In 1870, Law 2033 of September 20 declared that the writ of habeas corpus would be granted even in cases in which the petitioner, though not actually under illegal restraint, believed himself threatened with it. Subsequently, a growing demand among lawyers for a reconsideration of the nature of the writ resulted in the limitation of its application and the creation of a new writ, the *mandado de segurança*, to protect other rights.

Taxation is another field that has provided considerable political activity. In recent years a whole new body of tax legislation, especially in regard to income and excise taxes, has come into existence and is steadily growing. A new income tax law was adopted in 1964 (Law 4506 of November 30). One of the more publicized of the actions of Castelo Branco's administration was the determined campaign mounted to collect taxes from all individuals subject to it, especially the more well-to-do, who had traditionally either ignored this requirement or had reported only a fraction of their income. A special investigation of one hundred of the wealthiest of these suspected delinquents—among whom the former President Kubitschek was prominently included—was launched in December of 1965.

A further enlargement of the sphere of power of the federal government is represented by the adoption of a National Transit Code (Law 5108 of September 21, 1966). This governs the use of any highways, roads, streets, or passageways throughout the country that are open to public use. It includes the regulation of motor vehicles and the licensing of vehicles and drivers. Federal, regional, and municipal agencies are set up for the purpose of its enforcement.

Another important sector, labor law, is not included here, since it is discussed elsewhere in this volume.

Brazil has frequently legislated upon immigration, colonization, and the naturalization of aliens. The most recent important statute on this subject is Law 4404 of September 14, 1964, which declares that the minor child of naturalized Brazilian parents domiciled in Brazil will be considered to be a Brazilian for all purposes. When he achieves majority, in order to preserve his Brazilian nationality, he must opt for it within four years.

Treaty Law

Brazil has been and is an active member of numerous international organizations, including the Pan-American Union and the League of Nations in the past, and in the present, the Organization of American States, the United Nations, and several of its specialized agencies, including the International Monetary Fund, the International Bank for Reconstruction and Development, and its two affiliates, the International Finance Corporation and the International Development Association, and also the Inter-American Development Bank. She has also subscribed, ratified, or adhered to numerous important multilateral and bilateral treaties on subjects too diverse to list here.

Chapter 6

The Evolution of Labor Legislation in Brazil

J. V. Freitas Marcondes

B RAZILIAN LABOR LEGISLATION can be divided into eight different periods, from the beginning of colonization to the present date. These are: (1) the slavery period; (2) the individualistic regime; (3) the experimental period; (4) the Social Democratic regime; (5) the authoritarian state; (6) the Democratic restoration period; (7) the revolutionary period; and (8) the consolidation of the revolutionary period. We will adopt this division, not only for historical reasons, but also because it follows the different constitutional phases which the country has experienced. Constitutional changes are frequent in Latin America. Pearson and Gil point out that some countries have had more than twenty.[1] Brazil has suffered much less in this respect, having had only seven constitutions.

THE SLAVERY PERIOD (1532–1888)

Brazil was discovered by the Portuguese in 1500, but the first attempt at populating the region came in 1532, when Portugal sent, under the direction of Martim Afonso de Sousa, 600 men and animals and many plants, including sugarcane, with the objective of beginning the colonization of the new country. The first colonizers, the majority of them released from Portuguese prisons, were not very interested in working. Their freedom, the beauty of the Indian women wandering nude on the beaches and in the woods, the absence of a colonization plan, and various other factors softened the spirit and boldness of those Portuguese. The early settlers and those that came later wanted to enslave the Indians in order that the latter would carry out the first tasks of colonization. The period of "red" or Indian slavery was

1. William W. Pearson and Federico G. Gil, *Governments of Latin America* (New York: McGraw-Hill, 1957), p. 160.

thus initiated. But, as the Indians were not used to working very much, especially at organized and fatiguing tasks, they tried to flee or attacked the colonizers. Thus, the attempt to enslave the masses of Brazilian Indians met with only partial success.

In view of the failure of "red" slavery, the Portuguese undertook to import a Negro labor force from Africa. The Negro slave was more docile than the Indian and was accustomed to regular and methodical agricultural work. The labor of one Negro corresponded to that of four or five Indians. In 1538 the first African slaves arrived and thus began the period of black or Negro slavery in Brazil. The estimated number of Negro slaves imported during the three and one-half centuries of slavery varies from 4 to 18 million. Pandiá Calógeras calculated the annual average at from 50,000 to 60,000 Negroes. This gives from 5 to 6 million per century, or 18 million during the three centuries of the regular traffic.[2]

At the dawn of Brazilian nationality, in the first days of the empire, there were some laws concerning labor. However, those laws lacked the spirit of modern social law; they were merely "fragmentary legislative dispositions,"[3] preoccupied with aiding exclusively the capitalist class. Nor could it have been otherwise, in as much as slavery persisted among us until 1888.

After the importation of African Negroes, slaves were the only labor force in the agricultural sector. The slaves worked from sunrise to sundown, and in the *casa grande* slaves served in all kinds of domestic occupations. Why then was labor legislation necessary for them when the master had power of life and death over the Negro slave? In spite of this, the Constitution of the Empire (1824) ironically assured the freedom of labor in Article 179, no. 24. In the same article, no. 25 abolished craft guilds (*corporações de ofícios*) so as to restrict any attempts at professional association, a development which was occurring in Europe. (In France, the Penal Code of 1810 also prohibited professional associations.)[4] Other laws concerning contracts and agricultural services also were formulated in this epoch (September 13, 1830; October 11, 1837; and in 1879). These laws aimed more at the protection of the European immigrants who were coming to Brazil than that of the Negro slaves. It is fitting to remember the loftiness with which one scholar wrote about the law that regulated the "written contract about the hiring of services made by Brazilians or foreigners inside the Empire."

The contract established by the present law cannot be observed,

2. Arthur Ramos, "The Negro in Brazil" in *Brazil: Portrait of Half a Continent*, edited by T. Lynn Smith and Alexander Marchant (New York: Dryden, 1951).

3. A. F. Cesarino, Jr., *Direito Social Brasileiro*, 3rd ed., vol. 1 (São Paulo: Livraria Freitas Bastos, 1953), p. 121.

4. Paul Durand and R. Jassaud, *Théorie Génerale du Droit du Travail* (Paris: Librairie Dalloz, 1947), pp. 69, 414.

under any pretext whatsoever, with the barbarous Africans, with the exception of those who presently exist in Brazil.[5]

A few words are necessary about the Commercial Code of 1850, still in effect, which at the time was a mark of juridical wisdom. In it we find the germ of the institution of *aviso prévio* (prior notice). Prior notice today is increasingly strengthened not only by the doctrine but also by the jurisprudence of the tribunals. It is true that this principle of social law, presently so respected, was at that time a "dead letter." It is difficult to find any claims or cases that were taken to the tribunals. Employees in those days had no way to plead in the courts against their employers. The labor movement in this period was weak, although some labor newspapers had been in existence and had circulated for some time and some strikes had been noted by one student of the matter.[6]

The Individualistic Regime (1889–1930)

The gradual extinction of slavery, which culminated with the *Lei Aurea* (Golden Law) in 1888, and the subsequent flight of the slave laborers from agriculture, created an acute need for new workers and gave rise to the current of immigration to Brazil.[7] However, at the time of the proclamation of the republic, there was a pressing necessity for a legal measure that would give a general cleansing to labor, one that would eradicate the odor of slavery. This legal measure was consummated in Decree 213 of February 22, 1890, which revoked all the laws relative to contracts for the employment of agricultural labor; that is, the laws of September 13, 1830; October 11, 1837; and March 15, 1851. This decree of the provisional government had international repercussions, and it was the key that opened the national ports to immigration. One cannot speak of modern social legislation without special mention of it.

The Constitution of the Republic (February 24, 1891) included in Article 72, no. 24, a reference to the freedom of labor. That was all. Why was labor thus ignored when in Europe the labor movement was already flourishing? The situation in the United States Constitution, which served as a

5. The law of September 13, 1830, was prudent and equitable for the time, and it would be exaggerating to proclaim that it contained the seeds of the institution of labor law that only a century afterwards would come to flourish. Jarbas Peixoto, "Fundamentos da Legislação Trabalhista Brasileira," *Revista do Serviço Público* 2, no. 3 (1938): 17.

6. José Linhares, "O Operario Brasileiro no Seculo xix," *Revista Brasiliense* 49, (1963): 24–33.

7. "Immigration to Brazil has been confined largely to the period 1887 to 1934. During those years she received a recorded immigration of more than four million persons from other countries." T. Lynn Smith, *Brazil: People and Institutions*, rev. ed. (Baton Rouge: Louisiana State University Press, 1963), p. 118.

model for that of Brazil, was similar. Inventions and industrialization, however, were expanding and demanding a juridical regulation of labor. The answer is simple: the individualistic mentality of the legislators of the first republic and the sociological climate of the *casa grande* obstructed the inclusion in this constitution of elements other than those mentioned in Article 72, no. 24. They were sufficient for that period. And it is very true that before the Treaty of Versailles (1919) no country enjoyed the provisions of social legislation in its federal constitution.

In the same year, the government promulgated Decree 1313, intended to regulate child labor in the incipient industry of the federal capital. During the four republican decades that preceded the Revolution of 1930, innumerable labor laws were discussed and voted by the legislative and executive powers. Examples of these are Decree 979 (1903), which created the first rural labor unions;[8] Decree 1150 (1905), concerning the rights of farm laborers to their wages; Decree 1637 (1907), pertaining to unions; and Law 3724 (1919), relating to accidents while at work. In 1923, the Conselho Nacional do Trabalho (National Labor Council) was created. In this same year the Eloy Chaves Project, the well-known law of the *Caixas de Aposentadorias e Pensões dos Ferroviários* (Railroad Workers Retirement and Pension Funds) was approved, an exhibition of foresight which undoubtedly constituted a significant advance in the new social legislation of the time.[9] However, all of these laws were filled with the individualistic-patriarchal characteristics that influenced the Civil Code, published in 1916, which in the words of Clovis Bevilaqua was "incomplete, anachronistic, and technically defective."

During the constitutional reform of 1926, there was a preoccupation "to legislate about labor" (Article 34, no. 28), and, as a result of this, many important laws, including the *Código de Menores* (Child Labor Code), were published in 1927. In this period, two distinct currents of thought had emerged in the Brazilian juridical world: one denied the social question, and proclaimed that all the agitation was merely a *caso de polícia* (police matter); the other urged advanced legislation modeled on European enactments. These enactments represented the social imperative of the period, which was growing strong in the Old World, principally in England, Italy, Germany, and France.

Capitant and Cuche point out four fundamental causes which, in conjunction with economic and political developments, resulted in the formu-

8. J. V. Freitas Marcondes, *First Brazilian Legislation Relating to Rural Labor Unions*, Latin American Monographs Series, no. 20 (Gainesville: University of Florida Press, 1962).

9. J. V. Freitas Marcondes, "Eloy Chaves" and "O Precursor da Previdência Social no Brasil," *Ferrovia* 24, nos. 280–81 (São Paulo, 1959).

lation of European social law: (1) a considerable increase of the laboring class and principally of the industrial workers, as a consequence of the development of large-scale industry; (2) universal suffrage and the establishment of democratic regimes; (3) the creation of numerous professional associations of laborers and the activities of these associations in connection with public powers; and (4) the progress of ideas of intervention and decline of the liberal classical school of individualism ("Laissez faire, laissez passer").[10]

Prior to the Revolution of 1930, a similar situation existed in Brazil. The workers, increasing in number, lacking protection, and trampled underfoot, heard the distant cry to unite and clamored in the streets for the secret ballot and the right to free elections. In this environment, the harmful herb of exotic theories prospered. The torrent was swelling and nothing could check it. Only revolution remained. And this came.

THE EXPERIMENTAL PERIOD (1930–1934)

This period was short, historically speaking, but it is very significant in the history of Brazil. Getúlio Vargas, in leading the Revolution of 1930, promised the people that he would offer a new constitution to the nation as soon as he was in power, and with it new labor legislation. However, the nation remained for nearly four years without a constitution and obtained one only after the popular protest which was manifested in the São Paulo Revolution of 1932, in which thousands of Brazilians lost their lives. It is very true that we had many laws in the labor field in this period. Nevertheless, many of them were of an experimental nature and short-lived.

All revolutions presuppose the creation of new laws, or new juridical structures. The first act of the provisional government along these lines was the creation on November 23, 1930, of the Ministry of Labor, Industry, and Commerce (Decree 19443). The establishment of this administrative organ represents, without question, a victory over a century of deep-rooted prejudices which arose from the individualistic mentality associated with Indian and Negro slavery. This patriarchal and servile mentality, which Gilberto Freyre has pictured with a masterly hand in his principal books, "was projected even into the field of law."[11] For more than a century, individualism had exaggerated and corrupted the contracts between persons in Brazil, leading to frequent exploitation of human labor in the name of contractual freedom. As we have seen, the appearance of labor legislation among us came more as an imperative of revolution than as a national movement of the people. It was even less a national movement on the part of the

10. Henri Capitant and Paul Cuche, *Précis de Legislation Industrielle*, 4th ed. (Paris: Librairie Dalloz, 1936), p. 18.
11. *Casa Grande e Senzala, Sobrados e Mucambos*, and *Nordeste*.

laborers, who, being illiterate, lacked an ideology or a class consciousness, not to mention group organization. Moreover, even in 1970, we still lack a group spirit in spite of the presence of more than 5,000 labor unions including rural ones.

Unhappily, a good part of this labor legislation remained on paper or was later revoked, thus characterizing the experimental nature of this period. On the other hand, it should be re-emphasized that state paternalism and demagoguery in the labor field began at this time principally with respect to unionization.

THE SOCIAL DEMOCRATIC REGIME (1934–1937)

On July 16, 1934, the Second Constitution of the Republic was promulgated by the national legislature, and after almost four years of dictatorship Brazil entered again into a constitutional regime. The Paulista Revolution of 1932 stimulated the return of the country to a legal regime.

Modern constitutions, with the objective of improving the lot of the workers, have not merely conferred upon legislatures the power to legislate about labor but have established bases on which such legislation could be built. The first republican constitution, as we have seen, devoted only one paragraph to labor. The second republican constitution devoted a special section, the fourth, to the social and economic order (*Da Ordem Econômica e Social*), composed of Articles 115–43. Its roots in democratic socialism and Catholic doctrine are manifested in the following:

> Article 115—The economic order should be organized, in conformity with the principles of justice and the necessities of national life, in a manner that makes a dignified existence possible to all.

The principles of justice alluded to are those of distributive justice (Pope Leo XIII in 1891 and the Social Code of Malines in 1927). It is a cry of revolt against the romantic-liberal aspects of economic individualism. It is the social surpassing the individual as an historical imperative. It is man gaining a better understanding of the group and participating intensively in it, as Durkheim pointed out. It is the choice of the whole over the part, of the family over the isolated man. The social law emphasizes the "we" and impels the individual to participate in the juridical relations of the group.[12] This socialization was a final blow to the liberalism which was favorable to laissez faire, laissez passer in labor matters.

The twenty-nine articles pertaining to the social and economic order contained one of the most advanced programs of social legislation of the period.

12. Georges Gurvitch, *Sociology of Law* (New York: Philosophical Library and Alliance Book Corporation, 1942), pp. 211–12.

The legislators included in the constitution all the innovations and experiences which followed the Revolution of 1930 and also foreign experiences, principally the German (Weimar Constitution).

The best proof of the vitality of social law in this period is found in the establishment of chairs in the national university system for the teaching of this subject. Federal Law 176 of January 8, 1936, created the chair of industrial law and labor legislation in the law school of the University of Rio de Janeiro. The first professor of the subject was Dr. Irineu Machado. State Law 3023 of 1937 created the chair of social legislation in the law school of the University of São Paulo. In a brilliant public examination, in which eight candidates participated, Professor A. F. Cesarino, Jr., was selected; he still occupies the chair of social legislation in the university's law school and now in its business administration college also. This professor is the author of dozens of juridical works of international renown. He also has reformed the teaching of law, instituting a seminar on social legislation to provide practical experience to the students, combatting in this way sterile theorizing.

At present there are about 100 law schools in Brazil. All of them include in their curricula the teaching of social legislation or labor law. These courses have made an enormous contribution to the diffusion of knowledge about, and the formal teaching of, labor law. Innumerable works have been published. Jurisprudence, principally administrative, is abundant.[13]

Some important laws were published in this period in accord with constitutional principles. An example is Federal Law 185 of 1936, which created the Commission on the Minimum Wage. Article 1 states:

All laborers have the right, in payment of services rendered, to a minimum wage capable of satisfying, in determined regions of the country and in definite periods, their normal necessities of diet, housing, dress, hygiene, and transport.

The commission neglected to include among the normal necessities of labor certain indispensable elements such as recreation, education, and social security, elements that now are as normal as food itself. Nevertheless, the minimum wage approved later by Decree-Law 2162 of 1940 had great repercussions among the laboring classes.

Because of constitutional dispositions, numerous legal aspects referring to labor were studied and regulated. Among them were the limitation of profits, union organization, labor courts, and the nationalization of industry.

It was provided that agricultural labor was to be the object of special reg-

---

13. The doctrinaire debate over the organization of the labor courts and other aspects of social legislation between Dr. Waldemar Ferreira and the sociologist Oliveira Vianna resulted in the publication of the latter's interesting book, *Problemas de Direito Corporativo* (Rio: Livraria José Olympio, 1938).

ulations, taking as a basis, insofar as possible, the general principles then established. These sought to fix the rural man on the soil, to care for rural education, and to guarantee preference for native Brazilians in the colonization and improvement of public lands.

The Constitution of 1934, however, existed only for a short time. The international political climate contributed to this. The profound changes that the constitution underwent and the quality of amendments brought popular discredit to it. The majority of legislators, including the *classistas* (the representatives of various occupational groups), collaborated in the work of bringing it into disrepute. They put petty controversies and private interests ahead of the welfare of the nation. The Communists also took the lead in organizing a national alliance against the Vargas administration. Luiz Carlos Prestes was their chief. A large group of trade unionists and many "professional" politicians reinforced the alliance. In November 1935 they organized a rebellion against Vargas in the northeastern part of Brazil and in Rio de Janeiro. Under those circumstances, on November 10, 1937, President Vargas executed a coup d'etat, abolished the Democratic Socialist Constitution of 1934, and imposed on the nation a constitutional charter of an authoritarian nature.

THE AUTHORITARIAN STATE (1937–1946)

The coup d'etat of November 10 was justified by President Vargas, who, among his reasons, alleged the almost complete uselessness of the national legislature, which no longer corresponded to the national necessities but preoccupied itself too much with private interests; the dangerous clashes of the political parties, more regional than national and more personal than social in character, thus compromising the presidential succession set for the following year; the fear of federal disintegration which led him to extinguish regional symbols (flags, emblems, and state and municipal insignia); the threat of the *verderubro* (Fascist and Communist) extremist groups and doctrines; and, as a consequence of all this, the decline of internal and external economies. On the other hand, he, like many others, thought the corporative European states were producing good results.

Supported by the armed forces and the prestige that he enjoyed among the masses, Vargas imposed on the nation the *Estado Novo* (New State) and, as a redeeming measure, the *Carta Constitutional* (Constitutional Charter) of November 10, which had a corporative and authoritarian character. In the chapter *Do Conselho da Economia Nacional* ("On the National Economic Council"), Article 61, letter *a* established that the first duty of the council was to promote the corporative organization of the national economy. In the chapter *Da Ordem Econômica* ("On the Economic Order"), Article 140 provided that "production shall be organized into corporations which are the representative organs of the strength of national labor" and that labor shall be placed under the assistance and protection of the state, and that it would have "functions delegated to it by the state (*poder público*)."

Labor legislation occupied a prominent position in the *Carta* of 1937 in the part dealing with the economic order, which includes twenty-one articles, numbers 135 to 155, inclusive. Article 136 considered labor as a social duty and placed all its forms (intellectual, technical, and manual) under the protection of the state. Similar dispositions are to be found in the *Carta del Lavoro* (Labor Code) in Italy, in the German Constitution (Article 163), and in the Spanish Constitution (Article 46).

During the *Estado Novo* abundant legislation appeared dealing with labor courts, social security, protection of the family, cooperatives, the public services, air transport, hunting and fishing, waters, mines, and other things all trying "to show that the juridical order must reflect the economic order, guaranteeing it and strengthening it."

In this entire period, undoubtedly the most remarkable event in the realm of Brazilian labor laws was the publication on May 1, 1943, of the Consolidation of Labor Laws (*Consolidação das Leis do Trabalho*; CLT), containing 922 articles (Decree-Law 5452). The exposition of motives written by A. Marcondes Filho, minister of labor, affirms that:

Item 8: Consolidation corresponds to a stage in the development of juridical progress.

Item 9: Midway between the compilation or collection of laws and their crystallization into a code—which form, respectively, the beginning and end of a process incorporating law—there exists consolidation, which is the phase that corresponds to the concatenation of texts and the coordination of principles, when for the first time, the underlying idea of the system takes shape, after social relations have been regulated on a wide scale according to any given plan of political life.

Undoubtedly, the Consolidation of Labor Laws performed an important educational function among the representatives of capital and of labor. However, it tied the labor movement even more to the Ministry of Labor, Industry, and Commerce, which exploited labor in a demagogic fashion. The *sindicato* came to be the greatest weapon of the Vargas government. An American scholar, examining the politics of this period, expressed himself in this way:

The *sindicatos* established under the *Estado Novo* were not conceived as organizations for collective bargaining with the employers. To take the place of collective bargaining, the *Estado Novo* provided an elaborate system of labor courts which would handle not only cases involving violations of labor law, but things which, under a collective bargaining system, would be handled through negotiations for a collective agreement and through a grievance procedure. The function of the *sindicato* in relation to the employer was thus reduced to providing the worker with legal representation before the labor courts. To compensate for its loss of collective bargaining functions, the *sindicato* was charged with providing its members extensive social services. In fact, this became the principal office of the *sindicatos* during the *Estado Novo*.[14]

In 1939 in São Paulo, a group of jurists founded the Instituto de Direito Social (Institute of Social Law), with chapters that later gradually spread to all the states of Brazil. In 1941 this institution organized and held the I Congresso Brasileiro de Direito Social (First Brazilian Congress of Social Law), in which were discussed the most varied theses on the conceptualization and systemization of this new branch of law. The official definition of social law, approved in plenary session, is as follows:

> Social Law, *latu sensu*, is the body of imperative principles and norms which has as a subject the groups and members of the groups; which has as an object the adaptation of the juridical form to the social reality; and which visualizes in this adaptation, the collaboration of all for the common good.

Strictu sensu, according to Professor A. F. Cesarino, Jr., is defined as follows:

> Social Law is the assemblage of imperative principles and laws whose immediate objective is, having in view the common good, to aid and to satisfy adequately the vital and proper necessities of the families and individuals who are dependent upon the products of his (the worker's) labor.

The four volumes containing the material of this congress are a good indication of the seriousness and the value of the meeting. In 1945, also in São Paulo, the II Congresso Brasileiro de Direito Social, also organized by the Institute of Social Law, took place. Of the seventy-eight papers discussed, ten were by representatives of other countries. At the present time, the institute offers specialized courses on social law with the objective of preparing technicians in the most varied branches of labor law such as labor courts, unions, social security, social services, and industrial and commercial establishments.

Another remarkable occurrence in this period was the delegation of pow-

14. Robert J. Alexander, *Labor Relations in Argentina, Brazil, and Chile* (New York: McGraw-Hill, 1962), p. 61.

ers to semi-official institutions. The growing concern over the general economic and social welfare (*socialização*, as it was called) reflected in the juridical world created in Brazil a state paternalism. President Vargas was even known among the workers as the *Pai dos Pobres* (Father of the Poor). Demagogues predominated beginning with the Ministry of Labor itself, in which Vargas used paternalism exaggeratedly as a political weapon. The reaction against this paternalism came from cultural and scientific organizations and even from the employer classes which sought to enlighten the laboring masses. The man responsible for this reaction was Roberto Simonsen. This politician, industrialist, and author of the important *Historia Econômica do Brasil* was the precursor, founder, and promoter of the institutions that today achieve notable benefits for the workers in the economic, social, and juridical fields.

The first of these institutions was established by Federal Decree-Law 4048 of 1942, which created the Serviço Nacional de Aprendizagem dos Industriarios (National Service of Apprenticeship of Industrial Workers), or simply SENAI, under the direction of the National Confederation of Industries. The financial resources for the maintenance of the *serviço* were furnished by the employers, discounted monthly from the payrolls of the industrial establishments, and collected by the Instituto de Aposentadorias e Pensões dos Industriarios (Industrial Workers Retirement and Pension Institute). "The product of the collection made in each region of the country, after deducting the amount necessary for expenses of a general nature, will be applied in the same region" (Article 4, no. 3). By virtue of this disposition, the most industrialized region, the state of São Paulo, for example, can best fulfill the objectives of the service. What are these objectives? The answer is simple, but it requires an explanation. With the rapid industrialization of some states, the industrialists took meticulous care of the machinery but did not concern themselves with the workers. They forgot the semiliterate, technically incompetent laborers. Many of them had left the hoe in the fields in order to start working awkwardly in the factories, because of the better salaries that industry could offer and because of the siren song of urban social legislation. On the other hand, communism was infiltrating and preached demagogically the necessity of improving the techniques of labor—a practical solution, however, was not furnished by Moscow's followers.

It was in this period that the Simonsen plan was introduced. The function of SENAI came to be the establishment in all parts of the country of schools of apprenticeship and improvement for industrial workers. In this way, SENAI sought to increase the skills of laborers and to render a great service to Brazilian industry. The apprentice enjoys all the prerogatives of the position that he occupies in industry and he is not charged for his apprenticeship in the school that he attends. These schools maintain the most varied courses In 1969 there were about 453 courses such as textiles, carpentry, woodwork ing, masonry, and shoemaking in the state of São Paulo and 993 in othe Brazilian states. The capacity of the 160 schools all over Brazil, including 5! schools in the state of São Paulo, is 90,000 and 44,000 students respectively annually. The duration of the courses varies from three months to thre years, in accordance with the regional necessities of industry. At the end o the course the worker receives a *Carta de Ofício* (Trade Certificate), a doc ument of real importance in industry, which increases the occupationa prestige of the bearer. While the worker is studying, he has at his disposa a doctor, a dentist, a healthful and hygienic diet, sports, social activities, an other useful elements indispensable to a decent level of living. With SENA and its schools spread over the country, Brazilian industry is preparing per sons with ability and skills for the future.

The 1964 budget for the SENAI program in the state of São Paul amounted to 3 million dollars, which is 48 per cent of the entire budge for SENAI programs throughout Brazil. The SENAI program spread to all 2 Brazilian states and even stimulated similar developments in foreign coun tries. This program is the best protection against extremist doctrines and th best aid in the solution of the problems of the workers. Under these circum stances, the Serviço Social da Indústria (SESI), or Industrial Social Service was created by Federal Decree-Law 9403 of 1946, with the objective o bettering the level of living of industrial workers. The SENAI and SESI to gether satisfied the requirements for the harmonious solution of the labor capital relationship. Both are organs of the Confederação Nacional da In dústria (National Confederation of Industry), maintained by employers with 1 per cent and 2 per cent, respectively, discounted from the total pay roll and collected by official social security institutions. The programs o SENAI and SESI are executed by delegates of the employees and supervise by the minister of labor.

SENAI, as already seen, educates and trains the worker, visualizing a greate volume of production; SESI, besides educating socially, promotes the well being of the worker, including the acquisition of a house. Thus, the laborers with the integrated education that they receive, are more likely to condem anti-Christian theories, contributing in this way to the maintenance of socia peace.

Commerce accompanied industry in the reaction against state paternal ism. By Decree-Laws 8621 and 9853, both of 1946, the federal governmen ordered the National Confederation of Commerce to create and maintai the Serviço Nacional de Aprendizagem Comercial, SENAC (National Servic of Commercial Apprenticeship), and the Serviço Social do Comércio, SES (Commercial Social Service). The financial resources for the maintenanc of SENAC and SESC come exclusively from monthly contributions of merchants. SENAC undertook the education and improvement of white-collar workers, creating schools of different grades and varied courses in accordance with regional necessities. These courses are free and the students enjoy all employment privileges as if they were on the job. In the more advanced courses the students work and study at the same time. In the state of São Paulo during 1969 more than 60,000 students employed in commerce took specialized courses, 22,219 being in the city of São Paulo and the rest in other counties of the state. Generally, at the end of the course, there are examinations and the best students receive scholarships.[15]

SESC completes the practical program of SENAC. It attempts to give to the white-collar worker and his family the most ample social assistance, visualizing, thereby, the solution of domestic problems arising from the difficulties of modern life. It also aims to improve health with specialized doctors, health centers, diet, and hygiene, and restaurants serving healthy and inexpensive foods; it strives for better housing conditions, transportation, and recreation (for example, a model vacation resort at the beach); and by these means, it seeks to defend the real wage of the business employee.

Brazilian labor legislation concerns rights and duties of the workers; the semi-official institutions SENAI, SESI, SENAC, and SESC enforce the laws, spread their benefits, and form an amalgam of the good life.

THE DEMOCRATIC RESTORATION PERIOD (1946–1964)

From 1946 to 1964 Brazil, like all Latin American nations, was shaken by a series of violent crises. The end of the Second World War, in which Brazil also participated on the European front with a loss of more than a thousand dead and mutilated men, marked the end of the ironic "short lapse of time" (fifteen years) of the Vargas government, in which a damaging political mentality was formed, culminating with the "sea of slime" which swallowed even Vargas himself, creator of the regime. All this and a demagogic social legislation without roots in Brazilian reality, nearly always copied from other nations with socio-philosophic problems very different from ours, all this, we repeat, resulted in a social illness which kept growing worse. As a consequence of this period, the most agitated of all our national history, the nation suffered political impacts of the most serious kind, including a period of twenty-four years in which there were thirteen presidents of the republic.[16] Of the thirteen presidents, only two governed for a complete term:

15. To the one in first place is given a scholarship to the USA; to the following six are given trips through Brazil; to the next three, trips to the interior of the state; to the following twenty, a vacation of fifteen days in the *colônia de férias* (vacation resort) of the SESC at the seashore.

16. 1945–46   Minister José Linhares (as president of the Federal Supreme Court).
      1946–51   Marshal Eurico Gaspar Dutra (a regular period of five years).

Dutra and Kubitschek. Ranieri Mazzili, as president of the Chamber c
Deputies, assumed the presidency seven times, sometimes in situations ver
difficult for the nation.

During this disturbed period, Brazil had serious difficulties in the field c
labor legislation. The Ministry of Labor, fundamentally guided by a polic
of paternalism, rigidly controlled the labor movement, at the same tin
usurping from labor unions their universal right of seeking redress for tI

TABLE 1

MINIMUM WAGES BY SUBREGIONS, 1940-1969

Decree-Law or Decree Number	Date	1st Subregion CR$	2nd Subregion CR$	3rd Subregion CR$	4th Subregion CR$	Other Subregion CR$
2162	5-1940	220	200	170		150
5977	11-1943	360	320	275		245
30342	12-1951	1,190	930	860	830	700
35450	5-1954	2,300	2,150	1,900	1,900	1,800
39604-A	7-1956	3,700	3,600	3,400	3,330	3,200
45106-A	12-1958	5,900	5,800	5,600	5,400	5,100
49119-A	10-1960	9,440	9,280	8,960	8,640	8,160
51336	10-1961	13,216	12,992	12,544	12,096	11,420
51613	12-1962	21,000	20,900	20,200	20,000	19,000
53578*	2-1964	42,000	40,000			
55803	1-1965	66,000	60,000			36,000
57900	3-1966	84,000	76,000			48,000
60231	2-1967	105,000	95,000			63,000
62481	3-1968	129,000	117,000			79,000
64442	5-1969	156,000	144,000			98,000

* This law modified the system of regional and subregional criteria.

membership. One example which will clarify this point pertains to mir
mum wages. With the galloping inflation that had demoralized the cr
zeiro, principally during the administration of Juscelino Kubitschek ar
mainly because of the construction of Brasília, the worker, whether unior
ized or not, demanded readjustments of the minimum wage. Since the fir
federal law on minimum wages was promulgated, the federal governme
has promulgated fifteen laws readjusting the value of the minimum wag
which has also meant that it has taken away from the *sindicatos* one of the

1951-54	Getúlio Vargas (who committed suicide on August 24, 1954).
1954-55	João Café Filho, Carlos Luz, and Nereu Ramos, filling the interi period until an election could be held and a new president elected.
1956-61	Juscelino Kubitschek (governed the full presidential term).
1961	Jânio Quadros (resigned August 25, after governing seven month:
1961	Ranieri Mazzilli (as president of the federal Chamber of Deputi who filled in as president seven times during the last nineteen years
1961-64	João Goulart (deposed April 1, 1964).
1964-67	Marshal Humberto Castelo Branco.
1967-69	Marshal Artur da Costa e Silva.

principal reasons for existence. For the purpose of applying minimum-wage legislation, Brazil is divided into five regions. Table 1 gives an idea of the evolution of the minimum wage in Brazil since 1940. A similar escalation has occurred in social security benefits. Inflation undermined those benefits also, including the retirement pensions. On the other hand, the national social security system was drawn up in a demagogic spirit. The Vargas government and all its successors have taken for the state the financial responsibility for the various social security institutions. The unions have nothing to do with the national social security system.

Perhaps the best way to underscore the most important aspects of Brazil's labor legislation is to describe in a brief and general manner labor unions or types of labor unions. Those institutions are organized structurally and operate in a very different manner from similar organizations in other countries. The Brazilian federal government controls everything. One could say that it is the "commander-in-chief of the Brazilian labor movements." It is not easy for a specialist in European or American labor unions to understand the differences.

Let us take a look at some of the points, some of the details of Brazilian unions or *sindicatos*.

I. *Organization.*

They are organized in four different ways according to Federal Law 5452, May 1, 1943 (*Consolidação das Leis do Trabalho*, or CLT), as follows: [17]

A. With respect to the kinds of individuals who can belong to the organization,

    a) Labor unions. On December 31, 1961, there were 1,607 urban unions or *sindicatos* made up of workers located in cities; [18]

    b) Employer organizations or *sindicatos*. On December 31, 1961, there were 1,038 organizations of this type;

    c) Organizations of self-employed individuals (*sindicatos autônomos*) such as taxicab drivers who own and operate small enterprises whose sole employees are himself and/or members of his family. There are no statistics available on the number of these organizations and the number of individuals they comprise;

    d) Organizations of the liberal professions (doctors, lawyers, dentists, etc.). On December 31, 1961, there were 117 *sindicatos* of this type.

B. With respect to the organizational structures,

    a) *Associações profissionais*. Under Brazilian labor legislation a *sin-*

17. See *Consolidation of the Brazilian Labor Laws* (São Paulo: American Chamber of Commerce in Brazil, 1960).

18. Ministério do Trabalho, Serviço de Estatística, *Cadastro Sindical Brasileiro* (Rio, 1961), p. 15. (This is the only official available source of information.)

dicato cannot be organized until it passes through a stage of organization in which the members are known collectively as an *associação profissional*, in accordance with Decree-Law or *Decreto-Lei* 1402, 1939, and Article 512 of the CLT;

b) *Sindicatos* or labor unions (only of workers organized horizontally; vertical or industrial-type unions do not exist in Brazil). On the other hand, no more than one *sindicato* representing the same economic, occupational, or professional category may be recognized in the same territorial zone (Article 516 of the CLT). For example, the Willys or Volkswagen factories, which employ over 20,000 workers each, cannot be organized into a single *sindicato*; their office-workers, plumbers, sweepers, etc., each belong to separate *sindicatos*;

c) *Federações*. Federations are considered syndical associations of a superior rank (Article 535 of the CLT) and operate only within the boundaries of a given state. Five or more *sindicatos*, representing groups of activities or identical professions, may form a federation (Article 534 of the CLT). On December 31, 1961, there were 156 federations, 91 composed of workers, 61 of employers, and 4 of the liberal professions;[19]

d) *Confederações*. Three or more federations may form a confederation, whose head office will be located in the federal capital (Article 535 of the CLT). On December 31, 1961, there were nine confederations, five composed of workers, three of employers, and one of the liberal professions.[20]

C. With respect to the territorial or geographic area covered (Article 517 of the CLT), *sindicatos* may be organized on the basis of: (a) districts; (b) *municípios* (similar to the American county); (c) *inter-municipais* of several *municípios*; (d) state; (e) inter-state groupings; (f) nation-wide groupings, which the minister of labor may authorize because of the special characteristics of the category, i.e., airline employees, maritime workers, etc. Those groupings organized on a *município* or inter-*município* basis are the most common in Brazil. However, there are no statistics available on their exact number.

D. With respect to an ecological base,

a) Urban unions (regulated by the CLT);

b) Rural unions (regulated by the *Estatuto do Trabalhador Rural*—Statute of the Rural Laborer—or ETR, Federal Law 4214 of March 2, 1963). At the present time there are 1,522 rural *sindicatos*, 38 federations, and 1 national confederation (CONTAG). Many of these *sindicatos* and federations exist, but do not have the legal recognition by the Ministry of Labor demanded by Article 119 of the ETR.

---

19. Instituto Brasileiro de Geografia e Estatística (IBGE), *Anuário Estatístico do Brasil, 1962* (Rio: Counselho Nacional de Estatística, 1962), p. 271.
20. IBGE, p. 271.

II. *Functions.*

Their functions are of two different kinds: (a) prerogatives or privileges (Article 513 of the CLT); and (b) duties (Article 514 of the CLT).

A. The privileges of the unions are the following:

a) To represent, before administrative and judicial authorities, the general interests of the respective category or profession and the individual interests of their associates relative to the activity or profession exercised;

b) To close collective bargaining contracts;

c) To elect or appoint the various representatives of the respective category or profession;

d) To collaborate with the state, in the quality of technical and consultant organs, in the study and solution of problems relative to their respective category or profession;

e) To levy contributions on anyone included in the economic, occupational, or professional categories which they represent;

f) To establish and maintain, in the case of the employees' *sindicatos*, employment agencies.

B. The duties of the unions are the following:

a) To collaborate with public authorities in the development of social solidarity or a community of interests;

b) To maintain legal aid services for their members;

c) To promote the conciliation of labor disputes;

d) In the case of the employees' *sindicatos*, to promote the establishment of consumer and credit cooperatives and to establish and maintain primary and vocational schools.

Rural *sindicatos*, besides the duties and privileges noted above, also have others, but at the present time these exist only on paper, for example, social and educational benefits for their members (Article 178 of the ETR).

In spite of the fact that the CLT emphasizes as a privilege of *sindicatos* the establishment of collective bargaining agreements (Article 513, *b*), Brazilian labor leaders are not yet really prepared to carry out this mission. The number of collective bargaining agreements in Brazil is extremely small. On the other hand, the Ministry of Labor, by means of a series of bureaucratic exigencies, makes the process of collective bargaining very difficult. Brazilian employers for their part are also not prepared for this type of bargaining, the majority of them preferring to make individual contracts. Existing labor legislation protects the employer in this particular respect and contributes to a paternalistic attitude on their part, as was emphasized above.

A great number of labor unions enroll less than 10 per cent of the total number of workers that form a profession or occupational category represented by a *sindicato*. In the city of São Paulo, the largest industrial center in Latin America, possessing as a result the most well-organized *sindicatos* and *federações* of the country, a recent investigation showed that:

Nearly a fourth of the existing labor organizations in São Paulo had within their ranks less than a third of the individuals belonging to a given union category, which means that they were operating illegally in view of the demands of Article 515 of the CLT (which requires that one-third of the membership of an enterprise has to join a *sindicato* for it to have continuing legal recognition); 60 percent of the labor unions had less than half of the available membership of the union category, while only 22 unions had more than 50 percent of the category (of these 5 had more than 90 percent, an extremely good index of their union organization).[21]

Few *sindicatos* have carried on systematic campaigns to attract new members. Generally, when there is a strike or a movement to gain readjustment in minimum wages, membership increases, but once the desired gains have been obtained, there is a return to the status quo ante.

In a large number of *sindicatos*, the "leadership group" has no interest in increasing the number of members. The former *imposto sindical* (syndical or union tax) and many governmental officials who do not themselves want the unions to be larger are responsible for this state of affairs.

One of the principal excuses for government interference in the financial administration and general affairs of workers' and employers' organizations is the fact that all such groups enjoy the benefits of the *imposto sindical* or trade union tax. Sixty percent of the *imposto sindical* collected from the workers goes to the *sindicato* under whose jurisdiction they are. Fifteen percent is paid to the federation with which this *sindicato* is affiliated, and 5 percent goes to the confederation to which the federation belongs. If there is no *sindicato*, its share goes to the federation; if there is no federation, its share goes to the confederation; if there is no confederation, the whole of the *imposto sindical* goes into the so-called *Fundo Social Sindical*.[22]

This *fundo* was responsible for the interference of the federal government in the unions and for other condemnable things. Fortunately the *fundo* was recently abolished, and the expression "*imposto sindical*" was changed to "*contribuição sindical*" (trade union compulsory contribution).

With regard to rural social legislation, two acts deserve special emphasis: (a) the *Estatuto do Trabalhador Rural* (Statute of the Rural Laborer), promulgated March 2, 1963, as Federal Law 4214 (twenty years after the publication of the CLT, in which rural workers and small farmers were excluded from the law's benefits by Article 7, letter *b*), and (b) the *Estatuto da Terra*

21. J. V. Freitas Marcondes, *Radiografia da Liderança Sindical Paulista* (São Paulo: Instituto Cultural do Trabalho, 1964), p. 88.
22. Alexander, p. 85.

(Land Statute), promulgated November 30, 1964, as Federal Law 4505, which aimed at the implementation of agrarian reform in Brazil and the promotion of a new agricultural policy. These two acts complement one another and ought to produce great transformations in rural customs and in the national agrarian structure itself.

By the first act, the rural worker, who still represents 60–75 per cent of the labor force in many states, will enjoy retirement and other juridical-social benefits that previously only the urban worker enjoyed. By the second—agrarian reform—the present rural worker can change his social status, moving upward to become a rural proprietor or what might be called a family farmer in the United States.

Article 16 of the *Estatuto da Terra* says: "Agrarian Reform has as its objective to establish a system of relations among men, rural property, and land use, capable of promoting social justice, progress and the well-being of the rural worker and the economic development of the nation, with the gradual extinction of the *minifúndio* and the *latifúndio*."

This goal complements that established earlier by two paragraphs of Article 2:

To all is assured the opportunity of access to land ownership in accordance with its social function, as prescribed by this law.

Paragraph 2—It is the obligation of the government:

a) To promote and create conditions of access of the rural worker to land that is economically useful, preferably in regions where he lives, or, when regional circumstances so indicate, in zones previously laid out in accordance with the regulations of this law.

It is still early to evaluate the importance of these two statutes in national life, but one can, of course, underline the fact that in the future these two acts will be considered basic in the study of Brazilian social legislation.

We should also single out in this chapter the effort that is being made in Brazil in the area of labor leadership education.

In Great Britain, Oxford University created a school for labor leaders in Ruskin College at the end of the last century; in Sweden the Arbetarnas Bildningsforbund was established in 1912; in the United States after World War I hundreds of universities, beginning with Wisconsin, established labor education programs. In other European countries similar programs were founded just after the signature of the Treaty of Versailles.[23] However, in Brazil education of the labor leader was never thought of. For this reason,

23. Mauro Barrenechea, *Formación Sindical Métodos y Programas en EE. UU., Europa, Asia y Latinoamerica* (Mexico: Buena Prensa, 1962), p. 303.

the Brazilian labor movement was always weak, unexpressive, and subjugated by the Ministry of Labor or the federal government.

In 1963, thanks to the collaboration of the American Institute for Free Labor Development, an educational organ of the AFL-CIO which is associated with various American and international institutions, there was organized in São Paulo, for all of Brazil, the Instituto Cultural do Trabalho (Labor Culture Institute). In less than six years, this *instituto* offered regional courses (varying from one week of studies to one month) to more than 10,000 Brazilian union and peasant leaders.

From the regional courses, the best students (who showed promise in union leadership qualities) were reselected and were offered grants to attend a three-month intensive trade union leadership course (eight hours daily) in São Paulo.

Eighteen subjects are taught by specially selected university professors, by certain labor leaders, and by some employers, the latter seeking to discuss with the students the rights and problems of management. Basic subject matter includes "Brazilian *sindicato* organization," "*sindicato* administration," "*sindicato* protection," "collective bargaining agreements," "social security," "the Brazilian judicial system for labor grievances," "history of the labor movement," and "international labor movement," all of which are taught through lectures and round-table discussions. These courses are augmented by complementary subjects such as "development and underdevelopment," "agrarian reform," "inflation," "cost of living," "productivity," "cooperativism," "leadership typologies," and by study visits to selected factories and by research.[24]

As a result of this high level work, some Brazilian universities are now becoming interested in offering extension courses for workers.[25]

We believe that with this work Brazilian *sindicalism* will undergo a profound transformation, not only in the ideological sector, but even more in the cultural and professional aspects.

In addition, the new *sindicato* leaders, with a new mentality, will be able to liberate *sindicato* activity from the clutches of the Ministry of Labor and work for new labor legislation, elaborated in accordance with the real necessities of Brazil, which will aid in a more rapid national development through new techniques and will help educate the great number of backward employers that still are found in the country.

---

24. *Radiografia da Liderança Sindical Paulista* (Typology of São Paulo Leadership) was the first research published; the second was Ophelina Rabello, *A Rede Sindical Paulista—Tentativa de Caracterização* (São Paulo: Instituto Cultural do Trabalho, 1965).

25. Cf. J. V. Freitas Marcondes, "Um Novo Front Educacional: O Sindical" in *Problemas Brasileiros 56* (November 1957).

THE REVOLUTIONARY PERIOD (1964–1969)

On March 31, 1964, Brazil, applauded by millions of its citizens, instituted without bloodshed a new revolutionary government. After a brief period of provisional rule, the Brazilian Congress elected General Humberto Alencar Castelo Branco to serve out the term of former President João Goulart. The causes of the revolution were principally economic and political. A galloping inflation was demoralizing the nation. The cruzeiro lost value daily. Requests for wage and salary increases were on the order of 100 per cent. The minimum wage, which in December 1962 was 21,000 cruzeiros, was raised to 42,000 early in 1964. Even so, workers complained that the increase was insufficient due to the dizzying rise in the cost of living. Thousands of wealthy Brazilians sent large amounts in dollars to foreign banks. On the other hand, foreign investors did not want to invest in a nation which, although desirous of new investments, was politically unstable. Workers' strikes were frequent. "In some cases, strikes over economic grievances were reportedly stimulated by Communist agitators and by other political considerations and problems." In this climate of economic and political tension the Left gained ground daily reinforced by Goulart's notorious support. Hundreds of worker-leaders that went to Russia to attend courses were putting their knowledge into practice through the General Confederation of Labor, an illegal sindical organization supported by the government. "Sixty labor leaders attended the fifth World Congress of the Communist WFTU in Moscow, although they were not legally allowed to become members of that organization." One of the most authentic of American labor union leaders, Serafino Romualdi, in an important work offers his suspicionless testimony on the pre-revolutionary phase in Brazil: "Communist resources were great. Secret training schools existed in key industrial cities. Hundreds of free visits to the Soviet Union were arranged for Brazilian workers each year, and scores were receiving special training there in infiltration tactics and industrial conflict."[26] Political deterioration proceeded to such a point that the armed forces had to assume power. Goulart escaped to Uruguay. Dozens of labor leaders also escaped to other countries, and several of them were sentenced to prison in absentia for condemnable moral, economic, and political acts.

Supported by the majority of the people and, principally, by a large contingent of workers, President Castelo Branco instituted a regime of severe austerity and tried to correct old moral and social national vices. Hundreds of politicians and syndicalists, some of whom were notoriously corrupt and many others with serious legal and moral impediments, were deprived of

26. Serafino Romualdi, *Presidents and Peons* (New York: Funk & Wagnalls, 1967), p. 277.

their political rights. Innumerable draconian measures were adopted. The thirteen political parties then in existence—some purely in order to satisfy personal ambitions—were reduced to two. Many well-intentioned administrative decisions were announced, including some that affected workers by reducing wages and benefits (for example, the case of the stevedores) practically without eliciting complaints. On January 24, 1967, the new federal constitution, which took effect on March 15 of the same year, was promulgated. It is not easy to assess dispassionately the mistakes of the Revolution of '64, which include some of its juridical acts. Obviously, many mistakes were made, but in all honesty, we must recognize the success of President Castelo Branco.

The second revolutionary president was Marshal Arthur da Costa e Silva, who was to have remained in office until 1971. During this period, as in the previous one, dozens of important laws and decrees were promulgated with the intent of rectifying certain aspects of labor law. Some of these changes were incorporated in the constitution but most were incorporated into the consolidation of labor laws and in other specific laws. The most important changes, those that affected the life of the worker, were the Guarantee Fund for Time of Service (Law 5107 of September 13, 1966, regulated by Decree 59820 of December 20, 1966); Modification and Unification of Social Security (Decrees 66 and 72, both of November 21, 1966); Strike Rights (Law 4330 of June 1, 1964); and Modifications of the Consolidation of Labor Law affecting the following subjects: professional identification, rest periods from work, minimum wage, vacations, labor safety and hygiene, conditions of employment, protection of female and underage workers, suspension and interruption of labor contracts, union elections, powers of unions, collective bargaining agreements, judiciary and labor lawsuits, and fines and pecuniary penalties (Decree 229 of February 28, 1967).

In addition to these, many other laws were enacted benefiting rural work and rural workers and attempting to strengthen the more than 2,000 rural labor unions in existence in the nation. Minister Jarbas Passarinho served with distinction during this period and was in continual contact and communication with labor leaders. His departure from the ministry was felt by the workers as was pointed out by the president of the Union of Metallurgical Workers of São Paulo, the largest in Latin America. The principal problems of urban and rural workers continue to be wages, educational facilities for their children, home ownership, the prevalence of individual over collective contracts, and the precariousness of relations between employers and workers—principally in the northeast where the patriarchal spirit still persists. The lack of supervision and control over all these matters by the Ministry of Labor further aggravates these problems.

CONSOLIDATION OF THE REVOLUTIONARY PERIOD
(1969...)

On the night of August 31, 1969, the Brazilian people were informed in a radio broadcast that President Costa e Silva had suffered a serious "circulatory crisis with neurological manifestations." The physicians in attendance could not predict the duration of the illness but affirmed that it would be lengthy. Normally, the presidency should have been assumed by the civilian vice-president, Pedro Aleixo, professor at the University of Minas Gerais. However, the armed forces saw fit to empower a provisional government composed of a triumvirate consisting of the three service ministers: General of the Army Aurélio de Lyra Tavares, Air Marshal Marcio de Souza e Mello, and Fleet Admiral Augusto Hamann Rademaker Grunwald. The army, navy, and air force ministers directed the affairs of the nation for two months, until October 30, when the reins of government were passed to the president legally elected by the federal congress convened especially for this purpose. Power was assumed in Brasília on that date by General Emilio Garrastazú Médici as president and Admiral Augusto Hamann Rademaker Grunwald as vice-president. Their five-year terms were set by the recently promulgated Federal Constitution of 1969.

The new constitution, which instituted a number of significant changes, did not, however, change the section referring to the economic and social order (Articles 160 to 174), which contains the master guidelines for all Brazilian labor law (Articles 165 and 166).

Brazilian workers, including all types of manual and intellectual occupations, through their confederations supported the new president with manifestos, but hoped that the more serious of the problems of the workers would come closer to solution and that the government would not be unequivocally on the right.

The workers and the people of Brazil hope that the new government will consolidate the work of the revolution so that the country may soon enter an era of normality and national pacification. Three additional things are expected of the president by the workers: (1) "That he will not permit unemployment, (2) That he will provide adequate wages, and (3) That he will make the unions gain courage."

Chapter 7

Industrial Development in Brazil

Dorival Teixeira Vieira

N THE PRESENT CHAPTER we shall first study the industrial evolution of Brazil in order to understand its principal characteristics. Then we shall indicate the dominant aspects, positive and negative, that explain its present state and help us see it in perspective.

During the colonial period, the Brazilian economy was essentially self-sufficing. Commerce was limited, for the ports were closed to foreign trade. The prohibition of cattle raising and of the development of industries impeded more than agricultural production. It is not possible, for this reason, to point to the development of processing industries in this period.[1]

Apart from sugar, the only industry found in the last century of the colonial period was mining, but even this was designed not for the benefit of Brazil but to furnish resources for the metropolis. The gold mines of Minas Gerais were rapidly exhausted by the greed of the Treasury. The establishment of factories, mills, and even of great rural properties was prohibited in order to make mining the almost exclusive activity of Brazil's inhabitants. After the discovery of the mines, gold production grew con-

1. In order to understand why the mother country was averse to the installation of industries in Brazil, it is necessary to recall that such an attitude was bound up with a mercantilist political economy that was then widespread. Portuguese bullionist mercantilism made Portugal drain to itself the greatest possible amount of gold, once the precious metal became considered a synonym for national wealth, and this permitted military and political power, so necessary in a period of deep and growing national antagonisms. Portuguese economic policy in Brazil was expressed in a completely fiscal spirit and explains the prohibition of the opening of roads and even the obstruction of those already in existence. These were means of preventing evasion in the payment of revenues due to the crown in gold and diamonds, besides assuring a better collection of the king's fifths. The monopoly of commerce, represented principally by the West India Company and by the closing of the ports to ships of other nationalities, completes the picture of the prohibition of industries, even that on the making of hidromel and aguardente, by-products of the sugar industry, the greatest source of wealth of the crown. All this explains the three centuries of retardation that Brazilian economy suffered in the industrial sector.

tinuously until the middle of the eighteenth century. It declined rapidly, however, so that from 1811–1820 it was approximately on the same level as in its first days. Between 1691 and 1700, 1,500 kilos of gold were extracted, and between 1740 and 1760, 14,600. From then on, the gold production of Brazil fell steadily until between 1810 and 1820 only 1,760 kilos, on the average, were obtained.

At the dawn of the nineteenth century, when the economic structure of the principal European countries was already becoming transformed, Brazil went on with a purely agricultural structure, based on slave labor. The coming of the Portuguese royal family, transforming the country into a kingdom, contributed little to its industrialization.[2] As the impoverishment of mining and the decay of the sugar industry of the northeast become manifest, it is easy to understand that the economic structure of colonial Brazil could only have had an agricultural base.

During the period of the kingdom of Brazil (1815–1822) and even during the first empire (1822–1831), when the country was in transition, an economic impoverishment occurred, the most evident index of which was the lack of capital. So true was this that we find the country resorting frequently to monetary expedients—emission of paper money; lowering of the standard of metallic money; making of counterfeit money, encouraged by the state itself; and continuous foreign loans.

Between 1820 and 1860 a new agricultural activity developed and gained foreign markets—coffee production. In 1840, coffee already was of great importance among Brazilian exports; from 1860 on, because of its importance, Brazil could show growing surpluses in its commercial balance. As this new activity became more solid, the commercial policy of the country passed from unrestricted free trade to a modified protectionism.

2. Hard pressed by Napoleon, and with no war fleet capable of taking the court to safety, Dom João vi found himself obliged to accept English aid. This aid, however, over a long period of time, cost the Brazilians too dearly. The very opening of the ports on January 28, 1808, already represented a sort of privilege granted to England because of its being at the time the sole European power able to maintain and protect a powerful merchant marine. Thus, for six years, Great Britain, favored by the commercial treaty of 1810, could monopolize the Brazilian market. This economic domination by England, which, beginning with Portugal, had reached out to Brazil, was extended in Brazil, through Portuguese magnanimity and a profound sense of indebtedness and by the Anglo-Portuguese commercial treaty, which ordered the collection of duties of 15 per cent ad valorem on goods carried under the English flag when merchandise imported from Portugal was burdened with duties of 16 per cent. It cannot be said, however, that this commercial treaty, which retarded the beginning of Brazilian industrial development, was produced by the blindness of the Portuguese administration in Brazil. It should be recalled that, at the time, England needed food and prime materials in order to survive and continue the war against Napoleon. In addition to dominating maritime commerce, it was in her power to isolate Brazil from the rest of the world. It is not then to be wondered at that Brazil remained at the mercy of London, thanks to the commercial treaty of 1810—the fruit of true economic brutality.

Beween 1850 and 1870, Irinêo Evangelista de Souza, Viscount Mauá, having drunk in the ideas of Saint Simon, attempted to lead a reaction to create a Brazilian industry alongside agriculture, seeking to diversify Brazil's economy and to keep coffee monoculture from strengthening itself— as indeed happened. He promoted the building of railroads, ports, and textile mills, as well as banking establishments, among which the Second Bank of Brazil stands out.

The country, which around 1850 had only a few more than fifty industrial establishments, all of small size, with invested capital of approximately 7,000:000$000, had already begun by 1866 to develop greatly. The textile industry expanded parallel with the foodstuffs industry, which, as was natural, was the predominating industrial activity, inasmuch as it was bound directly and closely to the eminently agricultural structure of the country. From two textile mills in 1850, Brazil went on in 1866 to possess nine, representing 14,865 spindles and 485 looms, employing 768 workers, and producing 125,600 kilos of thread and 3,944,600 meters of cloth. The value of production in that year was 2,116:200$000. But while in Brazil textiles produced about $1,000,000, in the United States, in the same period, production was more than $115,000,000.

The textile industry continued to increase, and in 1881 the number of mills had risen to forty-four, with 62,528 spindles and 1,994 looms, using more than 2,000 horsepower and employing more than 3,000 workers. It cannot, however, be stated that such a development was considerable, as we did not produce textiles enough for our own domestic market. Thus, in the imperial period, Brazilian economic structure was exclusively agricultural and the industrial development insignificant.

It should be noted, however, that here, as elsewhere, industrial innovations were always ill-received owing not only to the predominance of an agricultural mentality but also to the fact that the scanty capital in existence came from agricultural activity. The latifundiary nobility of the empire did not regard kindly the possibility of losing out to the rising industrial activities. Such a point of view was reinforced, more than anything else, by an accentuatedly liberal spirit in studies of political economy. The international division of labor was defended, and it was accepted as an indisputable truth that to Brazil fell an important position in the furnishing of food products and raw materials, and it was affirmed that the national prosperity lay in agriculture. As if to give strength to such ideas, agricultural production was sufficient to make a favorable balance of trade and even to allow appreciable surpluses. With these surpluses, then, foreign exchange could be counted on for the purchase of industrial products in foreign markets. It should be noted that, being at the beginning of production and facing technical and economic difficulties linked to lack of experience, the products of Brazilian industry cost more than those of foreign competitors. Therefore, they did not find a market, and this fortified a feeling of rejection for national products. The movement of commerce was joined to this reaction of the agricultural class.

The merchant who sold industrial products naturally found greater ease in selling imported articles of better quality and lower price and saw wares produced domestically paralyzed on his shelves. During the whole period of the empire, then, Brazilian commerce depended closely on imports and on the largest consumers, the agricultural class. In consequence, it was natural that it opposed any effort at industrialization. And it was also natural that the processing industry in Brazil became consolidated only during the republic.

The abolition of slavery in 1888 represented something more than a simple disorganization of labor. With the liberation of the slaves, the rural proprietors, already undermined by republican propaganda, lost the bonds that united them to the empire, because the liberty abruptly granted to about 800,000 Negroes, who for the most part abandoned their former owners, annihilated fortunes overnight. The exodus of the freedmen from the fields to the cities disorganized labor, led to the loss of 40–50 per cent of the crops of 1888, increased consumption in urban centers, and brought about a lack of food and a high cost of living. There was also a devaluing of mortgages, formerly secured by *fazendas* and slaves, which resulted in a contraction of the credit necessary for the expenses of the harvest; the middleman in coffee or sugar who furnished funds saw it was impossible, granted the lack of hands, for the harvest to be gathered and sent to the coast. Naturally, agricultural labor fell appreciably and the former *fazendeiros*, disillusioned and ruined, moved to the cities and turned their attention to industry and commerce.

Large-scale speculation and withdrawal from European commerce favored, then, the formation of numerous industries. International factors also explain, on the other hand, the occurrence of the beginning of the rise of industry only during the republic. The proclamation of the republic provoked on the part of England, Brazil's exclusive creditor, a contraction of credit that ended by transforming itself, with the passage of time, into true withdrawal. France withdrew its credit in the same manner, but for different reasons. Pedro ii had been beloved and respected in that country, and his exile and the negation of his administrative work seemed to the French to be extreme ingratitude. To this fact was added the unpopularity of the Conde d'Eu, which closely concerned the French, his compatriots. For all these motives, therefore, the growing republic did not recommend itself to the French. Germany, in its turn, preoccupied with its own unification, was almost unaware of the existence of our country and remained on the fringe of the events happening here.

These were the motives that carried the republicans, in a movement of disgust at European reprobation or indifference, to reject European models and to accept, almost idolatrously, North American initiative. This Yankee influence found a propitious climate for its spread, because it adapted itself in the highest degree to Brazil's republican intentions. The policy of "self-preservation," that began with the very independence of the United States, reached a culminating point in 1890 with the McKinley Bill and with the raising of North American customs duties to 40 per cent on imported products. Such a tariff, which by itself already showed strong protectionism, marked the beginning of an increasingly industrial and nationalist policy. The ultra-protectionist Brazilian tariff of 1897 reinforced even more the position of the Brazilian republicans and encouraged the imitations of the United States model. Therefore, in the last year of the monarchy (1889) Brazil possessed approximately 636 industrial establishments with a capital of 615,345:336$000, or an increase of 71 per cent and 53 per cent, respectively, in five years.

This industry was concentrated, by preference, in the south, and in this region it was localized principally in São Paulo, as this state possessed, in addition to the agricultural activity peculiar to the other states, mining, textiles, a lumber industry, and other products. This led authors such as Amaro Cavalcanti to say at that time: "What São Paulo is today, from this point of view, is what all Brazil will be." If, then, the proclamation of the republic permitted, on the one hand, a slight change in the Brazilian mentality opposed to industrial development, on the other, one cannot speak of a pronounced industrial development, because the positive factors mentioned were opposed by other, negative factors that, if they did not annul it, at least slowed down industrialization.

With the beginning of the republic there occurred a great inflation to which the name of *Encilhamento* has been given. As a consequence, a wave of unhealthy speculation, of real gambling, was created that harmed the Brazilian economy a great deal. Disorder was felt in all sectors of economic life. At the moment, however, we are concerned only with the aspects that most retarded the development of industry. Alongside new enterprises, viable and solidly established, fantastic firms were created that discredited the undertakings of the time. From June 8, 1889, to August 17, 1890, banks and companies were founded in Rio de Janeiro with a total capital of 1,148,000:-000$000. In 1891, 313 new companies were formed with a nominal capital of 1,849,156:900$000. Things reached a point where there were no more names for the new firms; competitions were then organized for the best suggestions. As almost all of these enterprises were organized as corporations, there was a great flood of every kind of shares, so that the stock market became unstable, with violent highs and lows in which watered stocks predominated.

Thus an illusion of wealth was created that did not deceive even the contemporaries of the period. Fantastic firms rose and fell, going bankrupt with the growing discrediting of their shares. These bankruptcies motivated greater pessimism for the future of Brazilian industry. The appearance of "bubbles" and swindles destroyed the initial enthusiasm for industrialized countries that had characterized the first days of the republic. The attitude of suspicion and even of disdain of the national industry began once more to predominate.

If the rhythm of the industrial rise did not lag, it was because the institution of partial tariffs in gold in the customs was a markedly protectionist factor that made foreign competition difficult. Only the liquidation of the *Encilhamento* in 1900 re-established a climate of confidence and of expectation of a better future. For this reason, beginning only in 1905, the growing rhythm of our industrial evolution was observed, and it became marked between 1910 and 1914, owing, at least in part, to the favorable result of the Exchange Conversion Agency (Caixa de Conversão), which permitted greater foreign exchange balances for the acquisition of machinery, instruments, and even raw material for our industrial development.

The first industrial census made in Brazil, in 1907, showed the existence of 3,250 industrial establishments with a capital of 655,576:663$000, production valued at 7,411,536:108$000, and 150,841 workers. The Federal District and the state of São Paulo were at that time in the first rank, contributing 46 per cent of industrial production, while Rio Grande do Sul, in third place, produced 7 per cent, and Minas Gerais only 4 per cent. The other 43 per cent was distributed among the other states. Industrial production was still dominated by foodstuff industries representing 26.7 per cent of the total industrial production. The textile industry, however, which continued to grow, represented at this time 20.6 per cent, while the clothing and toilet-articles industry reached 15.9 per cent of the remaining industrial production, and chemical and related products 9.4 per cent. The remaining 27.4 per cent was distributed among other industrial activities, among which handicrafts predominated. This industry used a total of 109,284 horsepower, of which 73 per cent was produced by steam and 22 per cent by waterpower, with electricity representing only 4,697 horsepower, or 5 per cent of the total energy used.

In 1914, with the beginning of World War I, Brazil found itself in serious difficulties in supplying a large part of its internal consumption. As its economic structure was eminently agricultural and monocultural, with the country depending on imported products not only to survive but also to develop the internal market, the lack of a series of products indispensable to national consumption was felt. It then became necessary, with the scarcity of foreign products, to appeal on a greater scale to national production.

Thus, industrial production, which was valued at 956,557:000$000 in 1914, rose to 2,424,190:000$000 in 1917, an increase of 153 per cent. Even taking into account the devaluation of the currency that occurred in this period, an increase of 109 per cent in the industrial production of Brazil may be noted. The nominal value of production in 1919 reached 2,989,176:000$000, which signified an increase of 112 per cent in relation to 1914. This is why 5,936 industrial establishments arose during World War I.

It cannot be said, however, that a phase of industrial growth had begun, because the majority of establishments were medium or small in size, with handicrafts or establishments linked directly to agricultural activities predominating. This was better demonstrated in 1920 on the occasion of the general census of the republic. This census showed 13,336 industrial establishments with a capital of 1,815,156:000$000, employing 275,512 workers, and with a production valued at 2,989,176:000$000. The food industry, which was already predominant, grew greatly in relation to the others. While in 1907 it represented 26.7 per cent of industrial production, in 1920 it represented 40.2 per cent of the total. The textile industry, however, rose at an accelerated rhythm to 27.6 per cent. There was, however, a diminution in the size of the clothing and toilet-article industry, which sank to 8.2 per cent, and in that of chemicals and related products, which fell to 7.9 per cent. Other groups of industries reached 16.1 per cent.

The principal characteristic of this phase is the lack of heavy industry, so that industrial activity depended for continuity and efficiency on imports. The lack of machines and ironware for the making of machinery and parts and the production of steel and iron combined with the scarcity of power to prevent industrial development. It suffices to say that in 1920 all Brazilian industry consumed only 310,424 horsepower. It should be noted, however, that Brazilian industrialists had already begun to electrify their enterprises. While in 1907, 73 per cent of the power was produced by steam, in 1920 this had been reduced to 36.2 per cent. The greatest source of energy was already electricity, accounting for 47.2 per cent of the total power consumed; 7.7 per cent was supplied by hydraulic turbines; 5.3 per cent by internal combustion motors; 2.7 per cent by waterwheels; and 0.9 per cent by other means. Industrial growth continued in a crescendo until 1923, at which time Brazil reached a production valued at 5,898,551:000$000. This same year, however, marked the beginning of a difficult phase for Brazilian industry, reflected in a marked reduction of industrial production. Two motives may have caused this retrenchment, the first being international and the second domestic.

On the international plane, in 1923 the greater part of the industrial plant of the belligerent nations of the European continent had already been rebuilt. International commerce, dislocated by the effects of the war, was re-established, hence the struggle for the reconquest of markets. Consequently, North America, which found its industrial plants overexpanded by the effects of the war and which was partly losing its European markets, turned to Latin America. The result was that foreign industrial products, principally textiles, perfumes, china, porcelain, crystal, and even certain food products, reached the Brazilian market at prices much lower than those of goods produced in the country. Quite often, they were better. As a result, domestic consumption turned to these imported products. Such a fact inevitably influenced Brazil's industrial production, especially if we consider that it was based upon internal consumption, as Brazil did not possess the means to compete in international markets.

Beside these international motives were domestic ones. The consumption of coffee, which because of a curious but easily explained phenomenon did not suffer much with the outbreak of the European war, increased appreciably at its close. Moreover, the Brazilian government, intensifying its policy of protection for high prices, acted so that coffee growing passed through a rise of prosperity without equal in the economic history of the country. It is not strange, then, that the old prejudices against industry reappeared vigorously and that the economic literature of Brazil sharply attacked national industry in the name of the well-being of the people.[3] Such factors explain why, during the decade 1920–1930, the real growth of Brazilian industry took place very slowly; the decade growth averaged less than that for the year 1923.

After the collapse of 1924–1925, industrial production rose only 67 per cent between 1925 and 1930. The 1930 crisis affected Brazilian industry only slightly and assisted rather than restricted it. The 1929 crisis, because of its repercussion on the coffee market, violently reduced Brazilian international trade. It should be noted that, in this period, the great coffee *fazendas* represented almost the whole of production, and coffee functioned indisputably as the supporter of the whole economy.[4]

It is not strange that in the 1929 crisis Brazilian coffee culture, principally in São Paulo, suffered much more than its competitors in the international market.[5] The industrial rise and even its concentration in the south-central

3. It was accused of being artificial, burdensome, and at times extortionate. It was a period, also, when writers returned to the defense of free trade and combated protectionist measures as dangerous, because, in reprisal, they provoked difficulties for the free entry of coffee into consuming countries. On this point, it suffices to recall the reaction of the Italian government in taxing Brazilian coffee as the result of the increase of Brazilian duties on oil and wines.

4. It was, even so, rudimentary culture, much more of the extractive type than an economic undertaking, in its true sense.

5. It also reflected, among other things, the bad quality of the product, the result of negligence in the care of the plantations, and the bad preparation of the product. Whoever analyzes the international coffee market may verify that during the 1930 crisis the

region, however, cannot be understood without a careful analysis of what coffee represented for Brazil's economy, whether domestic or international. The very distribution of the population was a reflection of coffee. It was also the reason why the major Brazilian currents of immigration flowed by preference to São Paulo. While in 1900, in São Paulo, there were already 231,000 foreigners for 768,000 Brazilians, in 1920 there were among 4,592,108 inhabitants no less than 829,851 foreigners and naturalized Brazilians. Owing to difficulties originating in the depression, in 1930 the Brazilian government began a policy of restricting immigration by greatly reducing quotas. In addition, large numbers of immigrants returned to their countries of origin or left Brazil for other parts. Coffee was responsible, at least in part, for a disequilibrium in the distribution of the population.

By consulting the indexes relative to their distribution, it may be observed that the number of inhabitants of the state of São Paulo represented in 1890 10 per cent of the Brazilian total, while in 1940 São Paulo represented 17 per cent of that number, thus becoming the most populous state in the country. In the 1960 census that percentage had increased, representing 18.3 per cent of the Brazilian population. With this growth, São Paulo succeeded in surpassing even Minas Gerais, which, having reached a population equivalent to 32 per cent of the national total, saw the figure reduced to 16 per cent in the 1940 census and to 13.8 per cent in the 1960 census. Observing the demographic evolution of Brazil, it may be seen that the southern states—São Paulo, Paraná, Santa Catarina, Rio Grande do Sul—and those of the central-west—Mato Grosso and Goiás—were those that without exception saw their population increase in proportion to the total for the country. According to the 1960 census, 39.8 per cent of the Brazilian population inhabited this area.

Now, if immigration to São Paulo diminished after the 1930 crisis, if foreigners settled here departed, and if, on the other hand, the great increase in the number of its inhabitants cannot be attributed solely to the development of coffee, we are obliged to agree that there was a dislocation from other states to São Paulo, principally starting after 1930. Indeed, while in 1921, 6,923 Brazilians and 32,678 foreigners entered the state of São Paulo, in 1939 Brazilians totaled 100,139, and the foreigners only 12,207.

It was to be expected that the country would receive, after the Second World War, large numbers of foreign immigrants, principally of industrial laborers and technicians that would aid in the industrial development of the country and increase the supply of skilled labor. However, immigration

better classes of coffee were the least affected by the fall in prices. In comparison with the 1925 prices, the fall of Costa Rican and Colombian "mild" in 1930 was 28 per cent; Tanganyikan, 37 per cent; Indian, 38 per cent. Even Kenyan, of a considerably lower quality, was 41 per cent, whereas Rio coffee type seven was 43 per cent and Santos superior, 48 per cent.

legislation was not revised so as to facilitate the entry of the foreign skilled labor force, so that immigration followed its previous trends. Thus, in 1963, according to the Department of Agrarian Policy, Brazil received only 23,859 immigrants, of which a majority came to Brazil spontaneously, for only 10 per cent of the total was sponsored by immigration plans. Of the immigrants who came, only 1,802 were skilled industrial laborers and 602 technicians, so that approximately 10 per cent of the immigrants were to seek industrial employment while 90 per cent were agriculturists, domestic servants, or unskilled laborers. Southern Brazil, including the states of Guanabara, São Paulo, Santa Catarina, Paraná and Rio Grande do Sul, was the region that received the largest number of immigrants. The national labor force continued to predominate in the supply of laborers to industry in the southern region. A study made of net internal migration among the geo-economic regions of Brazil permitted a comparison of the dislocation of native-born Brazilians from one part of the national territory to another, by analysis of the censuses of 1940 and 1950.[6] This study reveals that the north-northeast region continued to be the great supplier of labor and that the states of Guanabara, São Paulo, and Paraná received the largest contingents of Brazilians.

It should be remembered, however, that the great bulk of internal migrants is composed of unspecialized rural labor that migrates to the cities or transfers to pioneering regions where the opening up of new lands becomes intensified. Some 70 per cent of the total number of these migrants are adults between the ages of 20 and 59. In the period from 1941 to 1951, for example, 95 per cent of the Brazilians that migrated to the state of São Paulo found employment in agriculture. These facts prove the horizontal mobility of the Brazilian population, which, having been initially a reflection of the coffee prosperity of the south, continued to occur owing to the rise of industrialization stimulated by the fall of coffee in the international market. But such internal population movements created new difficulties by virtue of the ever-increasing concentration of the population in the capitals of the states. According to the 1960 census, the city of Recife, in the north-northeast region, has a population density of 3,814.5 inhabitants per square kilometer, the highest verified in Brazil. The corresponding figure for Fortaleza is 1,532.2 and for Salvador 1,039.2. These cities are located in a poor area where rapid urbanization has created serious social problems without any stimulation to industrial development because the northeast does not have the necessary material and financial resources nor markets that will

6. The census of 1960 unfortunately has not been completely published, and the data released are provisional. For a complete statement, read M. J. Villaça, *Fôrça de Trabalho no Brasil,* Universidade de São Paulo, Faculdade de Ciências Econômicas e Administrativas, Boletim no. 19 (São Paulo: Universidade de São Paulo, 1961).

permit and accelerate industrial development. For purposes of comparison we should note that the highly industrialized city of São Paulo in 1960 had a population density of 2,358.4 inhabitants per square kilometer; Belo Horizonte, 2,069.6; and Porto Alegre, 1,290, these being capitals of states with a satisfactory level of industrialization.

The movement of merchandise followed, in its turn, the movement of people. But São Paulo until 1930 was the leading consumer of the majority of the products of the other states. Imports and coastwise trade, which in 1907 were valued at 52,189:000$000, reached in 1928 the figure of 601,273:-000$000, equivalent to an increase of 1,052 per cent between the dates. Coastwise movement of goods from São Paulo to the other states also followed the same rhythm but, during the whole period, São Paulo consumed much more than it sold, rising as a worthwhile consuming market for other states of the union.

The 1929 crisis, however, had profound repercussions on the movement of coastwise trade. The appreciable damage to the coffee trade made Paulista imports by coastwise trade almost prohibitive, and São Paulo consequently began to consume less than before from the other states. The reduction in coastwise imports between 1930 and 1932 was 53 per cent. Because of this, as we have already said, there was an inversion in the position of Paulista coastwise trade, and from 1930 on São Paulo began to sell more and to buy less from the other states. The impoverishment of the north-northeast zone occurred as an inevitable consequence, thus accelerating the exodus of its population bound for the south of the country.[7]

As the industrialization of south Brazil progressed and as the capitals of the southern states increased their urban population while the area and population of the rural zones decreased considerably, they became large importers of raw materials and foodstuffs from the agricultural areas of the nation. This fact can easily be verified from statistics on internal trade. Bahia became a center of commercial dominance of the northeast and of the north, not only exporting a large quantity of primary products but importing from southern Brazil a considerable volume of industrialized products for its own consumption and for re-distribution to neighboring states. In 1961 Bahia sold to other states the equivalent of 3,340,000 tons, a figure that reached 3,984,000 tons of merchandise in 1963, especially cacao and petroleum. It imported from other states in 1961, 232,000 tons, a figure which was reduced to only 145,000 tons by 1963. Pernambuco, although it may also be considered a center of economic dominance, does not approach the importance

7. The 1940 census shows us that the states of Pará, Maranhão, Ceará, Rio Grande do Norte, Pernambuco, Alagoas, Sergipe, Bahia, and even Minas Gerais, had their population reduced in percentage in relation to the Brazilian total, a safe index of horizontal mobility caused by the 1929 crisis.

of the state of Bahia and has lost ground in the last years with regard to the supplying of industrial products to neighboring states. Pernambuco sold to other states in 1961, 380,000 tons of merchandise, but in 1963 it was only able to place 171,000 tons. It continued, however, to be a great purchasing center, importing from other areas of the country in 1961, 512,000 tons of merchandise and in 1963, 572,000. If one considers the physical volume of the merchandise bought and sold, no one of the southern states accounts for the tonnage attributable to the state of Bahia. But it is necessary to take into account that the south sells industrialized products of greater specific value and lower weight. This fact can be clearly observed when we compare the movement of the physical volume of commerce with the value of the transactions that take place. While Bahia received for its exports about 20.3 billion cruzeiros in 1961 and while in 1963 this figure was raised to 35.4 billion, the sales made by the state of Guanabara reached 25.2 billion in 1961 and 65.3 billion in 1963. São Paulo, for example, sold merchandise for which the value received was 23.8 billion in 1961 and 23.5 billion in 1963.

The value of the merchandise received through coastal shipping is also considerable. Pernambuco paid to other states 18.6 billion cruzeiros for purchases made in 1961 and 25.1 billion in 1963. Bahia paid 8.3 billion and 6.1 billion, respectively, while the state of Guanabara spent 31.7 billion in 1961 and 30.3 billion in 1963, and São Paulo, in second place, paid for products received from other states 23.8 billion in 1961 and 29.5 billion in 1963. These figures show that, as industrialization developed and the federal and state governments began to pay greater attention to economic planning, it was no longer possible to state that the southern portion of the country continued to impoverish the other states. Rather the contrary, the south increasingly has been paying more for the merchandise that it buys than the amount it receives for the sales it makes.

The 1929 crisis, aside from anything else, disorganized international exchange, obliging nations to take measures of economic defense, imposing exchange restrictions and controls, and causing violent contractions in the movement of international commerce, and it stimulated new industrial growth in Brazil. Because the depression had been eminently agricultural, it only retarded this expansion and did not begin to damage it seriously. Only in 1933 did the rhythm of this industrialization begin to accelerate. We shall see that between 1933 and 1938 the value of industrial production, taking monetary devaluation into account, increased by 44.3 per cent. When World War II began, the Brazilian industrial park was already in a promising state and could thus supply the needs previously met by imports.

The second conflict, more than the first one, had decisive repercussions on the transformation of the economic structure of the country. The contraction of imports was aggravated by Brazil's not having yet completely recovered from the 1929 crisis. To observe this, it suffices to consider that, taking the 1935–1945 decade as a base, Brazil imported 0.45 per cent of live animals, 17.6 per cent of foodstuffs, 20.6 per cent of raw materials, and 51.2 per cent of manufactures of the total of the imports. The predominance of the latter is explained by the growing need for machines, apparatus, hardware, and various tools used in industry or agriculture. Such machines, apparatus, and hardware represented, on the average, 17.4 per cent of the country's total imports. Next came the importation of fuels and lubricants, which represented no less than 12.9 per cent of the total, distributed as follows: coal, briquettes, and coke, 4.5 per cent; gasoline, 3.5 per cent; fuel oil, 2.3 per cent; lubricating oils, 1.4 per cent; kerosene, 0.9 per cent; petroleum, 0.2 per cent. Fuels and lubricants thus constituted almost half of the imported raw materials. The others totaled 17.9 per cent of the average imports, with an important place for imports of iron, steel, and cement, all necessary to industry. As far as manufactures are concerned, next to machines came manufactured iron and steel, representing on the average 7.9 per cent of all imports; chemical products, pharmaceuticals, and similar products, 5.5 per cent; automobiles and accessories, 4.5 per cent; other vehicles, 3.4 per cent. Other manufactures show percentages that vary between 2.2 per cent for paper and 0.01 per cent for other manufactures.

The analysis of these data shows us the most important problems of Brazilian industry after the war. In the first place, steel making increased and through its development permitted us to reduce considerably imports directly connected with the consumption of iron and steel. It suffices to consider that 28.2 per cent of Brazilian imports were represented by iron and steel, whether as raw material or as manufactures or in the form of machines, apparatus, and hardware. The second problem, of equal importance, was the scarcity of sources of power. From this comes the very large importation of fuels which, as we observed, reached 12.9 per cent of the total. A third problem, still of great importance and closely linked to the solution to be provided for the first two, is that of transport. In the decade of the forties, 8.5 per cent of Brazil's imports consisted of automobiles, other vehicles, and accessories. It should be noted further that in our analysis we had to consider the war years, which greatly disturbed the normal rhythm of our importation.

With the transformation of the economic situation of agriculture, the overthrow of the position of coffee, and the restriction of imports, Brazilian public opinion began to accept the idea of the need for greater industrialization. Hence arose the attempts at a solution of Brazil's most serious problems, of which those of steel making, electric power, transports, petroleum, and cement were outstanding.

What may be noted of more importance in the industrial evolution of

Brazil is that more watchful care has been taken of the setting up of heavy industry and that we may already affirm that we are on the road to an industrialization established on solid bases. Comparing the industrial census of 1940 with the previous one of 1920, it may be noted that a great transformation has occurred, extremely favorable to the development of large industry in Brazil. We had, in 1940, 39,937 enterprises, totaling 49,418 establishments that, according to existing statistics, consumed 1,205,594 horsepower. Given the reduced number of these enterprise establishments, we cannot speak of industrial concentration in Brazil, because this industrialization was still weak. Such enterprises earned at that date 7,273,025:000$000. Of them, 39.7 per cent were in the hands of foreigners. The capital invested, however, rose to 18,033,237:000$000, or an average capital of 451:500$000 per enterprise.

Considering the capital invested, which is more significant than earnings, we observe that 32.2 per cent of the capital was invested in production and distribution of electricity and gas and refrigeration, as well as in water supply and sewers. The foodstuff industries, which came second, showed an investment of capital of 19 per cent, while the textile industries almost equalled the level of the previous census, for they absorbed 17.3 per cent of all capital invested. Metallurgy, which began to grow thanks to restrictions on imports, was distributed among 1,299 enterprises, representing an invested capital of 871,926:000$000, equivalent to 4.8 per cent of the total invested in industrial activity. The chemical and pharmaceutical industry, fully developed, was still very small, for it represented only 752,045:000$000, distributed among 1,243 enterprises, corresponding to 4.2 per cent of the total capital employed in industry. The processing of nonmetallic ores represented 2.6 per cent of the capital, equalling in importance the lumber and related products industry, which was very much older and had an already established position.

Taking the average capital by enterprises as a base, it may be seen that outstanding activities in the Brazilian industrial plant were the following: the production and distribution of electricity, gas and refrigeration, and water supply and sewers, representing an average capital by enterprise of 4,744:-900$000; rubber, 2,769:300$000; oils, greases, and vegetable fats, 2,117:-200$000; textiles, 1,930:400$000; paper and cardboard, 1,237:300$000. It should be noted that in the case of rubber there are only fifty-two enterprises in Brazilian territory, which, notwithstanding, account for almost 145,000:000$000.

Considering the value of production, however, it may be perceived that in Brazilian production the foodstuff industry was in the lead with 4,911,842:000$000. Textiles came in second with 3,618,574:000$000, and chemicals and pharmaceuticals followed with 1,170,337:000$000. It should also be noted that metallurgy, which appeared in only an incipient form in the 1920 census, took on considerable size, achieving a production the value of which rose to 987,573:000$000. In the same order of importance should be placed civil construction, with a value calculated at 974,057:000$000. The shoe, clothing, and toilet-articles industry, which in the past occupied third place among Brazilian industries, dropped to seventh. The value of its total production, which had once been set at 731,953:000$000, was surpassed even by the machine industry, with a figure of 773,331:000$000. We must remember that the total Brazilian production was valued in the 1940 industrial census at 17,479,393:000$000.

Such activities employed 960,633 persons. Of this total, 781,185 were workers. The 1940 census, aside from the data just referred to, emphasized the industrial importance of São Paulo. It suffices to recall the indexes cited. It should be noted that, in 1939, 29 per cent, or 11,588, of the industrial enterprises in Brazil were concentrated in São Paulo, with a total real-value capital of 2,227,815:000$000, equivalent to 30.6 per cent of the industrial capital invested in the whole of Brazil. It is also necessary to point out that the capital invested reached 7,778,815:000$000, corresponding to 43.1 per cent of the total. In relation to the combination of other states, Paulista industry appeared quite powerful. To show this, it is sufficient to point out that it employed 329,344 persons, or 34.3 per cent, of the people in industry and that the value of its production rose to 43.5 per cent of the total, reaching the figure of 7,601,721:000$000. In this situation, the industrialists of the country began to work actively to supply the national market and even the international market, by virtue of the demands of World War II.

The increasing acceptance of the idea of enlarging the Brazilian industrial plant and at the same time eliminating a considerable portion of the importation of industrialized products allowed the establishment of new enterprises, as well as the extension of the plants of others. The industrial census of 1950 showed the existence of 83,703 industrial establishments, employing 1,177,644 workmen, to whom were paid wages corresponding to 11,268,898 thousand cruzeiros. These industries produced merchandise whose total value, on January 1, 1950, was 108.4 billion cruzeiros. Processing industries predominated over mineral extractive industries; of the former the most representative continued to be the food-processing industry, followed by the production of nonmetallic minerals, furniture and wood industries, the clothing industry, and textile goods and shoes. In 1960 a new industrial census showed the existence of a great industrial expansion. The number of industrial establishments increased to 110,339, employing 1,509,713 workmen and paying wages that reached 102.6 billion cruzeiros. The total value of production reached 1,186.9 billion cruzeiros.

Table 1 shows the total of production and the percentage contributed by each one of the principal industries as a share of the total industrial production verified by the last two censuses.

It may be observed that food-products industries not only continue to occupy first place in Brazilian industrial production, but also their relative importance remains essentially constant, for in 1949 they contributed 24.6 per cent of the total value of industrial production, while in 1959 they contributed 24 per cent. Textile industries also continued in second place, but their relative importance diminished considerably between the two dates. While in 1949 the value of textile production accounted for 20.7 per cent

TABLE 1

PRINCIPAL CLASSES OF INDUSTRIES BY VALUE PRODUCED, IN
BILLIONS OF CRUZEIROS, 1950–1960

Class of Industry	Value 1950	Per Cent of Total	Rank	Value 1960	Per Cent of Total	Rank
Food products	42.1	24.6	1	285.2	24.0	1
Textile	35.5	20.7	2	147.5	12.4	2
Metallurgy	15.9	9.3	3	123.9	10.4	3
Chemical and pharmaceutical	15.0	8.8	4	119.3	10.1	4
Nonmetallic mineral processing	8.8	5.1	5	53.4	4.5	6
Clothing, shoes, and cloth artefacts	7.2	4.2	6	40.2	3.4	8
Transportation materials	5.4	3.2	7	79.3	6.7	5
Wood	5.2	3.0	8	31.2	2.6	11
Beverage	4.7	2.7	9	28.0	2.4	12
Printing and graphic	4.3	2.5	10	26.9	2.3	13
Paper and cardboard	4.2	2.5	11	35.3	3.0	9
Electrical and communications materials	3.6	2.1	12	45.2	3.8	7
Rubber	3.4	2.0	13	25.5	2.1	14
Furniture	3.2	1.9	14	21.7	1.8	15
Mechanical	2.6	1.5	15	33.6	2.8	10
Leather, furs, and allied	2.5	1.4	16	12.8	1.1	19
Tobacco	2.3	1.3	17	13.2	1.1	18
Mineral extractive	1.4	0.8	18	14.4	1.2	17
Perfume and cosmetics				18.0	1.5	16
Plastics				7.8	0.7	20

SOURCE: Instituto Brasileiro de Geografia e Estatística, *VI Recenseamento Geral do Brasil, 1950*, vol. 3, *Censo Comercial, Industrial e dos Serviços* (Rio, 1954–1958); and *VII Recenseamento Geral do Brasil, 1960* (Rio: Censo Industrial, 1962).

of total industrial production, in 1959 that percentage had dropped to 12.4, in spite of the great increase in the value of textile sales and even taking into account the effect of inflation on the increase in prices.

Metallurgical industries continued to occupy third place, increasing their participation in industrial production, for their contribution to the total value produced went from 9.3 per cent in 1949 to 10.4 per cent in 1959. The chemical and pharmaceutical industries continued in fourth place, also increasing their degree of participation from 8.8 per cent to 10.1 per cent between the two dates. The industries of transformation of nonmetallic minerals went from fifth to sixth place, for their relative importance was reduced from 5.1 per cent to 4.5 per cent of the value of total industrial production between the two dates.

Table 1 indicates differences in the rank order of importance of the other industrial activities and shows an expansion in the areas of production, since the industrial census of 1950 did not accentuate the contribution of the perfume, cosmetics, and plastic industries, while the industrial census of 1960 shows that these activities had become so important that the first occupied the sixteenth place among the twenty principal industrial activities, and the second the twentieth place. The importance of the contribution of mechanical industry has increased considerably: it went from fifteenth to tenth place. Also showing substantial increases were the electrical and communications industries, whose contribution allowed them to move from twelfth to seventh place, and that of the transportation materials industry that, although it was already important in 1949, increased its relative importance in 1959, inasmuch as its contribution went from 3.2 per cent to 6.7 per cent of the total value of the Brazilian industrial production. The paper and cardboard industries are in a similar position, having gone from eleventh to ninth place, reflecting an increase in their participation in the total value of from 2.5 to 3 per cent between the two dates. The furniture and rubber-products industries remain relatively constant with regard to their degree of participation in Brazilian industrial production. The same is not true, however, of other types of production whose relative importance decreased with regard to the total industrial plant. This was the case with the wood industry; leather, fur, and allied industries; shoes; beverages; tobacco; and printing and graphic industries. As is natural, the great effort to industrialize, especially in the mechanical and metallurgical industries, stimulated the extractive minerals industry that increased the value of its production from 1.4 billion cruzeiros in 1949 to 14.4 billion in 1959; while on the first date it accounted for 0.8 per cent of total industrial production, in 1960 its relative participation increased to 1.2 per cent, or a relative increase of 50 per cent in one decade.

Brazilian industry has supplied, preferably, internal markets. Only 0.4 per cent of the country's total exports in 1940 were manufactures. In 1950 Brazil's exports were 7 per cent of manufactures. Of the total value, 4.5 per cent is attributable to cotton textiles. Exportation of cotton textiles in 1938 was insignificant, only 247 tons, with a value of 4,260:000$000. The only three customers of any importance were Venezuela, Colombia, and Argentina, in decreasing order. With World War II and the restriction of possibilities of supplies from other centers of textile production, the exportation of cotton textiles rose continually, and in 1947 Brazil exported 16,678 tons, equivalent to Cr$1,252,587,000. Not only did the volume and value of exports increase, but customers increased considerably in number. We began to count on exports not only to Latin America but to Europe, Africa, and even Asia. Nine countries imported Brazilian textiles in 1938 and twenty-nine countries in 1947.

In these last years the number of industrial products exported has increased, principally after the creation of the Latin American Free Trade Area. Inorganic and organic chemical products, principally carbonates, chlorides, alcohol, menthol, salts, pharmaceutical and medicinal preparations, essential oils and aromatic products for perfumery, polishing, preservation, and cleaning found a place on the list of products exported by Brazil. The development of mechanical industry, in its turn, has allowed Brazil, although on a small scale, to sell during these years home sewing machines, automobile accessories, trucks and similar vehicles, railroad rolling stock, passenger elevators, utility-type automobiles, buses, and even small airplanes. The exportation of textiles continues, although on a small scale, as well as that of some common metals employed in metallurgy. As yet, however, all these industrial exports represent only a small part of the total exports. Coffee, cotton, and cacao continue to be the principal Brazilian export products which supply the great part of the foreign exchange that we need for importation.

Another important result of this increase in industrial production and diversification of the national industrial plant is that the structure of imports changes substantially. Manufactured products were substituted by a great increase in the importation of raw materials and industrial equipment. Among food products, only wheat continues to represent a most important share of our purchases abroad. In 1963 we spent 164 million dollars on wheat, the estimate of these imports for 1964 being 205 million dollars.

The industrial concentration noted in the south-central region, with São Paulo as a fulcrum and expanding around the capital city of the state, has caused serious problems which must be analyzed. It has been noted, among other things, that the construction industry so increased that it surpassed that of clothing and toilet articles. One of the most serious problems facing us in this phase of the transformation of the national economic structure is the geographic concentration of enterprises that unbalances the distribution of the Brazilian population.

Starting in 1930, the attraction of cities increased considerably, as agriculture became precarious and industry developed in the urban centers. With this, the exodus from rural zones became aggravated and, principally in the state of São Paulo, assumed an alarming aspect.[8]

8. Analyzing the distribution of the population of the state of São Paulo in accord with the data of the census of 1940, it may be noted that its capital had a population of 1,326,261 inhabitants, with 1,258,482 inhabitants concentrated inside the urban perimeter,

The phenomenon is extremely grave, because it concerns not only a flight from the country to the cities but a movement from the country and the small cities to a few capitals. Consequently, the demographic balance necessary for a harmonious development of the economy of Brazil is destroyed. One part overexpands to the detriment of all and, instead of many medium-sized cities, there are numerous small centers in opposition to a very few great cities. On the national plane, however, the problem appears even more serious so long as the movement of population occurs from some states to others. And all this is occurring in a country that is far from attaining a population optimum and in which density is still very low, with only 4.8 inhabitants per square kilometer.

It is not, however, only the search for greater comfort and a better life that has caused this maldistribution of the population. Industrial development has contributed more than anything else to this phenomenon. Industry attracts workers, and one of its characteristics is a great number of workers concentrated in a small area, in opposition to agriculture, the area of which is immense and the numbers of individuals restricted. Though the determining factors of this concentration of men and activities may be many, one which arises from the struggle to obtain the power necessary for industrial labor must be emphasized.

We enter here into a curious and characteristic aspect of Brazilian industrialization—the location and development of the electric industry.

The very movement of imports shows us that a fundamental problem of Brazilian industrialization is that of power. It is known that Brazil is a country poor in coal and, therefore, must make heavy imports of this fuel. The known mineral coal reserves in Brazil are on the order of 1,836,000 thousand tons. But, of this total, only 42 per cent of the coal from Santa Catarina can be used in the steel industry. Under present technical conditions, the mixture made by the steel mills consists of 60 per cent imported and 40 per cent domestic coal. There is a good market for this type of coal because of

---

while only 67,779 inhabitants were located in the rural zone. Thus, a density of 893 inhabitants per square kilometer was found, an index higher than that of the majority of large cities and of the principal countries of the world. The gravity of the phenomenon may be better understood if we recall that the density of the whole state was 29 inhabitants per square kilometer. If we add to the population of the capital, properly speaking, that of Santo André, a neighboring city that has 62,440 urban inhabitants for 27,434 suburban and rural inhabitants, with a coefficient of 101 inhabitants per square kilometer, we may complete the picture of this concentration. To verify that this fact is generalized, it suffices to consider that Santos, the second largest city of the state, with a total population of 165,568 inhabitants, had 155,894 inhabitants concentrated in the urban zone, with the remaining 9,674 inhabitants in the suburban and rural zones, and shows a density of 189 inhabitants per square kilometer. The cities of São Paulo, as a group, had an urban population of 2,930,937 inhabitants, of which 1,258,482 were in the capital, leaving 1,672,455 inhabitants to be distributed among 305 *municípios*.

the expansion of the steel industry, but the consumption of steam coal, which represents 34 per cent of the national production, has decreased, and there is no market for the pyritic residue; although sulphur could be produced from it, it represents 24 per cent of the wasted production.

Even in 1945, after the outbreak of World War II, when the difficulties of obtaining foreign coal had increased and, therefore, a program had been worked out for the intensification of Brazilian coal exploitation, the thirty-nine enterprises in this line of production, which in this country are almost all located in Paraná, Santa Catarina, and Rio Grande do Sul, produced only 2,072,881 tons, with a total value of Cr$220,598,000. At the same time, we imported 698,278 tons of coal and 17,517 tons of coke, with a total value of Cr$266,138,000. Furthermore, importation of coal in 1945 was not typical, because this was at the end of the war.

In 1961 we produced 2,389.6 thousand tons, a figure that increased in 1963 to 2,828.5 thousand tons of mineral coal. Of the volume extracted, part was utilized in the chemical industry. Only 1,256 thousand tons in 1961 and 1,541.7 thousand tons in 1963 were utilized for fuel and the production of gas. The apparent consumption for these purposes was 2,175.1 thousand tons in 1961, increasing to 2,549.1 thousand tons in 1963, so that the difference between production and consumption had to be supplied through importation. The impossibility of supplying Brazil's demand for mineral coal through domestic production has been one of the most serious difficulties confronted in its industrial expansion, inasmuch as coal furnishes approximately 50 per cent of the energy utilized by Brazilian industry. In 1964 Brazil consumed 1,681,965 tons of domestic coal and 1,016,083 tons of imported coal. It is worthy of note that imported coal is used only in steel milling and in the production of gas, for all of the coal needed for the production of steam energy is supplied by Brazilian production.

In spite of this expansion of the coal industry, its contribution to the economic development of Brazil is very small. In 1963, in a report to the Brazilian Congress for the Definition of Basic Reforms, engineer Murilo Nunes de Azevedo showed that, if Brazil converts the coal and petroleum it consumes into electric energy equivalents, it can continue to derive energy principally from the petroleum and its derivatives, which supply 53.5 per cent of the total, followed by electric energy, which supplies 41 per cent, and coal, which, even considering the amount imported, furnishes only 5.5 per cent of the needed energy.

It is this scarcity of fuel that makes Brazil not only depend upon wood as a common source of power but also seek a better use for hydraulic power as a source of the electricity which today is becoming indispensable to economic activity. In this respect Brazil does not appear especially favored. The Water Division of the Department of Mineral Production of the Ministry of Agriculture, in a study published in 1948, estimated the hydraulic power of Brazil at 19,519,300 horsepower, equal to about 14,366,000 kilowatts. This estimate goes beyond reality, because the sources of power were not studied directly and the estimate was made from the difference in the level of the terrain shown on existing maps.

According to this study, our five largest waterfalls are, in order of importance: the Guaira Falls or Sete Quedas, in the Paraná River, with 1,500,000 horsepower; the Paulo Afonso Falls, on the São Francisco River, with 560,000 horsepower; the Iguaçú Falls, on the river of the same name on the boundary between Brazil and Argentina, with about 340,000 horsepower; the Urubupungá Falls, on the Paraná, with about 250,000 horsepower; and the Marimbondo Falls, on the Rio Grande, with about 150,000 horsepower. Not all these natural sources have yet been exploited.

The two largest uses of natural waterfalls in Brazil are represented by the Fontes plant at Ribeirão das Lages, state of Rio de Janeiro, with 140,000 kilowatts installed in 1947, belonging to the Companhia de Carrís, Luz e Fôrça do Rio de Janeiro; and the Itupararanga plant, on the Sorocaba River, state of São Paulo, with 50,400 kilowatts installed, belonging to the São Paulo Tramway, Light, and Power Company. The latter plant was the first in hydroelectric use in the country. On the basis of its present capacity, the Cubatão plant is ranked seventh in hydroelectric power in the world. If, however, we consider its ultimate capacity in comparison with that of the two companies mentioned above, it will become the third in the world, being surpassed by only the Grand Coulee and Boulder dams in the United States.

Brazil had, in 1947, 911 hydroelectric and 874 thermoelectric generating plants, with a total of 1,813 generating plants, including mixed plants. Private hydroelectric plants, which reach the number of 69, are, however, excluded. Such plants supplied 2,816 localities.

We should consider that the light and power group has put into effect an important expansion program. While in 1948 it provided 801 megawatts of energy, corresponding to 50 per cent of the power installed in Brazil, in 1960 its contribution had increased to 1,988 megawatts even though that contribution represented only 42 per cent of the hydroelectric power in the country.

All these facts indicate that the industrial concentration around the capital of the state of São Paulo is not to be wondered at, because the greatest source of power in Brazil is near at hand at Cubatão.

Even in the decade of the 1940's the need to exploit electrical energy in other areas and to decentralize the Brazilian industrial plant was felt. The São Francisco Hydroelectric Company was created by Decree-Law 8031 of October 3, 1945, with a fifty-year concession for the progressive utilization of the hydroelectric energy of the São Francisco River and for the furnishing of electric energy in high tension to public service concessionaires, as well as for carrying out the direct distribution of electricity in the area that it encompasses.

In May 1955 the first three generating plants, of 60,000 kilowatt capacity, of the Usina de Paulo Afonso began operation (the first stage in the work of that company), and two main transmission lines were then installed, one going to Recife and called the "north line" and another one leading to Salvador, the "south line."

At the present time, the São Francisco Hydroelectric Company encompasses seven states in the federation: Bahia, Sergipe, Alagoas, Pernambuco, Paraíba, Rio Grande do Norte, and Ceará. In 1961 that company served 147 *municípios*, and in 1964 it served 365. Thanks to this network, principally on the Salvador circuit, it was possible for Petrobrás to intensify their petroleum extractive and refining activities. It is still hoped that an important industrial plant may yet develop in the northeast because of this new hydroelectric enterprise. The capital stock of the company is now at 60 million cruzeiros, with an outlook for constant increase by virtue of the massive investments that the federal government has made in it with the cooperation of national and international agencies.

Worthy of special mention is the official inauguration of the Furnas Electric Plant in mid-1965, which placed into operation six generators, making the total installed potential 900,000 kilowatts. This plant has a special significance, for its dam controls the flow of the Rio Grande, whose potential is superior to 7,000,000 kilowatts. At the present time the Furnas, Camargos, Ibitinga, and Peixoto plants are in operation totalling 1,175,000 kilowatts.

Furnas is already supplying energy to São Paulo and Belo Horizonte, supplementing the supply previously provided by the Centrais Elétricas de Minas Gerais. Presently under construction is a line that will join that plant to Guanabara. In the south, in Santa Catarina, the Usina Termo Elétrica de Capivarí has gone into production on an experimental basis. It is burning steam coal taken from the mines of that state, a coal that has practically no market, for there is a stockpile of 500,000 tons that is not marketable because of the conversion of locomotives and steamships to diesel power. In the state of Piauí, the Usina Hidroelétrica de Boa Esperança is under construction. It should have a potential of 200,000 kilowatts and will greatly aid the development of that region.

The old estimate of 48,000,000 kilowatts as the hydroelectric potential of the entire country has been revised leading to the certainty of the existence of at least 60,000,000 kilowatts, without including the rivers of the Amazonian basin that certainly would increase greatly Brazil's capacity for electric energy production.

The Brazilian electric energy companies, which in 1948 furnished 109 megawatts, produced 520 megawatts in 1960. Foreign companies furnished in the later year 2,508 megawatts of installed power, corresponding to 53 per cent of the national total.

The federal and state governments initiated a program of electric energy development and by 1960 were able to supply 972 megawatts of power installed and to contribute 20 per cent of the nation's hydroelectric energy. Other national, private producers supplied 1,320 megawatts, or 27 per cent of the installed hydroelectric potential in Brazil.

To facilitate the expansion of electric energy, the Brazilian government created Eletrobrás, a central financing agency for the producing companies. In 1964 this public agency provided 54.4 billion cruzeiros in financing for those projects underway. Of this amount, 12.5 billion was in the form of societary participation, 30.9 billion in the form of financing, and 11 billion in short-term loans. The financial plan for 1965 provided for investments on the order of 162 billion cruzeiros, of which 45.3 billion was to be for increases in the capital of electric energy companies, 84.4 billion for financing, and 32.3 billion in new investments.

The present Brazilian government in its Economic Action Program for 1964–1966 intends to concentrate its efforts in the south-central region of the country with the cooperation of the United Nations and of the International Bank for Reconstruction and Development. Since national industry is concentrated in the south-central region, the preoccupation of the Brazilian government with increasing the potential of this region is readily understandable. For this reason, the South Central Region Energy Study Committee was created. This committee has been carrying out a systematic study of the hydroelectric potential in existence in the region so as to formulate an overall plan for development of its electric system. There is, in this region that stretches from the basin of the Jequitinhonha River to the basin of the Itabapoama and its affluents, an installed potential of 3,860 tons of energy. There are dams under construction that will permit an increase of 4,900 tons, and there are other projects already prepared that indicate a possible increase of an additional 3,805 tons, which will elevate the total of this region to 39,511 tons.

Thanks to this program it is expected that by 1970 the installed generating potential will be on the order of 12,665 million kilowatts with corresponding transmission and distribution facilities. The program would extend to the entire national territory from the north to the extreme south, but the greatest effort in the installation of new power plants and the enlargement of the existing ones would be concentrated in the south-central region, in the area of greatest industrialization.

The close connection between the development of electric power in Brazil and that of the cement industry deserves our attention. Let us review the history of cement in the country. The first cement factory, organized in Paraíba do Norte, dates from 1892. It was not, however, successful. Five years later, in 1897, another was founded in Santo Antonio, on the Sorocabana Railway. It had a capacity of 25,000 tons a year, using Dietz-system vertical furnaces. This plant, however, did not last long and stopped completely in 1910. Only with the outbreak of World War I, which made foreign cement scarce, was the old Rodovalho factory in São Paulo reopened. The government of the state of Espírito Santo, four years earlier, had begun construction of another cement factory, with a capacity of 25,000 tons, at Cachoeira do Itapemirim; this, however, failed.

Brazilian cement was not trusted, so much so that even in 1926 it equalled only 3.3 per cent of the consumption, whereas cement of foreign origin accounted for 96.7 per cent. In this year, however, the Companhia Light, undertaking large-scale works, especially at Cubatão, agreed to experiment with national cement, attesting the excellence of its quality. Its consumption increased rapidly, and, by 1929, 96,000 tons were consumed against 13,000 in 1926. The proportion of national origin was then 15 per cent.

Brazil's cement industry was unharmed by the 1929 crisis. On the contrary, it was stimulated because the fall in coffee prices, making it difficult for Brazil to obtain foreign exchange, brought, as a result, a violent contraction in cement imports, which fell from 535,000 tons in 1929 to 114,000 in 1931. With the lessening of foreign competition, the national cement industry could grow, and its production has been increasing daily, while the percentage of its use in relation to the total demand for cement in Brazil becomes increasingly greater. In 1942, thanks to the difficulty of importing foreign cement, 98 per cent of the cement consumed in Brazil was of domestic origin. With the end of the war, though the importation of foreign cement increaséd, the production and consumption of domestic cement continued to rise. Suffice it to say that in 1947 the nation consumed 888,000 tons of cement made in Brazil, representing 72 per cent of the total consumption. In 1950 there were ten cement factories. The most important, in volume of production, were the Companhia Nacional de Cimento Portland, in Rio de Janeiro; the Companhia Brasileira de Cimento Portland Perús; and the Votorantin factory, located in São Paulo. These three enterprises represented 73.7 per cent of the nation's cement production.

The cement problem has come to be one of the most important for our industrialization. While its production is steadily rising and it has established itself successfully, it should be noted that there is a real cement famine in the country. It is being used on a large scale in civil construction, principally in São Paulo and Rio de Janeiro, where the very powerful urban concentration requires modern buildings of multiple stories. Besides this, it is an indispensable raw material in the construction of highways in a country where transportation is a serious problem. Technicians of the highway department, according to studies that have been made, have proved that a cement highway reduces transportation costs by more than 20 per cent. It is also necessary for the construction of engineering works, for railroads, and for the work of improving rivers in order that inland navigation, so necessary in Brazil, may be developed. It is also a factor in the building program of hydroelectric power plants, thus facilitating the electrification of the national railroads. Today, cement, as a factor in the industrialization of Brazil, may be placed on the same level with steel.

For these reasons, there has been a great preoccupation in the last decade with the expansion of cement production. The National Economic Development Bank, in order to provide a better orientation for its investment plans in the cement industry, divided Brazil into eight regions. The first of these was formed by the states and territories that constitute the northern region of the country. It has only one factory in the proximity of Belém, the Fábrica Capanema. Its installed capacity is 80,000 tons per year, and operation began in 1962. This capacity is sufficient to supply the demand foreseen for the region between 1964 and 1968. The possibility of expanding it to supply the demands of Goiás, making use of the Belém-Brasília highway, is under consideration. The second region is formed by the states of Piauí and Maranhão, where there is no production. Their needs are supplied by the Fábrica Capanema, located in Belém. The third region is constituted by the states that make up the northeast-east region and may become a great producing center and perhaps even exporting center, for it contains great reserves of gypsum, capable of supplying all of the factories in Brazil and innumerable calcareous deposits of the best quality. The energy to power this production could be supplied by the Paulo Afonso Hydroelectric Plant and by fuel oil from the Landulfo Alves Refinery in Bahia. This region exported cement for a long time and until 1961 sent some 30 per cent of its production to the southern region. But beginning in 1962 because of the enormous increase in maritime transportation costs, sales to the southern region of the country became impossible. On the other hand, the production of the Fábrica Capanema, utilizing more modern methods, began to supply part of the northeastern market itself. In spite of this, there are plans for the installation of two new cement plants in Mossoró, in Rio Grande do Norte, and in Sobral, in Ceará, with a nominal capacity of 50,000 tons each foreseen.

The fourth region includes the states of Sergipe and Bahia and has one cement plant located in Aratú in the *Recôncavo* of Bahia, with an installed capacity of 190,000 tons a year, since 1962. This production is insufficient to supply the local demand. There is under construction at the present time a new plant that should begin to produce in 1965, with a nominal capacity of 54,000 tons per year.

The fifth region includes the states of Espírito Santo, Guanabara, and Rio de Janeiro. It has, at present, four ordinary cement plants, three in the state of Rio de Janeiro and one in Espírito Santo, with a total production of 1,128,000 tons a year and one of white cement with a capacity for producing 36,000 tons per year. The total regional production capacity is 981,000 tons, but consumption in 1963 was 1,191,000 tons. The deficit was covered by the importation of cement from the Barroso and Cominci plants in Minas Gerais. There are plans to construct a new producing unit in Cantagalo in the state of Rio de Janeiro with a productive capacity of 150,000 tons.

The sixth region includes the states of Minas Gerais, Goiás, and the Federal District. There are nine cement plants in the region, seven of these in Minas with a total production of 1,682,000 tons a year, and two in Goiás producing only 24,000 tons. There is a project for the enlargement of one of the plants in Minas Gerais and of the two in Goiás, which should increase the regional annual production potential to 2,032,000 tons by 1968.

The seventh region includes the states of São Paulo, Paraná, and Mato Grosso. In mid-1964 the productive capacity of this region was 2,106,000 tons a year, even so, insufficient to supply the demand. Therefore, plans have been made for an increase of 270,000 tons in the productive capacity of the region through the expansion of the plants in Corumbá, in Mato Grosso, and in Rio Branco, in Paraná.

The eighth and last region includes the states of Santa Catarina and Rio Grande do Sul. In the first of these there is a factory located in Itajaí, with a productive capacity which exceeds the needs of the state. It is a region where suitable calcareous reserves are small, totalling approximately 6,000,000 tons, which leads one to suppose that in the near future this will be the principal market for the surplus cement production that may occur in the more favored regions.

It is natural that the development of the highway system, the increase in civil construction, and industrial development have contributed to an enormous expansion in cement production. While in 1958 Brazil produced 3.8 million tons, in 1964 production reached 5.5 million tons.

Related to the power problem is that of steel. The problem of installing heavy industry in Brazil is reduced, above all, to a problem of fuel and power, since we are rich in ore. The history of Brazilian steel making indicates that the problem of iron and steel in this country lies principally in its dependence on fuel. In 1597 in the captaincy of São Paulo, a small forge was built for the production of iron. However, the enterprise did not succeed, and it was only in 1795 that the metropolis permitted the establishment of iron manufacture. In 1809 the prince regent was an associate in the iron factory at Ipanema, which also failed after two small blast furnaces and Catalan forges were built. At the same time, however, the good quality of the ore permitted the installation of a small steel plant at Morro do Pilar in

Minas Gerais and, later, two more at Congonhas do Campo and São Miguel de Piracicaba. Beginning in Minas Gerais, this activity extended to the other states, with blast furnaces in Rio de Janeiro, São Paulo, Paraná, and Mato Grosso.

The Brazilian steel industry, with the exception of Volta Redonda, which has been working since 1946 with metallurgic coke, has rested on plants using charcoal. Until now, the entire production of pig iron has been obtained with the use of charcoal. It is not strange, then, that our type of enterprises, while growing continually, has shown insignificant results if we consider the great need for raw and manufactured iron and steel. In 1915 Brazil produced only 3,259 tons of pig iron; in 1933, it produced only 74,774 tons—an index of very slow growth. Only since 1939, though here through the effects of the contraction of Brazilian imports, has this type of activity grown. In 1939, we produced 160,000 tons of pig iron, but we raised this figure in 1947 to 305,000 tons.

The fuel problem became prominent principally when the construction of Volta Redonda was under consideration. After careful study, the possibility of using electric blast furnaces was dismissed, because these were small-scale apparatuses and required the construction of an electric generating plant, and could not, furthermore, be used by large-scale enterprises. The possibility of using charcoal was also set aside, because it would not allow large-scale production. Coke of national origin suitable for use in steel making was then considered.

Swayed by this reason, the Companhia Siderúrgica Nacional acquired coal mines near Siderópolis, fourteen kilometers from Criciuma, in Santa Catarina, in order to obtain, through treatment, the coke it needed. Only in 1947 was this company able to complete its installations. Volta Redonda in 1946 produced 95,745 tons of pig iron, which, added to the 273,509 tons made in other plants, raised Brazil's production to 369,254 tons. The steel city in 1947 was already capable of producing rails, coupling plates, supports, thick and thin plates, hot- and cold-rolled, besides the products of the coking plant and subproducts factories, such as ammonia sulphate, coke, naphthaline, motor fuel, benzol, toluol, silol, naphtha solvent, coal tar, pitch, and oil.

In addition to the National Steel Mill of Volta Redonda, at the present time the quadrilateral area Itabira-Belo Horizonte marks the limits of the substantial area of enormous deposits of iron ore in Brazil. In this area are found the great national steel mills, the Mannesmann, the Siderúrgica do Vale do Lafaiete, the Companhia Siderúrgica da Guanabara, the Siderúrgica Belgo-Mineira, Usiminas, Acesita, and Ferro e Aço de Vitória.

Even though the nation had in 1964 ten great steel milling industries among which were, in order of importance, the Companhia Siderúrgica Nacional, Usiminas, Companhia Siderúrgica Paulista, Belgo-Mineira, Mineração Geral do Brasil, Mannesmann, Ferro e Aço de Vitória, Acesita, Siderúrgica de Barra Mansa, Siderúrgica Riograndense, and Siderúrgica Aliperti, internal production was insufficient to supply the apparent demand, principally of steel ingots. Even though Brazilian production increased from 1,866,000 tons in 1959 to 2,812,000 tons in 1963, the apparent consumption increased from 2,518,000 tons in 1959 to 3,428,000 tons in 1963, necessitating substantial importations that corresponded in 1959 to 26 per cent of the consumption and in 1963 to 18 per cent of the total. For this reason, the Brazilian government is tackling the problem of the expansion of steel milling and hopes to increase production to 6,285,000 tons of steel ingots in 1970.

Another very important base metallurgical industry developed after the Second World War, in the decade from 1950 to 1960—the aluminum industry, whether it be primary aluminum or whether it be the manufacture of intermediate or finished products.

In 1956, of an apparent consumption of 25.3 thousand tons of aluminum, Brazil could already produce 6.3 thousand tons, while 19 thousand tons were imported. The following aluminum factories were installed in Brazil: Saramenha, in Ouro Prêto, and Alumínio de Minas Gerais, S.A., both in Minas Gerais, and the Companhia Brasileira de Alumínio de Sorocaba, in the state of São Paulo. In 1964 the national production of aluminum had risen to 27,000 tons, with 21,000 tons being imported and an apparent consumption of 48,000 tons. The federal government plans to expand this industry, providing financing for the expansion projects of the Companhia Brasileira de Alumínio de Sorocaba and of the Alumínio de Minas Gerais, S.A., in Poços de Caldas.

As a part of this general plan, it expects also to construct a new mill with a capacity for 40,000 tons in Poços de Caldas, thanks to the Alcoa-Hanna Project. There are plans, therefore, to expand the aluminum industry continually so that by 1970 Brazil may produce 72,000 tons and import only 22,000 tons, for the apparent consumption should reach 94,600 tons in that year.

The petroleum industry must be considered in close connection with the fuel problem. The beginning of the search for petroleum in Brazil was a consequence of World War I. Though the Brazilian government had begun its search in the zone of favorable geologic formation and had already made 63 soundings by July 10, 1933, the results obtained by the technicians were always pessimistic. Notwithstanding, the search continued, and in 1935 the National Technological Institute, based on samples from the Lobato well in Bahia, reached the conclusion that the initial exploration must be intensified, with, however, the application of modern methods of extraction. Commencing with this, positive indications of the potentiality of the beds of Aratú, Candeia, Santo Amaro, and Itaparica were later obtained.

Judging by the first observations, the Bahian wells are commercially exploitable, for, according to 1941 statistics, they produced on the average 10, 30, 50, and 150 barrels a day, according to the well. By 1947, 100 wells had been drilled, of which 45 were already producing oil and 14, gas. It should be noted, however, that Bahia petroleum has a paraffin base which constantly plugs the production pipes, causing periodic expenses in maintaining the wells.

In view of the first favorable results of petroleum exploration, Brazil began to provide for the installation of refineries and pipelines. The first refinery installed was that of Landulfo Alves in the state of Bahia, soon followed by Usina Presidente Bernardes' in the state of São Paùlo, Duque de Caxias in Rio de Janeiro, Refinaria Gabriel Passos in Minas Gerais, Refinaria Alberto Pasqualini in Rio Grande do Sul, and Refinaria de Gasolina Natural in the state of Bahia. All these producing units are part of Petróleo Brasileiro, S.A. (PETROBRÁS), a company belonging to the federal government. In addition to these large refineries, there are also five private refining companies: Refinaria Ipiranga, with a plant in Rio Grande and another one in Uruguaiana; Refinaria Matarazzo in São Paulo; Refinaria União in Capuava in the state of São Paulo; and COPAN in Manaus and Refinaria Manguinhos in the state of Guanabara.

The Santos-São Paulo pipeline, a concession of the Santos-Jundiaí Railroad, has been functioning since 1951, in addition to the pipeline network of the Recôncavo Baiano, which joins the producing fields with the Refinaria Landulfo Alves and the terminal of Madre de Deus. In addition, there are under construction the great pipeline from Rio de Janeiro to Belo Horizonte, the São Sebastião-Refinaria Presidente Bernardes pipeline, the Tramandaí-Refinaria Alberto Pasqualini pipeline, and the São Paulo-Campinas pipeline. With the exception of the first of these, all belong to PETROBRÁS. This company also provided for the construction of an asphalt plant in Bahia, of a fertilizer factory in Cubatão, a synthetic rubber factory in Rio de Janeiro, another one of eteno, in São Paulo, as well as the installation of units for ethylene pyrolysis and for extraction of aromatic oils to furnish raw materials for the petro-chemical industry. The industrialization of bituminous schist from Tremembé in São Paulo and from São Mateus in Paraná is also planned, as well as asphalt plants in Madre de Deus and in Fortaleza, in addition to the development of the petro-chemical complex of Bahia.

It is, therefore, natural that the production of crude petroleum and its derivatives has increased considerably. While in 1949 we produced only 109,000 barrels a year, corresponding to 0.4 per cent of the national consumption, in 1963 production had increased to 43,000,000 barrels a year and Brazil supplied 36.5 per cent of the demand. As for petroleum derivatives, in 1949 Brazil produced only 587,000 barrels a year, corresponding to 2.2 per cent of the consumption. In 1963 production had increased to 104,000,000 barrels per year, corresponding to 95 per cent of the national consumption. The year 1964 showed a slight decline in the production of crude petroleum and its derivatives: 7.5 per cent for the former and 3.2 per cent for the latter.

From what has been said, it may be seen that the industrialization of Brazil is very recent. Only in this century has public opinion, thanks to the obstacles which Brazilian agriculture has overcome, become favorable to the development of large-scale industry, though, among industries, those directly connected with agricultural activity, the food industries, may predominate. Other industrial activities, however, gain ground every day.

The textile industry today, as we have seen, is on a high plane and already is beginning to compete in international markets with more advanced industrialized countries. It cannot progress much further, however, unless fundamental problems of the economic structure of the country are solved. The power, fuel, cement, iron and steel, and petroleum industries are beginning to take on size, and one of them, cement, is making itself felt on the national scene and almost completely meets the needs of domestic consumption.

With regard to the effort to industrialize during the past years, we should underline the role played by the automobile industry. Brazilian engineers and economists prepared the ground for Brazilian entrepreneurs who, aided in part by foreign capital, gave a powerful impulse to this most important industrial activity. This stimulus is attributable to a so-called Program of Objectives put into effect by the federal government between 1956 and 1960. The Brazilian automobile industry is composed of eleven assembly plants, seven manufacturers of chassis, and some 1,500 producers of automobile parts. In 1957, 30,700 units were produced with a nationalization of 65 per cent for trucks and automobiles and of 75 per cent for jeeps. In 1959 Brazil produced 96,243 units, with a predominance of medium-weight trucks, pick-up trucks, and passenger cars. The index of nationalization increased consistently. In 1963, 100 per cent of the material utilized was produced nationally; a total of 174,126 units were produced and distributed in the following way: heavy trucks and buses, 3,478; medium trucks, 20,546; pick-up trucks and station wagons, 50,157; utilitarian vehicles, 13,942; passenger automobiles, 80,023. The total financial resources mobilized in 1963 reached 139 billion cruzeiros, which included 17 billion attributed to reevaluations of fixed assets. This expansion is also due in part to the considerable increase in the profit margins of the automobile industry, that reached 22.1 per cent of gross investments in that year, 25.1 per cent of net investments, and 44.1 per cent of nominal capital.

In 1964 the number of units produced was raised to 183,755 vehicles, with increases of 0.7 per cent in the number of heavy trucks and buses, of 2.3

per cent in the number of medium trucks, and of 13.7 per cent in the number of passenger automobiles. The number of utilitarian vehicles was reduced, however, by 7 per cent and that of pick-up trucks and station wagons suffered a reduction of 3.4 per cent.

So that we may have a more exact idea of the degree of participation of Brazilian industry in the formation of the real product, table 2 was prepared based on the purchasing power of the 1949 cruzeiro. While in 1949 industry produced 30.9 billion cruzeiros, corresponding to 14.4 per cent of the real product of Brazil, in 1963 the value of industrial production in terms of constant value had increased to 100.9 billion cruzeiros, corresponding to 22.1

TABLE 2

PARTICIPATION OF INDUSTRY IN THE REAL PRODUCT, 1949–1963
BASED ON 1949 PURCHASING POWER OF THE CRUZEIRO

| Year | Real Product | | Participation of Industry | | | | |
	Value Billions of CR$	Index 1949 = 100	Value Billions of CR$[a]	Index 1949 = 100	Per Cent of Real Product[a]	Index 1949 = 100	Variation over Previous Year[a]
1949	215.2	100.0	30.9	100.0	14.4	100.0	
1950	226.0	105.0	34.5	111.4	15.3	106.25	106.25
1951	237.6	110.4	36.7	118.5	15.4	106.94	106.65
1952	280.9	116.6	38.5	124.4	15.3	106.25	99.35
1953	258.9	120.3	41.8	135.2	16.1	111.81	105.23
1954	278.9	129.6	45.4	146.7	16.3	113.19	101.24
1955	297.8	138.4	50.2	162.3	16.9	117.36	103.68
1956	303.4	141.0	53.7	173.5	17.7	122.92	104.73
1957	324.3	150.7	56.7	183.2	17.5	121.53	98.87
1958	345.6	160.7	65.9	213.2	19.1	132.64	109.14
1959	371.2	172.5	74.4	240.7	20.0	138.89	104.71
1960	394.7	183.4	81.1	262.3	20.6	143.06	103.00
1961[b]	425.0	197.5	91.2	295.0	21.5	149.31	104.37
1962[b]	447.1	205.9	98.1	317.3	21.9	152.08	101.86
1963[b]	456.0	210.0	100.9	326.2	22.1	153.47	100.91

a. Calculation based on data furnished by the Fundação Getúlio Vargas.
b. Provisional data.

per cent of the real product. There was, therefore, between the two dates, an increase in industrialization on the order of 226.2 per cent for the fifteen-year period. The indexes calculated to reveal the annual variation in the industrial participation in the real product of the nation show that there were annual increments, although variable, in this participation, with the only exception being the year 1957, when there was a small reduction in relation to the prior year of 1.13 per cent.

We should not, however, suppose that this promising evolution of Brazilian industry has positive aspects only. Much still remains to be done to accelerate the rhythm of industrial development.

The National Economic Council, an organ of the federal government, analyzing the situation of industry, underscored certain deficiencies that need to be eliminated.[9] In summary, these authorities believe that the internal productivity of industrial enterprises is still not completely satisfactory, for in many of them there is a considerable margin of waste so that the efficiency of the use of the factors of production should be increased in order to reduce costs. It is also necessary to generalize the system of cost allocation to avoid waste and calculate correctly indexes of productivity that may serve as a guide to the administrative activities of management.

There is still an excessive diversification of products with the same function, presenting difficulties for mass production. Another important problem is that of quality control. Although Brazilian industry is already capable of producing high quality products in many sectors, in others there are no testing laboratories to assure uniformity of the characteristics of the product. It would be highly convenient, in addition, to promote an industrial zoning having as its objective the rationalization of the interlocking among industries.

We believe, however, that one of the most delicate problems of Brazilian industry concerns the labor force.

A land of scanty population, without a tradition of solidly constituted labor, and in which the extinction of slavery dates back only eighty years feels the lack of skilled labor. It needs not merely technicians for industries but engineers. We have only slightly more than 40,000 engineers in the whole country.

The lack of workers adjusted to the needs of industry has been felt in such a manner that the National Confederation of Industry resolved to create at its own cost the National Service of Industrial Apprenticeship, which has contributed efficaciously in the whole country and, particularly in São Paulo, to the training of labor for work in Brazil's industrial plants. The level of living for the laborer in Brazil is precarious. Even in the state of São Paulo, where workers enjoy a situation without equal elsewhere in the country, it is much below the level of living in other industrial countries. The average consumption of a Paulista is, according to calculations made by Dr. Roberto Simonsen, three times higher than that of the Brazilian in general. The state of São Paulo, however, in spite of enjoying this privileged position, even today has large impoverished regions. The average consumption of the Brazilian is many times lower than that of the North American.

So much has the need for aiding the laborer been felt that, besides the services of social assistance created by the federal government and those of the various states, the National Confederation of Industries created in 1946

9. Conselho Nacional de Economía, *Exposição Geral da Situação Econômica do Brasil* (Rio, 1954–1963), passim.

the Social Service of Industry. Such a service has as its objective the promotion of the well-being of the laborers and their families. It seeks to improve the total environment in the whole country, to promote moral and civic betterment, and to develop a spirit of solidarity among employees and employers. Realizing that continued inflation has made the rise in wages more illusory than real, this service seeks to make possible a rise in the real wages of workers in the industrial sector. Its action extends even to medico-sanitary assistance.

The development of Brazilian industrialization, on the other hand, imposes on public authorities the task of regulating labor. The importance of this is increasing, even more so because certain political ideologies, introduced into the country from abroad, have contributed to disturbing the social order, thus making it more difficult to develop Brazilian production, especially industrial production. Various social reforms were introduced. Many of them, however, inspired by political motives of the moment, were carried through without the indispensable prior investigation and inquiry and, as a consequence, caused labor disturbances. For this reason, the benefits that the orientation of Brazilian social labor policy sought to give the working classes were much less than those promised. This disordered legislation disturbed labor law and contributed, in part, to the fall of productivity among a large number of individuals. Brazil is, at present, in a period that may be called that of the systematization of labor legislation, in which the better adjustment of the parties is sought and, with this, the obtaining of better social justice. While this consolidation, however, does not have the stamp of fact, such legislation will have to be considered as a disturbing factor in the rhythm of industrialization. It is these labor problems and the low standard of living of laborers that explains why it is difficult for large-scale industrial enterprises to be created. At the site of enterprises, it is not infrequently necessary to build real cities in order to obtain the indispensable labor. The case of Volta Redonda, the Companhia do Vale do Rio Doce, and the National Motor Factory may be mentioned, to cite only a few.

Aside from these problems concerning labor, we must still consider those of enterprise. The inflation that the country has suffered—one may well say chronically—makes planning difficult by facilitating extreme instability of prices. Thus, not only the risk increases but also the possibility of bankruptcy of a new undertaking becomes greater.

This same monetary phenomenon causes a reduction in tariffs despite the apparent protectionism of Brazilian commercial policy. Customs duties are calculated in nominal values and do not readjust themselves with the same rapidity with which money becomes devalued. This is so true that in the International Conference on Commerce and Employment it was proved that Brazil is one of the nations that has, on the whole, the lowest tariffs in the world. The participants in the conference consequently authorized the Brazilian government to make a tariff readjustment on the base of a 40 percent increase ad valorem.

Without taking into account the scarcities of power and deficiencies of transport that we have already pointed out, industrial undertakings are still being retarded by the precariousness of Brazil's credit and by the lack of capital. A vicious circle is thus created from which the country must escape. Only diversification of the economic structure of Brazil will allow greater economic solidity and, thanks to it, success in stabilizing the value of money in the domestic as well as in the international market. The weak purchasing power and instability of the cruzeiro, on the other hand, cause lack of confidence, which produces contraction of credit, and make difficult the obtaining of the capital necessary for the development of industry.

In conclusion, the following observations may be made:

1) The industrialization of Brazil is recent because public opinion has been unfavorable to movements to create and expand Brazilian industry.

2) Such industry is almost entirely limited to the internal market.

3) Its greatest volume is represented by the consumer-goods industries, among which food and textiles are outstanding.

4) Basic industries are still in their infancy, though developing with an accelerated rhythm, and present possibilities of great development, provided that they are oriented according to an intelligently drawn industrial plan.

5) Human factors, however, disturb this development at least in part, and the measures already put into practice to prevent their deleterious effects weigh on the cost of production and place the country in a difficult situation for competing with like foreign countries.

6) One of the great problems of enterprise is that of attracting capital which, once invested, will permit not only economic development but also changes in the structure of the Brazilian economy.

Let us not forget, however, that this problem is of the reflex type; international commercial movements have intense and immediate repercussions on the economy of the country. It is thus difficult to say to what extent it is possible to foresee the expansion and viability of Brazil's industrial plants.

Chapter 8

Brazilian Development
and the International Economy

Eric N. Baklanoff

N ATION-STATES, just as individuals, do not develop in isolation. An underdeveloped nation, by definition, lacks some of the most essential ingredients of an economically advanced society: a population exhibiting organizational and technical skills; a substantial capital structure embodying the insights of modern technology; and an institutional framework that links social rewards to economic achievement, while encouraging vertical and horizontal mobility. The classical "way out" for the economically backward nation is to tap the international economy for capital, human resources, and managerial-technical know-how. More, the extension of the market across international boundaries has constituted a viable historical option for a nation desiring to break out of its low-level equilibrium.*

The aim of this paper, then, is to illuminate the development of Brazil in the context of the international economy. Our survey begins around mid-nineteenth century—from which point in time Brazil experienced an acceleration in its rate of economic growth—and proceeds to the present.

Three rather distinct phases emerge from our study: the "export economy," the "industrialization drive," and "the systematic use of the international economy." The first covers the period roughly between 1850 and 1930; the second extends from the bottom of the Great Depression (around 1932–1933) to the overthrow of the Goulart government in the spring of 1964; and the last phase was initiated by the Castelo Branco administration (April 1964–March 1967) and consolidated by the regime of President Artur Costa e Silva (March 1967–August 1969).

*The author is grateful to Vanderbilt University's Graduate Center for Latin American Studies for a travel and research grant to Brazil during the summer of 1963, which made this and other studies possible.

190

ANATOMY OF AN EXPORT ECONOMY, 1850–1930

Brazil pursued an externally oriented pattern of development from mid-nineteenth century to 1930.[1] In organization and structure, Brazil typified what economists have come to call an "export economy." Such an economy exhibits the following properties: a high ratio of export production to total output in the cash sector of the economy; a concentrated export structure; substantial inflow of long-term capital, including the presence of foreign-owned enterprises; and a high marginal propensity to import.[2] Commonly, in such an economy a large fraction of government revenue is derived from customs receipts. The export sector constitutes the dynamic, autonomous variable which powers the nation's development; it is also the short-run disturber. The sheer weight of exports in relation to total economic activity dictates that the external market rather than private investment or government expenditure exercise predominant influence on aggregate demand. Because of its specialized structure, the export economy is heavily dependent on foreign sources for many kinds of consumer and capital goods.

The development of Brazil until the First World War was intimately linked with the international economic hegemony of the United Kingdom. Until the outbreak of World War I, the United Kingdom was Brazil's leading source of imports and supplied the lion's share of foreign capital, both portfolio and direct investments. The United Kingdom's share in the 1914 stock of foreign capital came to roughly 60 per cent, or more than three-fourths, of Brazil's external debt and about one-half of the direct investments outstanding. Total British investments in Brazil in that year constituted nearly one-fourth of the United Kingdom's overall holdings in Latin America. Thus, Brazil participated in Britain's "Golden Age of Foreign Investment" and became increasingly integrated with the international economy through expanding commodity trade.

Between 1880 and the Great Depression, Brazil experienced an explosive burst of externally induced investment activity (see table 1). Foreign capital outstanding increased sharply (from $190 million in 1880 to $2.6 billion in 1930), the railway network was expanded ninefold (from 3,400 to 32,000 kilometers), electric power was introduced, and the nation's exports increased 350 per cent. A little under one-half of the foreign capital outstanding in 1930 represented the country's external debt, and roughly $1.4 billion comprised direct investments in Brazilian railways, power plants, urban public services, factories, and financial and commercial enterprises.

1. This section is derived in part from the author's chapter, "External Factors in the Economic Development of Brazil's Heartland: The Center-South, 1880–1930" in *The Shaping of Modern Brazil*, edited by Eric N. Baklanoff (Baton Rouge: Louisiana State University Press, 1969).

2. Gerald M. Meir, *International Trade and Economic Development* (New York and Evanston: Harper and Row, 1963), pp. 5–6.

In the time span between the end of World War I and the Great Depression foreign capital continued to be attracted to Brazil but with significant changes in country origins. The United States emerged at the end of hostilities as an international creditor nation, reflecting a major shift in the world economic balance in its favor. The position of world banker and leading supplier of development capital was suddenly thrust upon this former bastion of international isolation. The rise of New York as the world's financial center and the relative decline of London help to explain the ensuing changes in Brazil's foreign investment pattern. United States holdings in Brazil increased by more than $500 million, from $55 million in 1914 to nearly $570 million in 1930, while in the same period Britain's capital investment grew by only $200 million.

TABLE 1

BRAZIL: INDICES OF ECONOMIC GROWTH,
1880–1929 (OR 1930)

Productive Factors	1880	1929 (or 1930)
Population (millions)[1]	11.7	37.4
Railway lines[2]	3,400 km.	32,000 km.
Electric power capacity[3]	negligible	700,000 K.W.
Value of exports[4]	£21,000	£95,000
Foreign capital outstanding[5]	$190 million[6]	$2.6 billion

1. Ministry of Foreign Affairs, *Brazil: An Economic, Social, and Geographic Survey* (Rio, 1940), p. 35.
2. *Anuário Estatístico do Brasil, 1937* (Rio: Conselho Nacional de Estatística, 1937), p. 850.
3. *Anuário, 1937*, p. 849.
4. *Anuário, 1937*, pp. 858–59.
5. Table 2.
6. In 1880 Brazil's debt in sterling bonds (public and private issues) was £39 million. Figures for direct investments are not available. See U.N., Department of Economic and Social Affairs, *External Financing in Latin America* (New York, 1965), p. 9, table 4.

While the period between 1880 and 1930 was one of prodigious economic development, it must be remembered that the geographic focus of this development was quite selective. The region mainly affected by the growth-promoting external factors was the south-central, and most especially the state of São Paulo. Brazil's incipient industrial establishments were concentrated in this region as was the nation's agricultural output and economic infrastructure.

The collapse of the international capital market during the Great Depression marked the end of over a century of continuous expansion of Brazil's external indebtedness. Foreign borrowing through the issue of bonds guaranteed by the government provided Brazil and other Latin American countries with an important channel of funds for capital formation and development. The extremely rapid buildup of Brazil's external bonded debt, from less than $200 million in 1880 to nearly $1.3 billion in 1930, was closely associated with the nation's coffee prosperity. Debt could grow and service obligations (interest and amortization) could only be met out of the rising export proceeds. The rising foreign exchange earnings, associated mainly with Brazil's coffee exports, was one of the essential conditions for successful debt service.

Between 1887 and 1936 Brazil received more than 4 million immigrants, comprised mainly of Italians (1,353,734), Portuguese (1,147,841), Spaniards (576,825), Germans (154,999), Japanese (177,304), and Russians (107,170).[3] Most of them settled in the temperate areas of the south-central and began their productive lives as sharecroppers, small independent farmers, craftsmen, artisans, or peddlers. Because of their contact with the more advanced industrial cultures of Europe, they brought new attitudes, new skills, and new perceptions to Brazil. The partially assimilated immigrant population introduced the family-operated commercial farm and the modern system of plowing into the south of Brazil.[4] They organized new commercial and industrial enterprises and provided the core of skilled workers and foremen. They and their descendants formed a solid base for a growing middle class and created an environment in which industrialization could take root. Emilio Willems, whose definitive work on Brazilian immigration is well known, writes of their special contribution to Brazil's development:

They were also bearers of economic attitudes that were relatively seldom encountered in the old Luso-Brazilian stock. As rural settlers they produced to sell rather than to subsist. As urban dwellers they tended to become entrepreneurs, willing to assume risks and to combine managerial skill with technical knowledge.[5]

The opening of Brazil to foreign direct investment was closely associated with the organization efforts of Irineo Evangelista de Sousa, Viscount Mauá, one of Brazil's most celebrated entrepreneurs. Between 1850 and 1870 he promoted the building of railways and ports and the establishment of textile mills and banks. The participation of foreign-owned subsidiaries and branches in Brazil's rapid economic growth between the middle of the eighteenth century and the First World War was very pronounced. From what must have been a negligible sum in 1850, the value of foreign direct investment outstanding reached a massive $1.2 billion in 1914 (represent-

3. Ministry of Foreign Affairs, *Brazil, Statistics, Resources, Possibilities* (Rio, 1937), p. 36.
4. T. Lynn Smith, *Brazil, People and Institutions* (Baton Rouge: Louisiana State University Press, 1963), p. 378.
5. "Brazil" in *The Institutions of Advanced Societies*, edited by Arnold M. Rose (Minneapolis: University of Minnesota Press, 1958), pp. 545–46.

ing a sum of about 4 billion in current United States dollars!). Foreign-controlled businesses in this period played a decisive role in the construction and operation of railways and utilities and in forging the vital financial and commercial links between Brazil and the rest of the world. Foreign enterprise and its associated capital in Brazil represented the extension of the emerging European and, subsequently, United States industrial revolutions.

Furtado infers that Brazil suffered a downward trend in per capita income in the first half of the nineteenth century, so that by 1850 it "had reached a lower point than in the entire colonial era, if the various regions of the country are considered as a whole."[6] The introduction and development of the coffee plant in Brazil provided the thrust for a new era of export prosperity: between the 1850's and 1930 the nation's economy was once again on the ascendant as Brazilian coffee penetrated the world economy through expanding lines of international trade. Through a fortuitous combination of topography, climate, and soil, Brazil quickly attained a comparative advantage in the growing of coffee, yielding a virtual monopoly position in world markets. In contrast to the earlier commodity cycles based on a single export commodity, the 1850–1930 period was characterized by growth of technical and organizational skills and the accumulation of real capital per head of population. Brazil offered the natural resource base and unskilled labor; the rest of the world supplied much of the capital, technical capacity, and entrepreneurship.

Exports, borrowing abroad, the inflow of direct investments, and immigration were interdependent and mutually supporting factors. Brazil's export economy rested precariously on the fortunes of coffee.

THE INDUSTRIALIZATION DRIVE

The Great Depression

The long-lived coffee prosperity of near one-century duration came to an abrupt halt in 1931. The sharp drop in the New York price of Brazilian coffee, from 22.5 cents in September 1929 to 8 cents in September 1931, reflected the general collapse of world markets for primary commodities. Brazil's foreign trade contracted strongly:[7]

(IN MILLIONS OF U.S. DOLLARS)

	1929	1932
Exports	446	181
Imports	417	108

6. Celso Furtado, *The Economic Growth of Brazil: A Survey from Colonial to Modern Times* (Berkeley: University of California Press, 1965), p. 118.

7. Reynold Carlson, "Brazil's Role in International Trade" in *Brazil: Portrait of Half a Continent*, edited by T. Lynn Smith and Alexander Marchant (New York: Dryden Press, 1951), p. 275.

As foreign sources of capital dried up, Brazil's much-compressed export earnings proved to be insufficient to pay for the most essential imports and to meet the rigid debt service obligations. Gold shipments proved, at best, a temporary solution, for by early 1931 Brazil's gold reserve was almost exhausted. Between 1929 and the autumn of 1931, the external value of the milreis fell by one-half, from 11.8 cents to 5.6 cents, and in September of 1931 the government imposed exchange control through the agency of the Bank of Brazil.

The ratio of public debt service (amortization and interest) to exports increased from a manageable 15 per cent in the period 1926–1929 to a scheduled 43 per cent in the bottom of the depression (1932–1933).[8] Brazil defaulted on its external obligations in 1931, the year when debt service would have absorbed nearly 30 per cent of the nation's exports. The government's moratorium on all foreign-held debts of the national, state, and municipal governments thereby lifted what may have been an unsupportable burden on the nation's greatly diminished external payments capacity. Official cessation of service payments on Brazil's external debt resulted in a collapse of bond prices. The market value of the dollar bonds, for example, which were nominally valued at $374 million at the end of 1930 dropped to $57 million at year end 1931.[9]

The drastic fall in export prices and the devaluation of the exchange rate altered the relative profitability of production for export and production of manufactures for the home market. For example, the dollar price of Brazilian coffee in the thirties averaged less than half its price in the previous decade. The factors mentioned together with the government's income maintenance policy now made it profitable to produce in Brazil many of the manufactured commodities which were formerly imported. Between 1925–1929 and 1935–1939, industrial output increased by 60 per cent.[10] This industrial advance was supported by (1) investment funds formerly channeled to the growing of coffee, (2) the availability in world markets of cheap used machinery and secondhand equipment, and (3) a policy of deficit financing. The government's support of coffee prices during the depression through purchase of unmarketable coffee had the effect of maintaining domestic purchasing power. The acceleration of industrial output in the latter 1930's rested on important pre-conditions already present in the 1920's: the existence of sizable urban centers in the south-central region of Brazil, the presence of skilled immigrants, and the huge foreign and domestic investments in transportation, power, and urban infrastructure.

8. Dragoslav Avramovic, *Economic Growth and External Debt* (Baltimore: Johns Hopkins Press, 1964), p. 46, table 8.
9. Thomas F. Lee, *Latin American Problems* (New York: Brewer, Warren and Putnam, 1932), appendix, table 1.
10. *Survey of the Brazilian Economy, 1960*, Brazilian Embassy, Washington, D.C., p. 104.

The fifth coffee support (valorization) program was initiated in 1931. Unlike the previous support programs, the depression measure aimed at drastically curtailing capacity by placing a prohibitive tax on new plantings. Capacity was reduced from 3 billion trees in 1933–1934 to 2 billion in 1949; the area devoted to coffee growing contracted from 8.5 million to 6 million acres between 1937–1938 and 1947–1948.[11] The joint effect of these efforts was to sharply reduce the volume of coffee production between the thirties and early forties. Between 1931 and the beginning of 1940, some 70 million bags of coffee were burned.[12]

Substantial diversification took place in Brazilian agriculture following the glut in the world coffee market. Diversification of coffee farms began in the thirties, with the introduction of cotton as an important export commodity. Coffee farmers also diversified their holdings with the introduction of animal husbandry and the growing of food crops—both for domestic consumption.[13] In the latter fifties, only about one-half of the average coffee farmer's income derived from coffee. The sharp fall in coffee prices relative to cotton, cereals, and meat products made alternative agricultural investments attractive. The share of coffee in Brazil's exports declined from 70 per cent in 1921–1930 to 50 per cent in 1931–1940. Cotton exports, on the other hand, increased their share from a negligible percentage in the twenties to 30 per cent in 1939.

Within a decade, Brazil became one of the world's three or four largest producers and·exporters of cotton. The production response to external demand was particularly intense in the state of São Paulo:[14]

OUTPUT OF GINNED COTTON
(TONS)

	São Paulo	Brazil	São Paulo as % of Total
1930	14,000	126,000	11
1940	307,000	469,000	66

All these measures facilitated the diversion of economic energies to the development of the domestic market. The evidence is clear that Brazilians were successful in overcoming a most difficult situation by reallocating resources to more promising lines.

11. Reynold Carlson, "The Bases of Brazil's Economy" in *Brazil: Portrait of Half a Continent*, edited by T. Lynn Smith and Alexander Marchant (New York: Dryden Press, 1951), p. 229.

12. Ministry of Foreign Affairs, *Brazil: An Economic, Social, and Geographic Survey* (Rio, 1940), pp. 96–99.

13. U.N., *Economic Bulletin for Latin America* 5, no. 2 (October 1960), p. 81.

14. *Facts about the State of São Paulo* (British Chamber of Commerce of São Paulo and Southern Brazil, 1949), p. 93.

The Capacity to Import and Development
1939–1961

From the outbreak of World War II in 1939 to the end of the Kubitschek administration in 1961, Brazil's pace of economic development continued, although in a diminishing degree, to be tied to the balance of international payments—to the country's overall capacity to pay for vital import commodities, including machinery and equipment, foodstuffs, raw materials, and fuels. When focusing on the merchandise account only, the capacity of a country to purchase imports is determined by the quantum (physical volume) of exports and the terms of trade (the relationship of export prices to import prices converted to an index). As figure 1 shows, in the decade

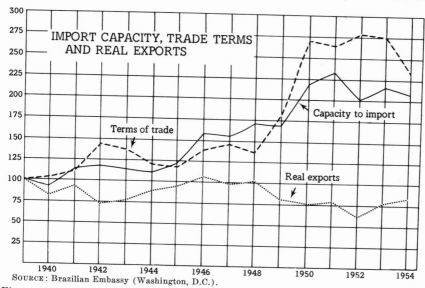

SOURCE: Brazilian Embassy (Washington, D.C.).

Figure 1. Current Capacity to Import, Terms of Trade, and Real Exports
(1939 = 100)

and one-half between 1939 and 1954 (despite a 15 percent reduction in the quantum of exports) Brazil's current capacity to import rose by more than 100 per cent, reflecting more than a doubling of the terms of trade, from 100 in 1939 to 225 in 1954. Brazil's good fortune in this span of years was mainly a result of the postwar coffee boom and of the sharp increase in the unit value of the country's secondary exports. The main explanation for the improvement in the terms of trade rests on the behavior of coffee markets in the immediate postwar decade. After 1945 the Western European market was once again accessible to Brazil, and, with the successful conclusion of the Marshall Plan (1948–1951), it became—next to the United States—Brazil's largest overseas market. Until the middle fifties, world consumption of coffee exceeded current production, forcing an increase in prices. Initially Brazil covered the supply-demand gap with the surpluses accumulated during the war. By 1949 Brazil's coffee stockpile was exhausted and, thereafter, coffee prices rose at an exponential rate. The production response of Brazil and of other coffee-exporting nations was necessarily delayed. Coffee as a commodity is characterized by low short-run supply elasticity. The coffee tree takes about five years to mature, reaching high yields at around ten to twelve years, and has a useful life beyond thirty years.

Brazil's major export-type coffee (Santos no. 4) averaged 22 cents a pound during 1924–1929, dropped to an average of less than 10 cents during the thirties, and edged up to 13.4 cents per pound during 1941–1945 (the maximum price fixed by the United States government during World War II). From 22.3 cents a pound in 1948, the price of Brazilian coffee increased rapidly, reaching its peak average (80 cents) in 1954. The period 1955 to mid-1957 marked a relative equilibrium between world coffee supply and demand, and the price of Santos no. 4 levelled off to a range of 55–60 cents a pound. Subsequently, world coffee output (resulting from the "run to coffee plantations" induced by rising prices) grew at a faster rate than world consumption. The price of Brazilian coffee deteriorated and fell to an average low of 34 cents a pound during 1962–1963, followed by a significant price recovery in 1964–1965 (averaging 46 cents a pound).

Concurrently with the end of the world coffee boom, Brazil's terms of trade and current capacity to import sustained a sharp reversal, as indicated below:[15]

(1948 = 100)

	1954	1961
Quantum of exports	75	102
Terms of trade	235	145
Capacity to import	177	148

Between 1954 and 1961, despite an increase in the quantum of exports, Brazil's current capacity to import declined from 177 to 148, reflecting the weakness of coffee, cacao, cotton, and other traditional Brazilian export commodities in world markets.

Two explanations may be suggested for Brazil's continued and rapid economic (and industrial) growth despite the fadeout of the coffee boom and an accelerating rate of inflation. The first lies in the massive inflow of private foreign capital, associated largely with the Kubitschek administration.

15. SUMOC, *Relatório do Exercício de 1961* (Rio: Superintendencia da Moeda e do Crédito, 1962), p. 56.

For example, in the "program of goals" period (1956–1961), the *net* inflow of private capital from abroad averaged $250 million per year, or about one-fifth of the nation's annual commodity imports. These autonomous capital movements—principally direct business investments and medium-term suppliers' credits for equipping electric power, transportation, and heavy industry projects—supported Brazil's "total capacity to import."[16] At this crucial juncture of Brazil's economic evolution the intensification of capital inflow constituted one of the necessary conditions for sustained growth.

By the early 1960's Brazil's margin for safety in compressing consumer goods imports had practically disappeared, leaving its foreign exchange position exceedingly vulnerable to the slightest adverse shift in the terms of trade and to the volume of international capital movements. Thus, if imports of raw materials were cut back, the economy would be forced to operate well below capacity; if capital equipment imports were reduced, investment would suffer. Notwithstanding the program of import substitution which has characterized the country's postwar industrializing strategy, the absolute import requirements have remained high.

The second explanation arises out of Brazil's inordinate success in creating a capital goods industry. This is reflected in Brazil's postwar drive toward the development of heavy industry for the production of intermediate products and equipment. The progress of import substitution in Brazilian industry is revealed by the sharp decline of the share of imports in domestic supplies of selected groups of manufactures, as shown below:[17]

(PERCENTAGES)

	1955	1965
Durable consumer goods	9.6	1.4
Intermediate goods	22.5	8.2
Equipment goods	39.5	8.8

The decline in the nation's relative dependence on equipment imports from 40 per cent in 1955 to 9 per cent a decade later was particularly dramatic.

With the exception of iron ore and manganese, Brazil failed to organize new export-oriented industries which could compete successfully in international markets. For example, from 1939 to early 1953, Brazil maintained an inflexible rate of exchange which became progressively overvalued with the course of domestic inflation. The controlled rate (a subsidy to importers), together with selective control of imports, strongly encouraged the

16. The total capacity to import represents the value of foreign exchange earned from exports plus the algebraic sum of the net balance of service account and net capital inflow from abroad.

17. U.N., Economic Commission for Latin America, *Economic Survey of Latin America, 1966* (New York, 1968), p. 115, table 83.

growth and diversification of manufacturing industry. On the other hand, this policy penalized export initiatives, particularly along nontraditional lines.

In sum, the evolution of Brazil's international trade from 1939 to 1961 yields the following significant highlights: (1) real exports stagnated, with small variations from year to year; (2) the current capacity to import rose, reflecting a secular improvement in Brazil's terms of trade with the rest of the world; (3) Brazil failed to materially alter its concentrated export structure, for coffee (after World War II) continued to contribute roughly one-half of total export sales; and (4) the long-run improvement in Brazil's terms of trade means that with roughly the same quantity of exports the country received in exchange one-third more commodities in 1948 than in 1939 and nearly one-half more imports in 1961 than in 1948. Brazilian policymakers, therefore, cannot validly argue that their nation has suffered in its trade relationships with the industrialized countries on account of a deterioration in its commodity terms of trade. Perhaps of even greater weight in determining the gains from trade is the matter of qualitative improvements. What Brazil has traditionally sold on world markets—coffee, cotton, cacao, lumber, manganese, and iron ore—has undergone little, if any, qualitative change; on the other hand, much of what Brazil buys abroad—machinery and equipment, parts, pharmaceuticals, etc.—has undergone progressive qualitative improvement.

The period spanning the beginning of the Great Depression and the close of President Kubitschek's "program of goals" produced a deepseated restructuring of the Brazilian economy. Nowhere is this change more dramatically apparent than in the reduced ratio of exports to total production between the latter 1920's and early 1960's:

(PER CENT)	
1925–1929	probably 25–30
1939	22
1950–1951	10
1960–1961	6

Brazil's Balance of International Payments
1941–1965

A nation's international economic relations are brought into sharp focus through balance of payments analysis. Balance of payments statements summarize the economic transactions between the citizens (including the government) of a nation and the rest of the world for a stated period of time, usually a year.

We can divide the balance of payments into three basic accounts or categories: the current account, the autonomous capital account, and the monetary account. The first comprises the flow of goods and services; the second shows transactions in capital claims such as long-term credit, loans, and equities; and the monetary account shows the balancing or equilibrating items such as short-term loans from the International Monetary Fund and / or reduction on gold and foreign exchange reserves. The outcome in the monetary (or compensatory) account reveals whether the nation has experienced a *basic* deficit (or surplus) in its overall payments position. In other words, the basic balance is the difference between autonomous receipts (credits) and autonomous payments (debits). Autonomous transactions (e.g., direct investments, tourist expenditures, commodity trade) are independently motivated; they exclude compensatory (or induced) transactions that respond to a disequilibrium in the balance of payments.

A balance of payments statement can reveal something about (1) a nation's international liquidity position (and hence the strength or weakness of its currency in world markets) and (2) its stage of economic development. For example, Brazil's current account normally shows a large net outflow (debit) of interest and dividend payments. We may infer from this, with some degree of confidence, that the nation's status is that of an international debtor—foreign claims against Brazil exceed its capital claims on the rest of the world. Furthermore, if year after year more capital flows in rather than out, the country is clearly an international borrower. So we may say that Brazil is an international debtor-borrower. The annual payments on capital income have become an important item in Brazil's current account. They, of course, represent primarily the service on the large stock of foreign business investments in Brazil and on the accumulated external debt. In Brazilian balance of payments accounts the *total* earnings of foreign direct investments are included in the "capital income" category, even though a large proportion of these is generally reinvested in Brazil. The protracted accumulation of foreign capital in Brazil creates a national obligation to generate a commercial (commodity) surplus with the rest of the world, out of which interest and dividend remittances can be financed. The other substantial debit in Brazil's current account—freight and insurance—is indicative of the fact that the bulk of the nation's international commodity trade is carried in foreign vessels and insured by foreign firms.

The war years, 1941–1945, were characterized by annual surpluses (see table 2) in Brazil's current transactions with the rest of the world. The cumulative current account surplus of $750 million is explained by a favorable commercial balance of $1,050 million—more than sufficient to offset negative service payments ($302 million) and a net capital outflow of $70 million. Brazil's international liquidity position improved dramatically during this period, as reflected in massive accumulation of gold and foreign exchange. External liquidity also generated greater domestic liquidity and inflation, as the balance of payments surpluses were monetized by the banking system.

Brazil's wartime surpluses in current account (in contrast to traditional deficits) responded to a number of special and temporary circumstances: (1) the diversion of world shipping to strategic requirements and (2) the

TABLE 2

BRAZIL'S BALANCE OF INTERNATIONAL PAYMENTS
BY SELECTED TIME PERIODS, 1941–1966
(IN MILLIONS OF U.S. DOLLARS)

Transaction	1941–1945	1946–1955	1956–1961	1962–1963	1964–1966
A. Current account	749	−1,357	−1,739	−640	369
Trade balance	1,050	2,043	766	22	1,459
Services (net)	− 302	−3,400	−2,452	−739	−1,226
Freight and insurance (net)	− 183	−1,556	− 624		− 227
Capital income (net)a	− 261	−1,095	− 914		− 683
Other (net)b	142	− 749	− 914		− 316
Unilateral remittances (net)	1		− 38	77	136
B. Autonomous capital account	− 70	686	1,305	278	619
Long-term private capital flow (net)	− 6	620	1,483	229	220
Public loans and donations (net)	− 64	103	− 178	49	399
Other		− 37			
C. Total (A + B)	679	− 671	− 434	−362	988
D. Errors and omissions	3	− 115	− 324	−260	− 58
Basic balance: Surplus (+) or deficit (−)	+ 682	− 786	− 758	−622	+ 950
E. Monetary account (gold, short-term capital and compensatory financing)	− 682	786	758	622	− 950

SOURCES: For 1941–1945, *Report of the Joint Brasil-United States Technical Commission*, Institute of Inter-American Affairs, FOA, Washington, D.C., 1954.
For 1946–1955, *Survey of the Brazilian Economy*, Brazilian Embassy, Washington, D.C., 1960.
For 1956–1961, Banco Central da República do Brasil, *Boletim* 2, no. 3 (March 1966).
For 1964–1966, IMF, *International Financial Statistics* 19, no. 10 (October 1966) and 20, no. 9 (September 1967).
a. Includes profits (remitted and reinvested), interest, royalties, and technical assistance contracts.
b. Includes travel, government expenditures, and other services.

allocation of United States resources to war production and consequent paucity of civilian-type commodities available for export to Brazil and other traditional markets. Brazil's exports, on the other hand, were greatly in demand. With technical and financial assistance from the United States, Brazil became an important source of strategic materials for the United States war effort; secondly, as other Latin American nations were cut off from traditional sources (the United States and Western Europe) of manufacturing imports, Brazil moved into this trade vacuum by supplying manufactured exports (particularly textiles) to her sister nations. The share of coffee in Brazil's total exports fell to about one-third in 1941–1945, while textile exports and strategic commodities each accounted for over 10 per cent of the nation's receipts from foreign buyers.

The cumulative surplus in Brazil's basic external balance during the 1941–1945 period of about $700 million greatly strengthened the nation's international liquidity position. Foreign reserves (gold and foreign exchange) of the Bank of Brazil soared from $60 million in 1940 to $760 million at the end of 1946. They were rather quickly eroded during the immediate postwar period. Because a part of the foreign reserves took the form of inconvertible sterling balances (and the United Kingdom's capacity to export had been impaired), the Brazilian government took the opportunity to purchase and nationalize four railway companies and port facilities which had heretofore been controlled by British investors. Another component of Brazil's accumulated reserves supported the purchase of consumer goods and capital goods abroad to satisfy pent-up demands. Much of Brazil's capital stock was worn out and its inventories depleted at the end of the war.[18]

Table 2 reveals that the periods 1946–1955 (roughly coinciding with the coffee boom) and 1956–1961 were characterized by heavy deficits in Brazil's basic balance on international account. To cover the cumulative deficit between 1946 and 1961 of over $1.5 billion, the monetary authorities had to resort to compensatory operations. These involved stabilization credits ("bail-out" loans) from the International Monetary Fund and the United States Export-Import Bank, as well as utilization of external reserves. Brazil's gold and foreign exchange holdings, as a consequence, declined by nearly $300 million (from $760 million in 1946 to $470 million at the end of 1961). Brazil's chronic external payments deficit in this period responded to a deepseated disequilibrium between demand (aggregate spending) and supply (productive capacity); the nation attempted to invest and consume more than was warranted by the limited resources at its command.

The inflow of private capital from abroad was greatly intensified during the administration of President Kubitschek and the "program of goals" (1956–1961) with which it became identified. The program established thirty targets for the concentration of investments, involving the elimination of structural bottlenecks in electric power and transportation and stimulation of strategic "growing points" in heavy industry. The steel, automotive, chemical, and machinery industries attained enormous advances over the program period in response to official incentives. President Kubitschek was Brazil's leading exponent of *desenvolvimentismo*, a kind of politico-economic mystique, which placed rapid economic development at the center of the political process. In contrast to many other "nation builders," he envisioned a crucial role for private enterprise:

18. Donald Huddle, "A Study of the Brazilian Exchange Auction System: 1953–57" (Ph.D. diss., Vanderbilt University, 1964).

I am decidedly in favor of the free-enterprise system, which is, in fact, made mandatory by our Constitution. I will do everything in my power to insure that Brazilian development will result from constant and intelligent endeavor on the part of free entrepreneurs, whatever their field, agriculture, industry or commerce—and whichever their origin—Brazilians or foreigners.

I am convinced, however, that the role of Government in the economic field should not be passive. On the contrary, the State must go forward and support private initiative in its effort to accumulate the nation's wealth and the equitable division of the fruits of progress.[19]

The incentive mechanism for attracting both direct investments and credits from abroad included preferential exchange treatment and freedom to remit earnings and capital. A very important instrument, the Law of Similars, applied the "carrot-stick" philosophy. It provided substantial protection to new industries locating in Brazil's growing national market, coupled with a threat of absolute exclusion. From 1956 to 1961 the gross inflow of private capital (including profits reinvested by foreign companies in Brazil) came to nearly $2.4 billion dollars, as shown below:

(IN MILLIONS OF U.S. DOLLARS)

Direct investment flow	215
Reinvested earnings	673
Loans and credits	1,419
Other	69
TOTAL	2,376

Foreign direct investments, outstanding at the beginning of the sixties, were highly diversified, both in their country origin and industrial distribution in Brazil.[20] For example, three-fourths of these investments were about equally divided between United States and Western European holdings, while Canadian, Japanese, and Argentine interests controlled most of the remainder. The foreign-controlled companies paced and stimulated Brazil's industrial advance during this period.

During 1962–1963 (the years associated mainly with the regime of President João Goulart) Brazil's basic deficit with the rest of the world assumed massive proportions ($343 million and $279 million, respectively). This period was marked by political demagoguery, an accelerated rate of infla-

19. *Survey of the Brazilian Economy, 1958*, Brazilian Embassy, Washington, D.C., pp. 93–94.
20. For a comprehensive analysis of foreign direct investment in Brazil, please see *New Perspectives of Brazil*, edited by Eric N. Baklanoff (Nashville: Vanderbilt University Press, 1966), chapter 4.

tion, and reduction in the rhythm of economic growth. The net inflow of foreign private capital (which had strongly supported the balance in 1956–1961) dropped sharply—from $225 million in 1961 to $42 million in 1963.[21] Thus, between 1946 and the end of 1963, Brazil's cumulative balance of payments deficit reached a figure of nearly $2.2 billion. As a consequence, the nation greatly increased its external debt while simultaneously depleting its foreign reserves.[22]

The Castelo Branco administration (April 1964–March 1967) reversed Brazil's chronic propensity for external deficits. By applying the "classical medicine" of stabilization and devaluation and improving the climate for investment, the new policymakers succeeded in sharply increasing the merchandise trade balance and restoring Brazil's credit abroad. The accumulation of a huge basic surplus of $950 million for the 1964–1966 period enabled Brazil to liquidate its commercial arrears with United States and European firms and to replenish its foreign reserves. At year end 1966, Brazil's gold and foreign exchange holdings of $600 million were nearly double the 1963 amount.

External Public Debt: Sources and Uses of Funds

The widespread defaults on foreign debts in the 1930's by Brazil and the great majority of the other Latin American nations closed the international bond market as a channel for attracting loan capital from abroad. Brazil did eventually negotiate refunding agreements with its foreign creditors, and service payments were resumed on the bond debt, although both interest and amortization obligations were scaled down substantially.

The bond market was replaced after World War II by an entirely new system of international credit, whose major elements included (1) intergovernmental loans and grants; (2) multilateral public lending institutions; and (3) medium-term equipment loans, extended by private enterprise but guaranteed by the governments of lending and borrowing nations. Brazil has received substantial accommodation from all of these sources, and this is reflected in its external debtor position as of the middle of 1965 (table 3). The major components of Brazil's medium- and long-term external debt include project financing ($1,446 million), compensatory financing ($1,198 million), and the funded bond debt of $75 million. "Project financing" covers outstanding official obligations to the Export-Import Bank, the World Bank, AID, and the Inter-American Development Bank—obligations which Brazil incurred in connection with infrastructure and industrial projects.

21. Banco Central da República do Brasil, *Boletim* 2, no. 3 (March 1966), p. 155.
22. Gold and foreign exchange holdings of Brazil's monetary authorities contracted by $440 million during this period.

Private entities, including mainly foreign suppliers of capital goods and foreign private banks, held an investment of $812 million in Brazil. The category "compensatory financing" represents outstanding obligations to the International Monetary Fund, the Export-Import Bank, the United States Treasury, and groups of commercial banks (both United States and European) for financing Brazil's recurring balance of payments deficits with the rest of the world.

The United States Export-Import Bank (Eximbank) has been the single most important source of external official funds for Brazil. The Eximbank,

TABLE 3

BRAZIL'S EXTERNAL MEDIUM- AND LONG-
TERM PUBLIC DEBT, JUNE 30, 1965
(IN MILLIONS OF U.S. DOLLARS)

I. Project financing, total	1,446
a) International or foreign official agencies	635
1) Inter-American Development Bank	167
2) IBRD (World Bank)	109
3) Export-Import Bank (U.S.)	221
4) AID (U.S.)	136
5) Other U.S. official agencies	2
b) Private foreign entities	812
1) United States	227
2) Italy	126
3) Japan	114
4) West Germany	101
5) France	81
6) Other countries	163
II. Compensatory financing operation, total	1,198
a) International Monetary Fund	189
b) Export-Import Bank (U.S.)	510
c) U.S. Treasury	217
d) Consolidation and re-scheduling agreements (1961–1964):	161
e) Banking consortia loans	121
III. External funded bond debt	75
TOTAL medium- and long-term debt	2,720

SOURCE: *Survey of the Brazilian Economy, 1965*, Brazilian Embassy, Washington, D.C., pp. 224–25, table 106.

in addition to balance of payments ("bail-out") credits, has also extended equipment loans for projects including such diverse fields as shipping, road building, steel production, railways, electric power, manganese mining, and agricultural mechanization.[23] Unlike loans extended by the World Bank and the Inter-American Bank, the credits made available by the Eximbank are tied; that is, the loan proceeds must be spent in the United States.

The more recently organized Inter-American Development Bank (IDB) has taken an active role in financing Brazil's economic and social develop-

23. Information received from Mr. Glenn E. McLaughlin, vice-president, Export-Import Bank of Washington, June 9, 1964.

ment. Commitments as of the end of 1966 exceeded $400 million, and the total cost of projects for which IDB has acted as catalytic agent comes to several times that amount.[24] About half the credits ($194 million) have been allocated to projects in industry, agriculture, electric power, and technical assistance. These are conventional "hard" loans drawn from the bank's ordinary capital resources. IDB is also interested in "social" investments such as low-cost housing, water supply and sanitation, and education. These "soft" loans (sometimes repayable in local currencies) generally carry very long maturities and provide for low (1¼ –4 percent) interest rates. Social project loans in Brazil have been channeled through a wide spectrum of public entities such as Banco do Nordeste, SUDENE, Banco do Estado de Guanabara, municipal departments, and the Comissão de Planejamento Econômico de Bahia. The sources of social investment credits are the bank's "Fund for Special Operations" and the "Social Progress Trust Fund." The administration of the latter was turned over to IDB in 1961 by the United States government and constitutes one of the important channels of "Alliance for Progress" assistance.

Brazil has also borrowed heavily from foreign private lenders to finance development projects, particularly in the "program of goals" period (1956–1961). Brazil's intensified utilization of foreign suppliers' credits to finance the importation of equipment coincided with the decline of its exports. The re-emergence of Western Europe and Japan in the international economy, with the assistance of the Marshall Plan (1948–1951), encouraged competition among the industrial nations for the markets in the less-developed nations. The erosion of Brazil's export earnings (after the fadeout of the coffee boom), together with the progressively larger fiscal deficits, now precluded the possibility of using other, less costly, forms of international finance. The World Bank, it should be remembered, suspended its loan commitments to Brazil from the fall of 1958 to the spring of 1965. As a result, medium-term suppliers' credits accounted for a major share of the $900 million increment in Brazil's external public debt between 1955 ($1.4 billion) and 1963 ($2.3 billion). A recent World Bank report warned of the dangers of indiscriminate accumulation of medium-term debt:

> In many cases, the maturities are too short and interest rates too high in relation to the debtor country's capacity for servicing its debt. Also, suppliers' credits are often employed in excessive concentrations at a particular period of time, so that maturities are bunched too closely together.[25]

24. Inter-American Development Bank, *Seventh Annual Report, 1966*, Washington, D.C., 1967.
25. International Bank for Reconstruction and Development, *World Bank and IDA, 1965–1966 Annual Report*, p. 34.

By 1962–1963 debt service (amortization and interest) absorbed 36 per cent, on average, of Brazil's exports.

The link between exports (goods) and loans (capital) does not create optimum conditions for the deployment of scarce resources. This basic principle of international economics is brought out in a recent publication of the Organization of American States:

> Tied loans limit the selection available to the purchaser. From the standpoint of the underdeveloped countries, this runs counter to the principle of free markets and free enterprise advocated by the industrialized countries. If the principle of purchase in the cheapest market is valid for domestic economic relations, it should be equally applicable to international economic relations.[26]

NEW DIRECTIONS: THE SYSTEMATIC USE
OF THE INTERNATIONAL ECONOMY

The Castelo Branco administration, which assumed power in April 1964, inherited an economy characterized by stagnation in output, rampant and accelerating inflation, and a major international liquidity crisis. The Brazilian industrial growth rate, for example, dropped from an average 9.6 per cent per annum during the 1947–1961 period to 6 per cent in 1962 and to less than 1 per cent in 1963. The country's international credit position was gravely impaired. Brazil's external debt of roughly $3 billion, both voluntary (autonomous loans) and involuntary (deficit financing), pushed Brazil to the edge of external default, as $1.3 billion in service payments were scheduled to mature in 1964–1965. Brazil's gold and foreign exchange reserves at the end of 1963 were the lowest year-end total in over a decade, and a large share of Brazil's gold was already pledged as guarantee for loans from the United States. Foreign direct investment, which had paced the nation's extraordinary industrial advance between 1956 and 1961, came to an abrupt halt toward the end of the Goulart regime.

Under the leadership of Minister of Economic Planning and Coordination Roberto Campos, an outstanding economist and former ambassador to Washington, the government prepared an Economic Action Program for 1964–1966 as a comprehensive guide to policy and for submission to the Inter-American Committee on the Alliance for Progress. The committee subsequently approved it for presentation to official international financial agencies. The three-year program focused upon stabilization as part of a broader plan to reactivate the growth of the economy on a sound basis.

26. OAS, Department of Economic Affairs, *The Effects of the European Economic Community on the Latin American Economies* (Washington: Pan American Union, 1963), p. 60.

Foreign economic policies and measures centered on Brazil's precarious international economic position. The new administration had to regain the confidence of the world financial community to reschedule the nation's external debts and reactivate the inflow of long-term private capital. More fundamentally, Brazil had to find a way to materially increase its capacity to import such vital commodities as machinery and equipment, raw materials, and fuels, on which its future economic prospects hinged. A trade promotion policy was shaped, with emphasis on export diversification. Obstacles which had deterred investment in export-oriented industries were removed. Import subsidies for newsprint, wheat, and petroleum were abolished, thereby strengthening both the central government's budget and Brazil's balance of payments.

The Castelo Branco administration took a series of dramatic steps to stimulate the flow of foreign business investment to Brazil. These included (1) an amendment to the abortive Profit Remittance Law of 1962, (2) an agreement to compensate the American and Foreign Power Company for ten utility plants nationalized during Goulart's term of office, and (3) the signing of an investment guarantee treaty with the United States. Two additional measures should prove of vital significance to Brazil's long-range development. One of them was a decision taken by the government to bring private enterprise into the petrochemical industry for the manufacture of products considered of vital importance to Brazil. Second, Brazil's prospects for diversifying and expanding exports have been significantly raised by the government's new iron-ore policy. A presidential decree signed in December 1964 called for private competitive development of the country's vast iron-ore reserves in preference to virtually exclusive dependence on government enterprise. The decree, reversing a trend toward state monopoly of mineral development, aimed at increasing Brazil's share of world iron-ore trade, thereby raising the country's foreign exchange earnings and national income.

The subsequent Costa e Silva administration (March 1967–August 1969) continued to provide a favorable investment climate for foreign enterprise. Not surprisingly, therefore, the flow of foreign investments (including reinvested earnings) to Brazil reached $1,250 million between 1966 and 1968, according to data released by the Central Bank.[27] In 1966 the total was $306 million; in 1967 it was $548 million; and in 1968, $397 million.

Following the drafting and submission of the new administration's Economic Action Program, the World Bank, the International Monetary Fund, and the Inter-American Development Bank sent missions to Brazil, whose findings generated a massive economic assistance package for Brazil, includ-

27. *Brazilian Bulletin* 24, no. 505 (June 1969), p. 5.

ing project loans from the United States and other friendly governments.[28] In addition to receiving two $125 million "stand-by" credits from the International Monetary Fund, the government succeeded in consolidating short-term external obligations into long-term debts. Significantly, accommodations were reached with both private and official creditors abroad.

Major loans for transport, power, industry and mining, and education totalling as much as $1 billion were announced by World Bank President Robert MacNamara during his conference in Rio with Brazilian authorities in 1968. According to preliminary studies, credit could be drawn over a four-year period in the amount of $405 million for transport, $200 million for electric power, $150 million for industry and mining, and $100 million for education.[29]

Misgivings of influential Brazilians concerning the single-minded import-substitution policy and the associated inattention given to the promotion of foreign trade were evident in Brazil before the new policy orientation. For example, the government's basic program, prepared by the Council of Ministers under Premier Tancredo Neves, recognized that Brazil's dependence on imports would increase sharply and that a corresponding rise in exports was imperative.[30] Unfortunately, the program did not go beyond the planning phase. A major shift in political power was required in order to implement the new economic ideas. Vasco Leitão da Cunha, Brazil's first foreign minister under the Castelo Branco administration, gave voice to this new direction:

> The promising stage of relatively easy development of industrial-ization—based on substituting local production for imports—appears about to reach its end in Brazil.
> An excessive zeal to produce exclusively for domestic consumption has contributed to a virtual stagnation of export activities. In reality, the export of manufactured products should be the natural complement for our industrialization.[31]

The government's Action Program advocated "an aggressive policy of diversification and expansion of exports to all areas of the world, especially to the LAFTA area, whether of traditional products, new primary products, or manufactured products."[32] Official measures in support of this dynamic export policy were continued and consolidated by the government of Pres-

28. *Brazilian Bulletin* 23, no. 677 (January–February 1967).
29. *Brazilian Bulletin* 24, no. 498 (November 1968), p. 3.
30. "Objectives and Instruments of a Development Policy," *Brazilian Bulletin*, Special Supplement (November 1–15, 1961).
31. *Brazilian Bulletin* 20, no. 457 (December 1, 1964).
32. *The 1964/1966 Action Program of the Brazilian Government*, analytical summary prepared for the Ministry of Planning by Benjamin Higgins, pp. v–1.

ident Artur Costa e Silva. These included the following: (1) realistic exchange rates for exports, automatically adjustable to offset domestic loss in purchasing power from inflation; (2) reorganization of bureaucratic export procedures; (3) simplification of drawback procedures (the process of refunding custom duties on imported raw materials for use in the production of export products); and (4) establishment of credit facilities and insurance coverage for Brazilian exports. Thus, obstacles which have deterred investment in export-oriented activities—overvalued exchange rates, administrative red tape, paucity of export finance, congested ports, and chauvinistic mineral policies—were being removed. Further, to help reduce costs of production and improve the competitiveness of Brazilian industry, the government in 1967 initiated a far-reaching import liberalization program which reduced average import duties and exchange premiums to about a third of what they had been in 1964.[33]

In response to the new iron-ore policy, an affiliate of the Hanna Mining Company and Brazil's Antunes group formed a joint-venture, Minerações Brasileiras Reunidas (MBR), in which the Brazilian group holds 51 per cent of the stock. The company plans to invest in iron-ore mining, pelletizing mills, steel-manufacturing facilities, a railroad link, and the construction of maritime terminals. The Antunes-Hanna combine, with holdings of nearly 1 billion tons of high-grade iron ore in the state of Minas Gerais, signed a $900 million contract in April 1970 to supply 105 million tons of ore to six Japanese steel companies over a sixteen-year period.[34] If the Brazilian government approves the contract, shipments will rise to a level of 7 million tons a year by 1973 compared with 600,000 tons annually in the recent past.

Another promising line for export expansion is meat products, and the World Bank has already indicated that it plans to finance a $50 million share of the $100 million cattle-development program.[35] A recent study on the livestock industry in Latin America reports that Brazil has immense natural resources which could enable it to become a leading exporter of meat.[36] Investment in improved pastures could substantially expand grazing area, thereby supporting a livestock population several times larger than at present. Over the medium- and long-term, the outlook is bright and depends in part on improvement in stock-farming techniques and creation of new processing facilities such as meat-packing plants and a network of cold-storage depots at shipping points. The cattle-development program will mainly affect the state of Rio Grande do Sul and central Brazil.

33. Inter-American Development Bank, *Social Progress Trust Fund Eighth Annual Report, 1968* (Washington, D.C., 1969), p. 81.
34. *The Wall Street Journal* (April 17, 1970), p. 18.
35. *Brazilian Bulletin* 22, no. 471 (July 1966).
36. ECLA and FAO, *Livestock in Latin America, II Brazil* (New York, 1964).

The sale of four ships to Mexico in 1964 opened the way for Brazil to become the main supplier for the Latin American Free Trade Association. Since 1960 Brazil has developed an impressive naval construction capacity with sixteen shipyards capable of building vessels of any type or size up to 65,000 tons deadweight each. Foreign capital, especially Japanese, is closely associated with the nation's shipbuilding industry and production of marine engines. Production costs in Brazil for these products are currently approaching world prices.

As a major supplier nation in the International Coffee Organization, Brazil has taken the lead to combat coffee's central problem: oversupply. With government assistance, Brazil's coffee growers are being induced to plow under coffee trees in order to curtail capacity by one-fifth, to match home demand and desirable exports. Simultaneously, coffee planters are being encouraged to shift their coffee land to the production of rice, beans, corn, and other crops in relatively short supply. If these measures succeed, the government will save more in reduced coffee support subsidies than the cost of the program, while at the same time stimulating agricultural diversification.

Thus far, the export drive has succeeded handsomely. The value of Brazil's total exports, which averaged $1.3 billion in 1962–1963, reached $1.7 billion in 1967, $1.9 billion in 1968, and surpassed $2.2 billion in 1969. Significantly, this large increment was achieved via export diversification rather than from increases in the nation's traditional export commodities: coffee, cotton, and cacao. Dramatic growth was registered in the export of iron ore, beef products, and in manufactures. Exports of manufactured goods, exceeding $280 million in 1969, have been one of the most dynamic components of the current account in Brazil's balance of payments.[37]

RECAPITULATION AND PROSPECTS

Brazil's economy was initially transformed and shaped by the international commodity, capital, and labor markets. The nation offered the natural resource base and unskilled labor; the rest of the world supplied much of the capital, technical know-how, and entrepreneurship.

Foreign capital played a decisive role in the construction and operation of railways, electric power plants, and urban infrastructure—and in forging the vital financial and commercial links between Brazil and the rest of the world. Foreign enterprise and its associated capital in Brazil represented the extension of the emerging European and, later, United States industrial revolutions.

Between the middle of the nineteenth century and 1930, Brazil's economy was on the ascendant as coffee provided the thrust for a protracted era of

37. *Brazilian Bulletin* 25, no. 513 (February 1970), p. 3.

export prosperity. Rising coffee exports (in terms of price and quantity) could be translated into a growing volume of imports and an expanding capacity to service Brazil's overseas debt and effect profit remittances. Exports, borrowing abroad, the inflow of direct investments, and immigration were interdependent and mutually supporting factors. The system rested precariously on the fortunes of Brazilian coffee.

The preconditions for Brazil's subsequent industrial revolution—abundant electric power, transportation and communication facilities, labor and entrepreneurial resources, and important urban centers—were largely created between 1850 and 1930.

With the disintegration of the international economy in the early 1930's, Brazil was compelled to seek a new development path. The "export economy" gave way to an "investment-government expenditure economy." In the next three decades Brazil's economy was characterized by the single-minded cultivation of the home market. The combined effects of the depression, World War ii, and the postwar industrialization drive evoked a fundamental change in Brazil's economic structure. On the positive side, Brazil achieved an impressive profile of manufacturing industries, commanding a wide range of consumer and capital goods. The heady coffee boom (1948–1954) was followed by a massive inflow of private capital (1956–1961) from abroad; both of these factors helped maintain the rapid general and industrial rates of growth.

There was also a negative aspect which must be considered. The overthrow of the Goulart regime in the early part of 1964 marked the close of the second phase in Brazil's economic evolution. Extending for about three decades, from the bottom of the Great Depression, this stage was characterized by a philosophy of government tutelage, the shielding of private enterprises from the cold winds of competition, favoritism in the securing of easy credit and foreign exchange, and highly subsidized public corporations. This philosophy and the policies which gave it expression led to progressive inflation, stagnation in the volume of exports, and the accumulation of an unsupportable external debt. Export initiatives were deterred by the import-substitution policies associated with industrialization. As a consequence, during the long period 1939–1963, Brazil failed to materially diversify its export structure. The excess monetary demand, generated largely by government-induced inflation, resulted in a huge deficit in Brazil's basic payments balance with the rest of the world. By the early 1960's an overhang of this "involuntary" debt plus the substantial buildup of medium-term suppliers' credits left Brazil with a crushing burden of foreign debt service obligations.

The current phase in Brazil's development, initiated by the Castelo Branco administration and consolidated by the Costa e Silva regime, seeks to put an end to three decades of official paternalism and move Brazil into the camp of nations which can effectively compete in the world economy. The implementation of the new economic philosophy will involve placing the public sector under more rational control while providing a framework within which a modern, competitive enterprise system with cooperation of private foreign capital can work to promote the economic development of Brazil. The new philosophy has important implications for Brazil's foreign economic policies. In sharp contrast to the past, Brazilians will have to cultivate an "export mentality." To encourage the inflow of loan capital into infrastructure projects at reasonable terms, the nation will have to maintain domestic and external equilibrium. Careful management of Brazil's external debt will have to replace the haphazard operations of the past. To build a viable industrial structure, Brazil must continue to rely on foreign managerial and technical resources, through the inflow of direct investment and the use of licensing agreements.

The new policymakers have shifted the emphasis to the world market without, however, abandoning industrialization programs. In their view, the alternative to an export drive is stagnation. They have recognized that exports must rise if Brazil is to pay for the growing requirements of specialized raw materials and capital goods associated with development. "Exports," as Minister of Economic Planning Roberto Campos so aptly put it, "continue to exercise a decisive influence on the economic development of the country, since it is only through foreign trade that we can transform an appreciable proportion of local savings into concrete investment."[38] Moreover, exports must grow if Brazil is to meet its service obligations on its external debt. The more effective the export drive, the better the borrowing terms on foreign loans. Export diversification with strong initiatives concentrated on mineral, livestock, and manufactured products represent a good prospect for the future.

The foreign economic policies pursued since April 1964 have achieved notable results. Brazil's credit in the international financial community has been re-established, resulting in large commitments to the nation from the World Bank and Inter-American Development Bank. Foreign-exchange receipts have increased sharply via export diversification rather than from increases in Brazil's traditional export commodities. Finally, substantial foreign business investments (many in joint ventures with Brazilian groups) are flowing into Brazil's petrochemical, steel, shipbuilding, automotive, iron-ore, and aluminum industries.

The unpopular but necessary economic measures applied by the Castelo Branco and Costa e Silva regimes have laid the groundwork for that more "humane" economy that can ultimately emerge from the dynamic interdependence of Brazil and the international economy.

38. *Brazil '66*, special edition of *Direção* (December 1965–January 1966), p. 43.

The Amazonian rain forest is a virtually untapped natural resource.

The product of this São Paulo coffee *fazenda*, while still a mainstay, is yielding to increasing diversification as the Brazilian economy grows.

Gaúchos are the backbone of Rio Grande do Sul's pastoral economy.

In Ceará, farm women learn to weave hats, baskets, and handbags.

Primary education is now within reach of a large majority of Brazilian children. These have built a classroom "zoo."

Secondary education has expanded rapidly in response to the rising aspirations of a growing middle class.

Manchete from Pictorial

Former President Getúlio Vargas, probably the most influential leader in modern Brazilian history.

USIA

Thousands rejoiced at the change in government in Rio de Janeiro in April 1964.

Following the illness of President Costa e Silva, Brazil was governed by a military tribunal headed by Admiral Augusto Rademaker, top.

Midtown São Paulo reflects the rapid pace of development in southern Brazil.

Many new expressways have been constructed to relieve traffic congestion in Rio de Janeiro.

Intensive migration to Rio de Janeiro from rural areas has contributed to the development of hillside favelas.

Manchete from Pictorial

The São Paulo produce market is a miniature city where 20,000 work and one million dollars changes hands daily.

Esso Standard do Brasil

"Made in Brazil" interurban buses in a São Paulo garage. Bus transportation is growing at an accelerating rate.

Volta Redonda, Brazil's first large steel mill, has provided raw materials for Brazil's growing manufacturing industry.

Another view of the Volta Redonda steel mill.

The Volta Redonda mills located between Rio and São Paulo produces high quality steel.

The Duque de Caxias petroleum refiners, one of several, helps meet the increasing demand for petroleum products.

The Volkswagen 1600 sedan, as well as other makes and models manufactured in São Paulo plants, are making the personal auto a common possession of Brazil's middle class.

An extraordinary highway network is bringing remote corners of the nation into closer communication.

The construction of Brasília, although controversial, crystallized national pride.

Heitor Villa Lobos, composer-conductor, won international renown for his modern works.

Joaquim Maria Machado de Assis, recognized as one of the hemisphere's leading novelists.

Nisão Chara creates a world of acrylic pyramids shown behind an arc of chrome steel at the Modern Art Biennial of São Paulo.

Chapter 9

Agriculture and the Economic Development of Brazil

William H. Nicholls

"Se o fundilho agüentar, vou até São Paulo!"
—HUMBERTO DE CAMPOS[1]

THE ROLE of agriculture in economic development depends heavily upon the stage of economic history in which a nation finds itself and—especially at the time that economic progress first becomes a major social aspiration—usually depends upon the ratio of agricultural land to population. The relative emphasis which public policy gives to agriculture, and the particular forms which agricultural policies should take, must therefore vary accordingly.

Fortunately for Brazil, the official adoption of economic (especially industrial) development as a national goal—largely a phenomenon of the period since 1947—came before its agricultural frontiers had disappeared. As a result, nationally if not always regionally, even today Brazil's land / man ratio is relatively favorable, so that, even without increases in agricultural productivity, Brazil has thus far been able to expand food production (by using more land) more or less in pace with its population growth, at constant relative prices. Hence, while much of its agriculture is still technologically very backward, Brazil has been able to start its process of development and national economic integration from a relatively favorable food base rather than from one of severe overpopulation and food scarcity, such as most Asian countries now face.

Less fortunately, however, Brazilian economic planners have allowed this still favorable situation in food production to lull them into a sense of false complacency which hardly squares with the prospect of the approach-

1. This quotation is the punchline of a Brazilian tale in which—attempting to travel by train from Rio de Janeiro without purchasing a ticket—one Gaudêncio is repeatedly kicked off at each successive way-station. At last, seizing him by the throat, the conductor demands, "How far are you going with this joke?" With shameless mien, Gaudêncio replies, "If the seat of my pants holds out, I am going as far as São Paulo!"

ing disappearance of its best remaining agricultural frontiers; a 3.5 percent annual rate of population growth, reinforced by the still large effects of rising per capita incomes upon the demand for food; and a rate of growth in urban population of 5–6 per cent per annum. This complacency also ignores the high costs of catching up from centuries of neglect of the infrastructure, not only in providing utilities and public services for the burgeoning cities, but also in at last beginning to meet the rural sector's needs for education, transportation, research and extension services, and other essential public investments.

Since, from now on, Brazil must increasingly be concerned with achieving higher agricultural efficiency as well as higher food output, its long neglect of the rural infrastructure means that it must now start from a relatively low level of agricultural productivity, largely associated with the primitive labor-intensive techniques of a hoe agriculture.

BRAZILIAN AGRICULTURE IN HISTORICAL
PERSPECTIVE

The backwardness of Brazilian agriculture is curious if one compares Brazil historically with other "new" countries such as the United States, Canada, Australia, and (until the 1940's) even Argentina. Initially underpopulated and having an abundance of land, the latter countries were soon able to achieve an agriculture characterized by high capital/labor ratios, optimum-sized farming units, a readiness to use mechanical devices, and a high rate of capital formation. Under such circumstances, since population growth was a positive asset, large-scale immigration was encouraged, a pervasive spirit of optimism prevailed, and substantial imports of foreign capital were attracted (particularly for the transportation developments which opened up their vast hinterlands).

Thus, almost from the very outset, these new countries were able to produce large food and fiber surpluses for which, thanks to the Industrial Revolution, they found rapidly growing markets in England and Western Europe. Finally, by their early attainment of political independence or enlightened dominion status, they freed themselves of the mercantilistic restraints on their general economic development, which the imperial powers of Europe commonly imposed upon their colonies. As a consequence, with agricultural (especially labor) productivity initially high and increasing at a relatively steady pace, agriculture provided a firm foundation for subsequent balanced economic development without ever becoming a bottleneck to further general progress.

For a complex of geographical, politico-historical, social, and cultural reasons, Brazilian agriculture did not play a similar favorable role in contributing to overall economic development—at least until modern times, when coffee became the basis for the vigorous growth and general development of the region centering in São Paulo. Each of the various previous "booms" (called *ciclos* by Brazilians appropriately, if one also notes the absence of an upward long-run secular trend) for a time had produced fabulous prosperity only to fade away as suddenly with few lasting general economic benefits. Even the initial sugar boom in the northeast—which Furtado has estimated produced in 1600 a per capita income of $350 (not again achieved in Brazil until 1960) for the then 30,000 Brazilians of European origin—proved to be abortive as foreign producers during the seventeenth century achieved and then surpassed the original technical superiority of Brazilian cane production. The initial impetus which Recife and Salvador gave to the settlement of the *sertão* as sources of food, oxen, and fuel for the sugar zones was lost with their economic decline, the *sertão* thereafter sinking into a purely subsistence economy, only occasionally revived by brief cotton booms when wars (1776, 1812, 1860) temporarily cut England off from its usual source of supply, the United States South.

The gold rush of the eighteenth century, apart from shifting the politico-economic center of gravity southward and stimulating considerable immigration, also made little contribution to long-run economic growth. While it temporarily lifted the south's agriculture out of a largely subsistence economy, the demand for cattle, work animals, and food largely disappeared as the gold played out in Minas Gerais. Bahia's cocoa boom and the Amazonian rubber boom of the late nineteenth and early twentieth centuries similarly produced disappointing long-run effects, as more efficient and rational foreign competition overcame Brazil's initial world leadership. The consequence of this economic history of repeated booms and busts was a persistent tradition of exploitation and speculation, well-expressed by the popular saying, *"Plantando dá, mas quem planta?"* Why plant, when the Nature of the exuberant tropics is so bountiful that one can reap without sowing? Or, if one must plant, why conserve when there is always virgin land to take the place of land worn out?

However, simply to blame Brazil's economic underdevelopment on such an exploitative attitude is to miss the main point. United States history is also replete with severe exploitation of natural resources and speculative activity. Indeed, so long as land is so relatively plentiful as to be virtually a "free good," its exploitation is *economic*, so long as the soil is merely depleted and not physically destroyed by erosion or other forces causing irreparable damage. Much of the westward march of American agriculture (notably cotton and wheat production) to expanding agricultural frontiers left in its wake exhausted lands and abandoned farms, just as did the march of sugar and cotton from the northeast to São Paulo and the march of coffee across São Paulo and Paraná. The California gold rush appealed no less to men's greed than that of Minas Gerais. The difference lies in how these "ill-gotten" gains were used and in whether, when more conservative farming practices did become economic because of the increasing scarcity of land, farmers' attitudes changed and whether sound technical advice was available to make conservative measures effective and efficient.

In the United States (and in São Paulo) these fruits of agricultural exploitation more largely found their way into savings and private domestic capital formation (initially in agricultural development but increasingly in the domestic nonagricultural sector as well), while in most of Brazil they were dissipated in private and public "conspicuous consumption." In the United States the fruits of exploitation also helped to support substantial investment in social overhead (especially transportation, education, and public agricultural services), an essential need seriously neglected in Brazil although somewhat less so in São Paulo than in the nation at large. Thus, the real costs of exploitation were much more than offset by the general developmental benefits which resulted from rapid capital formation, in terms of both tangibles and (through human investment) intangibles, making the nation, on balance, richer rather than poorer and turning economic development into a self-sustaining process. Even in the United States, a national interest in the conservation of soil and other natural resources did not develop until the frontier had disappeared with the completion of human settlement around 1900; by then, the agricultural colleges and experiment stations established several decades earlier were ready to fill the breach. With Brazil approaching the same stage today, its need for more conservative agricultural practices (and public technical orientation to this end) is still inadequately recognized. Even so, in old agricultural regions whose access to major urban markets is unusually favorable (as in the *Agreste* of Pernambuco or São Paulo's Paraíba Valley), many private landowners are already finding it economical to rehabilitate their land and modernize their techniques, particularly in milk and poultry production—much as New England did in modern times.

The relative stagnancy of agricultural productivity in Brazil must also be viewed in historical perspective. In the United States, farm output per unit of *all* inputs (not just labor or land inputs) showed very modest gains during 1870–1900, remained virtually constant during 1900–1930, and only thereafter showed a spectacular upward trend. Similarly, as late as 1910–1939, the index of crop yields per acre in the United States remained virtually constant over time, rising sharply only after 1940 as the use of hybrid corn, other improved seed, insecticides, and commercial fertilizers expanded rapidly. During 1910–1960, with the American frontiers gone, total cropland in the United States remained nearly constant, but, with its relative price rising, land was used more intensively as (in effect) other inputs were substituted for land—first, by the shift from home-produced feed crops (the "fuel" for work animals) to purchased tractor fuels, freeing much cropland for food production; and, second, by the increasing use of such purchased yield-increasing inputs as hybrid seed and fertilizers. It should also be noted that most of these land substitutes are products of agricultural research and the industrial sector, upon which agriculture must increasingly depend for the modern inputs needed at remunerative prices for its own technical progress.

If one recognizes that Brazilian agriculture is today at the stage of that of the United States in the late nineteenth century, the present relative constancy of Brazil's crop yields is more easily explained. In agricultural production Brazil still depends much more heavily than the United States on land inputs, since in Brazil land remains a less scarce factor, making most land substitutes (particularly given the greater scarcity of capital) less economical than in the United States. To a large extent, Brazil has been able to maintain average crop yields at a constant rather than declining level only because the high yields of new lands have approximately offset the declining yields of old lands. However, in certain crops (notably rice and potatoes) and livestock products the more favorably located old regions—with lower transportation costs and readier access to urban markets—are already finding it economical to use modern purchased yield-increasing inputs such as improved seeds, fertilizer, and feed supplements. More important, in other major agricultural regions, there are leading landowners who are quite ready to accept the use of such purchased inputs as their use becomes economical, although they, like all progressive farmers in Brazil, still lack the technical orientation, based on sound agricultural research, needed to know when and how to use such inputs properly and profitably.

The fact that Brazilian crop yields are far lower than in other parts of the world thus far largely reflects a situation in which it still pays to use more (cheap) land and less (expensive) capital to produce a given output. However, as the closing of the frontier proceeds in the face of rapid population growth and urbanization, land substitutes should become increasingly profitable, with favorable effects on crop yields. Whether agriculture does respond with increasing yields, as these become necessary for meeting burgeoning domestic food needs, will of course depend upon whether appropriate policies are adopted in time. Because Brazilian crop yields are so low, the potential for raising them is very great—a situation which is far more favorable than that of certain severely overpopulated countries (such as Egypt) which, having already largely exhausted not only the available land *but also most yield-increasing opportunities*, now have virtually no place to turn except to population control. However, the realization of potentially much higher crop yields in Brazil will require both much better public agricultural services (especially research) and adequate supplies (at remunerative prices) of fertilizers, insecticides, and other modern inputs, the latter requiring either sufficient imports or efficient domestic manufactures of these essential production goods. On both scores, there is presently much ground for uneasiness.

On the side of agricultural services, Brazil's long neglect of both education and technical and economic research makes one doubt that it will be ready to meet farmers' needs for general and specialized knowledge as these needs become more urgent. The United States' experience suggests that the gestation period for the application of science to agricultural problems is relatively long, but that the ultimate "pay-off" can be nothing short of spectacular. While the United States already had in the 1930's a vast storehouse of agricultural knowledge—and a large investment in the literacy and general education of its farm population and in well-developed transportation and marketing systems—only the strong economic incentives of World War II and the postwar period brought the rapid adoption of this improved technology. With the substantial shift of America's surplus rural population into more remunerative nonfarm employment after 1940, mechanization of agriculture (long underway) was also greatly accelerated, indicating the importance of sound industrial-urban development in stimulating agricultural progress. The United States' experience suggests the wisdom of public policies favorable to industrial-urban progress but also underlines the fact that only with a concomitant policy of agricultural improvement can agriculture be a full partner in, rather than a major barrier to, general economic development.

On the side of industrial development, recent Brazilian public policy also creates many misgivings. The forced-draft industrialization policies of the last two decades have been largely financed at the expense of the agricultural and rural sectors. To be sure, the attempt during the 1950's to divert much of the foreign earnings of coffee to financing domestic industrialization, through a multiple exchange-rate system which strongly discriminated against coffee producers and as strongly favored imports of industrial machinery, largely failed, as growing coffee surpluses had to be financed by national coffee price-support policies—public resources which might better have been used to improve the efficiency of food production. More important, however, was the use of inflation as a means of creating "forced savings" by the population at large—bearing down most heavily on real salaries and wages, especially those of the rural cash-wage laboring class, while favoring those (primarily selected industrialists) who were the principal beneficiaries of the public credits which allocated the inflation-creating output of printing-press money. Landowners, and tenants (such as sharecroppers and *moradores*) whose income was largely in kind, initially suffered less from inflation but were increasingly squeezed by the rising relative prices of purchased agricultural inputs, particularly so insofar as gains in efficiency failed to offset the advance in their production costs. The rise in the latter also reflected the substitution of higher-cost domestically pro- duced agricultural inputs for cheaper imports of the same goods. Finally, the new industries favored by public policy had an anti-employment bias, because they were relatively capital-intensive and largely directed toward production of consumer goods with a relatively restricted market in the upper-income classes. Thus, their ability to absorb surplus rural workers was much more limited than the high rate of urbanization called for.

For this and other reasons, the greatest lag in Brazilian agricultural pro- ductivity has involved its *labor* component. Throughout the history of those "new" countries which have shown the highest rates of general eco- nomic development, the relative scarcity of labor constantly encouraged the invention and widespread adoption of mechanical techniques in the form of stationary motors, animal-drawn equipment, and, ultimately, trac- torization. As a result, even while crop yields and overall agricultural pro- ductivity were remaining virtually constant for long periods of time, farm output *per worker* tended to rise steadily at a rapid rate. A partial exception was the United States South, which, like Brazil, developed a plantation sys- tem (rather than the family farms which typified the rest of American agriculture) and solved its problem of labor shortage by the institution of slavery. Slavery not only undermined the dignity of labor as an important cultural value but created an attitude which viewed the slave as an input not subject to technical improvement, either directly or in terms of the equipment with which he worked. It also created a social organization un- favorable to public investment in mass education and other essential social services, affecting adversely not only the worker families on the larger land- holdings but also the many but politically subsumed independent farmers who, having settled in the more remote and less productive lands of the same region, eked out a mere subsistence—even the latter being constantly threatened by their propensity to produce numerous children in a highly unfavorable social environment.

Despite these similarities between the United States South and Brazil, even the former—while lagging far behind the remainder of the United States in terms of farm-labor productivity and industrialization—was at least able to maintain a sufficient level of productive efficiency to more than hold its own in world markets (in part because of the cheapness of food produced in the United States Midwest) against the competition of Brazil and other tropical and subtropical countries. Nonetheless, like Brazil (and particularly its northeast), the United States South's relative agricultural backwardness rested largely on an excessive rural labor supply which rural-to-urban migration could not solve alone, even with rapid industrial-urban development, until the latter moved closer to the rural labor of the less advantaged regions. For this reason, the agrarian tradition common to the American South and Brazil—both of which long accepted the role of specialization on a few primary export products, exchanged for needed industrial imports, while favoring "free-trade" policy and a hierarchical social structure and viewing industrial-urban life as an inferior way of life—increasingly proved to be an inadequate base for general economic development. The result was relatively static labor productivity and (for the masses) low and stagnant per capita incomes.

Hence, the rather recent shift, in both the American South and Brazil, toward favoring the stimulation of its own industrial development had real economic merit, even if "nationalistic" emotionalism was often the principal motivation. As an important by-product, the stagnating socio-political and economic effects of the ancient agrarian tradition are being gradually eroded away. However, the dangers of an emotional rather than rational approach to this problem are likely to be too little emphasis upon expanding urban employment—because of a bias in favor of those industries and production techniques which are capital- rather than labor-intensive and which serve limited rather than mass markets—and so great a neglect of agriculture that it may become the effective limiting factor (bottleneck) on the growth of the other sectors. These dangers are today a very real threat to further Brazilian economic development, particularly since—sheltered from foreign competition by severe import restrictions and from domestic competition by the concentration of public credits on the favored few—the new industry faces few pressures to achieve greater production efficiency or to lower product prices to farmers and urban consumers.

THE REGIONAL DIVERSITY OF BRAZILIAN
AGRICULTURE

Thus far we have made some broad generalizations about Brazilian agriculture as a whole. Before proceeding further, however, we must pause to recognize the extreme diversity of agriculture in Brazil.

Given the vastness of Brazil's land area, it is most remarkable that it was able to survive as a single nation some four centuries with the most inadequate facilities for transportation and communication. Having visited every state and territory of Brazil, I have been surprised by the regional similarities—although my various Brazilian companions were struck by the differences—in accent, cuisine, customs, and outlook in a situation which might have produced the same political fragmentation of Portuguese America as did occur in Spanish America. This incredible ability to preserve for so long a sense of unity and nation-consciousness—thereby keeping Brazil politically integrated despite its huge size—undoubtedly reflects the genius of the Portuguese American to accommodate; his acceptance of moderation and compromise in matters of internal conflict; and the effectiveness of the Andes and the Amazon region as physical barriers (Rio Grande do Sul is the exception which proves the rule) to conflict with his Spanish-American neighbors. If Brazil has still not achieved the same degree of internal *economic* integration as that already attained and maintained in political affairs, it is at last beginning to do so. As this process continues, the nation's political unity has provided a much more viable base—in terms of diversity of resources and in geographic extent and population—for supporting economic (especially industrial) development than most parts of a fragmented Spanish America can now offer.

It is only natural that, as "half a continent," Brazil has vast differences in climate, soil, and topography which make for many Brazils, so far as the agricultural sector is concerned. Far more important than such physical differences, however, is the historical failure of Brazil to have achieved the national economic integration which would substantially reduce the sharp interregional differences in returns to labor and capital, in production techniques, and in the degree of commercialization within Brazilian agriculture. This great *economic* diversity of Brazilian agriculture still holds, even if we ignore those large and sparsely populated areas such as most of the Amazon basin and the more remote parts of the *sertão* and *campo cerrado*, whose agriculture is limited to very extensive cattle grazing and purely subsistence crop production. To illustrate, let us turn to data (tables 1–4) which Ruy Miller Paiva and myself collected in 1963 from ninety-nine agricultural properties (involving some 2,100 farm families) in seven major agricultural regions, all of which produced substantial surpluses of staple food products for urban consumption.[2]

Land and Capital Resources per Unit of Farm Labor

Among these seven regions, the amount of all capital which farm workers had to work with, *per man-year of their actual labor inputs*, ranged from only $156 in Maranhão to $5,055 in Rio Grande do Sul (table 1). Even the

2. The data here used are being presented and analyzed in great detail in a series of seven regional reports—under the general title of *Ninety-Nine Fazendas: The Structure and Productivity of Brazilian Agriculture, 1963*, by William H. Nicholls and Ruy Miller Paiva—being published in English by the Graduate Center for Latin American Studies, Vanderbilt University; and in Portuguese by the Instituto Brasileiro de Economia, Fundação Getúlio Vargas, Rio. Thus far, the following reports have appeared in English: *The Itapecuru Valley of Maranhão: Caxias* (July 1966); *The Cariri Region of Ceará: Crato* (November 1966); *The Agreste Region of Pernambuco: Caruaru* (April 1967); *The Triangle of Minas Gerais: Ituiutaba* (April 1968); and *The North of Paraná: Maringá* (September 1969).

TABLE 1

GROSS AND NET OUTPUT AND CAPITAL INPUTS PER MAN-YEAR OF LABOR INPUT
SELECTED AGRICULTURAL REGIONS OF BRAZIL AND THE UNITED STATES, 1963

Region[a]	Value of Output[b]		Ha. of Land in		Value of Capital Inputs				
	Gross $	Net $	Crops	Other[c]	Land & Bldgs.[d] $	Machinery & Work-stock[e] $	Productive Livestock[f] $	Production Expenses[g] $	TOTAL $
Itapecuru Valley (Mar.)	156	133	1.44	18.6	35	32	66	23	156
Cariri (Ceará)	323	254	1.98	7.5	466	108	177	69	820
Agreste (Pern.)	392	254	2.49	11.0	495	129	294	138	1,056
North of Paraná	620	478	2.61	10.4	2,065	286	796	142	3,289
Minas Triangle	1,012	654	6.37	17.1	1,889	645	379	358	3,271
Paraíba Valley (S.P.)	1,203	525	2.99	11.3	2,784	1,001	293	678	4,756
Rio Grande do Sul	1,490	685	10.18	35.1	2,052	1,468	730	805	5,055
Humid northeast	156	133	1.44	18.6	35	32	66	23	156
Semi-arid northeast	349	254	2.17	8.8	477	115	220	95	907
South	1,099	597	5.45	17.3	2,216	841	460	502	4,019
U.S., all farms	12,339	4,725	38.90	140.0	44,101	7,319	5,188	7,614	64,222
U.S. cotton farms:[h]									
S. Piedmont	3,608	2,604	21.30	n.a.	14,061	1,113	562	1,004	16,740
Delta, small	5,039	3,017	14.60	n.a.	10,364	2,924	468	2,022	15,778
large	8,400	5,624	25.20	n.a.	19,843	3,583	824	2,776	27,026
Calif., large (irr.)	21,654	11,606	41.90	n.a.	86,833	6,498	0	10,048	103,379

a. Based on interviews on 99 agricultural properties in 1963 by Nicholls and Paiva in the following *municípios*: Caxias (10 properties), Crato (15), Caruaru (15), Iuiutaba (14), Taubaté (15), and Cachoeira do Sul-Erechim (15). Data for Paraná, São Paulo, and Rio Grande do Sul subject to revision. United States data computed or estimated from United States Department of Agriculture, *Agricultural Statistics, 1965*, pp. 479, 483, and 484. A *man-year* is defined as 260 days or 2,600 hours per year.

b. *Gross* value of all crops, extractive products, and livestock and livestock products on the selected properties; and net value of product after subtracting all production expenses except cost of hired labor and interest on own investment. Output and input data were "normalized" for the low actual crop yields of 1963, and were priced at their market values of September 1963 (when United States $1 was worth Cr$1,000).

c. Pasture and all other uses.

d. Service buildings only, excluding residences and other nonproductive improvements.

e. Field and stationary machinery, motor vehicles, and work animals. (United States data exclude work animals.)

f. All livestock other than work animals. (United States data include work animals.)

g. Considered a measure of working capital. Includes costs of livestock feed, seeds, fertilizers, feeder animals purchased, insecticides, vaccines and medicines, tools, short-term interest on borrowed funds, and property taxes; machine hire; and fuel and lubricants, maintenance and repairs, and depreciation on machinery and service buildings. Excludes share or cash land rentals, cash wages of hired labor, interest on farm-mortgage debt, and interest on own investment.

h. These are data for "representative" cotton farms, based on farm-survey samples by type and location, designated as follows: family farms in the southern Piedmont and Mississippi Delta (small); and large-scale farms in the Mississippi Delta and (on irrigated cropland) the San Joaquin Valley of California.

two regions (Cariri and Agreste) representative of the better agricultural areas of the semi-arid northeast provided $907 of farm capital per man-year—six times the $156 of the humid northeast (Maranhão). The agriculture of the four regions of the south, in turn, had three to five times as much farm capital per man-year as the semi-arid northeast, the average for the south being $4,019. The seven regions ranked in essentially the same order for each major component of per man-year farm capital—real estate (land and buildings), machinery and workstock, and working capital (production expenses)—except productive livestock, in which only Paraná and Rio Grande do Sul showed a very substantial advantage over the Cariri and Agreste regions. Real estate investment per man-year showed the widest range—from only $35 in sparsely populated and remote Maranhão to $2,784 in the very favorably located and populous Paraíba Valley of São Paulo. However, the comparable range for per man-year nonreal estate (all other) capital was also very wide—from $123 in Maranhão to $3,003 in Rio Grande do Sul—the range being greatest for machinery per man-year and least for livestock per man-year.

If Maranhão is omitted as a special case and the remaining six regions are grouped into semi-arid northeast and south, we find that the agriculture of the south supplied each unit of labor input with nearly five times as much land and improvements, over seven times as much machinery, five times as much working capital (much of this representing the purchase of modern inputs), and twice as much productive livestock as the northeast. Relative to the United States average in the same year, however, even the south of Brazil had only 5 per cent as much real estate capital (and 9 per cent as much nonreal estate capital) per man-year of labor input. In nonreal estate capital, the south of Brazil was (relative to the United States) at the least disadvantage in machinery investment (11.5 per cent) and at the greatest disadvantage in working capital (5.8 per cent).

If one uses, instead, United States cotton farms as the basis of comparison—especially those of the relatively less advanced United States Southeast—the south of Brazil compares somewhat more favorably. Thus, let us compare for each capital component that region of southern Brazil (Rio Grande do Sul or Paraíba Valley) in the best position with that class of farms in the United States Southeast—family farms of the southern Piedmont or Mississippi Delta—in the poorest position of the selected classes of cotton farms. While Brazil's best region had only 32 per cent as much capital per unit of labor as the Southeast's poorest, this unfavorable showing was largely due to the real estate component (26.9 per cent), the leading Brazilian region having only 19.8 per cent less working capital per man-year and 55.9 per cent *more* livestock and 31.9 per cent *more* machinery per man-year. However, a more appropriate basis for comparison with Brazil—

in terms of size and organization of agricultural properties—would be the large-scale farms (plantations) of the Mississippi Delta. On the latter basis, the most favorable region of Brazil had only 18.7 per cent as much capital per unit of labor—14 per cent for real estate investment and 41.8 per cent for nonreal estate capital—making the best showing on livestock (88.6 per cent), a moderately good showing on machinery (41 per cent), but a relatively poor showing on working capital (29 per cent).

Such international comparisons in *value* terms are, of course, subject to many technical difficulties, such as choice of exchange rate, differences in internal relative prices, etc. The alternative of comparing *physical* units of capital is also far from satisfactory because of international differences in the quality of inputs (a head of cattle or a hectare [ha.] of land) and because of the problems of aggregation of physical units (numbers of cattle and swine, or tractors and trucks) into broad classes ("livestock" or "machinery") if the common measuring rod of money is abandoned. The problem may be illustrated by a comparison of the Brazilian south with United States averages in physical and value terms. Thus, while the Brazilian south had a per-man-year value of livestock only 8.9 per cent of the United States average, the corresponding percentages for *numbers* of livestock per man-year (although admittedly of considerably lower quality) were substantially higher—32 per cent for cattle, 19.8 per cent for swine, and 13.6 per cent for sheep and goats. On the other hand, while the Brazilian south had per man-year 11.5 per cent as much machinery and workstock by value, it had only 5.0 and 2.2 per cent, respectively, as many tractors and trucks per man-year as United States agriculture. Perhaps the most important international difference—real estate being the dominant component of total farm capital in both countries—was in land and buildings per unit of labor. The Brazilian south had only 12.7 per cent as many ha. of farmland per worker but, with land values per ha. 30.9 per cent as high (table 2), had a total real estate investment per man-year only 5 per cent as high as the United States average.

Even within Brazil, however, the differences in these several indexes of real estate inputs were considerable (table 1). The amount of farmland per unit of labor ranged from 9.5 ha. in the Cariri region (sugarcane, cattle, corn, rice, beans, cotton) to 45.4 ha. in Rio Grande do Sul (rice, cattle, swine, soybeans, and wheat). The average farm workers of the Minas Triangle (23.5 ha.) and Maranhão (20.0 ha.) also had relatively large amounts of farmland to work with, reflecting the relative scarcity of labor and abundance of land in these two regions. However, the quality of the farmland in the triangle (rice, cattle, corn, beans, swine) was very good and that in Maranhão (rice, manioc flour, cotton, *babaçu*, beans, corn, cattle) was generally low. In the other three selected regions, each unit of farm labor had an average of 12.1–14.3 ha. of farmland, including not only the populous and well-located Agreste (milk and beef cattle, beans, corn, manioc flour) but also the two regions with, by far, the highest land values—the north of Paraná, with its very rich soils, planted pastures, and heavy emphasis on coffee, cattle, swine, and rice production by labor-intensive methods; and the Paraíba Valley, with its relatively intensive land use in rice, potato, and milk production and a high degree of mechanization.

If we look at the seven regions, instead, in terms of the ha. of *noncropland* (pasture and other land) per man-year, we find wide differences depending on the relative scarcity of farmland, the quality of the pastures for cattle-grazing, and the extent to which supplementary forage crops, crop residues, and purchased concentrates were used as pasture substitutes. Thus, the relatively large amounts of "other" land per man-year (table 1) in Rio Grande do Sul (35.1 ha.) and Maranhão (18.6 ha.) reflect a relatively extensive type of livestock production. In Rio Grande do Sul, cattle and sheep are grazed on good natural *campo* supplemented only with post-harvest crop residues and the natural grasses which spring up on irrigated rice land in the two out of three years in which such land is in fallow. In Maranhão, except for the pockets of *cerrado* pasture, cattle, goats, and sheep must largely derive their nutrients from poor-quality grasses in the palm forests, supplemented during the post-harvest months by feeding on crop residues. The Minas Triangle presents a more mixed picture, with the 17.1 ha. of other land per man-year almost equally divided in our sample between extensively grazed low-quality natural *cerrado* pasture and intensively grazed excellent planted pastures on the rich soils of forest origin, which (being much more heavily cropped) also provide substantial crop residues.

In the other four regions, pastureland is scarcer and more intensively used. In the Agreste region (with access to the large Recife milk market) and in the Paraíba Valley (within the São Paulo and Rio milksheds) the available natural pastures (11.0–11.3 ha. per man-year) are used as fully as possible, but are heavily supplemented by purchased feed concentrates and (in the Agreste) by a major drought-resistant forage crop, the cactus *palma* (prickly pear). In the north of Paraná the land (10.4 ha. per man-year) which can be spared from coffee and other crop production is largely in intensively used planted pastures. In the Cariri region the limited carrying capacity of the low-quality and arid *caatinga* pastures (7.5 ha.) is substantially supplemented with cane forage (a by-product of its local emphasis on the processing of *rapadura* and *aguardente*), crop residues, and purchased feed concentrates. In general, the seven regions ranked in about the same position in ha. of noncropland and in value of productive livestock per man-year, the principal exceptions being Maranhão, where large areas of "other" farmland were offset by their very low grazing capacity, and the north of

Paraná, where livestock (cattle and swine) production was based on very intensive land use.

The amount of *cropland* per unit of labor ranged from 1.44 ha. in Maranhão to 10.18 ha. in Rio Grande do Sul, the interregional differences being closely associated with differences in the crop-production techniques used. Thus, there was a very strong tendency for farm workers to have more cropland per unit of labor, the more machinery they had to work with. The importance of the level of technology may be illustrated by the fact that, despite the relative plenty of land and scarcity of labor in Maranhão, each of its farm workers could handle relatively little cropland with the prevailing primitive techniques which they used. Maranhão's shifting agriculture had unusually high labor requirements, since every year or two new cropland must be won by clearing the forest, burning the debris, and building slash fencing. Because the soil is inadequately prepared for planting, there is a constant battle against the invasion of competing plant life. In planting and cultivation, even the hoe is little used relative to the pointed stick and machete; in the rice harvest, men pick the heads of grain like cotton instead of cutting the whole plant with hand sickles. With its farm labor virtually unassisted by machinery, workstock, or working capital, it is little wonder that there is so little cropland per man-year in Maranhão.

In the Cariri and Agreste regions cropping techniques were also almost entirely manual, labor working only with hoe, sickle, machete, and axe. The only departures from wholly manual techniques were in soil preparation and cultivation. Of the total cropland, 8 per cent in the Cariri and 28 per cent in the Agreste were plowed and graded with tractor-drawn equipment, much of the latter by state-owned tractors provided locally for a fee by a state agency. Animal-drawn equipment was used only in cultivation, and even there to only a very limited extent (14 and 2.5 per cent, respectively). All harvesting and almost all planting were entirely manual. The principal uses of machinery were for irrigation and water supply and, less frequently, for processing sugarcane and manioc flour, for chopping forage, and for shelling corn. Work animals (primarily burros) were largely used for internal transportation, mainly in Cariri's sugarcane harvest and in cattle herding, with hired trucking services rapidly displacing burros in external transportation. Thus, while cropping techniques in the semi-arid northeast still remained primitive, sufficient advances had been made to permit somewhat more cropland (1.98 and 2.49 ha.) per man-year than in Maranhão.

Of the four southern regions, the two with the most expensive land had only moderately more cropland per man-year than those in Ceará and Pernambuco. In the north of Paraná each unit of labor had only 2.61 ha. of cropland to work with and had the least assistance from machinery and work animals of the four southern regions. Because of a major emphasis on the production of coffee (often interplanted with subsistence crops), the north of Paraná made little use of tractor- or animal-drawn equipment but did produce a high value of product per ha. by very labor-intensive methods. Even where rice and other products were produced in isolation, however, felled trees and tree stumps from the recently cleared forests offered a major obstacle to any but manual cropping practices. Apart from very few tractors and trucks, the principal machines found in Paraná were motors, generators, and pumps used in water or electricity supply, corn shelling and disintegrating, and forage chopping. Even work animals were extremely few.

The Paraíba Valley, despite the fact that its cropping operations were the most completely tractorized (from soil preparation through harvesting), had a surprisingly low average of only 2.99 ha. of cropland per man-year. This apparent paradox is explained, however, by the intensive use of its expensive cropland in the flood plain of the Paraíba River, where—in sharp contrast with the rather extensive use of irrigated rice land (one rice crop each three years) in Rio Grande do Sul—the same land (with large outlays for fertilizer) was used year after year, often with irrigated rice and potato crops produced successively within each calendar year. Hence, for purposes of comparability, the 2.99 ha. of cropland per man-year should be raised to 3.50. To be sure, in the hillier parts of the Paraíba Valley, one also finds horse-drawn and ox-drawn equipment and even completely manual operations, but frequently these agricultural properties of rough topography are primarily involved in milk and cattle production, in which their techniques are often relatively advanced. In addition to very large investments in trucks, tractors and complementary field equipment, and combines and threshing machines, the cultivators of the Paraíba Valley also have many motors and pumps for irrigation and general operations, the availability of public power making electric motors more common than the gasoline motors more generally found in Brazil.

The substantially higher 6.37 ha. of cropland per unit of labor found in the Minas Triangle reflects a relatively high degree of tractorization in the face of a relatively scarce labor supply. With typically very large landholdings, largely cultivated by sharecroppers with land allotments of substantial size, the Minas Triangle has already completely tractorized the plowing and grading operations and much (about 33 per cent) of the planting, the remainder of which is planted with horse-drawn equipment. All crops receive, in addition to several manual (hoe) cultivations, cultivation with horse-drawn equipment (87 per cent) or, less frequently, tractor-drawn machinery (13 per cent). Only the harvesting operation remains largely manual, except for rice, about half of which is harvested with combines or threshing machines. There is also a large investment in trucks and a moderate use of stationary motors, pumps, and generators. As a result, the average farm worker in the triangle can handle a relatively large amount of cropland.

Finally, with the largest investment in machinery and workstock per man-year of the seven regions and less intensive land use in cropping operations, Rio Grande do Sul provided a very high 10.18 ha. of cropland for each unit of labor. Soil preparation was largely (81–85 per cent) with tractors, the remainder with ox-drawn equipment. On most properties, planting was manual (small grains being sowed broadcast or with hand seeders) or with animal-drawn equipment, although the few properties planting with tractors accounted for over one-half of the total cropland. Except for one very large and completely mechanized property which produced primarily wheat, soybeans, and corn but no rice (which under irrigation requires little or no cultivation), cultivation was still largely manual, although frequently manual operations were combined with animal-drawn equipment. Harvesting was still entirely manual, except for rice and wheat, of which much was harvested with combines but, more commonly, was cut and stacked manually but threshed with machines. The rice and wheat harvest required a heavy peak-load in labor requirements, which was largely met by temporary seasonal workers, many of whom were themselves small landowners in the nearby hill country. In this region, investments in trucks, tractors, field and harvesting equipment, and stationary motors were large, while the investments in irrigation equipment and facilities were also a major component. Even so, oxen were still used in large numbers for animal traction and internal transportation, especially in the harvest season. With so much mechanical assistance, the average farm worker in Rio Grande do Sul could handle a relatively large amount of cropland, although the exclusion of the completely mechanized wheat-soybean-corn property reduces the amount of cropland per man-year in the sample from 10.18 to 5.57 ha., somewhat below the average found in the Minas Triangle.

For our seven-region sample, the average amount of cropland per man-year was 3.58 ha., as compared with 3.09 ha. for the same seven states and 2.67 ha. for all Brazil in the 1960 census, after adjusting the latter's reported numbers of persons occupied in agriculture downward to approximate our base of man-years of actual labor input. The corresponding national average for United States agriculture was 38.9 ha. but substantially lower (14.6–25.2 ha.) on the several classes of cotton farms in the United States Southeast (table 1).

Intensity of Land Use

Before looking at the effects of the amounts of per-man-year land and capital on the productivity of farm labor in the several regions, let us examine

TABLE 2
GROSS OUTPUT AND SELECTED LABOR AND CAPITAL INPUTS PER HECTARE OF ALL FARMLAND, SELECTED AGRICULTURAL REGIONS OF BRAZIL, 1963[a]

Region	% of Land in Crops	Man-Hours of Labor Input[b]	Value of Gross Output $	Value of Capital Inputs				
				Land & Bldgs. $	Machinery & Work-stock $	Productive Livestock $	Production Expenses $	TOTAL $
Itapecuru Valley (Mar.)	7.2	129	7.77	1.73	1.57	3.26	1.17	7.73
Cariri (Ceará)	21.0	275	34.21	49.34	11.38	18.77	7.34	86.83
Agreste (Pern.)	18.5	192	29.02	36.65	9.52	21.74	10.21	78.12
North of Paraná	20.1	201	45.42	159.38	22.06	61.43	10.94	253.81
Minas Triangle	27.1	111	43.17	80.56	27.48	16.15	15.25	139.44
Paraíba Valley (S.P.)	22.5	182	84.31	195.03	70.13	20.52	47.55	333.23
Rio Grande do Sul	22.5	57	32.93	45.35	32.44	16.13	17.78	111.70
Humid northeast	7.2	129	7.77	1.73	1.57	3.26	1.17	7.73
Semi-arid northeast	19.8	237	31.85	43.56	10.53	20.12	8.65	82.86
South	24.0	114	48.29	97.36	36.95	20.22	22.06	176.59
U.S., all farms	27.8	18	88.10	314.88	52.26	37.04	54.37	458.55

a. The footnotes of table 1 also apply here.
b. All man-years of labor input converted to man-hours at the rate of 2,600 hours per year.

the interregional differences in the amounts of labor and capital applied *per ha. of all farmland* (table 2).

For our seven-state sample, 17.9 per cent of the total farmland was in cropland, as compared with 17.1 and 11.2 per cent for the seven-state and all-Brazil averages produced by the 1960 census. If Maranhão is omitted from our sample, however, the sample average rises to 23.2 per cent, only moderately less than the United States average of 27.8 per cent. The fact that the farmland in our sample was relatively intensively cropped reflects the fact that it was consciously chosen to be representative of those agricultural regions which produce substantial surpluses of staple food crops (rice, beans, manioc, and corn), beef cattle and milk, and swine for Brazil's urban centers. Hence, their more intensive use is in conformity with their more favorable climate, soil, and access to urban markets, as compared with Brazil as a whole.

Even among these seven regions, however, it is evident that there are wide differences in the amounts of labor and capital relative to total cropland, as a result of variations in the quantity and quality of the land, labor, and capital resources and in the agricultural technologies of the different regions. Thus, in Maranhão, where land is very plentiful and labor and capital relatively scarce, a ha. of *all* farmland (not only cropland) receives very low inputs of *both* scarce resources, while extremely low land values encourage very extensive land use. On the other hand, a comparison of the south and semi-arid northeast shows that the south applies only half as much labor (in man-hours) and twice as much capital to each ha. of farmland. The smaller application of labor per ha. in the south results from the greater labor scarcity (and the lesser scarcity of capital) within its agriculture, with the offsetting application of nearly four times as much machinery investment per ha. While livestock investment per ha. was almost the same in the two areas, the productivity of that livestock was enhanced in the south by greater expenditures per ha. for vaccines, purchased feeds, and purchased feeder animals, which—along with greater outlays for fertilizers, insecticides, and selected seeds for crop production—were, in effect, substitutes for its relatively more expensive land (twice that of the semi-arid northeast).

If the Brazilian south is compared instead with the United States, with land values over three times as high, one finds that even the former used over six times as much labor and about one-third (38 per cent) as much capital per ha. of farmland. By major components of nonreal estate capital, the Brazilian south compared least favorably in working capital per ha. (41 per cent) and most favorably in machinery investments per ha. (71 per cent), falling in an intermediate position in livestock investment per ha. (55 per cent). Although there was a very close positive relationship between per-ha. land values and the average value of gross output which a ha. of land produced, differences in the former were generally much more than proportional to differences in the latter. For example, the Brazilian south had per-ha. gross output equivalent to 55 per cent, while its average land value per ha. was only 31 per cent of the United States average. Similar results are indicated within Brazil. In terms of net output (gross output *less* production expenses) per ha., these differences are vastly increased (the Brazilian south / United States relationship increasing from 55 to fully 80 per cent, with comparable results in comparisons within Brazil).

These findings probably indicate the tendency for agricultural land values to be higher, the greater the extent of industrial-urban development, which usually increases the scarcity of farmland because of the growing demand for nonagricultural uses of land and also encourages investment in buildings and other land improvements. They also reflect the increased demand for farmland as a speculation, tax haven, or hedge against inflation in the more favorably located agricultural regions and the strong tendency (for example, in the north of Paraná and the United States) for public price-support policies to be capitalized in higher land values. Whatever the reasons for high land values, however, the pressures to find land substitutes are greatly enhanced. Even where such substitutes are increasingly used, the race between increasing *net* farm output and rising farmland costs is a difficult one to win, requiring additional nonreal estate capital on more favorable terms, as well as public technical orientation to assure that such capital is as productively used as possible in increasing crop and pasture yields.

Our data also suggest that the usual attacks on the structure of Brazilian agriculture are largely misdirected, since, given the market opportunities and adequate public assistance, Brazil's large landholders underutilize their land far less than is generally alleged and indeed respond to profit opportunities in ways consistent with a relatively good allocation of resources, insofar as they have in hand the necessary technical knowledge. At the same time, the large numbers of small operating units ("minifundios") are largely attributable to the primitive hoe agriculture, which greatly limits the amount of land a tenant family can handle. Insofar as actual land allotments fall below this level, the primary need is sufficient additional nonagricultural employment to make the existing supply of farm labor smaller, thereby encouraging its use in ways which will (in conjunction with more capital) raise labor productivity significantly.

Resource Combinations per Unit of Output

Perhaps the most effective way of indicating differences in resource allocation, at different relative prices, of the several inputs is to compute the ratios of these inputs used per $1,000 of gross output (table 3). Thus, we find that, in producing $1,000 of output, labor inputs ranged from 6.40 to only

TABLE 3

LABOR AND CAPITAL INPUTS PER $1,000 OF GROSS OUTPUT, SELECTED
AGRICULTURAL REGIONS OF BRAZIL AND THE UNITED STATES, 1963a

Region	Man-Years of Labor Input	Ha. of Land in		Value of Capital Inputs				
		Crops	Other	Land & Bldgs. $	Machinery & Work-stock $	Productive Livestock $	Production Expenses $	TOTAL $
Itapecuru Valley (Mar.)	6.40	9.2	119.4	222	203	420	151	996
Cariri (Ceará)	3.09	6.1	23.1	1,442	333	549	214	2,538
Agreste (Pern.)	2.55	6.4	28.1	1,263	328	749	352	2,692
North of Paraná	1.61	4.2	16.7	3,329	461	1,283	229	5,302
Minas Triangle	0.99	6.3	16.9	1,866	637	374	353	3,230
Paraíba Valley (S.P.)	0.83	2.5	11.8	2,314	832	243	564	3,953
Rio Grande do Sul	0.67	6.8	23.5	1,377	985	490	540	3,392
Humid northeast	6.40	9.2	119.4	222	203	420	151	996
Semi-arid northeast	2.87	6.2	25.2	1,368	331	632	272	2,603
South	0.91	5.0	15.7	2,016	765	419	457	3,657
U.S., all farms	0.08	3.2	11.3	3,574	593	420	617	5,204
U.S. cotton farms:								
S. Piedmont	0.28	5.9	n.a.	3,897	308	156	278	4,639
Delta, small	0.32	2.9	n.a.	2,057	580	93	401	3,131
large	0.12	3.0	n.a.	2,362	427	98	331	3,218
Calif., large (irr.)	0.05	1.9	n.a.	4,010	300	0	464	4,774

a. The footnotes of table 1 also apply here.

0.67 man-years and capital inputs from $996 to $5,302 in the seven regions. Agricultural production was most labor-intensive in Maranhão and least so in Rio Grande do Sul. The four regions constituting the Brazilian south produced the given output with 68 per cent less labor, but with 40 per cent more total capital, than the semi-arid northeast. Relative to output, the south used more inputs of every category of capital except livestock (34 per cent less), with 131 per cent more machinery investment, 68 per cent more working capital, and 47 per cent more investment in land and land improvements. If land inputs are measured in physical units (ha.), however, the south used 19 per cent *less* cropland and 38 per cent *less* pasture and other land, but this economizing on the use of land was more than offset by greater investments in land improvements and in greater outlays (production expenses) for purchased inputs which raised the yield of both cropland and pastureland.

In comparison with United States averages, however, the Brazilian south required eleven times as much labor, working with only 30 per cent less fixed and working capital, to produce output worth $1,000. Indeed, as highly mechanized as United States agriculture was by 1963, its machinery was much more efficiently used, as indicated by the fact that it required 22 per cent *less* machinery investment to produce the given output. The two areas required about the same livestock investment, but the United States used 35 per cent more working capital, enabling it to find cheaper substitutes for its high-priced land. Thus, the given output was produced in the United States with 36 per cent *less* physical cropland and 28 per cent *less* pastureland, even though its monetary investment in land and improvements remained 77 per cent *higher* than in the Brazilian south. However, it should be emphasized that these international comparisons reveal more than the mere effects of different sets of relative input prices (such as cheaper capital and dearer labor) on the most efficient combinations of these inputs (more capital and less labor) for producing a given output, since the state of the agricultural and industrial arts is so widely different in the two countries.

As a result of the latter difference, United States agriculture could, with the *same* input combinations, produce a substantially larger output or, with the same farm capital investments, could produce the same output with much less labor than its Brazilian counterparts. The latter may be illustrated from the data of table 3, which indicates that in the Mississippi Delta, both small family farms and large-scale plantations required about the same total capital investment to produce $1,000 of output as that required in the relatively advanced Brazilian regions—the Minas Triangle and Rio Grande do Sul. (The Mississippi cotton farms required less of every category of capital per unit of output except real estate capital, although, in physical terms, they also used less cropland.) However, with the same capital, the given output was produced in Mississippi with 52–88 per cent less labor. Among the factors accounting for the generally higher productivity of United States agriculture, we might cite the very large public capital investments in the health, education, and technical orientation of the rural population and in the general infrastructure (research, transportation, communications, electrical energy, etc.)—capital inputs which, although excluded from our comparisons, are key factors in raising the quality of the input of both farm labor and farm management and in increasing the efficiency with which the conventional farm capital inputs are used. In addition, we should emphasize the importance of the American private industrial sector, which has supplied American farmers with high-quality machinery and petroleum and chemical products at prices which encouraged their rapid adoption and has even provided much of the technical information required for their most effective use in raising agricultural productivity.

Productivity of Farm Labor

Finally, let us return to table 1, which permits interregional comparisons in the amount of output a farm worker can produce, largely a function of the land and capital he has to work with and the overall efficiency with which this package of agricultural inputs is used.

Among our seven selected agricultural regions, there were enormous differences in the annual value of output per man-year of labor inputs. For *gross* output, the range was almost tenfold, from a low of $156 in Maranhão to $1,490 in Rio Grande do Sul. In terms of ranks, there was a very high positive correlation between gross output and total capital, per unit of labor, in the seven regions. The same was true for the relationship between per-man-year gross output and working capital (production expenses), indicating the strong tendency for the more advanced regions to use more modern purchased inputs such as fertilizers, improved seeds, insecticides, feed concentrates, and vaccines and medicines. The gross productivity of labor was also consistently higher, the greater the amount of mechanical assistance (machinery) which farm labor received and, consequently, the greater the amount of cropland which a farm worker could handle.

Finally, there was a rather strong tendency for gross labor productivity to be higher, the greater the livestock investment per man-year, the relationship between the former and the physical amount of "other" land (noncropland) per man-year being relatively low. The fact that gross input and ha. of "other" farmland per man-year were not very closely related reflects the very great interregional differences in the quality of pastures and in the amounts invested in making them more productive, as well as the extent to which working capital (used for purchased feeder animals and feed concentrates) enabled farmers to carry more livestock with less area in pastures. That the latter is true is indicated by the close relationship between per-man-year livestock investment and working capital and the small relation-ship between the former and ha. of "other" farmland per man-year. In value terms, however, differences in physical quality of pasture and cropland were partially offset by differential land values. As a consequence, livestock investment per man-year was rather highly correlated with real estate in-vestment per man-year, while gross labor productivity was almost perfectly correlated with the latter.

It may also be noted that in the semi-arid northeast, a unit of farm labor—working with 45 per cent fewer ha. of farmland (but 51 per cent more physical cropland and nearly fourteen times as high a real estate invest-ment) and 255 per cent more nonreal estate capital—was able to produce over twice as much gross output as in Maranhão. In the four regions of the Brazilian south, however, a unit of farm labor—with the benefit of much more farmland (over twice as many ha., a higher per cent of which was in crops, and with nearly five times as much real estate investment) and four times as much nonreal estate capital—was able to produce over three times as much gross output as the semi-arid northeast. On the other hand, even the Brazilian south produced an average of only $1,099 of annual gross output per man-year, less than one-tenth of the United States average and only 30 per cent of that in the poorest region of the United States Cotton Belt, the southern Piedmont. The performance ($1,490) of even the best of the seven Brazilian regions, Rio Grande do Sul, was only 41 per cent of that of the southern Piedmont.

The differences among the seven Brazilian regions in terms of *net* output (gross output *less* production expenses) per unit of labor were substantially less, indicating the extent to which the more advanced regions had higher operating expenses because of their much greater dependence on purchased inputs and because of their much higher maintenance and depreciation costs as a result of their much larger investments in machinery and service build-ings and other land improvements. As a result, the range in *net* labor pro-ductivity was only from $133 in Maranhão to $685 in Rio Grande do Sul, with the differences in *gross* labor productivity largely eliminated among neighboring regions and substantially reduced even in longer-distance com-parisons. Even so, net output per man-year was nearly twice as high in the semi-arid northeast ($254) as in Maranhão ($133), while it was 2.4 times higher in the south ($597) than in the northeast. While the Brazilian south compared less unfavorably with the United States average in *net* labor pro-ductivity (12.6 per cent) than in *gross* labor productivity (8.9 per cent), the same was not true relative to cotton farming in the United States South-east, whose advantage was even greater in *net* terms.

Farm Wage Rates and Net Family Incomes

One would expect that farm wage rates and farm-family incomes would be closely related to average labor productivity, although it should be emphasized that the latter (as computed for table 1), even on a *net* basis, does not fully allow for the contribution to gross output of inputs other than labor, no allowance having been made (in deriving *net output* per man-year) for interest on capital investment. In fact, multiple-regression analysis would be necessary to compute accurately the incremental contribution of each input to output, all other inputs remaining constant—a step which we are presently undertaking, but the results of which are not yet available for all of the seven regions.[3]

In table 4 we present data by regions for net income (after deducting all direct and indirect costs) per man-year of labor inputs—which may be viewed as the average annual wage rate—for permanent and temporary hired workers. For *permanent* workers, the average annual wage in the semi-arid northeast was $180, 65 per cent above that ($109) found in the humid northeast (Maranhão), as compared with a 91 percent advantage (before interest charges) in net labor productivity (table 1). The corresponding annual wage in the south ($240) was only 33 per cent above the semi-arid northeast's, while its net labor productivity was 135 per cent higher. As a matter of fact, for the seven regions separately, there was only a very moderate tendency for permanent hired workers to have a higher annual wage, the higher the net output per man-year of labor. The two regions with the highest annual wage for permanent hired workers were the Minas Triangle ($338) and the north of Paraná ($233), both newer regions with relative labor scarcity and still dependent on a continuing flow of in-migrants, from the northeast and elsewhere, to meet their farm labor requirements. However, the other two southern regions did not pay their permanent hired workers nearly so well relatively, the average annual wage in Rio Grande do Sul ($199) being virtually the same as that of the Agreste ($197), while that of the Paraíba Valley ($149) was lower than the annual wages found in any other region except Maranhão ($109). The comparable United States average (hired monthly workers) was about $1,900 in the same year.

There was a much stronger tendency for the wages of *temporary* (seasonal) workers—whose daily rates were annualized to a standard 260-day

3. Those conversant with the statistical techniques of multiple-regression analysis may find the results for the four regions cited in the previous footnote in the reports already issued, in each case presented and analyzed in a concluding section entitled "Production Functions. . . ." It should perhaps be noted that, in the four regions thus far examined, there was little or no support for the view that farm workers are "exploited" in the economic sense of the word—that is, that their net annual wage is significantly *less* than their incremental contribution to total agricultural output.

TABLE 4

COMPOSITION OF FARM LABOR FORCE, ANNUAL NET INCOME PER MAN-YEAR AND PER FAMILY BY CLASS OF WORKER, AVERAGE SIZE OF PROPERTY IN FARMLAND AND LABOR INPUTS AND RELATIVE SHARES OF FARM-OPERATOR FAMILIES IN TOTAL LABOR INPUTS AND TOTAL NET INCOME, SELECTED AGRICULTURAL REGIONS OF BRAZIL, 1963

Region[a]	Hired Farm Labor Force[b]							Av. Size of Property in		Farm-Operator[d] Families, % of	
	% of Labor Inputs by			Net Income[c] (Wage) per Man-Year		Net Income[c] per Family					
	Permanent Wkrs.		Temp. Wkrs.					Ha. of Farmland	Man-Years of Labor Input	TOTAL Labor Inputs	TOTAL Net Income[c]
	Cash Wage	Crop Income	Cash Wage	Perm. Wkrs. $	Temp. Wkrs. $	Perm. Hired $	Farm Operator $				
Itapecuru Valley	6.2	88.6	5.2	109	76	179	1,522	1,687	84.0	2.2	15.2
Cariri (Ceará)	8.0	89.8	2.2	171	88	257	1,108	235	24.9	6.3	21.2
Agreste (Pern.)	23.4	71.7	4.9	197	86	190	317	197	14.6	7.9	9.8
North of Paraná	60.6	16.2	23.2	233	153	361	230	131	10.1	16.1	14.1
Minas Triangle	11.6	65.2	23.2	338	133	647	6,498	822	35.1	2.6	39.5
Paraíba Valley	89.2	2.1	8.7	149	124	212	1,868	359	27.4	5.5	40.8
Rio Grande do Sul	65.3	1.8	32.9	199	148	281	5,694	583	12.9	12.1	71.0
Humid northeast	6.2	88.6	5.2	109	76	179	1,522	1,687	84.0	2.2	15.2
Semi-arid northeast	13.7	83.1	3.2	180	87	226	482	216	19.7	6.8	17.3
South	50.7	29.5	19.8	240	138	384	2,979	468	21.1	6.6	45.6

a. For definition of regions and size of samples, see table 1. Data for Paraná, Paraíba Valley, and Rio Grande do Sul subject to revision.

b. "Permanent" hired workers include all full-time employees, resident or nonresident, being further divided into those (administrators, monthly workers, *colonos*, and regularly employed day workers) whose income is wholly or largely from a fixed *cash wage*; and those (*moradores*, nonresident cultivators, and sharecroppers) most of whose income is in the form of either a crop-share or total crop output less some fixed rent (if any) in cash or kind. "Temporary" hired workers are those who provide labor on a seasonal basis for a daily cash wage and are usually nonresidents, since we here exclude any cash-wage labor supplied *to the landlord* by *moradores*, sharecroppers, or other permanent farm families which have crop income from their own land allotments.

c. Net income is gross income less all direct expenses (*including* hired labor), land rent, property taxes, interest on short-term borrowed funds, and maintenance, depreciation, and (unlike net output in table 1) 6% *interest on own capital investment.*

d. Here, a "farm-operator" is defined as the operator of the whole agricultural property (ownership unit), thereby excluding those (such as *moradores*) responsible for particular subunits of land which, in agricultural censuses, are often counted as separate farms (operating units).

man-year—to be higher, the higher the net labor productivity, although the interregional differences in their annual wages were substantially less than those for permanent hired workers, with a range of $76–88 in the northeast and $124–153 in the south. (In the same year, the comparable figure for migratory workers in the United States was about $1,550.) However, there were only three regions in which such seasonal labor made a major contribution (23–33 per cent) to total hired-labor inputs—in the Minas Triangle and Rio Grande do Sul, where, despite a high degree of mechanization in crop production, the harvest season (particularly for rice) required much nonresident manual labor, and in the north of Paraná, where the use of generally labor-intensive methods included the coffee harvest, for which much outside labor was needed. In these regions peak demands for temporary labor were reflected in relatively high wage rates. In the Paraíba Valley, on the other hand, even the rice and potato harvest was fully mechanized, so that the demand for casual labor was small and wage rates were somewhat lower.

Returning to *permanent* hired workers, it should be noted that the fact that interregional differences in wage rates fell far short of the differences in net labor productivity was largely a result of substantial variations in the *composition* of the permanent hired labor force. In the northeast, of the total labor inputs supplied by hired labor, 72–90 per cent was furnished by permanent worker families (*moradores*, nonresident cultivators, and share-croppers) which had individual land allotments for the use of which they paid rent (a crop-share or a fixed amount in cash or kind) or furnished certain labor services to the landlord. While this class of worker families sometimes received substantial cash-wage income for labor for the landlord's account, their income in kind (value of crop and livestock production, net of all production expenses, *and land rent*) was still high enough to put their annual wages at a level considerably above those of the cash-wage workers of the same region.

Although worker families, dependent primarily upon crop income, are much less protected against weather fluctuations, they enjoy the offsetting advantage of having a built-in hedge against the price inflation to which relatively inflexible cash-wage rates are very vulnerable. Hence, at "normal" crop yields, they are substantially better off than the administrators, monthly workers, full-time day workers, and *colonos* who (unless they also have land allotments) are paid largely through cash wages. That this is so also suggests that the northeast's landlords are by no means so exploitative of their worker families as the prevailing folklore commonly alleges, since higher land rents could have eliminated much of the advantage which their *moradores*, cultivators, and sharecroppers enjoy over cash-wage workers. In any case, the relatively heavy dependence in the northeast on this favored class of workers significantly raises the average net income per man-year of *all* permanent hired workers.

In the south, however, the hired-labor force is (except in the Minas Triangle) largely composed of cash-wage workers, with only 2–16 per cent of the hired-labor inputs furnished by crop-income workers with their own land allotments. The primary reason for this difference is that, once agriculture is substantially mechanized, the larger landowner usually operates the whole landholding as a single unit for his own account, depending largely upon cash-wage labor for administration, machine operation, and supplementary manual operations. The consequence is to substantially reduce the average annual wage for all permanent hired workers combined in these southern regions. The fact that farmers of the Paraíba Valley could hire full-time workers for an average annual wage of only $149 (60 per cent of the then-prevailing official minimum wage) suggests, however, that—despite an extremely favorable location between the cities of São Paulo and Rio de Janeiro—this region still lacked sufficient nonagricultural job opportunities to force farm wages up to much higher levels. (While most of those born in the rural areas of the valley apparently migrate to nearby cities, local farm labor requirements—after having been reduced sharply by mechanization—can still be met at relatively low wages by in-migrants from the surrounding uplands on either side of the valley.)

As already noted, the Minas Triangle represents an exception since its hired labor force still consists largely (65 per cent) of sharecroppers with relatively large land allotments which—with horses and horse-drawn equipment of their own and with most plowing and planting operations supplied (for a fee) by their landlords—they can handle with a moderate amount of hired seasonal labor. As a consequence, they earn a relatively large annual wage, raising the average for all permanent workers to $338, the highest of the seven regions. This relatively favorable position which the triangle's hired-worker families enjoy is a good index of the region's relative labor shortage but probably represents a transitional stage toward the system found in other mechanized regions of the south. Already, in 1963, it appeared probable that the large landholders would have been better off, insofar as they could hire temporary labor at the prevailing annual wage of only $133, if they had operated their entire holding as a single unit, using cash-wage labor in place of most sharecroppers and thereby retaining a much higher net share of the total output. This outcome would appear to be even more certain if increased in-migration increases the available labor force or if the rice harvest is more generally mechanized, with tractors also continuing to displace horses in planting and cultivating operations.

The effects of such differences in the composition of the farm-labor forces on the farm operator's (landowner's) share of net income are also clearly shown in table 4. Since there were relatively few small family farms in our sample, farm-operator families supplied only 2–8 per cent of the total labor inputs, except in Rio Grande do Sul (12 per cent) and the north of Paraná (16 per cent). (Comparable averages for family cotton farms of the southern Piedmont and Mississippi Delta were 49 and 70 per cent; for large-scale cotton farms of the delta and of California, 12 and 9 per cent.) Therefore, the prime factor accounting for the size of the landlord's share of total net income (after all costs, including 6 per cent on investment)—which ranged from 9.8 to 71 per cent—was the composition of the *hired*-labor force. The data of table 4 make clear that, the higher the net labor productivity (table 1), the greater tends to be the use of both farm machinery and cash-wage workers and the greater the landowner's share of net income, the latter reflecting, at least in part, the reward for the landowner's greater managerial inputs on larger, more mechanized units.

Finally, table 4 presents the data on net incomes *per family* both of permanent hired workers and farm-operators. These averages reflect not only the effects of wage *rates* and the composition of the labor force but also the number of workers per family and the extent to which such workers are less than fully employed. For all permanent hired workers, average annual net family incomes ranged from $179 in Maranhão to $647 in the Minas Triangle. The comparable range for farm-operator family incomes[4] was far wider, from only $230 in the Paraná region to $6,498 in the Minas Triangle, which may be compared with $1,520–2,012 on family cotton farms of the United States Piedmont and delta regions, $28,555 on large delta plantations, and $45,405 on large California cotton farms. There was a fairly strong tendency for those Brazilian regions with higher farm-operator family incomes to have higher net labor productivity but relatively less dependence on crop-income workers.

It is also interesting to compare the interregional differences in the ratio of farm-operator to permanent-hired-worker family incomes as a rough index of rural income distribution—only 1.7 in the north of Paraná and the Agreste region; 0.6–4.3 in Cariri; 8.5–10.0 in Maranhão, the Paraíba Valley, and the Minas Triangle; and 20.3 in Rio Grande do Sul. There was a

4. It should be emphasized that the "net incomes" of table 4 exclude *interest income* since they are net of a 6 percent interest charge on own capital investment. Hence, they indicate the residual income remaining to remunerate the given families for their labor-management inputs. It may seem incredible that the average net income (labor-management returns) of farm-operator families could be so low in the north of Paraná, the fabled El Dorado of Brazilian agriculture. The reason is the relatively high frequency of freezes (*geadas*), which we assumed in "normalizing" our data, especially in terms of coffee yields. The "normal" net income show ($230) should be compared with $891 in an excellent coffee year (1961–1962) and a *negative* $821 (loss) in a bad coffee year (1962–1963). The corresponding average family net incomes for permanent hired workers were $361, $394, and $335.

moderately strong tendency for this ratio to be higher, the higher net labor productivity, the larger the average size of landholding, and the greater the relative importance of cash-wage labor. Thus, while it is the agriculture of southern Brazil which has been sufficiently progressive to achieve (largely through the use of more capital and superior farm management) higher labor productivity, the principal rural beneficiaries of this agricultural progress have thus far been agriculture's entrepreneurial and landowning class. At the same time, given the public neglect of agricultural research and technical orientation, most of the progress which has been made is largely attributable to that class.

The lag in rural-worker incomes largely reflects the anti-employment bias of the government's particular forced-draft industrialization policy— which has helped to attract migrants to the southern cities in numbers far greater than those which can be absorbed in more than marginal nonagricultural employment, holding down rural as well as urban wages even in the south—and, inversely, the lack of sufficient public concern for rural education and health, for a greater decentralization of industry, and for those types of improved agricultural practices (especially in the northeast) which would raise labor productivity without reducing (as machinery does) agricultural employment, thereby making rural life less unattractive to would-be migrants. In my opinion, it is the latter areas upon which Brazilian public policy needs to center. Without them, such measures as agrarian reform and minimum agricultural wages will either not work or will be largely ineffective; with them, agrarian reform and minimum wages will hardly be needed.

Interrelationships between Agricultural Development and Industrial-Urban Growth

The generally higher levels of farm labor productivity and production techniques in the agriculture of the south of Brazil are readily explained by its more favorable location relative to Brazil's generating centers of industrial-urban development, particularly the city of São Paulo.

As we have already seen, historically this need not have been so, had the northeast produced a different breed of men in its earlier days. With almost monotonous regularity, some agricultural or extractive product had flourished and produced enormous wealth in the northeast, only to collapse with the exhaustion of the particular resource or the rise of competition from other countries which were more progressive technically and more efficient economically. Brazil's men of agricultural wealth had perennially played a passive entrepreneurial role, failing to plow back a significant part of their current earnings into the capital improvements and better techniques which might have preserved the income base within agriculture or established an effective nucleus for industrial development. Instead, they were content to preserve a European enclave on the South American continent, preferring industrial goods of foreign origin, educating their sons in Portugal, and spending much of their lives abroad or in the court life of the national capital. When the time most propitious for capital formation had passed, they could still maintain a level of "genteel poverty" which (given the continued absence of competing economic forces) was materially satisfactory and which continued to give them an important base for socio-political prestige and influence. As Professor Vieira shows elsewhere in this volume, for this and other reasons, Brazil entered the twentieth century with an insignificant industrial base and a still strong agrarian tradition which was extremely unfavorable to either a progressive agriculture or industrial development.

Thus, the modernization of Brazil, both agriculturally and industrially, had to await the rise of the state of São Paulo as a growth center, from which a new fabulously large agricultural surplus at last became an effective basis for general economic development. The consequent industrial-urban development, in turn, has increasingly served as the instrument for modernizing a still largely traditional and static agriculture in ever-widening circles, first within São Paulo and then in the rest of the south and west-central, with steadily growing repercussions even in the old but long stagnant and impoverished northeast and north.

Contributions of São Paulo's
Agricultural Development
to General Economic Growth

In the early nineteenth century São Paulo could hardly have indicated much promise as the future engine of Brazilian economic development. It had long been handicapped by sparsity of population, a largely subsistence and capital-poor agriculture, the lack of a profitable agricultural export product, and inadequate transportation. Yet, by 1900—when Brazil's coffee exports were four times their physical level of the 1840's—São Paulo already accounted for 50 per cent of national production and over one-third of world production. In the meantime, slave-produced coffee had first flourished in the state of Rio de Janeiro and then in the adjoining Paraíba Valley of São Paulo, following the familiar Brazilian pattern of declining physical yields as exploitive techniques brought soil exhaustion and land abandonment. These unfavorable developments—capped by the abolition of slavery in 1888—might have been as abortive as Brazil's other booms if there had not been vast virgin lands to the west, new transportation developments which made these new lands accessible for exploitation and development, and a people with a more venturesome tradition.

From the completion in 1867 of the British-built railway connecting the port of Santos with the city of São Paulo via the formidable coastal escarpment, an expanding railway network became the instrument for the persistent westward march of coffee across the state—centered in its eastern third in 1886, in its middle third by 1920, and in its western third by 1935. This coffee expansion proceeded on the basis of free labor, initially attracted from abroad by a well-organized and effective recruitment campaign. Less hampered by the heavy hand of tradition, which had weighed hard on the older regions whose former prosperity had depended upon a slave-based agrarian system, the *paulistas*—greatly invigorated by an influx of foreign immigrants—quickly put their own hardy pioneer tradition to good account. It was not until the 1930's that Brazil's century-old coffee boom approached its end with the onslaught of worldwide depression, serious overproduction, and collapsing prices. By that time, with Brazil now responsible for 64 per cent of world coffee production, São Paulo still accounted for 68 per cent of national production.

The next thirty years were to see coffee culture reach São Paulo's westernmost borders and spread rapidly southwestward into the richer (but climatically more hazardous) soils of the north of the state of Paraná, whose coffee production first surpassed São Paulo's in 1959 and was over twice as large by 1962–1964. Meanwhile, however, there can be little doubt that coffee had played a major role in getting a self-sustaining process of economic growth underway in São Paulo, hence in Brazil. Thus, exploitive as the march of coffee indeed was, the unrelenting search for virgin soil succeeded in at last completing settlement and development of the entire state. In the process, an infrastructure and general economic climate were created which were also highly favorable to the more general industrial-urban development of the state, with strong stimulating effects on the agriculture and broader development of the Minas Triangle, the north of Paraná, and the states of Goiás and Mato Grosso, as these regions were increasingly drawn into São Paulo's economic orbit. As a result, São Paulo's economic development enabled it to establish its primacy—first, in agriculture and, then, in manufacturing—in such a way as to produce lasting fruits for the nation as a whole.

During 1872–1920, the state of São Paulo's share of the national population had increased from 8.4 to 15 per cent and stood at 18.3 per cent by 1960. The city of São Paulo grew from 31,000 to 579,000 during the earlier period and had reached a population of nearly 4,000,000 by 1960, its share of the state's population having expanded from 3.8 to 12.6 per cent during 1872–1920 and attaining 30.7 per cent by 1960. In industrial development São Paulo also made spectacular strides during 1907–1919, being only half as important as the city and adjacent state of Rio de Janeiro at the earlier date but standing slightly higher in the later year, when São Paulo's share of national value added by manufactures had reached 30 per cent. By 1962 São Paulo's share was a remarkable 57 per cent. Clearly, such a spectacular rate of urban and industrial development could never have taken place without the initial impetus, long sustained, of a rich and effectively exploited agricultural base and substantial agricultural savings which found their way into further agricultural development and increasingly—indirectly or directly—into industrial development as well.

Thanks largely to the coffee boom, São Paulo had attracted from other countries much valuable human capital in the form of immigrants, who not only supplied much of the agricultural labor force but became an important source of industrial labor and business leadership. It had also attracted an increasing flow of foreign investment capital, particularly for railway construction and electrical power installations. Finally, it had enjoyed a relatively sound evolutionary industrial development, beginning with the simpler industries which used local agricultural raw materials and required lower labor skills and smaller capital outlays but gradually moving to the manufacture of more and more sophisticated products, as growing managerial and labor skills, the increased availability of capital, and favorable fortuitous events permitted. Thus, the stimulation which the Great Depression and World War II gave to the demand for domestic manufactures in Brazil was much more productive of effective industrial development because of the diversion of agricultural savings to nonagricultural development—first, from the tremendous injection of purchasing power associated with coffee-defense policy of the late 1930's and, then, from the fruits of the wartime boom in Brazil's agricultural exports during the 1940's.

With this decided headstart, São Paulo was in an ideal position to consolidate its gains when the Brazilian government became the principal engine of industrialization after 1950. The government's attempts to accelerate further the previously voluntary contributions of agriculture to the financing of industrial development—through its new policies of multiple-exchange rates and inflation-cum-public-industrial-credits—were largely frustrated. Thus, much of the public *confisco* of coffee's foreign-exchange earnings, intended for industrial development, was recaptured by producers through coffee price supports as overproduction again became a problem, although a considerable part of the consequent agricultural benefits probably found its way back into nonagricultural investment. Furthermore, public investment policy was so exclusively focused on financing industrial development that—with the concomitant lack of public attention to increasing productivity in the nonexport (domestic food) sector of agriculture—food (particularly livestock) production has increasingly threatened to become a serious bottleneck in the developmental process.

The result has been to further stimulate inflation, with rising relative food prices, causing a diversion of nonagricultural savings to agricultural middlemen and large landholders. Under these circumstances, the investment of agricultural savings in the nonagricultural sector has been unduly encouraged by the low priority which government policy gave to making domestic food production more efficient through the wider use of modern agricultural inputs, more appropriate public price policies, and better technical orientation. At the same time, the level of those agricultural savings has been dropping with the rapidly rising relative costs of modern inputs, further discouraging the agricultural investments needed to remove the food sector's restraining effects on general economic development. Even so, as a major beneficiary of Brazilian industrialization and coffee-defense policies, São Paulo has gained most (or suffered least) from the regionally discriminatory policies of recent years.

Contributions of São Paulo's Industrial-Urban Development to Agriculture

If São Paulo's spectacular industrial-urban growth could not have been possible without prior agricultural development, there is equally little doubt that its agriculture has increasingly received important benefits directly attributable to its rapidly growing industrial-urban complex.

In a recent paper[5] I showed in elaborate detail (based on comparative analysis of twenty-three physiographic zones in São Paulo) that local industrial-urban development—by facilitating the flow of capital into agriculture and the flow of labor out of agriculture—had by 1940–1950 already had significantly favorable effects in raising the incomes and productivity of nearby farmers. On the *capital* side, those zones with more industrial-urban development had higher personal incomes and larger savings, thereby raising the total resources of the local banking and credit institutions, while creating a greater demand for milk, eggs, fruits and vegetables, and other more expensive foods. The nearby agriculture clearly benefitted from these changes, which facilitated investments in land improvement, the expansion of the production of such more profitable capital-intensive enterprises as milk and poultry, an increase in capital/labor ratios, and an increasing scale of farming unit—all of which increased farm output and incomes per farm worker relative to those in the less industrial-urban zones. The nearby agriculture also benefitted from the favorable effects of increasing population density and an expanding tax base on the urban-oriented infrastructure,

5. William H. Nicholls, "The Transformation of Agriculture in a Semi-Industrialized Country: The Case of Brazil" in *The Role of Agriculture in Economic Development*, edited by Erik Thorbecke (New York: National Bureau of Economic Research, 1969), pp. 311–79 (particularly pp. 339–64).

which improved both the quantity and quality of such facilities as electricity, railroads and highways, education and health available to the nearby rural people.

On the *labor* side, although still somewhat obscured by the countereffects of certain agricultural frontier zones which were still attracting in-migrants, the productivity of farm labor was raised by nearby industrial-urban development not only because of concomitant higher rates of capital formation in agriculture but also because of the greater facility with which excess farm labor could move into higher-income nonfarm employment. Furthermore, farms located nearer to industrial-urban centers could use the labor which remained in agriculture more productively. Thanks to their greater access to nonreal estate capital and to their more favorable local product markets, they could concentrate on more land-intensive and capital-intensive products which utilized farm labor more fully and raised its productivity in response to rising wage rates.

All of these relative benefits of industrial-urban development, as they accrued to São Paulo's agriculture, were probably further strengthened after 1950. However, given the almost inexhaustible supply of rural labor, as reflected in continuing interstate migration to São Paulo since 1950, the earlier analysis of the present chapter made clear that even the present levels of nonagricultural employment in São Paulo still leave much to be desired, if labor is to become sufficiently scarce in both industry and agriculture to bring the wage rates and incomes of the more industrial zones up to fully satisfactory levels. Nonetheless, at least within São Paulo, there is strong evidence that industrial-urban growth has already made substantial contributions to agricultural development, and there is reason to hope that these contributions will continue to grow both within and, increasingly, beyond the borders of the state of São Paulo. Much will depend, however, upon the wisdom with which Brazilian public policy promotes further industrialization. Much more than in the recent past, there must be a greater emphasis on industries which employ larger numbers of workers, which more adequately tap mass markets, and which (through better processing and through more efficient production of basic agricultural inputs) help, in conjunction with much-improved public agricultural services, to raise agricultural productivity.

Despite the shortcomings of recent Brazilian industrialization policy, however, the benefits of São Paulo's industrial-urban development are gradually spreading to the rest of the country. That such is necessary and desirable is dramatically demonstrated by the heavy concentration of wealth and income in São Paulo today. Thus, in 1960, with only 2.9 per cent of Brazil's land area, the state of São Paulo had 18.3 per cent of the nation's population, 23 per cent of the nation's agricultural output, 57.1 per cent of the value added by manufactures, and 32.3 per cent of the national income. With a per capita income of $605, São Paulo would—if it were a separate country—already be approaching the status of a developed country. It achieved this dominant position largely on the basis of the superior vigor, initiative, and thrift of its own people. However, its more recent development has been, in part, at the expense of other regions, whose sons have through migration kept its labor supply cheap and its economic enterprises more profitable and whose agricultural raw materials have had to be exchanged for the products of its publicly subsidized and protected manufacturing plants on relatively unfavorable interregional terms of trade. Nonetheless, on the converse side of this coin, many migrants have improved their relative economic lot by their move, at the same time relieving their native region of a surplus rural population which had discouraged improved agricultural practices; while growing urban markets (and improved transportation) for the agricultural products of the less-advantaged regions have brought increasing commercialization of their agriculture, giving their rural people access to a wider range of industrial products both for consumption and for improving agricultural production.

Thus far, of course, the main beneficiaries of São Paulo's economic development have been the other states of the south which are its nearest neighbors. Thus, during 1950–1960 São Paulo's share of the nation's agricultural production dropped from 33.4 to 23 per cent, largely due to the rapid expansion of agriculture in the frontier zones of Paraná, Mato Grosso, and Goiás, under the stimulation of São Paulo's burgeoning markets and its ever-widening network of transportation and marketing facilities. As a result, Mato Grosso (with little industrialization of its own) in 1960 already ranked seventh among the twenty-one Brazilian states in per capita income, and Paraná (with the help of considerable industrial development) ranked in fourth place, even though these two states, plus Goiás, probably gained about 2,000,000 people by in-migration during 1950–1960.

At the same time, while São Paulo's share of national value added by manufactures had increased from 47 to 57.1 per cent during 1950–1960, there had still been sufficient industrial-urban development in the other older states of the southeast to have increasingly favorable effects on the agriculture of the entire region. An industrial triangle connecting the cities of São Paulo, Rio de Janeiro, and Belo Horizonte—and embracing major parts of the states of São Paulo, Guanabara, Rio de Janeiro, and Minas Gerais—had emerged as Brazil's central industrial-urban complex, with important secondary centers in the older parts of Rio Grande do Sul, Santa Catarina, and Paraná as well. These seven states (with Mato Grosso) ranked highest among the Brazilian states in per capita incomes.

The same seven states, plus Espírito Santo, which has recently begun to prosper as the ocean outlet for Minas Gerais' rapidly developing iron-ore production, now dominate the Brazilian economy. Together, with 18 per cent of Brazil's land area, they now (1960–1962) account for 61 per cent of the population, 89 per cent of the value added by manufactures, 85 per cent of the wholesale and retail trade, and 82 per cent of the installed electricity-generating capacity in Brazil. On the agricultural side, they also have 62 per cent of the nation's cropland, 49 per cent of the agricultural workers, 58 per cent of the cattle, and 91 per cent of the tractors. With these resources, they produce 65 per cent of total crop production and 81 per cent of milk production; their slaughtering plants kill 72 per cent of the nation's cattle and 78 per cent of its hogs. Thus, the benefits of the original impetus which coffee provided in São Paulo have gradually spread to this entire southeast region, with a further strengthening of both agriculture and the nonagricultural sector. The entire eight-state region had in 1960 a per capita income of $456, two to three times as high as those of the other major regions—$211 in the frontier mid-west (Mato Grosso and Goiás), $156 in the humid north (Amazonas, Pará, and Maranhão), and $180 in the arid northeast.

Despite these very large interregional per capita income differentials, there had been some narrowing since 1947, primarily because of changes in the regional distribution of population rather than because of changes in the distribution of national income. Thus, as a percentage of the national average, São Paulo's real per capita income declined from 221 to 178 per cent and the southeast's from 140 to 134 per cent. Of the other three regions, the arid northeast (thanks to a high rate of out-migration) showed a slight gain from 51 to 53 per cent and the mid-west (despite large in-migration) a larger gain from 56 to 62 per cent. The humid north, faced with moderate in-migration, but with the brief new rubber boom of World War II behind it, suffered a relative drop from 54 to 46 per cent of the national average. At the same time, with a national rise of 51 per cent in per capita real income during 1947–1960, even the humid north showed a 28 per cent improvement, as compared with 45 per cent for the southeast (62 per cent in Paraná), 57 per cent for the arid northeast, and 67 per cent for the frontier mid-west.[6]

It is clear that, since 1947, the southeast has finally made substantial strides toward achieving a well-integrated regional economy both for food prod-

6. Nicholls, table 1 and the accompanying textual comment. Cf. also Nicholls, "The Changing Structure of Farm Product and Input Markets in Brazil" in *Agricultural Cooperatives and Markets in Developing Countries*, edited by Kurt R. Anschel, et al. (New York: Praeger, 1969), pp. 63–78; and Nicholls, "The Agricultural Frontier in Modern Brazilian History: The State of Paraná, 1920–65" in *Cultural Change in Brazil: Papers from the Midwest Association for Latin American Studies, October 30 and 31, 1969*, edited by Merrill Rippy (Muncie, Ind.: Ball State University, 1970), pp. 36–64.

ucts and agricultural inputs, thanks in considerable part to the region's industrial-urban development and the consequent impetus given to highway construction and truck transportation. By 1964, São Paulo had 10.7 per cent (37 per cent paved) and the southeast 55.3 per cent (20 per cent paved) of the nation's federal and state roads—Brazil's main links in long-distance transportation. With these recent developments, the independent truck owner-operator has become Brazil's modern *bandeirante*, introducing an important new competitive element into the assembling, transportation, and distribution of food products, while vastly improving the access of farmers to urban food markets and to the various manufactured agricultural inputs which constitute the trucker's return load. With the truck driver has come that other remarkable catalyst for the modernization of agriculture, the ubiquitous *paulista* traveling salesman, pushing the sales of protein supplements, insecticides, vaccines and veterinary medicines, chemical fertilizers, motors and pumps, improved seeds, and other modern inputs and offering much valuable technical assistance about their efficient use. In the process, much of the frontier mid-west is also being rapidly integrated into the nuclear southeast region.

Even between the south and the north and northeast, integrating forces are again underway. The latter regions—long only tenuously linked with the south by very inefficient and expensive coastal shipping and a few navigable rivers (primarily the São Francisco and Amazon)—had also lacked an adequate railway network, depending primarily upon cattle drives and donkey trains for their internal transportation. Probably the most beneficial by-product of the creation of Brasília has been the initiation of the arterial highway system which is beginning to link the northeast and north with the new federal capital, which is already connected by paved roads with the major cities of the south. Human settlement and the agricultural development of the hinterlands are following hard on the heels of these new highways. The manufactures and food products of the southeast are moving in large volumes by trucks to the northeast, the return loads consisting of both agricultural and mineral raw materials and human migrants, many of whom are bound for the newer agricultural regions (such as the Minas Triangle and the north of Paraná) where farm labor is relatively scarce and well-remunerated. As a consequence of highway development, even in the remote parts of Brazil, any product of agriculture has acquired some value, and, with a rapidly increasing variety of consumer manufactures available in the local street fairs and stores, there is a growing stimulus for the monetization and commercialization of agriculture.

Within the north and northeast, the mere anticipation of improved roads is bringing a transportation revolution. Trucks are rapidly displacing donkeys in local transport, while bringing such remote states as Maranhão and

Piauí and the less accessible but climatically favored areas of the interior (such as the Cariri) into more effective communication with the major regional capitals of Belém, Fortaleza, Recife, and Salvador. As a result, while production techniques remain primitive, even the more remote areas are beginning to produce substantial commercial surpluses of staple food products for the cities and—as truckers are increasingly bringing as their return loads manufactured farm inputs, feed concentrates, and better breeding stock—improved agricultural techniques are being stimulated. Thus, even in the north and northeast, one can already perceive a significant trend toward regional economic integration. At the same time, there is a growing regional sentiment that, as the northeast is integrated more fully into the national economy, the integration process should not be limited merely to out-migration. Thus, one now finds in many provincial towns of the northeast that the citizenry (including even the large landholders) is becoming increasingly united about the necessity of local industrialization if their young people are to remain at home. The consequence is an increasingly favorable environment for the growing efforts of the federal government, operating both through its regional development agency for the northeast (SUDENE) and directly, to help this long disadvantaged region to catch up in the race for economic development, both agricultural and industrial.

CONCLUSION

There can be little doubt that the general economic development of São Paulo and the south of Brazil since 1900 has been firmly based on prior agricultural development and that the latter has, in turn, been greatly accelerated by industrial-urban growth. As to the future, however, one can find the basis for almost any degree of pessimism or optimism within the Brazilian economic panorama, depending upon where one's focus lies. Even so, having known intimately rural as well as urban Brazil for some two decades, I have been astonished by the progress that has been made, touching in varying degrees every corner of this vast country. Hence, on balance, I remain cautiously but firmly optimistic about the continued economic development of Brazil.

The plain fact is that Brazil and the Brazilian people have such a high potential for development that, if only the federal and state governments at long last meet fully and in appropriate ways their responsibilities for the infrastructure, further sustained economic development can be confidently expected. Although it is both necessary and desirable that the federal government continue to promote industrial development, ways must be found for putting greater competitive pressures on existing industry to become more efficient and, through lower prices, to broaden its markets and thereby achieve more employment and greater economies of scale. Particular emphasis needs to be given to making manufactured agricultural inputs cheap enough to stimulate their much more widespread use in agriculture, while providing adequate public technical services to assure that these modern inputs are used effectively and efficiently. This will require not only improvement in agricultural extension and *fomento* agencies—which have already been substantially developed in Brazil since 1950—but, much more important, far greater development and financial support of the agricultural research, both technical and economic, to give extension workers sound scientific knowledge.

Such improved public research and extension services, while generally necessary, are far more needed in the livestock sector than in the crop sector of Brazilian agriculture. As technically backward as much of Brazil's crop production is, the output of staple food crops has, since 1950, expanded at a rate sufficient to reduce substantially their relative prices to urban consumers. This has been no mean achievement although it reflects more the relatively abundant amount of land available for the production of staple food crops—whose production can, therefore, be rather easily and cheaply expanded in response to temporarily higher prices—than the achievement of higher productivity per unit of land or labor. It also reflects the fact that, on the demand side, the pressures of urban population growth are less augmented by the desire of consumers to consume more of these staple food crops as their real incomes rise than is true for most livestock products. Given the prospect of further rapid population growth, there can still be no complacency about the need for modernizing and making more efficient Brazil's crop production, particularly in its older and less remote agricultural areas. Meanwhile, however, the greater problem for the crop sector is probably the short-run price instability resulting from rather inelastic consumer demand in the absence of adequate storage facilities for stabilizing crop supplies (hence prices) against seasonal and year-to-year variations in the volume of production and marketings. In all of these regards, there is an important role for public policy in promoting more efficient and more stable production of the staple food crops.

Even so, it is Brazil's livestock sector which currently stands most in need of public assistance, stimulation, and development. That this is true is indicated by the fact that in Brazil the relative prices of livestock products have *increased substantially* in recent years, indicating both the technological backwardness and inefficiency of the livestock sector and also the evident and strong desire of the urban consumer to substitute livestock products for cereals as his income rises. Wherever the urban market opportunities exist, the producers of milk, pork, and poultry are not only growing in numbers but are already following many of the improved practices which their United States counterparts use. In general, however, these practices are not yet adequately productive of great efficiency—primarily because livestock producers are tackling managerial problems, of a complexity far greater than that found in crop production, on a purely empirical basis because of the lack of adequate and reliable public technical assistance. Without such assistance, products of livestock origin will continue to command higher and higher relative prices, frustrating the urban consumer's desire to upgrade his diet and enhancing inflationary pressures because of this serious agricultural bottleneck.

In recent years there has been far too great an emphasis in Brazil on the shortcomings of the agrarian structure and the need for agrarian reform of existing patterns of land ownership and landlord-tenant relations. To a dominant extent—with the northeast's long-stagnant sugarcane industry the exception which proves the rule—regional agrarian structures are largely the effect rather than the cause of primitive production techniques, semifeudal systems of tenure, and small inputs of capital. Wherever regions with such traditional structures are gaining improved access to urban markets and wherever market forces are increasing farm wage rates relative to the cost of capital, farmers (and most of all the large landholders so often condemned as parasitic *latifundiarios*) are responding with surprising dispatch, even in most of the northeast. Not only are they very much profit-motivated, but, at a rapidly increasing rate, they are eager to accept improved techniques if they also receive the complementary technical orientation and if the relationship of input prices to their selling prices is such as to make the improved practices financially remunerative.

Hence, today, if not twenty-five to fifty years ago, it is not primarily the shortcomings and inequities of the agrarian structure or the lack of managerial and innovative enterprise on the part of landowners large and small which will make of agriculture the Achilles' heel of Brazilian economic development. Rather, if such an unhappy outcome should emerge, it will be because the Brazilian government fails to provide the rural infrastructure and public agricultural and rural services which are both necessary and sufficient to prevent it.

Chapter 10

The Changing Bases of Social Class in Brazil

Sugiyama Iutaka

I T IS ALWAYS difficult to understand the dynamics of social class in a rapidly changing society. It may be argued that Brazil is not experiencing drastic social changes or that modernization is not taking place at the expected rate. However, the industrialization of the southeast, rapid urbanization, and population growth are important enough to make Brazilian society more complex and more difficult to understand.

The present essay presents some of the consequences of these changes for the social class structure of Brazil. Since, frequently, the changes are not compatible, conflicts emerge. In order to analyze these dynamics, it is important to start with a model and to see how its components are affected. As usual in the search for a model, one looks back into the historical formation of the society.

The author proposes to use the *fazenda, usina,* and/or *estância,* traditional large agricultural producing units, as the basic social systems in the formation of Brazilian society. In the *fazenda* one finds many of the crucial factors which guided the structuring of the society. Life is centered on the land and the production which results from its utilization. The stratification system is basically dualistic—master-servant—the owners of the land at the top and everyone else at the bottom.

It is important to note that the *fazenda* is not a feudal social system[1] but rather a latifundia system. Although some feudal characteristics exist, the basic element—the vassal relationship—is not there. It is possible that the development of the stratification system in Brazil owes its peculiarities to the particular type of social system that is the *fazenda.* Three basic elements of

1. Marc Bloch, *Feudal Society* (London: Routledge and Kegan Paul, 1961); Rushton Coulborn, *Feudalism in History* (Hamden, Conn.: Archon Books, 1965).

the *fazenda* seem to be crucial: (1) the dualistic system; (2) the extended family; (3) the value system based on the importance of the land.[2]

The urban social systems of a society in which the *fazenda* is the basic social unit tend to reflect the *fazenda*'s traits. Since rural life was the predominant mode, the social structure of the cities merely reflected it, instead of presenting independent models. Basically, the towns and cities had two functions: commerce for agricultural products, and administration. The city was dependent on the countryside. Economically the cities responded to the amount of trade the *fazendas* required and were politically dominated by them. The figure of the *coronel* reflects such a system. The influence and power of the *fazendeiros* extended from a total control of their land to that of the different cities. A powerful *fazendeiro* would control the city near which the *fazenda* was located, followed by his dominance of the regional city, then of the capital of the state; finally he would have influence in the nation's capital. In other words, the influence of the landlords worked in concentric circles, and the larger the diameter and area of those circles, the more powerful he was. It was, therefore, important that he had absolute control of his *fazenda* and *município* (county). Many of the conflicts in traditional Brazil had their roots in the fight for such control, as is well illustrated by Palmério.[3]

This dualism—*fazendeiro*, on the one hand, and the remaining members of the population on the other—and the control of the city by the landlords was reflected, during a large part of Brazilian history, in the cities where a similar structure could be found. At one extreme, one finds the owners of the land, and, at the other end, those who depend upon them. Position in the hierarchy of landlords depended ultimately on the amount of land owned *and* the production each was able to obtain from his piece of land. The size of the *fazenda* was important because of the agricultural system which was prevalent and still is in most parts of Brazil. Agriculture and land rotation required large farms if the owner wanted to produce enough to maintain his subordinates and to have a large production at the same time.

In such a system it was important to link the rural areas to the cities and control the latter. If a *fazendeiro* did not have political power, it meant that the government's facilities could not be used on his behalf; therefore, it was essential to have as much political power as possible, since political power meant not only the private use of public institutions and resources but also control of the police, regulation of prices and credit, etc.

However, the situation was not so simple. Conflict existed because several groups wished to control the government. *Fazendeiros* of different states and regions, as well as urban economic groups, wanted to exercise in-

2. Gilberto Freyre, *Casa Grande e Senzala* (Rio: José Olímpio, 1938).
3. Mário Palmério, *Vila dos Confins* (Rio: José Olímpio, 1960).

fluence. The utilization of cities as places for economic exchange created the merchant class, which at the beginning depended entirely on the rural landowning class but, with time, gained a degree of autonomy and challenged the power of the landlords in the towns.

The second component of the stratification system, which is closely related to the first one, is the extended family. A basic rule of political dominance is "if you cannot beat them, join them." Marriages and *compadrismo* (godparenthood) were very useful instruments for avoiding conflict, which tends to absorb too much energy, chiefly when the outcome is not certain. The extended family was, therefore, very functional to the maintenance of the system. Daughters could marry members of the *fazendeiro* group at the same time that male offspring could be located in strategic positions in the power structure. The landlords could in this way have assurance that their best interests were being protected by members of the family in the cities, while they themselves remained in rural areas.

The extended family and the *fazenda* are so interrelated that it is difficult to understand the existence of one without the other. T. Lynn Smith suggests that the family is the social institution that had most influence in the formation of Brazilian society.[4] Given the structure of the *fazenda*, such a statement does not come as a surprise. A large family meant expansion of activities in rural areas and, more important, an increasing influence in the urban centers. Positions in the local, state, and federal government could be filled by the members of the family, which in turn would give considerable power to the landlords. Male offspring were sent to the cities in order to get an education which would enable them to obtain higher positions in the cities. They composed the so-called "intellectual elite" in urban Brazil and often were civil servants. However, most had rural roots and belonged to the traditional rural interests and were an extension of rural life into the cities.

Another mechanism prevalent in the *fazenda* system was *compadrismo*. To be a *compadre* (co-parent) had two meanings: to be equal to another or to be under the protection of a person of a higher position. The first type was and is used among the landlords. As was mentioned previously, the basic function of this social institution was to prevent conflict among those who had similar interests. The second type was and is a vertical relationship. The subordinate could through this mechanism enjoy certain privileges. It would give a rural worker high prestige among his peers if he could say, "Colonel X is my *compadre*." Implicitly he was saying that he and his family were under the protection of the landlord. For the latter it meant that a loyalty system was established vertically and that he could be perceived by

4. T. Lynn Smith, *Brazil: People and Institutions*, rev. ed. (Baton Rouge: Louisiana State University Press, 1963), p. 459.

the members of the lower stratum as being a generous and good man. In fact, the reputation the landlord would have on the *fazenda* could probably be measured by the number of *afilhados* (godsons and daughters) he had. Such a system involved not only the *fazendeiro* but also all the members of his family. The landlady and the sons and daughters of the landlord would also be invited to become a *padrinho* (godfather) or *madrinha* (godmother).

The third factor in the *fazenda* syndrome which is crucial in the understanding of the development of social class in Brazil is the dominant value system. The dual system, which was centered around the land, explains to a large extent the salience of manual work, prospects for individual betterment, lack of conflict between classes, personalism, and lack of middle-class values, which are some of the dominant characteristics of Brazilian society. Manual work was and still is a prerogative of those who are in the lower strata. Lack of manual skills rather than being a disadvantage was seen as an asset. It was and still is a mark of class. This characteristic applies to all sorts of roles: the landlord, the urban "intellectual," as well as the housewife. Lack of manual skill meant that the person had other people do his work for him. Such values have persisted until today: a higher status man does not make any repair of the house because he can hire or he can count on others to do it. An intellectual does not know how to use a typewriter because a secretary would fulfil his needs, nor would a housewife take care of the children because a *babá* is employed for that purpose, and a maid is employed to cook and clean the house.

Individual betterment is perceived not as a result of one's ability but by the number and "quality" of relatives, *compadres*, and friends one has. The author suggests that Brazilians give far more weight to these factors than to hard work or ability. It seems that there are some justifications for the prevalence of those values when one examines the qualifications of persons who occupy high positions today. Therefore, in personal contacts and in the making of friends, a constant give-and-take syndrome is reinforced. Since personal contact is so important, recruitment of individuals for positions is more locally oriented than qualification-oriented, because the latter may mean the bringing of strangers into the system.

An important feature of Brazilian social structure which has its roots in the *fazenda* is the lack of vertical or class conflict. The dependence pattern has created a system that minimizes conflict between groups or categories of individuals in different strata. It is not that the relationship between master and servant has been relatively cordial. The rule of the game is that the underprivileged should not make drastic demands, but rather should ask for reasonable favors. Since the act of giving was highly valued among those in the upper strata, lower status individuals would obtain the minimum which would prevent overt conflict. Furthermore, those who have received "favors" would be in debt, reinforcing the strong link between individuals of different classes. The mutual dependence created in the dual system is to a large extent responsible for the lack of middle-class values. Upper-class standards and models filter directly into the lower strata of the population (which tend to utilize them in a modified form) because personal contact in the closed system of the *fazenda* permits it.

It is important to know how the *fazenda* syndrome persists and what conflicts it brings to contemporary Brazil, which has been changing drastically. The major structural changes affecting social stratification in the country (which are related to the *fazenda* syndrome) can be studied in the context of the impact of industrialization, population growth, and urbanization, the presence of immigrants, and the fragmentation of land holdings, on the one hand, associated with a concentration of land holdings, on the other.

Population growth, urbanization, and industrialization are to a certain extent associated. In this century, chiefly after the Second World War, a drastic change has been occurring in rural areas. The low level of technology in agriculture resulted in the overutilization of the land, and, on many farms, production was not sufficient to maintain the *colonos*, sharecroppers, workers, or others at the subsistence level. Landless rural people had to migrate to other rural areas or to move into the cities. The ones who were able to purchase small plots of land had, and still have, a difficult time in harvesting enough to keep the family alive. Since the ownership of land is one of the highest achievements, people would buy land even if they could not operate a farm efficiently. The results of the low productivity which prevails in rural Brazil were: first, the creation of a category of individuals who would own land but would work as day laborers for other large farmers, and second, a shift from agriculture to extensive cattle raising. The large *fazendeiros* substituted people, which used to be one of the status symbols, for heads of cattle, and the excess of the population migrated to the cities.

The growth of cities, the demographic explosion, the decline in the importance of rural areas, and the expansion of industries and bureaucracies have remolded the social stratification of Brazil. Urban areas gained importance and achieved a certain degree of autonomy, and the situation is now reversed—the hinterland depends more and more on the decisions made in the urban centers. The picture, however, is not uniform. Different regions of the country have their own characteristics. It is obvious that the Amazon region is not as complex as, for instance, the south, but it seems that the direction toward which the society is moving is the model found in the Rio de Janeiro-São Paulo axis.

Since it is impossible to cover the several regions in this essay, I will take the second model, that which is developing in the most industrialized and urbanized areas of Brazil, contrast it with the first one—the *fazenda* social system—and suggest some of the impasses that modernization has brought to the stratification system of Brazil.

The stratification system found in the large urban centers of Brazil is a transitional industrial structure. That is to say, the stratification system presents both modern industrial characteristics and traits of the *fazenda* syndrome. A modern industrial structure presupposes the prevalence of achieved over ascribed status, the existence of a continuum of positions rather than a dual system, and a high degree of social mobility, both inter- and intra-generational.

These characteristics may be found in many large centers, chiefly in those located in the regions where industrialization has had its greatest impact, such as the south. Difficulty is encountered, of course, in a comprehensive analysis of social stratification in Brazil because of the fact that there are regional variations and that a significant part of the population lives in rural areas, which suffer more the impact of the *fazenda* system.

The occupational profiles of large urban areas like São Paulo or Rio de Janeiro are industrial. They are relatively similar to those of Western Europe and the United States. The proportion of individuals in skilled jobs is larger than that in the semi-skilled and unskilled occupations. This comparison is an important one since it reflects a structure that absorbs relatively more individuals into industry. In these areas the size of the middle class or stratum is considerable. The occupational structures of large urban areas show, for instance, that occupations like shoemaker are being made obsolete by the mass production of shoes and that work by *empreitada* (independent job work) is becoming less prevalent. A comparison between generations indicates the clear shift from a nonindustrial stratification profile to an industrial one.[5]

However, one can also expect different occupational profiles according to the degree of industrialization and urbanization that different regions have experienced. One could expect that the contemporary profiles of the northeastern and northern regions would resemble those possessed by southern and eastern regions of the country some twenty or more years ago—in other words, a structure that has more of the characteristics of the *fazenda* system. Middle-class occupations are less prevalent; the managerial category is less important; and there is a predominance of unskilled individuals. Of course, there would also be differences within each region, but such differences are not peculiar to Brazil and can be found in any nation.

An indication that Brazil is in a process of formation of an industrial structure can be noted when the integration of migrants is studied. In indus-

5. Bertram Hutchinson, "Mudancas de Status Social de Uma Geração para Cutra," *Mobilidade e Trabalho* (Rio: Centro Brasileiro de Pesquisas Educacionais, 1960), pp. 207–29.

trial societies migrants from rural areas tend to be less upwardly mobile or unable to achieve high social levels as compared with migrants from urban areas or non-migrants who are city-born.[6] This mechanism is absent in Brazil, where to be or not to be a migrant has little to do with actual possibilities of individuals to achieve better positions. Furthermore, to be of rural origin does not impede individuals from having better occupations.[7] The argument has been that in an industrial structure the urbanite would be brought up in an environment that would favor his mobility, while individuals raised in rural areas would be in a disadvantageous competitive position in the urban-industrial structure. This is not the case in Brazil, which fact suggests that, in the initial stage of industrialization, the requirements for attaining certain positions are determined less by training than by other factors.

I maintain that the present structure is a transitional one. In the shift from an agrarian, *fazenda* type of social organization to an incipient industrial one, paternalism may be the dominant factor. Knowledge of vacant positions through informal means, friendship patterns, and family connections may be more important than actual qualifications. These mechanisms are present at all levels of the society. It was mentioned previously that the *fazenda* syndrome meant, among other things, vertical solidarity. It is possible that this is the major form of recruitment found in emergent urban Brazil. An impersonal universalist type of recruitment is not likely to be as dominant as the reverse. An opening will be known by individuals in a factory, shop, or government bureaucracy. There are always individuals looking for a job, and there are also individuals who want to give favors. Individuals who are able to solve problems, to offer jobs, are the ones who have high social status in Brazilian society. The one who accepts a position through a friend is in "debt." Although such a mechanism may be found even in the most industrial modern societies, this pattern is very important in Brazil and is perhaps one of the prevalent characteristics of the structure.[8]

If, on the one hand, jobs are partially filled through informal means, it does not, on the other hand, prevent urban Brazil from presenting a high level of vertical social mobility. When the rates of social mobility among several countries are compared, Brazil's degree of mobility is not much lower than that of the modern industrial nations.[9] It shows that the large

6. P. M. Blau and O. D. Duncan, *The American Occupational Structure* (New York: John Wiley, 1967).

7. E. W. Bock and S. Iutaka, "Rural-Urban Migration and Social Mobility: The Controversy on Latin America," *Rural Sociology* 34, no. 3 (September 1969): 343–55.

8. Anthony Leeds, "Brazilian Careers and Social Structure: A Case History and Model," *American Anthropologist* 66, (1964): 1321–47.

9. S. H. Miller, "Comparative Social Mobility," *Structured Social Inequality*, edited by Celia S. Heller (New York: Macmillan Company, 1969).

urban centers have an open structure and that social mobility is possible. Again, the pattern of social mobility is that of a modern society. The unskilled stratum is the one that provides individuals who move towards the skilled level, and the lower levels of nonmanual strata are the ones that expand at the highest rate. Upward social mobility is more prevalent than immobility and downward movement.[10] However, it is important to note that the comparisons tend to be biased since the populations under study are different.

The major factor in the determination of social mobility in Brazil is the expansion of the occupational structure. The creation of new jobs and the consequent formation of an industrial structure account for the largest part of upward mobility. The implication of the expansion is that individuals can achieve positions which they would not otherwise achieve. Mobility through exchange of positions is not as important as mobility due to expansion of the occupational structure. This means that individuals would not be mobile if industrialization had no impact on the structure. Industrialization requires a structure with managers, high nonmanual positions, and skilled labor, and persons tend to be recruited into these categories from the lower strata. New openings, rather than competition for positions, is the main factor which explains the high rate of social mobility found in many parts of Brazil.[11]

In a structure which is expanding, how do individuals achieve higher positions? Who is benefitted? At the present level of knowledge, it can be said that education is the main avenue of upward social mobility.[12] Education per se, however, does not guarantee a higher position in society, since informal mechanisms play an important role in the achievement and/or maintenance of a given social level for several generations. It is not surprising that persons born into the upper social strata tend to benefit disproportionately from the educational system and, therefore, occupy high levels in society and have the highest level of formal education.

A comparison between Brazil and the United States shows that the mechanisms for achieving a given social level are similar in both countries, but the importance of education is greater in the latter than in the former. Data suggest that education had very little effect on social status in Brazil in the past generation and only recently has become an important requirement.[13] Father's social position is losing importance. In the past, parental social class

10. Hutchinson, *Mobilidade e Trabalho*, pp. 207–29.
11. Bertram Hutchinson, "Structural and Exchange Mobility in the Assimilation of Immigrants to Brazil," *Population Studies* 12, no. 2 (1958): 111–20.
12. S. Iutaka, E. W. Bock, and G. A. Watkins, "Determinants of Social Status," a paper prepared for presentation at the Southern Sociological Society Meeting, April 9–11, 1970, in Atlanta.
13. Iutaka, Bock, and Watkins.

was the most important determinant of status and may still be so in the less industrialized areas of the country today.

In the process of change that Brazil is experiencing, I suggest that two major categories of people are able to climb socially. First, persons who have connections with individuals of a higher social class than their own. This point has been presented above. The second category is composed of immigrants and their descendants. The new types of jobs created by industrialization are not recognized as conferring high social status. Those who desire higher status are more likely to seek the jobs which traditionally have conferred prestige, such as, for instance, being a civil servant rather than becoming a lower-level manager in industry.[14] As a result, certain positions are left open because the tradition-oriented member of the society seeks the occupations that the past generation tended to give importance to.

The transition to an urban industrial occupational structure creates a gap. Occupations which will, in the near future, enjoy high prestige are not awarded it by the tradition-oriented members of the society. These positions tend to be filled by immigrants and their descendants. The reason is simple and obvious. Immigrants do not have the same values as traditional Brazilians and tend to fill those vacancies which are open. They also seem to consider that those jobs are "good," given their past experience.

The "preference" of immigrants and their descendants for new occupations is revealed when students in universities are classified in terms of traditional and new careers and foreign and native background.[15] The traditional Brazilian expects to pursue a career that has the highest traditional reputation and only as a second choice to enter the newer professions, while foreigners and their descendants use education as a means of getting a higher position in society, with little regard for the traditional valuation of their career choice. Another important factor is that foreigners may perceive education, per se, as the major avenue for their children's upward social mobility, while Brazilians perceive certain traditional professions as being associated with high prestige and upward mobility.

In a changing society the traditional Brazilian is in a disadvantageous position. He tends to be concentrated in the traditional careers such as medicine and law, while newcomers tend to get technical educations, which are more easily absorbed into an industrial structure. It is not surprising, therefore, that immigrants and their descendants have been able to perform better than native Brazilians regarding upward mobility.[16]

The native Brazilian is in a disadvantageous position, because he still lives

14. Sugiyama Iutaka, "Social Mobility and Occupation Opportunities in Urban Brazil," *Human Organization* 25, no. 2 (1966): 126–30.

15. Hutchinson, *Mobilidade e Trabalho*, pp. 207–29.

16. Hutchinson, *Mobilidade e Trabalho*, pp. 207–29.

in a society that values highly the elements which were discussed in the *fazenda* syndrome. To obtain a university degree is still perceived as guaranteeing a high-prestige occupation. In a certain way it is similar to the cases in some African countries. To have a university diploma meant in many African countries to become a diplomat. In Brazil, to be a physician, or a lawyer, was associated with being in the highest levels of society. Since universities and enrollments have greatly increased in number, many graduates have not been incorporated into the occupational structure at the level they had expected. This problem is aggravated by the fact that many "faculties" have mushroomed throughout the country—such as faculties of letters, economics, and social sciences. Those who are not able to enter the traditional schools study for the new careers, but their high expectations are maintained. When they graduate and find out that their training is not in accord with the demand of the occupational structure, they become frustrated.

The way Brazilians perceive education seems to be a very clear example of some of the incongruence created by the transition from a dualistic type of social structure to an industrial one. Education, according to popular expectations, means high status, and traditional careers and those which resemble them are the ones people search for. The lack of consistency between the demands of the industrial occupational structure and the orientation of the educational system creates the conflict. The expansion of the university system has, furthermore, been more rapid, in many instances, than the expansion of the occupational structure, which tends to aggravate the problem. In addition, Brazil's population growth is also a contributing factor to the increase of inconsistency, because the number of applicants for admission to the universities increases each year. When the universities are not able to absorb them, protest movements are started by those who were not able to obtain admission. Graduates want to live according to the patterns with which they were inculcated. Residence in the large cities, which is concomitant with high status, is a normal expectation. For a physician to go to a rural area or an engineer to go to the interior are alternatives taken only by those who "cannot make it in the city."

The educational system is expanding more rapidly than the industrial occupational structure, creating status inconsistency.[17] Also, the expansion of the industrial occupational structure is not fast enough to absorb the increase of population. These two factors, plus the traditional expectations that education develops in individuals, are some of the crucial factors contributing to the unrest which exists in Brazil.

The unbalance created by industrialization is also noticeable in the lesser

17. Gerhard Lenski, "Status Crystallization: A Non-Vertical Dimension of Social Status," *The American Sociological Review* 19 (1954): 405–13.

developed areas of the country. Opportunities in rural areas are decreasing. Most of the good land has been over-used and extensive reclamation is necessary to recuperate it. Fire or slash and burn agriculture impoverishes the land. Reclamation requires the investment of considerable resources. Such resources are only available to owners of large landholdings and to owners who are able to operate a farm with a high degree of technology. Most Brazilian agriculturists lack one or both of these requirements. Traditional agriculture still prevails, and the soil is not fertile enough to sustain those who depend upon it. In addition, credit is difficult to obtain, machinery is very expensive, and fertilizers are frequently prohibitive. Under these conditions only the very efficient farmer is able to operate and sell products with profit.

The high cost of modern agricultural technology and the depletion of the soil have created a concentration of land and resources. Those who cannot operate a farm, at least at a subsistence level, are likely to sell to those who own or have access to capital. Machinery is taking the place of men almost as a result of the high cost of agricultural inputs. Farms are administered in a very efficient way, in an industry pattern. Many of the "farmers" are industrialists or urban people.[18]

Stratification in the rural areas is tending to revert to the past system—large landowners, on the one hand, and agricultural laborers, on the other. The difference is that these plantation-type farms resemble more an industry than a traditional farm. Since the large operators have capital, they are able to recuperate the impoverished land and operate it profitably. Those who cannot survive as farmers have to become agricultural laborers or move to the cities.

Summarizing, Brazilian social structure can be characterized as being in transition. The basic social unit, the *fazenda* syndrome which molded the social structure, has given place to an emergent urban-industrial structure. The latter can be observed in the most modern section of the country, while the former can still be found in the interior. However, "modern" Brazil is not completely industrial or urban, since many of the characteristics of the traditional pattern can be found. The importance of the family and friendship in achieving certain positions, the lack of acceptance of modern occupations associated with the industrial structure, the copying of upper-class values, etc., tend to create conflicts between what individuals can achieve and their expectations. During the transition period, people can move upward in the hierarchy, but upward social mobility is mainly due to the cre-

18. Unión Panamericaine, Comité Interamericano de Desarrollo Agrícola, *Inventoire de l' information de base pour la programmation du développement agricole en Amerique latine* (Washington, D.C., 1964).

ation of new positions rather than to personal merit. It is possible that in the recruitment system for those new positions personal ties are more important than individual abilities.

Where industry has not developed, the traditional dualist system is more prevalent. Perhaps the major difference between present-day rural cities of the interior and the ones of the past is that contemporary cities are much larger in number. Such a pattern reflects the reversion to a neo-dualist structure in rural areas in which landowners exercise control from the large urban centers, resulting in a lack of the vertical solidarity which characterized the *fazenda* system.

Chapter 11

The Growth of Cities and Urban Development

José Arthur Rios

R APID URBAN GROWTH has been a characteristic feature of Brazil since the fifties. The sixties carried the trend still further, and it is not likely that it will change in the next decade. Brazilians, and especially Brazilian administrators and planners, have become city conscious and acutely aware of the critical aspects implicit in this new trend. Urban planning, "urbanization," and urban development became common in the technocrat's jargon of the sixties. Some of these terms were spread and institutionalized by federal agencies such as the National Housing Bank (BNH) and its Federal Service on Housing and Urbanism (SERFHAU).

Spectacular though they may be, it is necessary first of all to distinguish in the process of urban growth the demographic from the sociological aspects and implications, all of which are usually summed up in Brazilian texts by the word "urbanization." The demographic growth of our urban population has three important features:

(1) The most outstanding is the quantitative growth of the urban population, which increased from 13 million in 1940 to 19 million in 1950 and to 32 million in 1960. This growth is not uniform in all the regions of Brazil. Some are more "urban" (*urbanizadas*) than others. For the decade of the fifties, the index of urban growth was above 50 per cent in Goiás, Paraná, Santa Catarina, Mato Grosso, Paraíba, Alagoas, Amazonas, Piauí, Ceará, Rio Grande do Norte, Minas Gerais, São Paulo, and Rio Grande do Sul. As is apparent, these percentage increases have nothing to do with the area of the state or the size of its population and seem instead to be linked to regional poles of growth caused by the opening up of new agricultural frontiers—a fact common in recent Brazilian history—or to the discovery of new sources of energy, or to the development of industrial complexes. Brasília (450,000

269

in 1968) is a unique phenomenon, a capital built up out of the wilderness—unique as a planned federal capital, not as a boom town, which it is not. Be as it may, the urban population of Brazil represented 31 per cent of the total thirty years ago, and 36 per cent twenty years ago. In 1960 it was almost half the total population and is estimated to be more than half at present.

(2) Urban population growth is backed by an expansion of the urban network. In 1960 Brazil had 2,763 cities, including 28,500,000 people, almost 90 per cent of the total urban population. The distribution of the cities' population is quite revealing: 6 included more than 500,000 people; 25 from 100,000 to 500,000; 37 from 50,000 to 100,000; 104 from 20,000 to 50,000; 199 from 10,000 to 20,000; 358 from 5,000 to 10,000; 867 from 2,000 to 5,000; and 1,167 below 2,000.

The real meaning of the data is fully grasped when we understand that our census considers as urban those people who live in "cities" and villages (*vilas*). City, however, is every seat of a *município* (county), no matter how small is the number of its inhabitants. Under this administrative criterion, some of the "cities" may be destitute of essential urban services, such as water and sewage, but the people who tread barefoot upon their unpaved streets and live in their huts are counted as urban.

The sociological error is corrected when only the population of cities above 2,000 is taken as a basis to gauge the growth of urban population. Even so, it is still appalling. The increase is general in all categories of the urban hierarchy, although it differs from region to region. Data show that the process of growth starts in the lower strata of the urban network and pervades the whole system.

(3) The most impressive trait of the process, however, is the amount of urban concentration. Population seems to flock to cities everywhere but in higher proportions to a few great cities. In 1960 two capitals included almost 20 per cent of the total urban population and four of them almost one-fourth of the same total. Still more impressive, the first two contained almost 10 per cent of the *total* Brazilian population.

Census data only recently took into account the metropolises. Figures dealing with the population of a city only include people within its *município* (county) limits. It includes suburbs and, small as they might be, rural areas, but excludes satellites or dormitory cities if they are located beyond the county boundary.

To understand the difference this makes, we can take the case of Rio de Janeiro (city), now officially rebaptized state of Guanabara, since the federal capital was transferred to Brasília. In 1960 the total population of Guanabara was 3,307,000. This figure omits Niterói, the capital of the neighboring state of Rio de Janeiro, but, as a matter of fact, a suburb of the city of Rio, located across the bay. It also leaves aside Nova Iguaçú, Duque de Caxias and Nilópolis, satellite cities outside the boundaries of Guanabara, not to mention Petrópolis, a summer resort up in the mountains. Greater Rio in 1960 had between 4 and 4.7 million inhabitants, depending on the definition used.[1] The same occurs in São Paulo. The city proper (*município*) had a population of 3.8 million. Greater São Paulo (plus Guarulhos, Mauá, Santo André, São Bernardo do Campo and São Caetano do Sul) had 4.4 million.

The failure to master the metropolis reflects only one facet of the general cultural shock created by urbanization. New forces have appeared which have changed and are changing the rhythm and trends of Brazilian development and which influence the life and behavior of millions, upsetting traditional patterns of family life and the life, customs, and working habits of our population. If it is true that *homo urbanus* is a distinctive feature of the West, we might assert that only now is Brazil as a whole beginning to integrate into Western civilization.

It means more than the affluence of a larger number of people to the cities which become their primary surroundings and source of living. A great number of Brazilians look to cities as a source of freedom from social and economic ties related to traditional rural life. There is a constant and irreversible movement from rural to urban areas, from small communities to regional centers, large cities, and metropolises. After taking the first and awkward steps of their education on the farm or in the village, millions of Brazilians are graduating in the urban complexes. Large-scale changes in the functions of cities are related to this. As all kinds of pressures are exerted on them, the urban agglomerates become more diversified, more complex, and undergo a spontaneous process of physical renewal which anticipates and oversteps the work of city planners and engineers.

On the other hand, urban concentration of such proportions itself produces tremendous social, economic, political, and administrative effects, which so far have scarcely been studied and evaluated. It can only be explained by a centripetal model of national development fostered by the federal government and favored by the highly centralizing trends of Brazilian society. It concentrates investments, income, political power, and administrative decisions, as well as the essential health and educational services, in some privileged urban centers. Paradoxically, such a concentration seems to increase as the rural hinterland becomes poorer and poorer—to such an extent that to many observers it appeared as a kind of "internal colonialism" pumping the life and blood of the interior to the poles of urban centralization and domination. Discarding the conception of cities as parasites, it is undeniable that, in our social history, there is a constant trend towards such urban concentration as against rural development. After 1930, many plans

1. Cedug-Doxiadis, *Guanabara, A Plan for Urban Development* (Rio: 1965).

and programs of a varied nature, but of only temporary effect and short-range, tried to countervail this tendency. Such was the real meaning of the "march westwards" (*marcha para o Oeste*) launched in Vargas' time, the municipalist movement (*municipalismo*) in the fifties, or the recent attempts to send young graduates or professionals to the backlands (*Operação Rondon, Interiorização de Técnicos*, etc.). Almost all profit city dwellers and merely contribute to raise personnel expenditures in the federal and state budgets.

This huge draining of human and material resources by some urban centers has impressed several scholars, foreign and Brazilian. Geographer Milton Santos, for instance, when studying the city of Salvador (capital of the state of Bahia, which had 10.5 per cent of the state's total population and 30 per cent of its urban population in 1960) tried to place the process in a Latin American perspective and showed the disparity of per capita income between the state capital and the remainder of the state, US$120 and US$35, respectively (1958). "In general, the resources accumulated in the city do not result from a real production or from productive activities. They come out of land rents, speculative trade in money and goods, from administration and commission costs, from an overgrowth of bureaucracy, from usury, from speculation with real estate, rents and buildings. The city, therefore, becomes a pole of attraction for investments which are not used, unless in small proportion, to change the present situation; on the contrary, they tend to aggravate it."[2]

Everywhere, cities are the result of an affluence of people and capital to centers of domination, but seldom on this huge scale. The growth of cities, like everything else in the Brazilian social structure, is related to the concentration of power and wealth in the hands of privileged groups who exert unlimited and uninhibited control over the economy of the country and over national as well as city planning. Urban booms and decline, frequent in Brazilian urban history, clearly show the tendency to have sudden shifts in the economy brought about by bursts of speculation in the internal or international markets.

Whether it reflects a continuous, long-term process or a discontinuous one, as in the case of boom cities like Goiânia (152 percent growth between 1940 and 1950, 188 percent between 1950 and 1960), this type of urban growth is only achieved through vast rural-urban migration and at the cost of the decline of many rural communities. As professor T. Lynn Smith clearly states: "The tendency of the Brazilian population to abandon its centuries-long practice of rural residence for life in towns and cities is best demonstrated, however, by a study of the comparative rates of growth of

2. Milton Santos, *A Cidade nos Países Subdesenvolvidos* (Rio: Editôra Civilização, 1965), p. 6.

the rural and urban populations during the decade ending in 1960. During that period, in every state and territory of the Brazilian confederation, the rate of growth of the urban population exceeded that of the rural."[3] According to the same authority, the following decade "will prove to be one in which not only all of the natural increase of the rural populations is drawn away to urban centers, but sizable proportions of the 'seed stock' as well. In other words, in many parts of rural Brazil depopulation is imminent."[4]

Brazilian scholars have discussed thoroughly the reasons for the rural-urban migration and the resulting "urbanization" of the country.[5] It is a general belief that industrialization played the role of accelerator in the process. To many, the growth of industries can be identified with the flowering of cities. Juarez Brandão Lopes, for instance, asserts that "The industrial system is the main force in recent Brazilian urbanization."[6] In his study he distinguishes two types of city growth, one which results not so much from the appearance of factories as from changes in the rural economy and the other resulting from the demonstration effect "which arises from the new society born out of mass communications, growing mobility of the population, weakening of patrimonialist relations, etc."[7] In short, he seems to relate Brazilian urbanization to the direct or indirect effects of industrialization, the first working in a limited number of urban centers, the other, through changes in total society.

As a matter of fact, industry and industrialization made large strides in Brazil during the 1950–1960 decade and changed the pattern of its economy. In 1920 Brazil had 13,500 industrial establishments, employing about 300,000 workers. Food and textiles represented 68 per cent of the value of total industrial production. Most of the factories were concentrated in São Paulo and Guanabara (42 per cent), as were the workers (49 per cent) and energy (51 per cent). In 1960 Brazil had 111,000 factories employing almost 1,500,000 workers and using 5 million horsepower. Most of the industrial establishments (69.5 per cent) were in São Paulo, Guanabara, Minas Gerais, and Rio Grande do Sul. In these same states was located a good part of the working population (70 per cent) and electrical capacity (73 per cent). Industrialization was concentrated in the south and southeast, attracting labor and availing itself of the potential consumption market.

3. T. Lynn Smith, *Brazil: People and Institutions*, rev. ed. (Baton Rouge: Louisiana State University Press, 1963), p. 598.

4. Smith, p. 598.

5. On urbanization, see Manuel Diegues, Jr., *Imigração, Urbanização, Industrialização* (Rio: Instituto Nacional de Estudos Pedagógicos, 1964); Philip M. Hauser and Leo F. Schnore, *The Study of Urbanization* (New York: Wiley, 1965); and Paulo Singer, *Desénvolvimento Econômico e Evolução Urbana* (São Paulo: Editôra Nacional, 1968).

6. Juarez Rubens Brandão Lopes, *Desenvolvimento e Mudança Social* (São Paulo: Editôra Nacional, 1968), p. 19.

7. Lopes, p. 18.

Industrial production became stationary between 1962 and 1965, but in 1967 the annual rate was 15 per cent over the 1962 indexes. The structure of industries according to the type of product also changed drastically. The processing industries, food and textiles, lost their first-rank position to minerals, metallurgy, and mechanical industries, and, in general, to new groups of industries such as extractive, building, and electrical energy.

In 1968 the largest group of processing industries was concentrated in three southern states (São Paulo, Guanabara, and Rio Grande do Sul), especially in greater São Paulo. The latter was responsible for 43.5 per cent of the total salaries paid in Brazil and 39 per cent of the value of total industrial production.

This represents a tremendous effort toward industrialization but cannot obscure the fact that economic development in Brazil was the result of three agricultural products—coffee, sugar, and cotton. The expansion of coffee in São Paulo gave origin to the capital applied in industrial growth. "From Independence (1822) to 1968, coffee, sugar and cotton were responsible for more than 50 percent of Brazilian exports and their contribution fell below 60 percent only after 1967."[8]

Until 1930, rates of growth were higher in agricultural production than in industry. After 1930, industrial rates were higher (65 per cent in 1947–1956 and double that figure in 1956–1967). After that they fell to 3.8 per cent per year, whereas agricultural rates remained at 3.7 per cent.

The fall of the volume of agricultural production, accompanied by an inflationary rise in prices between 1965–1967, brought a growing imbalance between industry and agriculture, which intensified rural-urban migration and the decline of the buying power of the urban middle classes, both factors of tremendous impact on urban growth and development.

The migration of the poor from rural areas following the disintegration of latifundia and minifundia[9] and the instability of the lower middle class accounts more than anything else for the type of city growth which has occurred in Brazil. The word "urbanization" has very different meanings when applied to mere quantitative growth and to a sociological process of social promotion and mobility, as measured by the number of people who come to cities in order to avail themselves of urban services. In Campina Grande (100,000 in 1960), an important regional center in the northeast which attracted migrants from its neighboring states, I found that the percentage of people who drank uncontaminated water was less than 35. The sewage network was used by 20 per cent.

8. Oswaldo Benjamin de Azevedo, "O Brasil no Mundo Industrial" in *Carta Mensal* 177 (1969).

9. Edgar Teixeira Leite, "Aspectos do Complexo Agrário Brasileiro" in *Carta Mensal* 177 (1970).

As in many other Brazilian cities, its expansion followed a radial pattern. It left empty spaces between the projections which started from a core. The center as well as upper- and middle-class residential sections were all provided with water, sewage, phones, and electricity. Streets were paved and squares and gardens reflected a great deal of care. The expansion of those utilities, however, as well as that of the built-up area itself, was all but uniform. An aerial view of the city would show many vacant spaces close to the center, resulting mostly from the irregular system of subdivision (*loteamentos*). These spaces slowly filled up with houses but most of the time were invaded by shacks or by precarious homes built by a transient, temporary population. "A simple look at the map shows the lack of coordination or planning in this growth and much more between the appropriated area and the land actually occupied. The area of vacant lots is much larger than the built-up one. The area of stone, cement and brick houses is surrounded and infiltrated by shacks and houses."[10] This irregular pattern has great repercussions on city life and raises the cost of services, putting a high burden on the municipal government, which transfers it through taxes to the small group of taxpayers.

In the average Brazilian city this type of urban growth is quite frequent and is not uncommon even in great cities and state capitals. Lofty buildings and fine monuments, as well as expensive homes, contrast with a lack of essential services and proper urban comfort: a privileged urban center reigns over a periphery of dark suburbia. It is the physical result of a high centralization of urban land in advance of actual occupancy. Inflation plays a central role in this process which is known as *loteamento*.

The real estate agent (in this case, *loteador*) plays in our urban structure the role of the rural land speculator (*grileiro*), described by Monteiro Lobato in an unforgettable passage.[11]

Like the *grileiro*, the *loteador* stimulates an artificial urban expansion, anticipates spontaneous city growth, and, at the same time, destroys traditional ownership and control in many areas. Lobato understood very clearly that the *grileiro* has an important social function, but he did not make clear that he is peculiar to rural areas where latifundia prevail. The same is true of the urban real estate broker. Both create serious problems for the community. The *loteador* does not hesitate in making false deeds and titles and creating fictitious urban subdivisions without any prior planning or provision of urban utilities. He tries to attract to his projects the savings of lower- and middle-class persons and plays with their dreams of security and home

10. José Arthur Rios et al., *Campina Grande: Centro Comercial do Nordeste* (Rio: Serviço Social do Comércio, 1963).
11. Monteiro Lobato, *Onda Verde*, p. 14, quoted in Oliveira Vianna, *Evolução do Povo Brasileiro* (São Paulo: Editôra Nacional, 1933), p. 115.

ownership. Many subdivisions never mature into true residential sections. They end up as slums (*favelas*), and the original design is defaced by the irregularity and crowding of the shacks. This happens many times not only in suburbia or faraway areas but also in the core of great cities, in industrial sections, and on highly valued land.   /

Urbanist Jorge Wilheim correctly asserts that "it is impossible to understand the development, nature, problems, and possibilities of Brazilian cities without going into the *loteamento* process."[12] The idea of merely buying land, waiting for a rise in values, and selling it piecemeal in small lots without any further investment does not correspond exactly to the situation. The actual or potential pressure of urban growth and the loss of value of agricultural land in the vicinity of cities, resulting either from division after successive inheritances or falling productivity, creates conditions for *loteamento*. We saw the same processes working in regions as remote from each other as Itabuna (Bahia), Governador Valadares (Minas Gerais), and Curitiba (Paraná). In the latter it tore out and displaced Polish and Italian settlements, which supplied fruits and vegetables to the city. Rural areas, latifundia, or small holdings (*sítios*) are transformed overnight into *loteamentos* and sold to urban newcomers, usually through a down payment and small long-term installments. Sometimes it is the landowner himself or his inheritors who do the selling and become real estate entrepreneurs. More frequently, bankers, insurance companies, liberal professionals, or sharp traders assume this role by buying decaying, valueless land, minifundia or latifundia, and waiting for the inevitable rise in values (*valorização*), an attitude which pervades all of Brazilian economic history.

On the other hand, it serves the interest of real estate customers, recent rural migrants, people from the lower strata of bureaucracy, or small shopkeepers and tradesmen who are eager to own property so as to avoid payment of rent and to attain a long-desired security and respectability. While still paying for their lots, the new owners build the house, usually with their own hands and the help of relatives and neighbors, under one form or another of traditional mutual aid (*mutirão*).[13] At the same time, they exert pressure on the local authorities to provide the new community or *bairro* with water, sewage, electricity, schools, etc. This is done through the mediation of actual politicians or potential candidates to public offices, in short through some type or other of patron (*padrinho*). Sometimes the new owners themselves urge the authorities to tax them. They are willing to pay

12. Jorge Wilheim, *Urbanismo no Subdesenvolvimento* (Rio: Editôra Saga, 1969), p. 45.

13. See José Arthur Rios, "Operação Mutirão" in *Cuadernos Latino Americanos de Economia Humana* 7 (1961); José Alípio Goulart, "Favelas do Distrito Federal" in *Estudos Brasileiros* 5 (1957); and Helio Galvão, "O Mutirão no Nordeste" in *Documentário da Vida Rural* 15 (1959).

taxes to enter into the full status of city dwellers and not be "marginals," i.e., underdogs. Immediately values rise and the able entrepreneur has no trouble selling the remaining lots, without any additional investment, for higher prices.

Needless to say, such a process converts the majority of our cities into a mess and distorts any attempt to develop a well-balanced budget or physical planning. The problem is most serious in great capitals like Rio de Janeiro and São Paulo.

From this perspective, what appears as quantitative growth in census data is a huge transfer of poverty from rural to urban areas bringing along with it all sorts of social problems. It is called by many *inchacão* (bloating). It results in poor housing, lack of community identity, heavy and unequal taxation, vagrancy, and urban delinquency. It is responsible for huge concentrations of houses built out of precarious materials—planks, tin cans, and even cardboard. It is at the roots of *favelas* (slums) and *favelização* (slum growth).

The important point to stress about the physical aspects of this suburbanization, dismal as it may be, is the presence in cities of a great mass of unskilled and casual laborers. Not all slum-dwellers of every kind are unemployed or unskilled laborers. (As a matter of fact, as the *favela* grows older, it includes a higher percentage of "respectable citizens.") However, this fact is truer of new *favelas* and other types of housing sought by the urban newcomer. The transient worker or *biscateiro*, more than the so-called *inativo* (unemployed), is the protagonist of this sub-urbanization, which ends up in the lowering of levels of living, social degradation (*cafagestimo*), and the general debasing of educational and cultural values in large cities.

It is difficult to evaluate the process quantitatively. However, in Rio I had the opportunity to compare the growth of urban districts and the growth of *favelas* and, above all, the growth of districts with and without *favelas*. The rate of growth of the *favelas'* population proved to be higher than that of the remainder of the city.

In 1950 Rio, where *favela* dwelling is typical, had 170,000 people living in *favelas*. In 1960 there were 147 *favelas*, with a population of 340,000. This is a rather conservative count. Other estimates mention 800,000 to 1 million, about one-third of the total population of Rio. If all types of underhoused and marginal people are included, I do not hesitate in subscribing to the latter figure. More impressive, however, is the rate of growth of the *favelas'* population: 10 per cent a year as compared to 4 per cent for the total population of Rio. The real meaning of this can only be grasped when we study the change effected in some Rio districts by the growth of its *favelas*.

Internal rural-urban migration is the basic factor behind the phenomenon.

In 1950, 18.2 per cent of the population of Rio consisted of migrants (people born in other states). The comparable figure for São Paulo was 11.8 per cent. The 1950 census indicated that in Rio's *favelas* 27 per cent of the population came from the state of Rio de Janeiro, 7 per cent from Espírito Santo, and 16 per cent from Minas Gerais. In the larger *favelas*, which are also the oldest, a new factor comes into the picture, tied to recent shifts of the internal population of the city and even more closely related to recent demolitions and to the dominant motive in choosing a place to live in the city: the closeness of residence to place of work.

What appears, above all, from the evidence is the particular nature of urban growth in Brazil. "Tertiarism," with Brazilian connotations, is the immediate factor responsible for accelerated urban growth. Occupations in the lower strata of the tertiary sector do not require developed skills and are favored by the volume and nature of economic life in the cities. Trade and services, in general, more easily absorb larger quantities of unskilled labor, and their transient character allows people to secure more than one job, therefore testing themselves, so to speak, learning new techniques, and adjusting to low salaries and less than minimum wages (*sub-faturamento*), all conditions imposed by the employer. According to Brandão Lopes, in 1950 tertiary activities were responsible for 29 per cent of urban growth in the less-developed states, and 33 per cent in moderately developed and in well-developed states. In other words, as he puts it, for one person entering industrial employment between 1940 and 1950, 5.2 obtained employment in the tertiary sector in cities belonging to the first group of states, 2.7 in the second group, and 1.7 in the third.[14]

The tertiary sector is, therefore, as Lopes exhaustively demonstrated, the main locus of *inchação*. But below the *biscateiros* (underemployed) we have to add to the picture the unemployed (*inativos*). The same authority, working with 1950 census data, estimated that the percentage of the labor force in the tertiary sector was about 18 in Recife and Fortaleza, 12 in Rio, 10 in São Paulo, and 14 in Pôrto Alegre. Summing up his analysis he states: "[There is] a process of urbanization in many areas of the country which is largely independent of any industrial development. The consequence is the constant growth of the unemployed and underemployed. Unemployment looms larger in smaller cities, underemployment in the larger ones."[15]

Urban growth in Brazil, under the features we ascribe to it, is more closely related to the main traits of our agrarian structure than to any other factor. It is frequently forgotten that, in the present phase of our technological development, cities are closely dependent on rural areas for food supplies; they also lean on them heavily for human resources. The type and

14. Lopes, pp. 19–30.
15. Lopes, p. 30.

nature of the rural migrant is an all-important factor in shaping the quality, values, and styles of life of our cities.

In the beginning our cities were simple projections of their rural surroundings. They originated from an agrarian society, and their specifically urban functions arose in a recent phase of our social development. There has been a close dependence, since colonial times, of cities on the countryside, of urban activities on agriculture. "All the structure of our colonial society had its roots outside the cities."[16] This situation prevailed until abolition, which fostered the exodus of former slaves to urban areas and was the first important benchmark in the history of our cities. During colonial times the landowners had their permanent homes in the city. They would come to it to do business, to buy everything which was not produced on the latifundium, for recreation, in vacation periods, or at election time. But the sources of power remained in the countryside.

In imperial times the urban elites were formed by landowners or their descendants educated for the liberal professions. The first wave of material improvements in our cities, as Afonso Arinos once remarked, was launched by men related to agriculture. These improvements covered a wide range of utility companies, banks, telegraph, railways, and tramways, but control remained in the hands of sugarmill owners and coffee and cotton growers.

Buarque de Holanda called attention to the fact that in Brazil, unlike all countries of recent colonial history, one cannot find forms of intermediary social life between the agricultural landholdings and the urban center, as anyone can observe in almost all Brazilian regions. In America, he added, the distinction between the plantation and the city equals the distance between village and city. Till a certain moment of our social history, Brazil contradicted North American and European tendencies of progressive urban growth through short-distance migrations. Only in recent days were the functions of cities expanded to include power of decision in political, economic, and financial matters. At the same time, they developed more efficient mechanisms of centralization and absorption of rural manpower and income.

Until the beginning of the twentieth century, the wealthy lived in the countryside. Cities were inhabited by soldiers, bureaucrats, merchants, craftsmen, and tradesmen. They lacked almost every comfort and facility, and descriptions of these towns by chroniclers and travelers up until the nineteenth century matched those of medieval cities as described by Pirenne and Mumford.

Paradoxically, Portuguese colonization, pervaded by mercantilist ideas and state-centered, became, in Brazil, ruralist. Having started with the *feito-*

16. Sergio Buarque de Holanda, *Raízes do Brasil* (Rio: Livraria José Olímpio Editôra, 1936).

rias, colonization became agrarian and aristocratic, with a feudalistic tinge, given the poverty and vastness of the country. As soon as colonists left the shores of Europe, they seemed to forget the democratic village community. The municipal government they brought to America was definitely based on landownership.

Dutch colonization in the northeast might have changed these prospects. Dutchmen had reached a high level of urban progress and sophistication. The improvements they brought to Recife were definitely well ahead of Portuguese conceptions of city development, but were wiped out by the fires which followed the Luso-Brazilian reconquest.[17]

At the end of the eighteenth century, the situation changed and landowners became more and more dependent on the merchant class. It can be stated that a succession occurred in real estate and that a competition for the control of agricultural production took place which reacted on urbanization. The merchants played the role of moneylenders, financing crops. The landowners' failures transferred to the former an increasing number of holdings. However, even during the imperial period, the *Brazilian* was by definition the countryman and the merchant, a newcomer. The contemporary literature revolves around rural themes and situations. Urban scenery and types until mid-century did not seem to attract novelists, probably because they did not feel them to be really representative of Brazil.

This trend changed in the later years of the empire and, above all, with the abolition of slavery and the proclamation of the republic, mostly because of the migration to cities of former slaves and, in the case of Rio and São Paulo, the new waves of foreign immigrants. São Paulo, at the beginning of the century, was an Italian creation, as Rio was a product of the Portuguese grocer and Salvador, a product of the Spaniard.

The republic (1889–1930) is the period of the great urban improvements, financed by the British and, later on, by American capital. From 1872 on, as Richard Graham puts it, "urban growth became characteristic."[18]

All this urban expansion was financed by agriculture, mostly by coffee. As a matter of fact, the gold brought by coffee exports helped finance government through taxes, as well as industries, railways, business in general, banking, and all kinds of urban improvements.[19]

Both the agrarian backbone of Brazilian social structure and the rural origin of city dwellers left its mark on urban development. Brazilian cities only imperfectly and as an exception played the role of social levellers. The urban middle class is a thin layer and a recent phenomenon in the country.

17. Nelson Omegna, *A Cidade Colonial* (Rio: Livraria José Olímpio Editôra, 1961).
18. Richard Graham, *Britain and the Onset of Modernization in Brazil, 1850–1914* (Cambridge: Cambridge University Press, 1968).
19. Paulo Pinto de Carvalho, quoted in José Fernando Carneiro, "Matérias Primas e Productos Manufaturados" in *Correio do Povo* (Pôrto Alegre, 1967).

Although fostering ethnic miscegenation, cities grew up as socially heterogeneous aggregates, where class distinctions and strata were sharply defined. Still today in many cities, the observer will look vainly for a middle class; whereas, upper and lower strata are quite apparent. Marginal areas and populations (*favelas, mucambos, malócas, cortiços*) reflect the presence of large groups which have only a slight chance to climb up the urban social ladder and who are not socially or culturally assimilated into urban patterns and life styles.

However, leaving aside these aspects of the social structure produced by a strangled labor market and a precarious economy, still, many traits of Brazil's rural social organization are commonly found in the cities. One is the general insubmission of city dwellers to the norms and rules of city life. "No man in this land is community conscious, nor concerned with the public welfare, but cares only about his private wealth. . . . So that the household of the wealthy is well provided with everything. . . . But in the villages nothing is found. Water streams, bridges, pathways and all public utilities are in very poor conditions, because everyone counts on his neighbour and nobody cares about their maintenance even though they drink dirty water and get wet when they try to wade the rivers or tread the paths, and all that because their main concern is not the things they will leave here (in the colony) but the wealth they want to take back with them to the Kingdom (Portugal)."[20] This statement by Frei Vicente do Salvador about sixteenth-century Bahia is still valid in our days for many Brazilian capitals where public authority is unable to impose its disciplines, either traffic rules or building provisions, on a great number of urbanites. In cities the conflict between public order and private interest, well-studied by Nestor Duarte, still prevails.[21]

But the city itself has its land problems. In a certain sense, it has its latifundia and minifundia. Urban latifundia, also resulting from absenteeism and speculation, reflect not only a great amount of concentration of wealth but, as in the countryside, the lack or ineffectiveness of taxes on real estate. As happens with agricultural lands, urban holdings remain consolidated as long as values remain high, feeding on the owner's social and economic prestige and on family solidarity. As soon as it collapses, the urban manor no longer withstands the pressures of demographic growth and the pitfalls of inheritance. It falls apart, prey to the broker and the speculator. In its first phase it becomes a low-class tenement (*cabeca de porco*) or is shredded into very small, low-cost houses (*vilas*), a lower middle-class type of urban development very usual in Brazilian cities in the first half of the twentieth

20. Frei Vicente do Salvador, *História do Brasil*, 3rd ed. (São Paulo: Companhia Melhoramentos, 1954), p. 17.
21. Nestor Duarte, *A Ordem Privada e a Organização Política Nacional* (São Paulo: Editôra Nacional, 1939), passim.

century and still existent. If the location is valuable of itself, in a later phase the tenement gives way to the apartment house, the supermarket, or the bank.

Behind all these changes there is a valuation of land which depends on inflation more than on anything else. It works more rapidly in the cities than in the countryside, attracting profits and savings generated by agriculture, quite frequently invested thousands of miles away from their original source and even from the region where the agricultural holding is located.

The high value of urban land and its capacity to produce high incomes, either through rents or sheer increase in value without the counterpart of an adequate and fair real estate tax, does not stimulate the building of low cost housings in cities, and is a permanent factor in the creation of slums and all kinds of marginal agglomerates.

Strange as it may seem, the high prize collected by land speculation in cities is not precluded by the imprecision of titles, legal entanglements, delays in settlements, frequent suits, and all kinds of handicaps to real estate liquidity, easily removed by the wealthy but impossible for the poor and half-literate to overcome.

In this sense it is quite legitimate and up-to-date to talk in Brazil about urban reform. Brazilian scholars prefer to distinguish between (1) *urban growth*, a demographic and ecological process usually spontaneous or "natural"; (2) *development*, a semi-voluntary expansion which results from economic factors set in motion or put together by entrepreneurial imagination or political leadership, such as subdivisions, artificial cities, public works, etc.; and (3) *urban planning*, a type of expansion dictated by welfare reasons and directed by a public authority. In the new semantics of the technocrats the concept of *integrated* urban planning was introduced as a sophistication of the same concept.[22] So far, the expression (4) *urban reform* has been used to mean plain socialization of urban property. In the years preceding the 1964 revolution it was used both by the Left and by the government with a demagogic connotation implying general expropriation of urban property or at least the blocking of rents.

There is no doubt that something has to be done to cope with the deterioration of the city and the lack of adequate housing for a great part of its population. The Brazilian government, through the National Housing Bank (BNH), has tried to change the situation and establish a national housing policy. Federal investments have been heavy in this sector, NCr$6,268,551,000 (US$179,100,000) in 1968 for housing programs.[23]

22. Harry James Cole, *Informe do Seminário de Planejamento Estadual* (Quitandinha: Serviço Federal de Habitação e Urbanismo, 1965), mimeographed.
23. Instituto Brasileiro de Geografia e Estatística, *Anuário Estatístico do Brasil, 1969* (Rio: Conselho Nacional de Estatística, 1969).

These figures represent a tremendous waste of money and hide the failure to cope with the problem. A system for financing housing, although successful, will never take the place of a social and physical plan of urban renewal. The people benefitted by the system will never be those in greatest need. The core of the so-called "housing deficit"—a frightening figure which becomes meaningless as compared with the effective number of people able to buy, rent, or build a house—is urban poverty. So far, the bank has mostly been a source of profit to the building industry. It has been a real bonanza to big building concerns in Rio, São Paulo, and the larger cities.

Bank policy in the slums has been sharply criticized. In Rio it has favored the state government trend of "eradicating" the slums. This really means the transplanting of thousands of people from their usual dwelling place to great apartment houses (*conjuntos*) in remote suburban areas, far from their places of work, thus breaking their neighborhood ties, their cultural patterns, disintegrating their families and adding new stress to their budgets by increasing transportation cost and by putting them in a highly capitalistic system of home installment payments, subject to periodic increases to adjust for inflation without any corresponding readjustment of their salaries. The result is the introduction on the Brazilian scene of a new type of marginal housing, the urban ghetto.[24] This anti-social policy destroys values, disintegrates popular culture, and threatens the bare living of slum-dwellers by increasing their economic burdens. On the other hand, it fosters concentration of wealth and "clientelism" in the higher brackets.

The false assimilation of urban and agrarian reform is easy to understand. The pressure of real estate owners on the legislature to subvert rent control laws grew steadily with inflation, which, in the last months of Goulart's regime went up to 80 per cent a year.[25] On the other hand, renters have entrenched themselves with the "freezing" of rents (*congelamento*). Demagogues and social extremists played with the renters' anguish by advocating the nationalization of urban property.

The analogy with agrarian problems, to say the least, is superficial. First of all, home ownership is widespread among city dwellers. In research on the cost of living done by the Fundação Getúlio Vargas, the percentage of owners in the total sample of 4,625 families looms large.[26] A slogan such as "land to the workers" would sound meaningless in the cities. Besides, there is a great difference in the nature of the functions of rural and urban land. The first is a direct productive resource either for food or for commercial

24. José Arthur Rios, "Reforma Urbana ou Planejamento?" in *Arquitetura* 54 (dezembro 1966).
25. Ministério do Planejamento, *Programa Estratégico de Desenvolvimento, 1968/70*, vol. 1 (Rio, 1968).
26. Fundação Getúlio Vargas, *Pesquisa sôbre Orçamentos Familiares, Habitação* (Rio, 1961 / 62); see also Wilheim, p. 45.

crops. Absenteeism and land speculation directly affect production and the food supply. Agricultural land, therefore, besides being a primary good, is itself capital. The general purpose of an agrarian reform is to place land in the ablest hands, in order to increase agricultural production and to avoid wastes resulting from its idleness.

The nature of urban land is rather different. The secondary and tertiary nature of cities superimposed different functions on the primary function of urban soil and suppressed its original purpose. Being useless for production of goods, it became a utility and an important generator of rent, a value in itself. In many cases, even without any productive investment, it generates higher rents than many areas devoted to agricultural exploitation. The market value of an urban acre is established by variables which have little in common with those which apply to an agricultural holding, such as density, location in relation to types of transportation and to certain centers of dominance, or pure fashion. This is the main reason why it becomes quite vulnerable to real estate speculation and inflationary trends.

In Brazil, urban land, by providing a large profit margin, attracted a great share of upper- and middle-class savings. As compared with other types of investment (in agriculture, industry, business), it affords a higher rent. In urban fringe areas the competition between agricultural uses and urban subdivision, due to several factors, is striking. In Londrina, Paraná, coffee farms have common boundaries with urban backyards and are pushed back by urban development. In Itabuna, Bahia, old cocoa plantations fall prey to urban real estate brokers when land productivity and earnings start to decline. In places such as these the usual cycle of the latifundium is interrupted, but instead of minifundia it gives origin to urban subdivisions.

In great part, urban land is disputed by families that come to cities looking for jobs, higher wages, social security benefits, education, recreation, and culture. These motives create in cities powerful poles of attraction for different types of short- and long-range migrations. On the other hand, this movement does not encounter its counterpart in the development of facilities such as housing and public utilities, because their cost and bare availability are quite beyond their reach.

Urban growth of itself, without a social policy and physical planning, creates a huge waste of human resources. Urban growth is similar to a chain reaction: any increase in the number of vehicles, in the volume of, and in the amount of services leads to an expansion of manufactures, an increase in the transportation network, and, through it, an increment of all industries. Urbanization of itself, even before industries develop or, on the contrary, have already collapsed, generates a tertiary expansion, under the form of services—educational, health, and cultural. Juiz de Fora, a regional urban center in Minas Gerais (200,000, in 1960) is a good example of the maintenance of high standards of urbanization.[27] The modern Brazilian city is also the home of an expanding bureaucracy. When it plays the role of national, state, or regional capital, it tends to grow and have a multiplying effect on the demand for labor which feeds back into housing, city utilities, and so forth.

In Brazil, as everywhere, this type of marginal or proletarian lower- and middle-class migration flows to cities in a volume quite superior to the cities' capacity of absorption insofar as equipment, the labor market, communications, and services are involved. Idleness and semi-idleness is just a social expression of an overall unpreparedness to cope with migrants and their impact.

In the last years several approaches have been tried in Brazil to cope with urban problems resulting from growth.

(1) So far, purely physical development has produced poor results, although it still enjoys great favor among administrators and politicians. A typical, purely physical solution is the opening up of large avenues, a historical European heritage of ancient Rome. Their main purpose is to open new paths to the center and, at the same time, to create new and wide surroundings for urban marches, carnival festivities, processions, and military parades. But the avenues require great and costly demolitions as well as the expulsion of many people to the suburban and marginal areas. Workers who had chosen a place of residence near the center are, therefore, compelled to look for a new home under conditions of stress. Besides aggravating the pressures on their budgets, their new mobility worsens the transportation problem from the suburbs to downtown. On the other hand, the new avenue raises the real estate values in the area, and outdates the former rent structure. New types of land utilization take place, better adapted to the new situation, but no entrepreneur would consider the possibility of establishing low-cost housing projects on the vacant lots. Soon, the new avenue is insufficient for the volume of traffic, and new solutions of the same monumental kind, involving great works and the payment of costly indemnities, start a new cycle.

Everywhere in Brazil, the congestion of the centers of cities seems to follow the one million mark, when a sort of critical stage in the disease is reached. Along the same line of purely physical solutions, the opening up of wide avenues has been coupled with the skyscraper, symbol of the "American" vertical city. Big buildings increase the density of the center to the breaking point, and many capitals, proud of their new skylines, suffer from energy deficits, lack of parking, traffic jams, and lack of space for educational and recreational activities. In the fight for space, the first to suf-

27. José Arthur Rios et al., *Estudos para o Desenvolvimento Integrado de Juiz de Fora*, vols. 1–2 (Rio, 1968), mimeographed.

fer, i.e., to move out, are *favelados* and occupants of low-rent houses, who occupy highly valued land. In Rio the new policy is no longer slum "urbanization" but "eradication," which means the destruction of shacks in the fashionable sections and the transfer of their inhabitants to huge apartment houses in the suburbs.[28] Cornered by the periodical upward readjustment of installment payments, their buying power falls, as well as their hopes of raising their status. These ghetto dwellers become a new layer in Rio's housing stratification, placed above the *favelados* from whom they have compulsorily been differentiated and below the middle-class homeowner with whom they are not able to identify.

From all this it is apparent that purely physical growth and urban development create more problems than they solve. Besides, their operational costs are extremely high, much higher than urban investments, which although encouraged by chronic inflation, also acts undercover as a camouflaged tax. On the other hand, the operational cost of cities accounts, above all, for the impossibility of coping with inflation. Brasília is a definite case of artificial urban development without planning. Its operational costs have been rising, as well as its *favelado* population (now around 100,000).[29]

Mere expansion and growth, or what is usually termed urban development, has already produced its fruits in Brazil as elsewhere. Something else has to be tried to save our cities from chaos.

(2) Planning was the next phase of the government's approach to the problem. Both SERFHAU, an agency subordinated to the BNH, and the Ministry of Interior assumed the responsibility of stimulating this new trend by financing preliminary pilot and overall planning studies in our cities, as well as the development of county-wide plans. The Ministry of Interior has been instrumental in fostering planning by making obligatory the presentation of a program of public works in order to liberate quotas paid by the federal government to counties. Urban planning has not received the same impetus. SERFHAU is the special agency in charge of the problem. It selects urban priorities, approves proposals, and pays for them. The city mayor has little to say in the process. The high interest charged by the BNH on its loans is pointed out as one of the reasons for failure. The other is the general resistance to change in city administrators, echoing, in this case, the same and even stronger resistance put up by vested interests. In São Paulo the failure of the bill proposed by a group of urbanists led by Anhaia Melo and placing limitations on building (*gabaritos*) was defeated by the city legislature clearly representing real estate and building interests.

Many of these planners have been accused of irrealism. Hirschman's ap-

28. Govêrno do Estado da Guanabara, *Rio-Operação Favela* (Rio, 1969).
29. Robert T. Daland, *Brazilian Planning* (Chapel Hill: University of North Carolina Press, 1967), p. 214.

proach to planning in Latin America, in general, is worth quoting. The core of the matter, as he puts it, is "to show how a society can begin to move forward as it is, in spite of what it is and because of what it is." Nonetheless, the efforts of Brazilian geographers, economists, sociologists, and urbanists to build up an interdisciplinary concept of integrated planning deserves mention. According to its promoters, integrated local planning is the summing up of economic, social, and physical planning, and its integration at the regional and local levels.[30]

Urban planning in Brazil cannot be, in fact will never be, mere physical planning. Integrated or not, it has to develop a wider approach to urban problems. It has to contemplate, before all else, the burden of the underprivileged and their promotion to higher standards of living. City growth has been traditionally tied up with upper-middle-class patterns, values, and styles. It is time to shift the trend of urban development to include the ghetto and *favela* also, as an urbanistic possibility. In many, the middle class itself is still marginal, and general conditions—monumentalism, high operational costs, lack of manpower resources related to heavy taxation—lead to its strangulation and to bitter class confrontation.

Urban zoning is not enough whenever a wider scheme of decentralization, political as well as administrative, is required. The corrupted and highly centralized governments of our cities, mostly in state capitals and metropolitan areas, are inept in consulting the real interest, values, and goals of local urban communities.

In the planning model of Caxias, state of Rio de Janeiro (300,000 population in 1968), Paulo Novaes advanced a step further in formulating a methodology for planned development inspired by his Brazilian and African experiences. Taking as his primary goal the transfer and the establishment of the largest possible number of families in the city as permanent residents—as an urban middle class and not just as a labor force—he sees the core of the problem as being the creation of self-supporting jobs, as well as adequate housing zones. This necessitates the development of self-supporting processes which will decrease, locally, the exportation of labor and the importation of goods. The stimuli to local production can only be provided through low-input, labor-consuming technologies (so far, in the usual plans, export industries have been the general goal), which raise forcibly the amount of investment needed to create new jobs. In the SUDENE area the average investment is NCr$70,000 to NCr$100,000 (US$20,000 to US$28,500). In the Aratú industrial center (state of Bahia) it is NCr$200,000 (US$57,000).[31]

This new scheme might be based on a cooperative system and become operational through shorter distances between home and place of work, reduc-

30. Cole, p. 7.
31. "Dez Anos de SUDENE," *Revista Visão* (19/26 dezembro 1969), p. 102.

tion of transportation costs, higher utilization of unskilled labor, decreased circulating capital, utilization of common stocks and central warehouses, simplification of mechanical processes, encouragement of teamwork, and a progressive rise in labor skills. This down-to-the-ground planning would have to be supported by adequate tax policies. In Caxias "any attempt to produce goods or services related to a highly mechanized technology would be unrealistic."[32]

However, official efforts have been exerted in the other direction. Capital-rather than labor-consuming industries have been exclusivly fostered as the primary goal of urban development. They result, as often as not, in unemployment and underemployment, high operational urban costs, urban ghettos, and slum development, as well as in national dependence.

Nothing new, however, can be expected under the present framework of legal ownership prevalent in urban real estate. The Roman concept of absolute rights of private ownership influenced Brazil's Civil Code and still prevails in urban legal relations. The common good is defenseless in a confrontation with usury and individual interests.

If the expression "urban reform" has any meaning at all in Brazil, it indicates a set of legal measures tending to assert the right of public intervention in order to correct the uses and abuses of usury and speculation in urban real estate and to utilize it according to the best interests and needs of the common good. On the other hand, urban taxation must cease to be a means of oppression used by an often unscrupulous bureaucracy and become the sound basis for a zoning policy which fosters the preservation of human and natural values in our cities.

Everywhere there is a great need for innovation in these areas, as well as less formalistic and more manager-like types of urban government, free of archaic survivals congenial only to traditional Brazilian structures.[33]

As Brazilian cities move into the one million category, many have already taken the shape of metropolises, and the megalopolis looms on the horizon. It is high time to confront urban development with something more than technology, skyscrapers, subways, and the fragile hope that they will solve the social and economic problems of the cities. Such a short view would mean, at the least, giving up in the prospective city the higher values of civilization and the noblest creations of the human mind.

32. Paulo Novaes, *Um Modêlo para Caxias* (Rio: Pontifícia Universidade Católica do Rio de Janeiro, 1969), mimeographed.
33. José Arthur Rios, "The Geography of Rio and its Effects on Local Government" in W. A. Robson, *The Great Cities of the World* (London: George Allen and Unwin, 1961).

Chapter 12

The Evolution of Brazilian Literature

Earl W. Thomas

URING THE FIRST three centuries after the founding of the first permanent settlements in Brazil, its intellectual life formed a part of that of the mother country. The importance to us of what was written then is mostly historical. These works give us some idea of what was happening in the colony, of what these writers and their fellows were doing and thinking. Until the middle of the eighteenth century, the literary quality of most of this writing is rather low, as is natural in a period in which most of the energy of the people is required for the conquest of the land.

Most of the early writings are simply descriptions of the country, its inhabitants, and its possibilities for development, or accounts in prose or poetry of events in the colony. One exception is the work of the Jesuit priest and missionary to the Indians, Father José de Anchieta (1530–1597). He wrote sermons, poems, and religious plays, both in Portuguese and in the "general language" of the Indians. The poetry is simple, so it could have been understood by an illiterate colonist, by a child, or possibly by an Indian who had learned to speak Portuguese. The main purpose was to teach certain basic principles of religion in an agreeable way.

Father Antônio Vieira (1608–1697) was celebrated in his day for his sermons. They are studied today mostly as brilliant examples of Portuguese baroque style at its best.

The outstanding literary figure of the early colonial period is Gregório de Matos Guerra (1623–1696). He was the son of a wealthy sugar planter of Bahia, in the period in which these planters were at the height of their affluence. He was sent to Coimbra to complete his education, took the degree of doctor of laws, and mingled with the intellectual elite of Portugal. He felt perfectly at home in Lisbon and Coimbra, where he published poems and where he spent a great part of his life. He might never have returned to Brazil if he had not become involved in personal feuds which made his position in Portugal uncomfortable.

Matos' poetry is in the tradition of Quevedo, including love poetry, religious poems, and witty satires often descending to personal attacks. His satires of dishonesty, pretentiousness, and licentious living were doubtless well merited, but he, nonetheless, earned the enmity of those he attacked.

His love lyrics make agreeable reading, but the best poetry is found in a few religious poems. In spite of the writer's licentious life, these express a convincing note of faith and sincerity. One of the finest is the beautiful sonnet which begins, "I have sinned, my Lord."

Many Brazilians also claim as one of their writers Antônio José da Silva, known as "The Jew" (1705–1739). He was born in Rio de Janeiro, but spent most of his life in Portugal, where his comic plays, e.g., *A Vida de Esopo* (*The Life of Aesop*) and *Guerras do Alecrim e da Manjerona* (*Wars of the Rosemary and the Sweet Marjoram*), were written. He is remembered not only because he was burned by the Inquisition as a heretic, but because his plays were the best written in Portuguese in his day.

LATE COLONIAL PERIOD

The second half of the eighteenth century showed the faint beginnings of a national feeling among the Brazilians, reflected both in the political and the literary life of the country. There was considerable expansion into the interior in the eighteenth century. With the discovery of gold in Minas Gerais, that province was settled rapidly. By the middle of the century, it contained numerous permanent towns, the most important of which was the capital, Ouro Preto. It became one of the largest towns in Brazil, and its wealth supported artists, musicians, and poets. Its artisans and artists, of whom the greatest was O Aleijadinho, "The Cripple," filled the town and the province with beautiful baroque churches, public buildings, palaces, and fountains. The very considerable baroque music composed in this period has only recently been rediscovered. The poets of the *mineiro* school are the most brilliant of the colonial period. The wealth of the region also provoked conflict with the Portuguese, who claimed a fifth of the gold for the crown, and brought about the conspiracy for independence known as the *Inconfidência*.

Two of these poets mentioned wrote epics. José Santa Rita Durão (1720–1784) was a close imitator of Camões, using the Camonian octaves, figures imitating those of the Portuguese poet, and the same general structure as the *Lusiads*. But whereas Camões wrote of the voyage to India of Vasco da Gama, and in a period in which the importance to Portugal of that voyage was quite apparent to everyone, Durão had no Brazilian subject of comparable importance. In *Caramurú* (the title is the name given to the hero by the Indians), he tells the story of Diogo Álvares Correia, a sailor shipwrecked on the coast of Bahia, and of his Indian wife, Paraguassu, a kind of Brazilian Pocahontas. The basis of the story is historical, and it is familiar to all Brazilians, but it does not gain from being drawn out to the length of an epic. Besides, Durão's talent was inferior to that of Camões.

The second epic poet is Basílio da Gama (1741–1795). His poem *Uraguay* (the name was so spelled in his day) is somewhat more original and more readable than *Caramurú*. It deals with the short war which the expeditions from São Paulo waged against the Jesuit missions and the Indian tribes which they had gathered into settlements in Rio Grande do Sul. The poet had studied in a Jesuit school in Rio, finishing his studies in the year in which the marquis of Pombal expelled the Jesuits from Portugal and its colonies. Since he was harsh toward the Jesuits in his poem, many thought it was to win favor with the government. In any case, he showed great sympathy toward the Indians. Although the formal hero is the leader of the Portuguese forces, the only memorable characters are Indians. As a poet, he freed himself from the tradition of octaves, using blank verse. There are passages in the poem which can still be read with interest and pleasure.

Cláudio Manuel da Costa (1729–1789) composed a large number of excellent sonnets. His pastoral poetry celebrates the rivers and meadows of Minas, rather than the usual ones of Greece. It compares well with similar poems of the European writers who were his contemporaries.

Without doubt, the best poet of the colonial period was Tomás Antônio Gonzaga (1744–1809?). He was a native of Portugal and died in exile in Mozambique, but lived most of his life in Brazil and wrote there. Like Cláudio Manuel, he was involved in the conspiracy of the *Inconfidência*. He was arrested, kept in prison for three years, and then exiled to Africa. Before his arrest, he had planned to marry a Brazilian girl who is better known today by his poetic name for her, Marília, than by her real name. In 1792, while he was still in prison, his book of poems to her was published in Lisbon under the title of *Marília de Dirceu* (*Dirceu's Marília*). This is still one of the most frequently published and widely read books of poems in the language. An Arcadian by reason of his education and the age in which he lived, he put into his poetry from the beginning a personal note and a depth of sincere emotion which overcame the artificiality of the Arcadians. The later poems, written in prison, are even more personal, reflecting his melancholy and despair.

There were other members of this school who wrote sonnets, madrigals, and rondeaus in the style of the period. The most important are Alvarenga Peixoto (1744–1793) and Silva Alvarenga (1749–1814).

THE ROMANTIC PERIOD

Brazil became a nation when the prince regent Dom Pedro proclaimed independence in 1822. Up to then the country had been mostly cut off from foreign influences, but now it was opened to trends dominant in other countries. In their effort to express literary independence from Portugal, many writers turned to other countries.

The great literary movement of the early nineteenth century in Europe was, of course, romanticism. It was no less dominant in England, Germany, and other European countries than in France, but the similarity of the two languages and the prestige of French culture led the Brazilians mostly to French authors.

In addition to the prestige given to romanticism by so many writers of various European countries, this school included elements which were especially attractive to the citizens of a new nation—its accent on nationalism, the attention it gave to folklore and local customs as expressions of the national character, its glorification of primitive peoples, the cult of the individual. The Brazilian romanticists, like their European models, were individualists above all. Their works and their interests took many different directions, were expressed with vigor and emotion, and generally contained a great deal of the personality of the writer.

The most frequently read of the Brazilian romantic poets is doubtless Antônio Gonçalves Dias (1823–1864). Born a year after independence, son of a Portuguese, he received from his mother the heritage of the other two races of Brazil. Perhaps it was because of him that it later became fashionable to boast of descent from all three races. He studied in Portugal, spent a good many years in Europe, and died in a shipwreck while returning from one of his trips there.

In his poetry Gonçalves Dias expresses a number of the main themes of romanticism. In the *Sextilhas de Frei Antão* (*Sextets of Friar Anthony*), he turns to the Portuguese Middle Ages, even to the extent of imitating the medieval language. He is the founder of Indianism in Brazil, expressing the theme of the noble savage in such poems as *I-juca-pirama*, *Marabá*, and *Os Timbiras* (the titles are untranslatable). This attitude was only poetic, not due to ignorance of the true state of the Indian culture. Gonçalves Dias had seen the Indians close-up as a child, and he also carried out very serious scientific studies of their culture and language. He dealt much less with the Negro, but did write a few poems attacking slavery, e.g., *A Escrava* (*The Slave Woman*). A great part of his work is personal, expressing his own longings, his loves, and his problems. Most of these last are amatory.

Most of his poetry has a soft and tender melody reminiscent of much of the poetry and popular music of Portugal and a large content of *saudade*, a kind of gentle melancholy and longing for what is absent. A skillful master of metrics, his poems give an impression of simplicity, with few problems of interpretation. His best known poem is the *Canção do Exílio* (*Song of Exile*), which all children read early in school.

Álvaro de Azevedo (1831–1852) was more emotional, morbid, melancholy. He felt a kindred spirit in Byron, one of his favorite poets. His own poetry is melodious and inspired, but it rose directly from his emotions and gives an impression of improvisation. His despair, brought about by his realization of his approaching early death, in the poem *Se Eu Morresse Amanhã* (*If I Should Die Tomorrow*) reminds us somewhat of Keats.

In Luiz Nicolau Fagundes Varela (1841–1875), this subjectiveness was already becoming tempered. He has a certain restraint and discipline which are not so much an anticipation of the Parnassians as a return to the Portuguese classics. He is by turns bucolic, mystic, and humorous. The most representative volume of his work is *Vozes da América* (*Voices of America*), a collection of lyrics on many subjects, in which his varied talents can be seen. *O Evangelho da Selva* (*The Jungle Evangel*) is a long poem on the missionary Anchieta. Perhaps the best is *Cântico do Calvário* (*Canticle of Calvary*), written in memory of his dead son.

The fame of Antônio Castro Alves (1847–1871) rests chiefly upon his "social poetry," the ringing protests against slavery and inhumanity most forcibly expressed in *Vozes da África* (*Voices of Africa*) and in *Navio Negreiro* (*Slave Ship*). His anguish from the idea of early death in *Mocidade e Morte* (*Youth and Death*) is sincere and passionate, but is not tinged with the morbidity of Alvares de Azevedo. More than almost any other romantic poet, he was concerned with the wrongs and the feelings of his fellow-man, rather than with his own. Because of this, and especially his powerful support of the abolitionist movement, he is one of the most widely read of the Brazilian poets. He could also write vigorously of nature, if mostly of the most dramatic aspects of it. *Crepúsculo Sertanejo* (*Dusk in the Hinterland*), a short poem, and a long work, *A Cachoeira de Paulo Afonso* (*Paulo Afonso Falls*), attest to this interest. Most of his poetry was written to be declaimed, rather than read. His intent was to reach the emotions first, and the intellect only secondarily.

The poets of the romantic movement are quite numerous. The recent anthology of Péricles Eugênio da Silva Ramos lists forty-four. Among others who still have a considerable following are Junqueira Freire, Casimiro de Abreu, and the recently rediscovered Sousa Andrade (known as Sousândrade).

In the prose of this period, mention must be made of Manuel de Macedo (1820–1882). He wrote great numbers of novels and plays which were popular in their day. They have all the traditional artificialities of the weaker romantic literature. His characters enter grottoes, overhear conversations, are identified by lockets, send passionate letters via slaves, and engage in parlor games. Of these novels, *A Moreninha* (*The Little Brunette*) has remained popular with very young readers and is a part of the childhood culture of practically all Brazilians.

Bernardo Guimarães (1825–1884) is best known for *A Escrava Isaura*

(*Isaura the Slave*), which was more of a contribution to the abolitionist campaign in Brazil than to literature. His best novels represent the current of *sertanismo*, interest in the people and customs of the interior of the country. These novels, such as *O Seminarista* (*The Seminary Student*) and *O Garimpeiro* (*The Diamond Panner*), are interesting as descriptions of the way of life of the time and place and also avoid most of the artificial devices of the poorer romantic novels.

Franklin Távora (1812–1888) wrote several historical novels concerned with his native Pernambuco in colonial times. These works, such as *Lourenço*, *O Cabeleira* (*Long-Hair*), and *O Matuto* (*The Backwoodsman*), are now antiquated in style, and even in language, but they are engrossing tales into which enter several elements that later became important—the bandit of the northeast and the exploitation of the poor by powerful landowners, for example.

Alfredo d'Escragnolle Taunay (1843–1899) wrote a great deal, but is remembered chiefly for two books. One is the romantic novel *Inocência*. The story told in this one is an uninteresting romantic tale; but the accounts of customs and the descriptions of the land in southern Mato Grosso are well worth reading today. The other book is an account of the retreat from Paraguay of the Brazilian forces which attacked that country from the north during the war against the dictator Solano López. Written originally in French and translated into Portuguese by the son of the author, *A Retirada da Laguna* (*The Retreat from Laguna*) is undoubtedly Taunay's most important work.

The best of the romantic prose writers was José de Alencar (1829–1877). His novels remind American readers in certain respects of those of James Fenimore Cooper, but there are very considerable differences. He is concerned with the Indians as a romantic theme and with descriptions of the beauties of Brazilian nature expressed in poetic prose. In *O Guarani* and *Iracema*, the theme is the impact of Europeans on the primitive society of the Indians. The latter is short, highly poetical in language, and altogether a charming book.

These and numerous other works of Alencar, some of which deal with foreign influences in the cities and some with conflicts between the city and the interior, still enjoy great popularity among younger Brazilian readers.

REALISM, NATURALISM, AND PARNASSIANISM

The romantic period gradually faded and was replaced by other styles which were developing from 1870 to 1880. However, one novel of a very different type appeared during the heyday of this movement. This was *As Memórias de um Sargento de Milícias* (*The Memoirs of a Sergeant of Militia*), first published in serial form in a newspaper in 1854–1855. Aided by the tales of an old-timer who had been a militia sergeant, the author, Manuel Antônio de Almeida (1830–1861), describes for us the Rio of the time of King John VI, more than thirty years before he was writing. The main character is an engaging rogue of no noticeable virtues, who makes his way with as little effort as possible through the society of rascals, knaves, tradesmen, petty officials, etc. The treatment of characters shows the influence of the picaresque tradition of realism, while the interest in the past and in colorful customs reveals a trend of romanticism. The result is a delightful volume, far superior to any of the novels of the romantic authors. The book did not receive much attention in its time, but was rediscovered in the present century, re-edited numerous times, and finally translated into English.

Beginning with *O Mulato* by Aluízio de Azevedo, published in 1881, a group of writers who are generally termed naturalists produced a number of novels of excellent quality. They were influenced by theories of determinism, recent developments in science, and by new interest in social problems. Their literary mentors were, of course, the French naturalists. Their works owed more to observation than to imagination. They had little interest in local color, in regionalism, or in the Indian. They wrote mostly of the cities and were concerned with people, whether as examples of general human types or of Brazilian ones in particular. Their works are more intelligible to the foreigner than most Brazilian literature, since understanding is not dependent to any great extent upon a knowledge of local conditions and culture.

Azevedo (1857–1912), in addition to the one mentioned above, wrote a considerable number of novels. Several were in the romantic pattern, produced because there was a public for them. However, even these are often worth reading because of the author's sense of humor. But his best, such as *O Cortiço* and *Casa de Pensão* (*A Brazilian Tenement* and *The Boarding House*) are naturalistic. Azevedo was an excellent observer and was especially skilled in the portrayal of social groups. Some of his pages which describe the activities of groups, such as the St. John's Eve party in *O Mulato* or the party in *O Cortiço*, have seldom, if ever, been surpassed in literature.

Herculano Marcos Inglês de Sousa (1853–1918) wrote several novels, but all but *O Missionário* (*The Missionary*) are unobtainable today. This work, set in an Amazonian town, presents a young and enthusiastic priest in struggle against both man and nature. Like most naturalistic novels, it is anticlerical. In spite of the importance of the element of nature, represented here by the Amazon River and the jungle, it differs completely from the nature we find in the romantics. For Inglês de Sousa, nature is another determining force against which man may struggle in vain. *O Missionário* is the best of the novels which have been written up to the present about the Amazon country.

Júlio Ribeiro (1845–1890) is known for one book, *A Carne* (*Flesh*). He frankly proclaimed himself the disciple of Zola and followed as closely as possible, given his talents, in the footsteps of the master. The book aroused considerable controversy upon its publication because of its sensuous tone and frank expressions, which were quite daring for his time. It has been kept alive partly because of this, but, in spite of some rather tiring didactic passages and too much dependence on the science of its day, it has more solid literary worth than has usually been credited to it.

Like Ribeiro, Adolfo Caminha (1867–1897) is known mostly for one book, although he wrote two others, which have been republished only infrequently. Also, like Ribeiro, he created controversy and drew violent opposition, both with his manner of living and with his works. *Bom Crioulo* (*Good Darky*) is thoroughly naturalistic in style and outlook, although the element of determinism is not expressed with much insistence. Its notoriety is due to the subject matter, which is homosexuality, at that time a scandalous departure from accepted subjects. However, the subject is not treated in an offensive manner. The simple but careful style, the logical development of the action, and the social theme of opposition to corporal punishment in the navy give it a permanent place in Brazilian literature.

Raúl Pompéia (1863–1895) is also remembered for one novel, *O Ateneu* (*The Athenaeum*), which deals with a boarding school. It is a curious work, which critics have trouble in classifying. It bears some relation to the naturalists, but does not properly belong with them. Its language is vague and suggestive, rather than explicit. It is a bitter book, the bitterness magnified by the restraint of the teller, and its horror is heightened, rather than weakened, by the fact that the corruption and stupidity of the school do not really touch the narrator.

Joaquim Maria Machado de Assis (1839–1908) does not fit neatly into any of the usual categories. He is the most important figure in Brazilian letters and one of the first rank in the literature of the world. Of humble origin, largely self-taught, he studied Brazilian, Portuguese, English, and French literatures, and absorbed much from each of them. His understanding of Shakespeare, for example, is unusually acute—ahead of the Shakespeare critics of his time. The total quantity of his writings is not very large—a few plays, slender volumes of poetry, nine novels, about ten volumes of short stories, along with criticism and *crônicas*. The most important works are the novels and short stories.

The principal novels, *Bras Cubas*, *Quincas Borba*, and *Dom Casmurro*, reveal remarkable penetration into the human character. They are relatively short, apparently rambling, with little or no attempt at suspense or surprise. The plot is of little importance in itself, and is generally commonplace. What at first glance seem to be digressions turn out to be carefully planned episodes that contribute important pieces to the puzzle of human psychology. Events and actions which are familiar to our human experience are shown to us in a new light, either through the reactions of the characters or through the peculiar twists that the author knows how to give to them without straining our credulity. One can read Machado de Assis again and again, each time finding more that is worth the effort. Every incident and every word was chosen by the author with the greatest care and contributes to the total result. The same attention to detail in reading produces the most rewarding results, although this author's works can be enjoyed and appreciated even with a rapid reading.

Machado is known as one of the great stylists of the Portuguese language. While his language is somewhat out of date to the contemporary Brazilian reader, it is not very difficult for the foreigner who has a moderate knowledge of the language. Fortunately, the three novels mentioned above and many of his short stories have been well translated into English.

In poetry, the reaction against the subjectivity of the romantics opened the way to the Parnassians, who dominated the scene during most of the last years of the nineteenth century and continued into the twentieth. The origins of this movement are also to be found in France, whence Leconte de Lisle, Sully-Prudhomme, and others were important influences. Portuguese poets of this school were also important in establishing the principles of the poetry of the Brazilian Parnassians.

The leaders of this school objected to the personal element in romantic poetry, to what they considered to be excesses of subjectivity, and to carelessness in poetic form. They tended to replace passion with reason, subjectivity with a more objective point of view, the particular with the general. They gave major attention to form, meter, rhythm, and diction. Their meters scan, their rhymes are careful, and their language is free of the trivial and slangy expressions of popular speech. Some of these elements were already appearing before the conscious beginnings of Parnassianism. Machado de Assis, whose poetry is overshadowed by his greater works in prose, already shows some of them by 1870.

The recently published anthology of Parnassians, by Péricles Eugênio da Silva Ramos, lists twenty-nine poets, including a few precursors. The three outstanding ones were Raimundo Correia (1860–1911), Alberto de Oliveira (1857–1937), and Olavo Bilac (1865–1918).

Correia was given to self-analysis, to consideration of the emotions and passions which affect the human spirit, but his attitude was one of detachment and analysis in contrast to the romantic expression of strong sentiment. He was pessimistic, finding hidden evil in humanity, and was discouraged by the quick passing of the better things of life. His poetry is polished, his words chosen with care, his figures and also his vocabulary often new and original. His pessimism is expressed in many short poems such as *As Pombas* (*The Doves*) and *Mal Secreto* (*Secret Suffering*).

Oliveira is most appreciated for his sonnets, although in the large body of his works there are many other poems of almost equal merit. He is especially attentive to the poetic form, original in his figures, and tends toward the use of rare and exotic vocabulary. The expression of emotion is restrained, with the artistry more apparent than the sentiment. In poems concerned with nature, such as those of the book *Meridionais* (*Songs of the South*), he exhibits artistry rather than a personal interest in nature for itself. The exactness of the descriptions and faithfulness to details shows a tendency for observation similar to that of the contemporary naturalist novelists. He is probably truer to his own character in *Alma em Flor* (*Soul in Bloom*), a long poem or connected series of short poems dealing with childhood and adolescent love.

Bilac was concerned with the artistry of his poetry, with an effect of simplicity, technical perfection, and choice of poetic words. He saw the contrast between good and evil, between the beautiful and the ugly, and between the benign and the cruel aspects of nature, but did not express great personal concern. Perhaps more than any other Brazilian poet, he observed from a position of philosophical detachment. Emotion is replaced by sensuousness, but even this is basically artistic, rather than personal feeling. Most of his poetry is lyrical, e.g., the collections *Poesias* and *Tarde* (*Afternoon*). One long poem, *O Caçador de Esmeraldas* (*The Emerald Hunter*), is narrative.

Among other Parnassians, mention should be made of Vicente de Carvalho (1866–1924) and Augusto de Lima (1858–1934). The latter wrote poetry with a religious note rare in the Parnassian school, which tended to be somewhat pagan in outlook. Raul de Leoni (1895–1926) began writing when Parnassianism, as a school, was practically dead, but his *Luz Mediterrânea* (*Mediterranean Light*) is essentially Parnassian and one of the finest works of this school.

An interesting poetic group was that of the symbolists, who wrote during the period when Parnassianism was flourishing—the later years of the 1880's and up to the turn of the century. Like the latter, they took their inspiration from French poets, principally Baudelaire, Moréas, Mallarmé, and Verlaine. They avoided the literal and exact representation of natural objects, the rigidity of form, and the scientific view of life which were important to the Parnassians. They were concerned with what they considered a higher reality, which they hoped to reach through suggestion, intuition, or metaphor. They took to free verse, irregular in length and in rhythm, often without rhyme. They never attained the wide popularity of the Parnassians, but their influence is to be found in many later poets.

The two outstanding symbolists are Cruz e Souza (1861–1898) and Alphonsus de Guimaraens (1870–1921). The books of poetry of the former, such as *Missal* and *Broquéis* (*Bucklers*), are highly regarded by modern critics as worthy to be compared to the works of the French symbolists. Guimaraens began publishing when most of the symbolists were leaving the field, and much of his work only became known after his death. Since then such works as *Pastoral aos Crentes do Amor e da Morte* (*Pastoral to the Believers in Love and Death*) have won an important place in Brazilian poetry.

The first decades of the twentieth century were a period of transition, a time when Brazilian literature was developing a more national character and a feeling for its own autonomy. It was not, of course, free from foreign influences, but it no longer followed so clearly in the paths of foreign schools and movements. In addition to the poets previously mentioned, there were prose writers whose work was more concerned with Brazil than with foreign literary types.

Henrique Coelho Neto (1864–1934) produced a very large number of novels, short stories, and other books. He was an excellent stylist, although both his style and his vocabulary tended toward archaism in his own day. As the principal target of the modernists, he fell into disfavor, and was little read for several decades. However, he possessed much greater merits than his detractors were willing to recognize. His subjects were very often taken from the interior of Brazil, either contemporary or historical. Among his most interesting books are *Sertão* (*The Backland*, 1896), *Banzo* (*Homesick*, 1913), and *O Rei Negro* (*The Negro King*, 1914).

This interest in the back country, which goes back to the romantic writers, was one of the principal currents of this period. It was stimulated by an important book by Euclides da Cunha (1866–1909). This book was not fiction but essentially observation and reporting. During the latter part of the nineteenth century a fanatical cult had developed a settlement in the interior of the state of Bahia. The government was compelled to send a military expedition against it to subdue the rebellion which took place there. Da Cunha accompanied the expedition as a reporter. Later he made a more serious study of the conditions of the people involved. The book was published under the title of *Os Sertões* (*Rebellion in the Backlands*) in 1902. It became a powerful influence both in the literature and in the social consciousness of the people. Its style, the breadth of the study, and the timeliness of the subject combined to give it a lasting influence.

This same interest in the interior and in the character of humble people of the interior produced several other works of varying importance during this period. One of these is *Canaan*, a novel by José da Graça Aranha (1868–

1931). Although it is not a very good novel, it aroused great interest at the time. Its principal concern is the problem of the Brazilian race. The racial theories that were then current in Europe and North America led many to believe that the Brazilians, as a mixed race, would not be able to maintain a viable society without heavy immigration from Europe. Graça Aranha seems to have subscribed to this theory in part. The novel has been translated under the same title.

This current of *sertanismo* appears in an excellent book of short stories, *Pelo Sertão* (*Through the Backlands*) by Afonso Arinos de Melo Franco (1868–1916), and in the novels of Afrânio Peixoto (1876–1947). The latter presented the *sertão* of his native Bahia in a series of light, but very readable novels. He is not a writer of the first rank but is always interesting because of his ability as a storyteller and for his presentation of social situations of a people he knew very well.

A similar current in literature was represented in the extreme south by several writers who set down the regional culture, the language, and the way of life of the *gaúcho*. The principal one is Simões Lopes Neto (1865–1916), whose *Contos Gauchescos* (*Gaucho Stories*) and *Lendas do Sul* (*Legends of the South*) have maintained their popularity. Some of the stories are based on legends or folk tales, others on real incidents. The author clothed these tales in a vivid, personal style which adds to the pleasure of reading.

A sympathetic point of view toward the people and the problems of the interior also appears in the essays of José Bento Monteiro Lobato (1883–1948). He had at first accepted the common view that the *caipira*, the countryman from the interior of São Paulo state, was lazy and unambitious. But, as he came to know this man better, he realized that his seeming indolence and lack of character were due to the appalling state of his health and to the hopeless social situation in which he lived. In his short stories Monteiro Lobato described and satirized social and personal foibles with biting humor and pitiless dexterity. Other works are concerned with political questions, attacking the dictatorship in his country and the foreign economic interests.

A very different writer of this period is Lima Barreto (1881–1922). He had acquired some of his technique from the naturalists, but had learned more probably from the great Russian novelists. He is not in the least regional or picturesque. His scenario is the city of Rio, his subjects the bureaucratic inefficiency of the government, the lack of scruples of officialdom, the decay of agriculture near Rio as a result of bad government, and the low estate of the Negroes. In spite of this strong element of *roman à thèse*, his novels are vigorous, his characters lifelike, and the plots interesting, although not always well constructed. The novels include *Triste Fim de*

Policarpo Quaresma (*Sad End of Polycarp Quaresma*), *Vida e Morte de Gonzaga de Sá* (*Life and Death of Gonzaga de Sá*), and *Clara dos Anjos.*

THE MODERNIST MOVEMENT

Modernism is generally considered to have begun in Brazil with the "Week of Modern Art" in February of 1922. This week was concerned with all the arts, but especially with painting, architecture, sculpture, and poetry. The principals were painters such as Di Cavalcanti and Anita Malfatti, writers such as Oswald de Andrade and Mário de Andrade, the poets Menotti del Picchia, Guilherme de Almeida, and soon joining them, the already established poet Manuel Bandeira and the composer Villa Lobos. They won the immediate support of Graça Aranha, who, although he did not contribute to their artistic production, gave them the prestige of one of the most famous names in the Brazil of the twenties.

It should be emphasized that Brazilian modernism is separate and quite different from the movement by that name in the Spanish-speaking countries. Brazilian modernism in its early days was characterized by enthusiasm, innovation, iconoclasm, and chaos. Although Mário de Andrade, who was soon known as the "pope of modernism," assures us that the inspiration and the germ of the movement came from France, it very rapidly became the most nationalistic movement of Brazilian literary history. Oswald de Andrade and a few others formed a sub-group which they called the "cannibals," claiming that they were returning to the time of the Indians—the true Brazilians. Mário de Andrade fought the battle of the language, insisting that Portuguese was dead and that one should write in "Brazilian," the language spoken in the country. The verse of several poets is so completely free that it has practically no rules at all. The modernists turned their backs on all previous literary movements, with some exception for symbolism.

The problem of deciding which of the writers subsequent to the "Week of Modern Art" are modernists and which are not is practically impossible. The first modernists were an interesting group of innovators, but there is still a transitional quality about them. Most of their works were minor, but the influence of the movement on the course of literature was very great. Among the best-known of the poets are the following, who differ greatly among themselves and whose relationship to the modernist movement was different in each case:

Mário de Andrade (b. 1893) was one of the very early leaders in modernism. He owes this position and the high regard with which he is generally held to his magnetic personality more than to his writings. His influence in modernizing the literary language is possibly his greatest contribution. He was also an able musicologist. There is an excellent translation of his book of poetry *Paulicéia Desvairada* (*Hallucinated City*) and other translations of many of his poems and some prose.

Guilherme de Almeida (b. 1890) had already published some of his best poetry before the modernist movement and written some not published until much later. He adhered to the movement enthusiastically, especially attracted by the nationalism. However, most of his work is of a different order. His poetry gave importance to three things—word, idea, and rhythm, of which only the second was much appreciated by most of the modernists.

Manuel Bandeira (b. 1886) was already well known before modernism. Although he supported its aims, such as the transformation of the literary language and the use of free verse, he did not really form a part of it. He is undoubtedly one of the most widely known and read among contemporary poets. Among the poems most widely known are *Na Rua do Sabão* ("On Soap Street"), *Evocação do Recife* ("Evocation of Recife"), and *Vou-me Embora para Pasárgada* ("I'm off to Pasargada"). Many poems are available in translation.

Paulo Menotti del Picchia (b. 1892) wrote his best poetry before modernism. He owes his fame and reading public in considerable part to the long poem *Juca Mulato*, which places the plantation worker in confrontation with the owner and with industrializing society. He supported the nationalistic side of modernism mainly, but contributed little to it directly.

Carlos Drummond de Andrade (b. 1902), a native of Minas Gerais, accompanied modernism and shows similarities to some poets of the group, but remains somewhat isolated from the São Paulo group. His poetry is generally irregular, rugged, and reserved in its expression. The early poetry generally refers to situations, people, or places in his native region, but his horizon has become wider with the passing years and his expression more frank. He is generally considered one of the outstanding contemporary Brazilian poets. Some of the early poems are available in translation.

Jorge de Lima (1895–1953) is often included among the modernists, but has little relation to the movement. In his early work the "Negro poetry" is most characteristic, not so much for African rhythms as for the content and the sympathetic understanding. In a later period he wrote, partly in collaboration with Murilo Mendes, some of the best religious poetry in Brazilian literature. A large part of it has been translated. His novel *Calunga* (*Hex*) belongs to the "Generation of 1930" both in date and in content, although the mystical approach to literature which appears in the later poetry is also present here. The long poem *Invenção de Orfeu* is a complex and difficult work which requires more penetrating studies than it has yet received.

Cecília Meireles (1901–1964) was termed by some critics after her death as the "greatest poetess of Brazil." She certainly merits a high place among the poets of either sex. She shows certain tendencies of the symbolists, but has borrowed freely from many different sources. She is more concerned with perfection of rhythm and with choice of words than the symbolists were. Her poetry is suggestive, sometimes difficult to penetrate, nearly always musical. She has little or no relation to the modernists.

Murilo Araújo (b. 1894), who has strong links both with modernism and with symbolism, is best known for his "Negro poetry," in which certain situations of the Afro-Brazilians are expressed in vigorous rhythms. The rhythm is so prominent in some that the reader is almost compelled to chant or sing them. In fact, *Toada do Negro no Banzo* ("Song of the Homesick Negro") has been set to music.

THE GENERATION OF 1930 AND THE NOVEL

A number of important writers who first began to publish within a few years of each other, around the year 1930, are commonly grouped together as the "generation of 1930." Although they differ from one another in significant ways, there are certain common characteristics. They are basically novelists, their other works being of less importance in most cases. They are mostly concerned with social problems, usually with those of their own region, in particular. They write in a style which is much closer to the language spoken by the average person than to the literary language of the preceding generation, but sometimes with a great deal of regional vocabulary. Since these trends were new at the time, they were forced to create a new literary language, a result which required considerable experimentation and the passage of time. The following writers are usually included in this group:

The earliest of these, both in date of birth and date of publication, is José Américo de Almeida (b. 1887). His three novels—*A Bagaceira (Bagasse)*, *O Boqueirão (The Gorge)*, and *Coiteiros (Protectors of Bandits)*—deal with problems of the state of Paraíba, such as agricultural development, the droughts, banditry, and conflicts of various groups. They are full of regionalisms, difficult to read, and untranslated. The author is more concerned with social problems than with producing good novels, so that the reader's interest is more social than artistic. Neither the style nor the structure is completely adequate to the subjects treated.

The novel *Calunga* by Jorge de Lima has already been mentioned. It is laid in his native state of Alagoas. In it the young son of a plantation owner, educated in the city, inherits the estate from his father. He returns and tries to fight the ignorance, superstition, and vices of the community but finds them too strong.

Raquel de Queiroz (b. 1910) wrote several novels concerning life in the state of Ceará. The most interesting is the first, *O Quinze (The Year 1915)*, concerned with the plight of refugees from the drought of that year. A later one, *Três Marias* (*Three Marys*), exists in English translation. The principal characters are three young women who are trying to adjust to the modern world.

José Lins do Rêgo (b. 1901) is known mostly for the novels of the *Sugar-Cane Cycle*. These works parallel to a great extent the research of the social anthropologist, Gilberto Freyre. They contain the most dramatic and vivid presentation ever made of the declining days of the sugar plantations and of the newer conditions dominated by the sugar refineries. Five novels, *Menino de Engenho* (*Plantation Boy*), *Doidinho* (*Little Nut*), *Bangüê* (*The Ox-powered Mill*), *Usina* (*Sugar Central*), and *Fogo Morto* (*The Fire is Out*), give the complete history of the sugar industry from the declining years of the old plantation to the development of the new system. The story is told in human rather than technical terms, so that the reader who is not primarily interested in social problems as such can read them with pleasure.

Lins do Rêgo also deals with other features of life in northeastern Brazil in several novels. *Pedra Bonita* (*Beautiful Stone*) is concerned with a fanatical religious cult. *O Moleque Ricardo* (*Richard the Negro Boy*) shows the difficult life of a young Negro who abandons the plantation to make his way in the city. *Os Cangaceiros* (*The Bandits*) was the best presentation in Brazilian literature of this problem up to the great work of Guimarães Rosa.

His best novel is *Fogo Morto*, in which his best character, Captain Vitorino, seems to have taken over the work from the author. He is a kind of Brazilian Quixote who became the main character, although the author had not planned to give him much importance.

Graciliano Ramos (b. 1892) is a regionalist only by accident. He is concerned with social and human problems, but he places them in the region he knows best, the states of Alagoas and Pernambuco. His subtle penetration into the human psyche shows his heavy debt to Machado de Assis, to whom he otherwise bears little resemblance, and makes him one of the most rewarding of Brazilian writers. Two novels exist in translation: *Vidas Sêcas* (*Barren Lives*) and *Angústia* (*Anguish*). His *Memórias do Cárcere* (*Memoirs from Prison*) is a very moving human document. His style is deceptively simple, his language popular and even slangy at times.

Jorge Amado (b. 1912) has been writing novels, mostly concerned with various aspects and social problems of Bahia, since the early thirties. Several of the early ones were Communist-oriented, while the more recent ones have an opposing point of view. Some of those of the first period are among his best, especially when there is less insistence on the political question. Among these are *Jubiabá* (the title is the name of a character) published in 1935 and *Terras do Sem Fim* (*The Violent Land*), 1942. In these, his ability as a storyteller was almost as great as in his most recent works, while his social consciousness produced impressive passages concerned with the lives and problems of the poor. In recent years his genius for spinning interesting yarns has been the outstanding characteristic of novels such as *Gabriela, Cravo e Canela* (*Gabriela, Clove and Cinnamon*) and *Os Velhos Marinheiros* (*The Old Seamen*), both of which attained great popularity in translation in the United States. His interest in the humble people of Bahia continues, but without political overtones. His style and the general quality of his work have tended to improve over the years, but his best work is probably still *Jubiabá*.

Érico Lopes Veríssimo (b. 1905) is a member of this generation from the far southern state of Rio Grande do Sul. He is mostly concerned with certain problems of individuals, such as personal responsibility, rather than with those of social classes. At other times he has considered problems of more international scope, especially in recent years. Several of his books have been translated, including *O Tempo e o Vento* (*Time and the Wind*), *Caminhos Cruzados* (*Crossroads*), and *Olhai os Lírios do Campo* (*Consider the Lilies of the Field*). *O Tempo e o Vento* is his best up to the present. It is a historical novel, dealing with the early development of his native state, with a panoramic view, a vast cast of characters, and splendid presentation of the forces at work in that violent and agitated region.

Other novelists who were the contemporaries of these but whose orientation was different include the following: Lúcio Cardoso (b. 1913), author of psychological novels; José Geraldo Vieira (b. 1897), concerned with universal human problems; Otávio de Faria (b. 1908), the author of numerous "bourgeois novels"; and Cyro dos Anjos (b. 1906), who writes of his native state, Minas Gerais, but with little regionalism.

Several of the novelists mentioned above are still writing. Very many others have begun to publish since they became prominent, and the quantity, variety, and excellent quality of the recent Brazilian novel are all impressive. The most discussed of all these is doubtless *Grande Sertão: Veredas* by João Guimarães Rosa (b. 1908), translated as *The Devil to Pay in the Backlands*. In it the author uses regionalism, not so much for its own sake, nor to discuss social problems, as to study the eternal problems of human beings. His incredible command of the Portuguese language, with numerous word-coinages and intentional deturpations of existing words, makes him very difficult reading, to native readers as well as to others. He is also an outstanding writer of short stories. His first published work was *Sagarana*, a collection of beautifully organized and artistically written tales. In the stories of *Corpo de Baile* the art of suggestion, analysis of the human personality, and linguistic virtuosity were carried even further. Except in some of the stories of *Sagarana*, it is probably not possible to translate Guimarães Rosa into any other language without very considerable loss of important qualities.

It is difficult to indicate which of the other contemporary writers are the more outstanding, and impossible to mention them all. One may mention the novel *São Miguel* of Guido Wilmar Sassi, a good novel based on the lumber industry of the far south and noteworthy for its structure; those of Herberto Sales, which expose new facets of regionalism, e.g., *Cascalho* (*Gravel*), concerned with diamond panners; the fine novels of the sea by Moacyr C. Lopes, *Maria de Cada Pôrto* (*A Woman in Every Port*) and *Cais, Saudade em Pedra* (*The Pier is Homesickness Made of Stone*); Josué Montello's *Os Degraus do Paraíso* (*The Steps of Paradise*), a story of Protestantism, set in the author's fondly remembered São Luiz, Maranhão. The novels of the *mineiro* Mário Palmério, *Vila dos Confins* and *Chapadão do Bugre* (the titles are both proper names), are basically concerned with politics and the social causes of political corruption, but they are excellent literary creations. The neo-Catholic writer Gustavo Corção is one of the best stylists writing in Brazil today. He has written several books of essays and at least one novel, *Lições do Abismo* (*Lessons from the Abyss*). The "new novel" of such writers as Adonias Filho and Clarice Lispector is densely written, with attention to the significance of small acts and to emotional states. By the former writer, one should mention *Memórias de Lázaro* (*Memoirs of Lazarus*) and *O Forte* (*The Fort*); by the latter, *A Paixão Segundo G. H.* (*Love according to G. H.*).

THE SHORT STORY

The short story has existed in Brazil at least since the time of the romantic writers, most of whom wrote some of them. Nearly all writers since then have added few or many to the stock. At the present time, the number of short stories published every year is very great. Many of them appear in the literary sections of newspapers, but collections in book form, either of a single author or of several, are very numerous. Among authors of the past whose short stories enjoy a prominent place in Brazilian literature are Machado de Assis, Coelho Neto, Afonso Arinos, Monteiro Lobato, and Simões Lopes Neto. Among recent ones, one might mention Guimarães Rosa, Osman Lins, Atila Brandão. Many other contemporary authors are writing excellent ones. This genre is so large that it would require a separate work to do it justice.

THE THEATER

The theater has not, until recently, been one of the more outstanding literary forms in Brazil and has never received as much attention from either the critics or the public as have several other genres. However, it is one of the earliest and most continuous types of writing in the national literature. A great many writers who are remembered more for other works also wrote for the stage. Among the romantics, Gonçalves Dias, Taunay, Macedo, and Alencar wrote plays.

One romantic writer whose reputation rests solely on his theatrical works is Luiz Carlos Martins Pena (1815–1848). His comedies, beginning with *O Juiz de Paz da Roça* (*The Country Justice of the Peace*) in 1838, dominated the theater until his death ten years later. They deal with the humble people, with customs and incidents of the time, sometimes in a serious way, sometimes merging into farce. Their humor is still fresh and their presentation of customs more interesting than ever.

The serious drama of the romantics, including those of Martins Pena, were of little lasting interest. The best is *Leonor de Mendonça* by Gonçalves Dias, but it suffers from most of the weaknesses of the romantic play as it was in Europe.

In the latter part of the nineteenth century Machado de Assis and Coelho Neto wrote plays. They had their merits as literature, but were not great successes as theater. The principal author of plays in this period was Artur Azevedo, brother of the novelist, whose comedies were widely applauded and successful enough to earn him a living. Others were Cláudio de Souza, known principally for *Flores de Sombra* (*Flowers of the Shade*), and João do Rio.

The theater—the art of acting and presenting plays, as distinguished from the writing—is highly developed in Brazil. A great many foreign plays are produced by professional and amateur groups, but there are also nowadays excellent plays written in Brazil. Among the best-known playwrights, we may mention Nelson Rodrigues, in whom we can see similarities to Eugene O'Neill in, e.g., *Vestida de Noiva* (*Bridal Dress*); Joracy Camargo, the author of plays of social significance such as *Deus Lhe Pague* (*May God Repay You*); Pedro Bloch, whose play *As Mãos de Euridice* (*The Hands of Eurydice*) was an international success; Jorge Andrade, whose plays such as *A Moratória* (*The Moratorium*) and *Senhora na Boca do Lixo* (*Lady at the Police Station*) have been very successful in Brazil; Dias Gomes, whose *O Pagador de Promessas* (*The Keeper of Promises*) was made into a movie that won international acclaim; Ariano Suassuna, whose *Auto da Compadecida* (translated as *The Rogue's Trial*) gave new impetus to the theater based on folk motifs and was also made into a film. Another writer who has used folklore to write excellent plays, although they have not won such wide acclaim as yet, is Luiz Marinho. His *Afilhada de Nossa Senhora da Conceição* (*Goddaughter of Our Lady of Conception*) is a delightful play in which the folklore and the way of life of the humble in the northeast are presented sympathetically.

In very recent years there has appeared a new theater of protest, usually directed at political or economic domination by certain groups. It is usually at least partly musical and is more concerned with ideas than with dramatic qualities. Its themes are taken from Negro or other leaders who fought for freedom—Zumbi, Chico Rei, or Tiradentes—from folk music, or from economic situations. Generally well-staged and acted, it has had some influence on public opinion, particularly among the younger generation. Some are group projects, rather than the work of one individual. Such are *Opinião*, which made popular a number of songs of protest against hunger and exploitation, and *Liberdade, Liberdade*. The story of the hero of a Negro revolt in colonial times was used in *Arena Conta Zumbi* and that of a famous revolt intended to free Brazil from Portugal, in *Arena Conta Tiradentes*. The *Arena* is a theatrical group which has specialized in this type of play.

The *Crônica*

The *crônica* is also an old form, although it was not considered properly a literary genre until recently. It appears at regular intervals—weekly or biweekly—in a newspaper or magazine, over the signature of the author. The subject matter is his own choice. He may write on the important questions of the day, but more often comments on the lesser events, describes something he has observed during the week, reminisces about other days, presents human foibles in a serious, satiric, or humorous vein. Sometimes the *crônica* is fiction, sometimes essay, at other times an anecdote. Some *cronistas* specialize in certain fields, others range over a wide area. The only requirements are to be intelligible and interesting to the readers of the paper or magazine—and, of course, to keep out of trouble with the censor. Since the readers differ widely in education and interests, it is necessary to write in a style that is clear and relatively simple. At the same time, it must be correct enough to be accepted by those who have had enough education to perceive errors in grammar, and adequate to express the writer's meaning to all. As a result, the *cronistas* have developed a new literary style, relatively close to the spoken language.

Both Machado de Assis and Coelho Neto wrote *crônicas* which were later included among their literary works. However, many contemporary writers are primarily *cronistas* and largely publish collected *crônicas* as books. Among the contemporaries, first place should probably be awarded to Rubem Braga. Others who have a large following of readers are Fernando Sabino, Raquel de Queiroz, Henrique Pongetti, Paulo Mendes Campos, and the late Sérgio Pôrto, who wrote under the name of Stanislau Ponte Preta.

In poetry, the outstanding work of recent years is João Cabral de Melo Neto's *Morte e Vida Severina* ("The Life and Death of a Northeasterner"), a fairly long dramatic poem which focuses attention onto the difficult life of the poor in that area.

Of Brazilian literature in general, we may say without hesitation that it is one of the most vital and vigorous ones being produced in the world today.

It includes a considerable number of writers of the first rank in their respective fields and a few who are taking their place alongside the best writers of all ages. Whether the reader is concerned with knowing Brazil through its authors, or with an understanding of universal man, or is simply in search of engrossing reading, he will be amply repaid for the effort of taking up Brazilian books. Imprisoned for a long time in a language known to relatively few, these authors are now becoming available to people of other countries in many languages.

BIBLIOGRAPHY: BRAZILIAN LITERATURE
IN ENGLISH

Adonias Filho (pseudonym of Adonias Aguiar), *Memories of Lazarus* [*Memórias de Lázaro*, novel], trans. Fred P. Ellison (Austin: University of Texas Press, 1969).

Alencar, José de, *Iracema, the Honey-lips; A Legend of Brazil* [*Iracema*, novel], trans. Isabel Burton (London, 1886).

————, *Iracema (A Legend of Ceará)*, trans. N. Biddell (Rio: Imprensa Ingleza, n.d.).

————, *The Jesuit* [*O Jesuita*], trans. E. R. de Britto, in *Poet Lore* 30 (Winter 1919).

Almeida, Manuel Antônio de, *Memoirs of a Militia Sergeant* [*Memórias de um Sargento de Milícias*, novel], trans. Linton L. Barrett (Washington, D.C.: Pan-American Union, 1959).

Amado, Jorge, *Gabriela, Clove and Cinnamon* [*Gabriela, Cravo e Canela*, novel], trans. William L. Grossman and James L. Taylor (New York: Alfred A. Knopf, 1962).

————, *The Violent Land* [*Terras do Sem Fim*, novel], trans. Samuel Putnam (New York: Alfred A. Knopf, 1945).

————, *Slums* [*Suor*, novel] (New York: New Americas, 1937[?]).

————, *Home is the Sailor* [Second episode of *Os Velhos Marinheiros*, novel], trans. Harriet de Onís (New York: Alfred A. Knopf, 1964).

————, *Dona Flor and Her Two Husbands* [*Dona Flor e Seus Dois Maridos*, novel], trans. Harriet de Onís (New York: Alfred A. Knopf, 1969).

————, *Shepherds of the Night* [*Pastores da Noite*, novel], trans. Harriet de Onís (New York: Alfred A. Knopf, 1967).

————, *The Two Deaths of Quincas Wateryell* [*A Morte e a Morte de Quincas Berro Dágua*, first episode of *Os Velhos Marinheiros*, novel], trans. Barbara Shelby (New York: Alfred A. Knopf, 1965).

Andrade, Carlos Drummond de, *In the Middle of the Road*, bilingual ed., ed. and trans. John Nist (Tucson, Ariz: University of Arizona Press, 1965).

Andrade, Mário de, *Fräulein* [*Amar, Verbo Intransitivo*, novel], trans. Margaret Richardson Hollingsworth (New York: Macaulay Co., 1933).

————, *Hallucinated City* [*Paulicéia Desvairada*, poetry], bilingual ed., ed. and trans. Jack E. Tomlins (Nashville, Tenn.: Vanderbilt University Press, 1968).

Aranha, José Pereira de Graça, *Canaan* [*Canaã*, novel], trans. Mariano J. Lorente (Boston: Four Seas Co., 1920).

Assis, Joaquim Maria Machado de, *Esau and Jacob* [*Esaú e Jacó*, novel], trans. Helen Caldwell (Berkeley: University of California Press, 1965).

————, *Epitaph of a Small Winner* [*Bras Cubas*, novel], trans. William L. Grossman (New York: Noonday Press, 1952).

————, *Posthumous Reminiscences of Bras Cubas* [*Bras Cubas*, novel], trans. Percy Ellis (Rio: Instituto Nacional do Livro, 1955).

————, *Dom Casmurro* [*Dom Casmurro*, novel], trans. Helen Caldwell (New York: Noonday Press, 1953).

————, *Philosopher or Dog?* [*Quincas Borba*, novel], trans. Clotilde Wilson (New York: Noonday Press, 1954).

_____, *The Psychiatrist and Other Stories* [*O Alienista* and selected stories], trans. William L. Grossman and Helen Caldwell (Berkeley: University of California Press, 1963).

_____, *What Went on at the Baroness'; A Tale with a Point*, trans. Helen Caldwell (Santa Monica, Calif.: Magpie Press, 1963).

Azevedo, Aluízio de, *A Brazilian Tenement* [*O Cortiço*, novel], trans. Harry W. Brown (New York: Robert M. McBride & Co., 1926).

Callado, Antônio, *Frankel, a Play in Three Acts* (Rio: Ministério de Educação e Cultura, 1955).

_____, *Quarup* (New York: Alfred A. Knopf, 1970[?]).

Carneiro, Cecílio J., *The Bonfire* [*A Fogueira*, novel], trans. Dudley Poore (New York: Farrar & Rinehart, 1944).

Cavalcanti, José Lins do Rêgo, *Plantation Boy* [*Menino de Engenho, Doidinho*, and *Bangüê*, three novels], trans. Emmi Baum (New York: Alfred A. Knopf, 1966).

_____, *Pureza* [*Pureza*, novel], trans. Lucie Marion (London: Hutchinson International Authors, 1948).

Corção, Gustavo, *Who if I Cry Out* [*Lições de Abismo*, novel], trans. Clotilde Wilson (Austin: University of Texas Press, 1967).

Cruls, Gastão Luiz, *The Mysterious Amazon* [*A Amazônia Misteriosa*, novel of fanciful adventure], trans. J. T. W. Sadler (Rio: José Olímpio, 1944).

Cunha, Euclides da, *Rebellion in the Backlands* [*Os Sertões*, narrative of a revolt, description of conditions, etc.], trans. Samuel Putnam (Chicago: University of Chicago Press, 1944).

Downes, Leonard S., *An Introduction to Brazilian Poetry* (São Paulo: Clube de Poesia do Brasil, 1954).

Drummond de Andrade, Carlos. See Andrade, Carlos Drummond de.

Fitts, Dudley, ed., *Anthology of Contemporary Latin American Poetry* [includes Manuel Bandeira, Ronald de Carvalho, Menotti del Picchia, Carlos Drummond de Andrade, Jorge de Lima, Murilo Mendes, and Ismael Neri], 2d ed. (Norfolk, Conn.: New Directions, 1942).

Freyre, Gilberto, *The Masters and the Slaves; A Study in the Development of Brazilian Civilization* [*Casa Grande e Senzala*], trans. Samuel Putnam (New York: Alfred A. Knopf, 1946).

_____, *The Mansions and the Shanties* [*Sobrados e Mucambos*, social study], trans. Harriet de Onís (New York: Alfred A. Knopf, 1963).

_____, *Mother and Son; A Brazilian Tale* [*Dona Sinhá e o Filho Padre*, novel], trans. Barbara Shelby (New York: Alfred A. Knopf, 1967).

_____, *New World in the Tropics* [An interpretation of Brazilian culture, written originally in English] (New York: Alfred A. Knopf, 1959).

Goldberg, Isaac, ed. and trans., *Brazilian Tales* [Machado de Assis, Medeiros e Albuquerque, Coelho Neto, Carmen Dolores] (Boston: Four Seas Co., 1921).

Grossman, William L., comp. and trans., *Modern Brazilian Short Stories* (Berkeley: University of California Press, 1967).

Guimarães Rosa, João. See Rosa, João Guimarães.

Jesus, Carolina Maria de, *Child of the Dark* [*Quarto de Despejo*, a diary of life in the slums], trans. David St. Clair (New York: New American Library, 1963).

_____, *Beyond All Pity* (London: Souvenir Press, 1962).

Lima, Jorge de, *Poems*, ed. and trans. Melissa Hull (Rio: R. Monteiro, 1952).

Lispector, Clarice, *The Apple in the Dark* [*Maçã no Escuro*, novel], trans. Gregory Rabassa (New York: Alfred A. Knopf, 1967).

Lobato, José Bento Monteiro, *Brazilian Short Stories* [From *Urupês*], trans. not identified (Girard, Kansas: E. Haldeman-Julius, 1924).

Machado de Assis, Joaquim Maria. See Assis, Joaquim Maria Machado de.

Miranda, Edgard da Rocha, *And the Wind Blew* (Rio: Ministério de Educação e Cultura, 1956).

Monteiro Lobato, José Bento. *See* Lobato, José Bento Monteiro.

Morley, Helena (pseudonym of Alice Dayrell Caldeira Brant), *The Diary of "Helena Morley"* [*Minha Vida de Menina*, a diary of life in the interior], ed. and trans. Elizabeth Bishop (New York: Farrar, Shaw & Cudahy, 1957).

Nist, John, *Modern Brazilian Poetry*, trans. John Nist and Yolanda Leite (Bloomington, Ind.: Indiana University Press, 1962).

Onís, Harriet de, ed., *The Golden Land: An Anthology of Latin American Folklore in Literature*, 2d ed. (New York: Alfred A. Knopf, 1961).

Pena, Luiz Carlos Martins, *The Rural Justice of the Peace* [*O Juiz de Paz na Roça*, comedy], trans. Willis Knapp Jones in *Poet Lore* 54 (Summer 1948): 19–119.

Pereira, Antônio Olavo, *Marcoré* [*Marcoré*, novel], trans. Alfred Hower and John Saunders (Austin: University of Texas Press, 1969).

Pontiero, Giovanni, ed., *An Anthology of Modernist Brazilian Poetry* (Oxford: Pergamon Press, 1969).

Queiroz, Rachel de, *Three Marys* [*Três Marias*, novel], trans. Fred P. Ellison (Austin: University of Texas Press, 1965).

Ramos, Graciliano, *Anguish* [*Angústia*, novel], trans. L. C. Kaplan (New York: Alfred A. Knopf, 1946).

————, *Barren Lives* [*Vidas Sêcas*, novel], trans. Ralph Edward Dimmick (Austin: University of Texas Press, 1965).

Rosa, João Guimarães, *The Devil to Pay in the Backlands* [*Grande Sertão: Veredas*, novel], trans. James L. Taylor and Harriet de Onís (New York: Alfred A. Knopf, 1963).

————, *Sagarana* [*Sagarana*, short stories], trans. Harriet de Onís (New York: Alfred A. Knopf, 1966).

————, *The Third Bank of the River and Other Stories* [*Primeiras Estórias*, short stories], trans. Barbara Shelby (New York: Alfred A. Knopf, 1968).

Sabino, Fernando, *A Time to Meet* [*O Encontro Marcado*, novel] (London: Souvenir Press, 1967).

Sayers, Raymond and Cassiano Nunes, ed. and trans., *Modern Brazilian Poetry*, read by Prof. Cassiano Nunes [bilingual pamphlet accompanying record] (New York: Folkways Record and Service Corp., 1965).

Setúbal, Paulo de Oliveira, *Domitila; The Romance of an Emperor's Mistress* [*A Marquêsa de Santos*, novel], trans. and adapted by Margaret Richardson [Hollingsworth] (New York: Howard-McCann, 1930).

Suassuna, Ariano, *The Rogue's Trial* [*Auto da Compadecida*, play], trans. Dillwyn F. Ratcliff (Berkeley: University of California Press, 1963).

Taunay, Alfredo d'Escragnolle, *Innocencia: A Story of the Prairie Regions of Brazil* [*Inocência*, novel], trans. James W. Wells (London, 1889).

————, *Inocência*, trans. Henriqueta Chamberlain (New York: Macmillan, 1945).

Trend, John B. ed., *Modern Poetry from Brazil* (Cambridge, Eng., 1955).

Veríssimo, Érico Lopes, *Night* [*Noite*, novel], trans. Linton L. Barrett (New York: Macmillan, 1956).

————, *The Rest is Silence* [*O Resto é Silêncio*, novel], trans. L. C. Kaplan (New York: Macmillan, 1946).

————, *Time and the Wind* [*O Tempo e o Vento*, historical novel], trans. Linton L. Barrett (New York: Macmillan, 1951).

————, *Crossroads* [*Caminhos Cruzados*, novel], trans. L. C. Kaplan (New York: Macmillan, 1943).

————, *Consider the Lilies of the Field* [*Olhai os Lírios do Campo*, novel], trans. Jean Neel Karnoff (New York: Macmillan, 1947).

————, *His Excellency, the Ambassador* [*O Senhor Embaixador*, novel of inter-American politics], trans. Linton L. Barrett (New York: Macmillan, 1967).

Villicaña, Eugenio, ed. and trans., *Twelve Modern Brazilian Poets* (New York: October House, 1969).

Chapter 13

The Evolution of Brazilian Music and Art

Gerrit de Jong, Jr.

I T SEEMS DIFFICULT to believe now that only a short time ago we North Americans were almost completely unaware of Brazilian culture and art. So many of us knew so little about Latin America and its peoples, and especially about Brazil, that it seldom occurred to us that worthwhile contributions in any of the fields of art might have been made by Luso-Americans. Whenever South American art was discussed the name of Portinari usually came up, but all too often it sounded like an exception to prove the rule. Few of us could recall more names than that of Villa Lobos to indicate that we realized the possibility of composers being born in Brazil. Even among musicians it was usually assumed that the name of Brazil did not need to be listed in any discussion of musical accomplishments on a national basis. Those who thought they were familiar with the history of music in Europe and America knew practically nothing of what, or how much, had actually been done in Brazil toward the civilization of the art of music in America, for when they spoke of the history of music in America, they usually thought of North America only.

Today we are fortunately much better informed about the South Americans, and the South Americans about us. Just as we to them are no longer extremely rich people who are too much in a hurry to figure out what to do with our wealth, so they to us are no longer simply sentimental guitar-playing serenaders who live in, or uncomfortably near, disease-infested and steaming jungles. It took a worldwide upheaval, however, to shock us into this improved consciousness. The present chapter is offered in the hope of providing for the general North American reader the minimum information he will need in order to develop an appreciative overview of what has happened in Brazil to give it title to a respected place in the fields of music and art.

312

MUSIC

The Brazil of today began its political career as a colony of a European power, Portugal. It is not at all strange, therefore, that its art music was almost completely under the dominance of Europe until the end of World War I. A similar statement could be made about art music in North America also, and because of similar circumstances. Both in South and North America it was the struggle for liberation from European colonialism that led ultimately to cultural as well as political independence. Along with his attempts to throw off a foreign yoke and his further fights for individual freedom, the Brazilian began seriously to study himself ethnographically, historically, socially, and artistically. This analysis has helped him considerably to understand the characteristics of his own culture. It will be precisely on the basis of such studies that the true Brazilian soul will be discovered, which in turn will make it possible for its message to be given to the world. In different ways the United States has encouraged Brazil in these efforts at defining its peculiar place in a world of art and culture. The interest shown in this country in the sociological studies made by Gilberto Freyre, in the paintings of Portinari, and in the musical compositions by such men as Villa Lobos, Fernândez, Mignone, and Guarnieri gives ample proof of our sincere desire to help in that direction as well as in others.

An almost feverish concern about folklore has lately become manifest in Brazil, which has naturally brought an extraordinary interest in musicology. Consequently, a great number of men, all of them fine thinkers, are dedicating their untiring efforts to the solution of national and continental problems in musical aesthetics, history, and folk music in its various manifestations. Among these scholars should be mentioned especially Mário de Andrade, Renato Almeida, Andrade Muricy, Luiz Heitor Corrêa de Azevedo, and Otávio Bevilaqua. These, and the North American Herskowitz, are making significant progress in the determination of the constants among the various lyrical elements and in the classification of the historical processes and influences in what is today called Brazilian music. Another eminent musicologist among us, Charles Seeger, should not go unmentioned here, for he has accomplished much in furthering the more widespread understanding of "American" music.

Any understanding of contemporary Brazilian music presupposes an acquaintance with its past, as well as a knowledge of its present, for the art forms used in Brazil today are largely based upon folk music, as is the case in most other countries where a national music exists. It is never easy to determine the exact nature of folk music, for, passed along from mouth to mouth but not often reduced to writing, it is hardly ever played or sung twice in the same way. Besides, rural folk music undergoes further radical changes when, under the influence of urbanization, it is made to fit into conventional forms. The folk song of any country is therefore constantly in the process of being formed, without ever reaching a fixed or final form. Because of the complicated racial background of Brazilian culture, it is particularly difficult to characterize Brazilian folk music. There are in Brazil, as in many other countries, two kinds of folk music. The first seems the product of the people as a people, without being the work of any individual composer. The second bears the stamp of being composed, or at times merely arranged, by an individual composer, but recognizably expressed in the folk spirit. It is, of course, always extremely difficult to state precisely what constitutes this folk spirit.

The population of Brazil is composed basically of three racial strains: first, the Caucasian, represented chiefly by the Portuguese; second, the Brazilian Indian; and, third, the African Negro. These three racial strains also form the foundation upon which Brazilian folk music is built and developed. Besides, representatives of many different European nationalities in addition to the Portuguese have come to Brazil to add to the conglomerate in the ethnic and cultural melting pot. Italians and Spaniards came in large numbers, to join or be joined by persons from many other European nations, among them Germany, France, Holland, and Poland.

To Brazilian folk music, the Portuguese brought the European characteristics of melodic line, harmonic tonality, and the concepts of classical form, all of which were already greatly influenced by Moorish rhythm and color. In the last analysis, all that is basic in the structure of "Brazilian" music really came from Portugal. This will not seem surprising when we remember that the Brazilians, in large measure, Portuguese by blood, got their entire fundamental cultural pattern (including their religion, their language, their educational system, and their customs) from Portugal. Although this Portuguese inheritance had to change materially in the immigrant's new home and is still changing today, the bold outlines and enduring melodic, harmonic, and rhythmic traits of Brazilian music are Portuguese.

Since the Portuguese colonizer never ceased to look forward to an eventual return to his home country in Europe, a definitely nostalgic tone pervaded all his music. In Brazil he even invented the *fado*, a sad, homesick serenade that became immensely popular in Portugal, where it is now generally, though erroneously, regarded as of local origin. This note of yearning has remained a constant characteristic of Brazilian music to this day.

The conquered and vanishing Brazilian Indian, not so highly developed as some other South American Indians, added more sadness to the blend. Melodically and rhythmically he had few ready-made elements to offer beyond those that occurred in some fixed monotonous war chants and laments. Since he had comparatively little to do with the feared white colonizers, what contribution to Brazilian folk music he did make, mainly through the early Jesuit missionaries, was of necessity relatively small. However, the indigenous increment to Brazilian folk music, although not extensive, is to-day eagerly sought after and used as inspirational material by contemporary Brazilian composers of national art music.

The Negro, on the other hand, was constantly in contact with his white "boss." Being distinctly musical, he began at once to adapt the European melodies he heard in his new home to that important expression of his most profound sentiments: the chanting that accompanied his work and dances, assuaged his sufferings and grief, and voiced his religious and amorous emotions. He, too, had little to offer melodically, but the numerous and varied rhythmic patterns of his intoning became a rich treasure for the Brazilian art music which was to develop later. Afro-Brazilian music was almost exclusively dance music, accompanied by the polyrhythm of an unbelievably large number and variety of percussion instruments. String instruments were rarely used by the Negro, wind instruments still less. The intriguing rich rhythms of modern Brazilian art music, perhaps the sailent feature of this national form, owe their development principally to the significant contributions made by the African on the South American continent.

Since the Negro had been brought from Africa to live out his life in slavery, Afro-Brazilian music was naturally shot through with yearnings and longings similar to those that were so much a part of the musical expression of his new neighbors. Melancholy definitely marked also the African contribution to the mixture that finally resulted.

It is easy to trace the three strains in the artless blending that constitutes Brazilian folk and art music today. Especially in the popular and traditional dance forms it is interesting to observe one of these three basic ingredients definitely asserting itself. While the *lundú*, the *macumba*, and the *batuque* are unmistakably African, the *chôro*, the *cateretê*, and the *coco* are typically native of Brazil.

Other influences upon Brazilian music should be mentioned. For example, from the beginning of the colonial period a great number of Spaniards came to settle in Brazil and penetrated far into the interior both in the south and in Bahia. Spaniards joined the *bandeiras* at the end of the sixteenth century. As soldiers, many of them helped in the fight against the Dutch. Beginning with Anchieta, there were a number of Spanish fathers among the Jesuits who worked in Brazil. As the influence of Spanish music was noticeable in Portugal, some song forms, like those of the fandango type, came to Brazil by way of the Portuguese, as did also the popular Brazilian *violão*, which is really the Spanish guitar. The romantic element in Brazilian art music is traceable largely to the influence of the Italians; this came later, principally in the nineteenth century. The leadership of Italian music was enormous among Brazilian musicians for a long time. A characteristic gaiety, sparkle, and polish constitute additions made by the French. Of late, North American music, especially through the medium of jazz, exercises a marked influence on the development of urban Brazilian music. In spite of the great variety of the sources from which Brazilian folk and art music have drawn contributions and notwithstanding the fact that Brazilian music is preponderantly in the major mode, it is definitely marked by the depth of sadness that characterizes the national temperament. Even the *samba* of the happiest *carnaval* festivities is positively nostalgic. Because Brazilian music reveals the amalgamation of so many racial and different cultural elements and forms, its richness and flexibility will always keep it expressive and satisfying.

The Beginning

The discoverers of Brazil, in the main rough, adventurous, seafaring folk, had little time to devote to the finer things of life. Their principal interest was not the promotion of culture but rather the establishment of political dominance for the sake of economic gain. Among these restless people and the Europeans who followed them to the New World during the next two centuries, the arts would have been badly neglected but for the fact that the Jesuits, well-represented even among the earliest colonizers, from the very beginning vigorously promoted them. In the pursuit of their particular undertaking, the conversion of the Indian to Christianity, the Jesuits noticed the influence the plain chant of the church services exercised upon the sensibilities of the native Brazilian. It soon became evident that music would be the Jesuits' greatest help in attracting the Indian to the Church and the ideals for which it stood.

The happy songs of the sixteenth and seventeenth centuries, though primarily written as a form of entertainment, became the vehicle for the new religious teachings. The religious processions that were organized in those early days also made good use of music. The mystery plays, called *autos*, a most popular form of entertainment produced in the churches for over a century and a half, would have lost much of their effectiveness without the music they employed for the overture, the finale, and at other important points. Choral and instrumental music needed in church ceremonies had to be created by those priests who had been trained in music. For this reason, the Gregorian chant naturally came to have marked influence on folk music. Schools for systematic instruction in vocal and instrumental music were established in numerous places, mainly by the Jesuits, but later also by Benedictines, Carmelites, and Franciscans.

It was discovered that the Indian had considerable talent for singing and playing the instruments used at that time, such as the flute and the viol. Masses were sung in organum. Somewhat later, more particularly in art music, the harpsichord came into use. Thus the Church furnished the strongest impetus for the development of music in Brazil during the colonial period, so that both its folk and art music remained predominantly religious. Since neither of these forms was written down, our specific knowledge concerning the music that was sung and played throughout that period, is, of necessity, limited. That it grew and was shaped under the influence of many different factors, however, cannot be doubted.

Father João Navarro is usually credited with having made the first translation of any songs and hymns into the Tupí language. The "Mistério de Jesús," the text and music of which are said to have been written and composed by Father José de Anchieta, is the most famous of a long list of mystery plays produced. Father João da Cunha turned it into the Portuguese language. It was first put on in Bahia, where the luxuriant growth of that part of the country served as a stage setting. The instrumentation of the supporting orchestra was excessively percussive, including such instruments as rattles, shakers, bells, and whistles of many kinds. In 1555 Father Anchieta also founded the first theater in Rio de Janeiro. Before that time one had already been established in São Vicente.

The churches and schools, eventually established in all parts of Brazil by priests of various orders, were first founded in Bahia. In 1549 the Jesuit Manuel de Nóbrega began a course in music in Bahia which turned into a recognized music school. As early as 1578 the first diploma of Master of Arts in instrumental and vocal music was given there; the Brotherhood of Santa Cecília became a "real" music center.

Bahia's outstanding musical figure of the seventeenth century was Friar Euzébio de Soledade, a man of vast erudition, a poet, artist, and orator, who played the harmonium and viol and composed much religious music. He also made secular songs, using his own poetry as texts. The historian Guilhermo de Mello says that Euzébio, Friar Antão de Santo Elías, and Friar Francisco Xavier de Santa Tereze, together with Anchieta, Navarro, and Álvaro Lôbo, introduced the diatonic scale of seven degrees in Bahia. He refers to them as "excellent musicians, splendid organists, who did a great deal for music instruction during the colonial period."

José Pereira Rebouças (1789–1843) of Bahia was the first Brazilian to go to Europe to complete his musical education. He first studied violin in Paris, then harmony, counterpoint, and composition in Bologna, Italy, where he was awarded the degree of Master of Music. The outstanding work among his numerous compositions is the "Magnificat."

There must have been much musical activity in Pernambuco after the Jesuits began their work there in 1551. In Olinda, for example, masses were sung in organum during the sixteenth century. We read of a wealthy gentleman who, in 1640, sent for "a clever French master to teach the great progress which the art had made in the science and the handling of instruments." During the next year the feast of Santo Antônio was celebrated "with the best musicians of the country, who sang in three choirs, having mass, sermon, and measured music." Mention is made of a military band, with trumpets, bagpipes, and other martial instruments, that functioned in 1645. During the latter half of the sixteenth century a regular music school was established in connection with the Cathedral of Olinda; religious processions were held in which harps, trumpets, and violins were played; even daily morning concerts were given on board ships riding at anchor in the port of Recife. The outstanding Pernambucan musician of the seventeenth century was Francisco Rodrigues Penteado. During the eighteenth century Augustinho Rodrigues Leite established an organ factory in Olinda. He built organs for the churches in Pernambuco and later also for those in various localities in Bahia. Wind and string instruments, as well as organs, were manufactured by Manuel Inácio Valcacer. In 1760 the Brotherhood of Santa Cecília was established; it later became a popular music center, just as it did in other localities.

In seventeenth-century inventories and testaments executed in São Paulo we read of viols, zithers, harps, timbrels, and other instruments. Manuel Vieira Barros in 1657 was appointed conductor "to beat time for a period of one year in the mother church of São Paulo and environs." In 1774 the choir of the São Paulo Cathedral was created, and André da Silva Gomes de Castro was brought from Lisbon to direct it. In reports concerning the musical activities carried on in São Paulo toward the end of the colonial period, the names of many well-trained singers and instrumentalists among the priests are mentioned.

Also, in Minas Gerais intense interest in music was manifest. In 1745 a chorister, organist, and four choir boys were known for the fine music they supplied for the cathedral services. Some of the earliest Brazilian theaters were established in Minas Gerais. Music, of course, formed an important part of the performances in all theaters in Brazil; in fact, many of those that were built in the latter half of the eighteenth century bore the designation "opera house." Manoel Joaquim, Jerônimo de Souze Paiva, and Father João de Deus were among the outstanding Minas composers of the colonial period.

Santa Catarina became known for producing good orchestral music. Paraíba developed a marked taste for good music, especially organ music. Even in Mato Grosso an opera house was opened in 1790, and other evidences of interest in culture were noted.

José Maurício.—A figure of rare creative talent and the only really great composer of the colonial period was José Maurício Nunes Garcia. Born in 1767 of humble colored parentage in Rio, he amazed everyone as a child prodigy by his phenomenal memory, his ability at improvisation, and his sweet voice. He received the best general and musical education then available. Having become a priest, he sang his first mass at the age of twenty-five. After his ordination he at once turned his attention to the composition of religious music. Remembering the hardships imposed by his own poverty, he established a free music school that continued for thirty-six years and produced some outstanding musicians.

Always a thorough student, he sent for all the music scores and important books about music that were printed in Germany, France, Italy, and England, until he amassed the largest and best music library in all of Brazil. Although never privileged to leave his native state, he proved himself to be an unusually fine, sensitive artist. Since Haydn and Mozart had been of greatest influence upon his art, he naturally wrote in the classical idiom; his work became an important factor in the cultivation of good taste in sacred music. All his compositions show profound emotion and reflect his own intense mysticism, but never fail to astonish by their freshness and spontaneity. His most productive period was the ten years following 1798. The best known among his 300 works are the Requiem in D Minor and the Mass in B-flat.

Personally unassuming, never self-interested, he became the victim of almost constant exploitation. Those who could and should have appreciated him personally and his unusual talents did nothing to promote his efforts. After the royal court had moved from Portugal to Brazil, Maurício was appointed Inspector of the Royal Chapel, where he played the large three-manual organ. This appointment was the first in a series of attempts on the part of the prince regent to protect Maurício somewhat against the overt jealousies and intrigue of the Europeans at court. Unfortunately, the more the prince praised the artist's work the more jealous the Portuguese became, for they despised everything Brazilian and could not believe that any art could be developed in America. In order to demonstrate his confidence in Maurício's abilities, the prince kept on giving him orders for music to be composed for special festive occasions. For fear that he might disappoint the only person who seemed to believe in him, Maurício tried to keep abreast of this unreasonable number of commissions, and, as a result, literally worked himself to death. Deprived of his memory and nearly all his creative powers, he died in 1830.

Not much of his work has been left to us, but the relatively little we have leaves no doubt that under more favorable circumstances José Maurício would have become one of the world's leading musicians. To the indefatigable efforts of Viscount de Taunay is to be credited the fact that

José Maurício is at all recognized in Brazil today. The famous music historian Renato Almeida says of this truly great man: "His music, whether for its material or for the art with which José Maurício developed it, is of value to us not only because of the beauty it encloses, for its religious lyricism, or for its expressive melody. It is of great significance, rather, for its creative power, for its spontaneity and balance, the profound affirmation of the musical genius of a people."

Dom Pedro I.—The escape of the royal family from Portugal brought much of the flower of Portuguese aristocracy to this hemisphere. The advent of wealthy and cultured Europeans, the development of new foreign commerce, and the establishment of libraries and schools meant new life for the entire country. A celebrated Portuguese opera composer, Marcos Portugal, joined the court at Rio. A group of writers, artists, architects, and musicians from France was brought to help found the Brazilian Academy of Fine Arts. Among these was Sigismund Neukomm, one of Haydn's favorite pupils, who praised the accomplishments of José Maurício, thereby making himself the focus of Marcos Portugal's jealousy and anger.

Dom Pedro I, the son of João VI, who had inherited the musical talent of the House of Bragança, studied with Marcos Portugal and perhaps also with José Maurício. He learned to play at least half a dozen of the standard orchestra instruments; later he studied composition with Neukomm. His better-known compositions include the famous Hymn of Independence of Brazil, a symphony, a mass, a *Te Deum*, an opera, and another hymn that was used as the national hymn of Portugal until 1910.

In spite of all the musical training and experience Dom Pedro had had, there was a decided slump in all artistic activities during the period of political agitation that followed João VI's return to Portugal. Not until after Brazil's independence had been declared could the nation again think about promoting music. But Dom Pedro's interests and mode of life were too erratic for him personally to help materially in cultural matters. Nevertheless, because of more and more contact with the music centers of Europe and increased systematic music study at home, at least Rio de Janeiro developed its culture considerably. Italian opera companies brought many foreign artists, singers, instrumentalists, directors, and dancers to the Imperial Theater São Pedro de Alcântara, where they sang Rossini, Donizetti, and other popular Italian composers. Varied reports concerning these performances lead us to believe that the ballets were generally deserving of praise, whereas the work of all the rest, orchestra, chorus, and often soloists, was of rather poor quality. Sacred music steadily gave way to the ever more popular secular music.

Francisco Manoel.—The only really strong figure to dedicate his talents to the development of music in Brazil during the first half of the last century was the composer of the Brazilian national anthem, Francisco Manoel da Silva, who was born in Rio de Janeiro in the year 1795. He studied violin, cello, piano, and harmonium. While he did not disapprove of the then fashionable importation of European artists, he felt that Brazil should not stop with that but provide for its promising young musicians opportunities for significant training and experience. Like his teachers José Maurício and Segismund Neukomm, he had abundant confidence in the native talent of his countrymen. It was his aim and desire, therefore, to establish musical instruction in Brazil on a sound basis. To encourage the cultivation of music and to provide social benefits for his companions in art, he organized in 1833 the "Sociedade Beneficente Musical," which functioned until 1890. Completely selfless in all he undertook, he promoted concerts, organized religious festivals, and directed opera companies. As a teacher he specialized in piano and vocal art. The imperial court recognized his services to the country, decorated him, and appointed him to many positions of responsibility.

Francisco Manoel did not equal Maurício as a composer, but he wrote constantly, so that the works he brought forth are considerable. He composed hymns for all occasions, numerous pieces for voice and piano, and many religious works for voices, chorus, and orchestra. For the benefit of his students particularly, he also wrote a music compendium. His greatest contribution to the artistic welfare of Brazil was the founding of the Conservatório de Música do Rio de Janeiro in 1841. Its name was later changed to Instituto Nacional de Música and, in 1932, to Escola Nacional de Música. This institution is today Brazil's leading music school. Francisco Manoel died in 1865. Mário de Andrade said of him that he was for Brazil "the musician of greatest social importance."

Domingos da Rocha Mussurunga (1807–1856) tried to establish a conservatory in Bahia but failed to receive government aid for such an undertaking. Like Francisco Manoel, he constantly exerted himself to promote instruction for prospective musicians. He composed a large amount of sacred and profane music. A compendium he wrote saw two editions (1834 and 1846).

Dom Pedro II.—Dom Pedro I abdicated in 1831, and, since his son was at that time only five years old, Brazil was governed by a regency for a period of ten years. The regency gave way to the forty-nine-year rule of Dom Pedro II. Under him, the country really became prosperous, and, in the main, the government for which young Pedro was responsible was wise and helpful. After the regency, principally because of the encouragement received from the new emperor, the arts began to show signs of life. In many places orchestra and band organizations sprang up, which helped noticeably in the promotion of secular music. Religious music, however, during this period definitely lost its dominating influence. Italian opera companies made frequent visits to Brazil, until finally their offerings served as the only means by which taste in musical affairs could be developed. Although there had been some before Marcos Portugal arrived in Brazil, it was he who worked most vigorously to make Italian opera popular.

The sentimental and melancholy love song known in Brazil as the *modinha* was made from the Portuguese *moda*, also largely under the influence of Italian opera. While this now characteristic Brazilian love song was first developed in the salons of Rio aristocracy, it eventually became the vehicle for the expression of typically Brazilian popular sentiment.

It must also be noted that the period from 1834 to 1869 saw the opening of many new theaters in all parts of Brazil. While it is true that they offered mostly dramatic productions, many operas also were produced. In 1857 the Imperial Academy of Music and National Opera was founded by José Amat, a Spaniard, who became its director. He tried hard to develop Portuguese opera in opposition to Italian opera, the taste for which had by this time become like a sickening craze. Although the government helped and poor students received their instruction and training free, this academy, the first organized attempt in Brazil at creating truly national music, was discontinued in 1865, but not until after it had introduced Gomes to the Brazilian public. It was Carlos Gomes who, in 1860, directed the opera "A Noite de São João" by Elias Alves Lôbo, recognized as the first genuinely Brazilian opera.

A large number of artists among those imported with the visiting Italian opera companies chose to make their home in Brazil. Because of this and the organized moves that had been made to improve the training of music teachers, the number of teachers of vocal art and instrumental music active in Brazil had by 1860 been tremendously increased. Everywhere musical societies were being established in order to give Brazilian amateurs a chance to show their interest in music and help actively in its promotion. Even music magazines began to make their appearance. Much of this activity was naturally centered in the capital, but Bahia witnessed a similar increase in musical interest and activity, until it became known as Brazil's second music center. The most serious drawback of the period between João VI's departure in 1821 and the 1860's was the fact that the contributions then being made by the great romantics in Europe were almost never used in Brazil.

Carlos Gomes.—Antônio de Carlos Gomes was not only the most famous opera composer of Latin America but also one of the greatest lyric composers of both the Americas, and the first American composer to achieve worldwide recognition.

He was born into a poor family of Campinas, state of São Paulo, in the year 1836. His father, who married four times, was of Portuguese descent; his mother, his father's third wife, was of native Brazilian Indian stock. Carlos had twenty-five brothers and sisters. To begin with, he learned what he could about music from his father, a composer and the leader of a band in Campinas. As a very young boy Carlos became a member of that band. While apprenticed to a tailor, he spent all his spare time studying and memorizing operatic scores. However, the impossibility of making adequate progress in his musical studies without going to Rio soon became evident to him. When, after a long struggle, he did reach the capital, Dom Pedro II helped him register at the Imperial Conservatory of Music, which was then under the direction of Francisco Manoel.

At the conservatory Carlos made phenomenal progress in the study of composition under Joaquim Giannini and was graduated with honors. In 1861 his first opera, "A Noite do Castelo," was produced with unprecedented success. The audience, which included all the court and most of the cultivated people of Rio, literally went wild in showing its appreciation. The emperor, who was also in attendance, made Gomes a *cavalheiro* of the Order of the Rose. The town of his birth sent him a golden crown, the ladies of Rio a golden baton. Francisco Manoel was the conductor on that memorable occasion.

His second opera, "Joanna de Flandres," produced two years later, was similarly successful. The audience gave the composer another boisterous ovation, and the emperor, who decorated Gomes a second time, was so impressed with his talent that he granted him an annual pension of 1:000$000 (about $250 in United States money then) to facilitate his going to Europe for advanced study. The next year Gomes went to Italy. He studied composition with Rosse, the director of the famous Milan Conservatory, where, in 1866, Gomes earned the title of "master composer."

In 1870 Gomes' opera "Il Guarany," with a libretto based on a novel by José de Alencar, was presented at La Scala and conclusively established Gomes' fame as an opera composer. An ovation lasting more than half an hour followed the premiere. The famous Verdi, who was present, said of the new composer: "He begins where I leave off." After its initial performance in Milan, "Il Guarany" was presented in all important opera houses of Europe and America. In December of that year it was presented in the composer's native country. As had been the case after performances of his earlier operas, the audience gave a stormy demonstration of appreciation once more, this time going so far as to carry the composer home after the performance.

"Il Guarany" describes the meeting of the Portuguese with the indigenous race in Brazil. It is today what it was when first performed, the biggest event in Brazilian music. The overture, the best-known orchestral composition created by a South American, has come to be regarded as one of the national symbols, more or less like a second national anthem. Though this opera is too distinctly Italian in style to be called a typically national work, throughout it we note unmistakable anticipations of the manner in which later national composers were to embody the atmosphere of Brazil in their creations. The original, yet strangely familiar, sonorities, the rich melodic beauty, at once graceful and rough, and the prodigious imagination used made "Il Guarany" the most popular of all Brazilian operas.

Early in 1873 La Scala produced "Forsca," complimented highly by Gounod and considered by Gomes his best work. In this opera Gomes makes interesting use of leitmotiv, not structurally but as melodic ornamentation. This work, though popular, was not as enthusiastically received as his previous operas. "Salvator Rosa," based on a historical episode in Naples, became so popular in Italy that it ran in five Italian cities at the same time. The first La Scala performance of "Maria Tudor" in 1879 was a failure, but the second, the following evening, was a complete success. This opera is distinguished for its great dramatic tension and, like the other Gomes operas, for its beautiful orchestration.

In an effort to return to Brazilian thematic materials and thereby satisfy the thousands of admirers who were eagerly waiting for him to compose another "Il Guarany," Gomes went back to Italy and wrote "Lo Schiavo." He experienced great difficulties in doing it—misunderstandings with his librettist, failure of promised financial aid to arrive from Brazil, and many others. Nonetheless, he produced a work full of native inspiration, definitely Brazilian in feeling throughout, and symbolically rough in its melodic construction. The Negro dances of this work abound in original rhythms and are accented by the use of authentic Afro-Brazilian instruments. The production of "Lo Schiavo" in Brazil was the fourth occasion on which the emperor decorated Gomes. Even though critics generally do not consider Gomes a typically national composer, it is interesting to note that the best parts of his lyric writings are invariably those based upon Brazilian themes.

In 1871 Gomes married Adélia del Conte Peri, a member of an illustrious Bologna family. They had five children. Itala Maria, the youngest daughter, wrote the life of her famous father. Throughout his entire life it was difficult for Gomes to manage his financial and economic affairs. Moreover, he frequently ran into serious misunderstandings with those whose goodwill was indispensable to him. The emperor of Brazil had promised him the directorship of the Rio de Janeiro conservatory, but with the coming of the republic (1889) the position was given to Leopoldo Miguéz. Because of a long series of disagreements, Gomes was accused of being a monarchist and antagonistic to the regime then in power. He was also disappointed in not being able officially to represent his native country and people at the Chicago Exposition. At last, after having accepted the directorship of the conservatory of music in Belém, a belated recognition of his talent and services, he discovered that his own illness and worry about the serious illness of his son had left him too weak to do any work in connection with the new position. Death took him in the year 1896. That he was one of the greatest manifestations of the Brazilian spirit no compatriot would now deny.

The Second Half of the Nineteenth Century

The fact that at least one Brazilian musician had gained international recognition stimulated new interest in making music liked, in promoting improved music education, and in attracting young people with real talent to a musical career. To help in these matters, a great number of societies, or "clubs," were organized during the latter half of the nineteenth century. Of these, the "Club Beethoven," beginning under Roberto J. Kinsman, did most to refine taste and promote Brazilian culture. Many chamber music and a few symphonic recitals were given. The works of Haydn, Mozart, Beethoven, Schumann, Mendelssohn, and Saint-Saëns now regularly formed part of the concerts played. Practically all artists of importance to come out of that period had some association with this club or with the "Club Haydn," which pursued a similar program in São Paulo. Many promising musicians were given stipends to enable them to study with the best European masters. The number of magazines that devoted all or part of their space to music was signally increased. Gradually, but surely, music in Brazil was widening its horizons, abandoning the almost exclusive influence of Italy for a broader acquaintance with the music of other countries.

Among the celebrated virtuosi brought to Brazil during the second half of the last century, we should cite two outstanding teachers of piano. Artur Napoleão (1843–1925) was born in Oporto, Portugal; Liszt and von Bülow had been his teachers. He established himself in Rio de Janeiro. Luigi Chiafarelli was Italian by birth and chose to do his work in São Paulo. Here he founded the School of Pianoforte, where some outstanding pianists received their training, notably Guiomar Novaes, Antonietta Rudge, and João de Souza Lima. It is important to be aware of the contribution to the development of Brazilian music made by these two illustrious pianists. For it is a curious fact that from its beginning until now music in Brazil saw its greatest development in the piano field. With this in mind, it should not come as a surprise that the world's best-known woman pianist is a Brazilian, Guiomar Novaes. In the 1969 Van Cliburn International Piano Competition, held in Texas, a young Brazilian senhorita, Christina Ortiz, nineteen-years old, won the first prize. Solid interest and accomplishment in Brazilian symphonic and chamber music is of a more recent date.

The success achieved by the majority of musicians who went abroad to study proves the artistic temperament of the Brazilians and the facility with which they cultivate music. Most of them, of course, developed their art within the international tendencies of the period and, thereby, in a measure, failed to become composers of "Brazilian" music. It is not until the "moderns" take the lead in musical affairs that the music produced in Brazil can be stamped truly national. There were, however, a number of composers whose works indicated that, although the whole atmosphere of all Brazilian culture was still markedly international, true Brazilian music was actually being developed.

Leopoldo Miguéz, born in Rio de Janeiro in 1850, for many years was the director of the Instituto Nacional de Música and did a great deal to develop public taste, especially for symphonic and chamber music. The first to write symphonic poems in Brazil, he was a finished craftsman but, unfortunately, lacked the creative capacity that might have led him to find his individual manner of expression. All that he created was molded in the European forms of his period. His symphonic poems were strictly in the style of Liszt; his principal work, a lyric drama in one act, "Saldunes," was completely Wagnerian. He died in 1902.

There is very little in the compositions of Henrique Oswald that can be designated typically Brazilian, but all critics recognize in him one of the foremost composers of the last century. His works, though outwardly classical in form, expressed the purest of poetic feeling, variation, and originality. The romantic vagueness that characterizes his creations was always perfectly controlled and in good taste. His fine qualities are heard at their best in his chamber music, in which the influence of Schumann is obvious. The Quintet opus 18 is usually considered his outstanding contribution to this genre. When other composers were led to excesses for the sake of novelty, Oswald countered with delicate sensitivity and balance. In a worldwide contest sponsored by the newspaper *Figaro* of Paris, the jury, headed by Saint-Saëns, awarded him first prize for his "Il Neige." No wonder that he has been called the "most refined and complete musician" of his period (1854–1931).

Brasílio Itiberê da Cunha, born in Paranaguá in 1848, distinguished himself in the promotion of culture and art while serving his country as a diplomat abroad. He was minister plenipotentiary in Berlin when death overtook him in 1913. His compositions represent the true dawn of Brazilian national music. He was the first to employ folkloric thematic materials in his works, for he believed that the folk music of a country was the true source of inspiration for composers of art music. He endowed all his creations with a Brazilian feeling. His orchestral rhapsody "Sertaneja" must be considered the starting point of the greatest significance for genuinely Brazilian music. The majority of the great European artists of his day were numbered among his personal friends, including Liszt, who played his "Sertaneja."

Alexandre Levy (1864–1892) was a brilliant Brazilian pianist to whom life was all sadness and melancholy. In his Schumannesque attempt to find the fitting expression of his personality, the twenty-eight years of his life proved too short. With Brasílio Itiberê he has the distinction of being among the very first to use primitive Brazilian materials in his compositions. All the creations of his last five years have a distinctly national flavor. Especially known are his "Suite Brasileira" for orchestra in four parts, which includes a famous samba and a popular song; "Tango Brasileiro," characterized by a typically Brazilian fatalism; and a considerable number of piano pieces.

Alberto Nepomuceno was born in Fortaleza in 1864 and died in Rio in 1920. He spent many years studying piano, organ, and composition in Italy, Germany, and France; when he later returned to Europe, he directed concerts in Brussels, Paris, and Geneva with great success. He is the forerunner of the modern national school, making contributions of the highest importance to the development of Brazilian national music. While the forms of his compositions remind us of the European patterns, the contents are always unmistakably Brazilian. Generally considered, his master work is the "Série Brasileira" in four parts, for it definitely points the way to a national school of composition. "O Garatuja," a lyric comedy based on a work by the celebrated Indianist José de Alencar, remained unfinished. This work breathes the spirit of Brazil. Its prelude has become immensely popular. His many compositions for voice and piano are among the most beautiful and most characteristic ever written in Brazil. In this work he laid the foundation for the Brazilian *lied*. He was such an enthusiast for singing in the national language that he made the National Institute of Music officially adopt this idea as its policy, which greatly encouraged Brazilian composers to write in this genre.

Francisco Braga (1868–1945) is held in the highest esteem as the connecting link between the premodern and modern attempt to reflect the reality of Brazil; he was for over thirty years Rio's seasoned conductor. At the age of twenty-two he was designated the outstanding candidate among twenty-one who sought admission to the conservatory in Paris. There he was taught principally by Massenet and later studied in Dresden to become acquainted with the Wagnerian approach. He wrote in all genres, but the symphonic poem was his favorite form of expression. Songs, with words by Olavo Bilac, the most popular Brazilian poet, are among his most noteworthy contributions. No composer ever represented the true Brazilian atmosphere better than did Braga in his Trio in G Minor for violin, cello, and piano, which includes a beautiful *lundú*; "Tango Caprichoso" for violin and piano;

and "Toada" for cello and piano. As professor of composition at the Escola Nacional de Música, his erudition guided an eager generation of composers.

In the field of popular music, the creator of the Brazilian tango, Ernesto Nazareth (1863–1934), the pianist who idolized Chopin and Beethoven, stands out. He wrote around 500 pieces in the *carioca* popular style. His work has had appreciable influence on that of many composers who sought to give their creations a national coloring. Villa Lobos called him the "incarnation of the Brazilian soul."

The Modern Movement

Since, in the strict sense of the word, nothing creative has ever been produced in Brazil by the European influence alone, it has long been evident that the true Brazilian musical idiom would not be simply a copy or extension of the European pattern. On the other hand, a truly Brazilian musical idiom could not be merely Indian, or Negro either, for if it were, it would be going contrary to the universal stream of music and become a thing apart, a mere curiosity. Obviously, all the many different elements offered by the land and people of Brazil would have to be integrated with the universal forms of expression and still produce an idiom sufficiently different from other national forms of expression to represent the spirit of the Brazilian people, developed under a variety of influences.

For four centuries Brazilian composers, some consciously, some unconsciously, had made efforts to come ever closer to that ideal. It was left for the so-called "moderns" to achieve it. Today discriminating non-Brazilians hear something in Brazilian music that is distinctive, however difficult it may be to define at times, but always unmistakably characteristic of the Brazilian nation, which is itself constantly growing more different from its sources.

Musicological studies have done much to reveal the great treasure of folkloric motives to the composers of popular and art music in Brazil. Especially deserving of praise in this field was the work of Luciano Gallet, who left us—in addition to many original compositions—valuable harmonizations of numerous Brazilian folk songs. And the most prolific of modern composers, Villa Lobos, has also exercised his talents in the uncovering of the various component elements of the Brazilian cultural pattern. The charm of religious rites and ceremonies, Christian and pagan, with all their symbolism and mysticism; the choreographies and polyrhythms of vigorous folk dances; the melancholy and nostalgia of wide-open spaces; the carnivalesque spirit of urban popular festivities; the throbbing tropical imagination—all these, and more, are now being incorporated into a sensitive musical idiom to translate a national consciousness.

The contemporary movement in art music, trying through a variety of forms to give fitting objectification to the temperament of its time and place, itself not definitely characterized, is, therefore, giving the world the most inspired creative approach to an appropriate musical expression of the real soul of a great people.

Luciano Gallet (1893–1931), under the influence of Glauco Velasquez and Henrique Oswald, determined to be a musician rather than an architect. He won a gold medal for piano in 1916 at the National Institute, where he later taught piano. From then on, he worked indefatigably as a composer, journalist, teacher, pianist, musicologist, promoter of musical societies and concerts, and stimulator of publishers and radio broadcasting, always with one goal in mind—to inspire Brazilian composers with the ideal of developing a musical idiom that would be characteristic of their country and people. He began composing in 1918, largely influenced by Darius Milhaud. His compositions show his French descent, the romanticism with which Velasquez had acquainted him, and his own tragic confusion. Beginning in 1924 he published several collections of folk melodies which he himself had discovered and harmonized and two monographs about Indian and Negro influences on Brazilian music. After his death some of his folklore studies were published. Even though his compositions are of no particular consequence, since only the later ones show any Brazilian feeling, his contributions to the study of Brazilian music were extremely valuable.

Oscar Lorenzo Fernândez (b. 1897), of Spanish descent, was to be a doctor. He studied piano and composition with Henrique Oswald, Francisco Braga, and Frederico Nascimento. When he discovered his great attraction to modern harmony, he gave up his medical career. In 1922 he received three first prizes for composition in a national competition. For his early compositions, he used the French style entirely, but he soon changed to the Brazilian style, in which he did very well. In the field of the Brazilian art song his contributions are remarkable. His "Cantigas de Minha Terra" are of a distinctly national character. His "Trio Brasileiro," the first music in the larger forms to have that burning national spirit, was awarded an international prize in 1924. His opera "Malazarte," with libretto by modernist Graça Aranha, is very successful in reflecting the Brazilian temperament. Among his outstanding symphonic works, all imbued with Brazilian color, are "Reisado do Pastoreio," which ends in a frenzied *batuque*, and "Imbapara," a splendid example of highly skillful orchestration, that breathes the indigenous atmosphere. Fernândez is one of the outstanding and most important conductors in Brazil. He has conducted concerts in Spain (1929), in Colombia (1938), and in the United States.

The flutist Francisco Mignone, professor of conducting at the Escola Nacional de Música, was born in São Paulo, where he began his career as a composer writing popular songs. For these and for his later art music, he drew much inspiration from the São Paulo *caipiras*, the country folk of European and Indian descent, whose favorite instrument is the *violão*. He spent nine years studying abroad, mainly in Milan. Italian, French, and Spanish music have influenced his style most. The early operas he wrote ("Contrator de Diamantes" [1924] and "L'Innocente" [1928]) definitely follow the European pattern. For all his later works, he uses authentic Brazilian materials and treats them in a genuinely Brazilian manner.

His songs are among the most poetic in Brazilian music. The most capable Brazilian criticism holds that he surpasses even Gomes as a song writer. The melody and rhythms of his piano numbers are always refined but preserve the ruggedness of the sentimental popular tunes. Those who are familiar with his artistic productions consider him Brazil's foremost symphonic composer and conductor. Mário de Andrade says of him: "I consider this Brazilian composer one of the most representative expressions of American music. No one in America thinks symphonically better than he does." His works have been performed by the Vienna Philharmonic Orchestra under Richard Strauss and by the National Broadcasting Company Orchestra under Arturo Toscanini. Mignone has conducted symphonic concerts in Germany and Italy and frequently in the United States.

The Rio carnival spirit and the typical nostalgia of the *caipiras* characterize especially the third of Francisco Mignone's "Fantasias Brasileiras." In the fourth of this series local color is added through the use of native instruments. In it we hear the whistling of the little Negro boy, and even the snort of the *cuica*, a marsupial mammal like an opossum. The noblest and most onomatopoetic of his works is the symphony in praise of labor. Of the greatest beauty is the religious symphony in which he gives impressions made upon him by four famous sacred Brazilian edifices. Nothing could be more Brazilian, it seems, than his ballets. "Maracatú de Chico-Rei" tells the story of an African mine worker who rises to create a state within a state; it brings in the ceremonials, processions, laments, and dances of the Negro workers and ends with a magnificent samba. "Babaloxá," also thoroughly Afro-Brazilian, shows the working of black magic and the *macumba* in one of the most highly developed symphonic works in Brazilian music.

Camargo Guarnieri, born in Tieté, São Paulo, in 1907 is a musicians' musician. He began his career as a pianist in the movies. In 1938, after he had already developed a distinctly personal style, São Paulo sent him to Europe to study. Eventually Alfred Cortot referred to his work as "one of the most personal musical manifestations of our time and one of the most characteristic manifestations of Brazilian national genius." Guarnieri refines the national folk materials he uses, escaping the danger of becoming monotonous by avoiding ready-made motives. He seems never to be tempted by extra-musical concepts and preserves the purity of his acousticism by an almost constant use of polyphony, in which his craftsmanship is phenomenal. This powerful creative artist produces works that are at once the most profound and the most elegant contributions made by present-day Brazilian composers.

What he has written for voice and orchestra is of amazing beauty: "A Morte do Aviador," a cantata for soprano, chorus, and orchestra; Three Dances (samba, *cateretê, maxixe*); and Three Poems (*Tristeza, Pôrto-Seguro, Coração cosmopólita*). In these strikingly beautiful works the ideas brought out in the luxurious vocal parts are further accentuated by the remarkably appropriate orchestral accompaniment. His contributions to piano literature are of the highest quality. Especially mentioned should be the Concerto for Piano and Orchestra, in three movements, all of the purest local color: *Selvagem, Saudosamente, Depressa*. But chamber music, after all, lends itself best to the expression of his temperament. His great technical mastery and originality are particularly noticeable in his Sonata for Violoncello and Piano, while in his Second Sonata for Violin and Piano the *caipira* spirit of São Paulo, with all its sadness and motivation, is plainly revealed. Among experts Guarnieri is regarded as doing as much toward the spiritualization of Brazilian national music as any one composer. Prizes have been awarded for Guarnieri's compositions in more than a score of international competitions.

Villa Lobos.— Among Brazilian composers Heitor Villa Lobos continues to enjoy the greatest international recognition. Of all American composers, he was the most prolific. Writing in nearly all genres, sacred and profane, he has given the musical world well over 1600 works: for symphony, small orchestra, chamber music combinations in many varieties, chorus, piano, organ, violin, violoncello, guitar, and voice. In spite of the unevenness in the quality of his works and occasional evidence of a lack of finished technique, if individuality, creativeness, and novelty count at all, Villa Lobos was still a singular—and the most impressive—figure among Latin American composers.

Villa Lobos was born in Rio de Janeiro in 1887. His widowed mother made it possible for him to receive a good general education and special instruction in music. As a youth he played the cello and the guitar. Angelo França and Francisco Braga directed his music study. At the age of nineteen, he joined orchestras as a cellist and gave a considerable number of concerts in many parts of Brazil. At the age of twenty-five, he began to compose. In 1919 Villa Lobos became acquainted with the celebrated pianist Arthur Rubinstein, who liked his music and advanced money to print it. Later, in Paris, Rubinstein brought Villa Lobos and the French publisher Eschig together. When Villa Lobos had reached his thirtieth year, his compositions had stirred up such violent criticisms, both favorable and unfavorable, that there was no longer any question about the importance, if not the greatness, of this new creative force in music. At the age of thirty-two, Villa Lobos was already becoming recognized in European art centers as the most talented conductor of contemporary music in the Americas. He never went to Europe to study; instead, he remained in his native country until he had matured artistically and was formally established as a representative composer. He assimilated the primitive forces of Tupí and Guaraní Indian music especially, before, at the age of thirty-six, he took his creations to Europe to show what he had accomplished. Villa Lobos asserts that the European "moderns" were unknown to him until he himself had written a good deal of music that was more modern than theirs.

From the beginning Villa Lobos was original, extremely inventive, a real creator in the best sense of the word. His composing evidently had its roots in popular music and in the rich Brazilian folklore. Through successive transformation of essentially folklore elements and the musical suggestions which the Brazilian people offered him gratuitously, Villa Lobos shaped his works of art in the larger forms. He clothed and harmonized for voice or instrument and orchestrated the complex and characteristic musical idiom native to Brazil, bringing out and emphasizing the artistic potentialities of all this sonorous virgin material like an absolute master. Thoroughly at home with the universally accepted patterns of composition, he was also acquainted with the experiments carried on by other serious Brazilian composers toward the creation of a truly national formula. He never failed to make all his productions absolutely characteristic of his native land. Not that he strove consciously to breathe a spirit of nationality into his compositions, for that would be like carrying coals to Newcastle. Villa Lobos remained his true self in whatever he undertook; it seemed to be almost instinctive with him to be as Brazilian as anyone could be. Not allowing himself to be swayed by his materials, he showed complete control over them at all times. An incessant experimenter and innovator, he refused to use established forms over and over again, even those that were successful and expressive and the products of his own inventive genius. He had no fear of trying out any new forms of objectification, no matter how bold or subtle, how rough or refined, how promising or unpromising of success. Consequently, the works of this "Berlioz of the New World" have the same variety found in the life and habits of the Brazilian nation.

His compositions cannot be said to be descriptive in a narrow sense; they are, nevertheless, replete with suggestions and atmosphere, never common or vulgar in spite of the live imagination that pervades them. It is meaningless to speak of a Villa Lobos style, for there cannot be one. Each of his important works is *sui generis*. He never stooped to use devices for their own sake, but always made his formal innovations subservient to the expressions of a vibrant and sincere message. Though usually vigorous, often even rough, he always remained poetic. What he had to say carried him over a great range; he changed easily from the representation of the products of the wildest parts of his native Brazil to that of the tenderest emotions, such as those he felt toward children.

A creative giant, Villa Lobos kept in close touch with the life of his fellow countrymen. For forty years he was actively interested in the promotion of music education, for example. As director of music in the Federal District, he revolutionized music instruction in the entire country. The resultant development of a strong love for music in the hearts of Brazilian adolescents is particularly noteworthy. He was of the opinion that children should be taught the fundamentals of music through the vocal rather than through the instrumental approach.

Brazil's most dynamic composer has been justly lauded for the great amount of musicological research he undertook, for it is extensive and significant. To his personal credit stands the collection of more than 5,000 melodic and rhythmic forms that are native to Brazil. In all his compositions, from his little guitar pieces to his powerful *chôros* for orchestra, Villa Lobos showed he had completely absorbed the flavor of the masses. All ethnic materials he changed and adjusted to his artistic needs without having to submit them to a violent transmutation. Villa Lobos was Brazil.

"His *Dansas Africanas* (*Farrapos, Kankukus, Kankikis*), of fine symphonic value, are outstanding works of his earliest period. The monumental symphonic poem *Amazonas*, which he calls a *poema bailado*, is barbarous music which finally seems to turn into a cosmic force that threatens to overwhelm everything, like the Amazon country itself," says the renowned musicologist Renato Almeida. The various phases of life in Brazil are reflected in his *chôros*, which, although none is like any other in the series, are all full of real poetry. No. 8 (for orchestra alone) and no. 10 (for orchestra and chorus) have been especially admired and praised as great New World music. While his songs are among the loveliest written in Brazil, the five operas he produced in his youth have not become popular. Villa Lobos paid homage to Johann Sebastian Bach in his "Bachianas Brasileiras," in many ways the acme of all Brazilian musical compositions, in which the spirit of the German immortal and that of Brazilian folk music are successfully and artistically fused. His works for piano, which indicate new technical possibilities, are generally considered among his best productions; the world's foremost performers regularly find a place for them on their recital programs. Of particular interest and charm are the pieces based on children's themes: twelve *Cirandinhas*, sixteen *Cirandas, Carnaval das Crianças Brasileiras* (eight pieces), *Momo Precoce*, and others.

Villa Lobos dominated Brazilian music for a generation. Among his followers these musicians must be mentioned: Luciano Gallet (1893—1931); Fructuoso Viana (b. 1896); Jaime Ovalle (b. 1894); and Brasílio Itiberê, Jr. (b. 1896). These four have added greatly to Brazil's reputation as a producer of fine songs.

Over fifty years ago, when Villa Lobos conducted his first concert in Paris, when neither he nor his music was known or understood, and Arthur Rubinstein, his friend, was a new rising star on the pianistic horizon, the public booed music, conductor, and soloist. Ignoring public opinion, Villa Lobos was extremely happy—he had thoroughly enjoyed the excellent playing of the French orchestra! "What an orchestra! They are wonderful!" exclaimed the musician who had just been practically hissed off the podium. In his last year, whether he conducted in New York's Carnegie Hall or in the Salle Gaveau of Paris, engagements contracted for twelve months or more in advance, the "standing room only" sign was always out.

When, before his death in 1959, Villa Lobos was asked why he so often conducted in foreign countries and so seldom in Brazil, he answered that he spent only two or three months per year in his native country. His countrymen seemed not to think of him and what he had done for them until he arrived in Rio de Janeiro again. Then they invited him to conduct a concert, which he regularly refused to do because they did not give him enough notice. "Last minute invitations cannot be accepted," he used to say. "I direct only when the contract has been made a long time in advance. In art nothing can be done in a hurry. When the United Nations asked me to conduct a concert six months hence, I had to refuse—I was already signed up beyond that time. Here is another thing: for every concert I need many rehearsals. The Boston Symphony allows me four rehearsals on the average, others give me eight. But in Brazil they give me only three. That's not enough."

Actually, Brazilians generally agree with critics the world over that Villa Lobos was one of the greatest composers of our day. But they do not think that he was a good conductor. French and United States audiences, however, seemed not even to notice that his dress suit fitted him too loosely, if at all, or that his appearance was quite disarranged, at times slovenly. Instead, they rewarded each of his offerings with a standing ovation that called for five or more curtain calls. I wonder whether we North Americans would have appreciated his work if he had been born among us.

ART

We have observed that the African Negro made a powerful contribution to the development of Brazilian music. This was not the case in the field of

Brazilian graphic and plastic arts. Among the three racial strains that were fundamental in the formation of the Brazilian nationality, the Portuguese was the only one that showed itself possessed of marked talent.

What is called Brazilian colonial art is really not a matured national form. Essentially it consists of the Portuguese, Spanish, and Italian styles brought to America by the various peoples of Europe, influenced by the work of relatively few significant Brazilian artists.

The architecture of the colony, almost exclusively of the baroque type, imported by the Jesuits mainly from Portugal and Spain, preserves its most important and imposing monument in the famous Cathedral of Bahia. The earlier Brazilian colonization period coincides with the time in which the Counter-Reformation made its greatest influence felt and the Jesuits exercised spiritual domination over virtually all new territory where Catholicism was being introduced. For a long time the artistic South European renaissance styles were applied to church buildings and their interior embellishments and to the religious pageantry of the worship service. Generally speaking, there was little of external architectural beauty but a great deal of beautiful interior sculpture, which in richness and abundance became a fitting reflection of the splendor of Catholicism. This aesthetic pattern, in a sense a new interpretation of art, resulted in the establishment of a school of painters, wood carvers, and sculptors, who for a considerable time continued to furnish the lavish interior decorations of the churches, while during the sixteenth and seventeenth centuries the modest exteriors continued to appear relatively unadorned. Mention is made, by way of exception, of some churches and convents that were "notable for the harmony of their over-all masses and effects, generally planned by European builders."

The so-called "Bahia school of painting" did not come into existence until the eighteenth century. It began with José Joaquim da Rocha, who was the creator of the roof panels of the churches of the Conceição da Praia, of the Rosário, of São Pedro, of São Domingas, and of the mother church of Santo Amaro. José Joaquim had several pupils who later gained great fame, at least locally. Some of the most distinguished among them were Veríssimo de Souza Freitas, Lopes Marques, Antônio Dias, José Teófilo de Jesús, and Antônio Joaquim Franco Velasco. In time the latter two were regarded as having surpassed their master in his art.

The state of Rio de Janeiro (*fluminense*) school of painting flourished somewhat later, although its actual founder, Friar Ricardo do Pilar, did his best work during the early part of the eighteenth century. A really great artist and teacher of this school was José de Oliveira, who counted among his followers the well-known João de Souza and João Florêncio Muzzi. Manuel da Cunha, the best portrait painter, and Joaquim Leandro, distinguished for his excellent landscapes, were pupils of João de Souza. Later came Manuel Dias de Oliveira, the first to paint from live models, and José Leandro de Carvalho, another outstanding portrait painter.

The spiritual cultivation of the Brazilian people profited immensely from the political situation of the early nineteenth century, for the development of all the arts was greatly stimulated by the coming of the Bragança court to Brazil. Antônio Araújo de Azevedo disposed Dom João vi to establish the Escola de Belas Artes in 1815. The Marquis de Marialva, then minister plenipotentiary of the king of Portugal at the French court, was ordered to select a group of artists to help in the organization of this Brazilian academy. The leader of the artistic mission, Joaquim Lobreton, included in its membership João Baptista Debret and Nicolau Antônio Taunay, painters; Augusto Taunay, a sculptor; Augusto Henrique Vitório Grandjean de Montigny, a celebrated architect; Simão Pradier, an engraver; and others. The work of this committee proved of lasting benefit to the direction and development of culture and art in Brazil. A magnificent generation of artists and technicians was launched upon its artistic endeavors as a direct result of the coming of this "French Mission."

"*Aleijadinho.*"—Francisco Antônio Lisboa, whom most Brazilians know only by his nickname "Aleijadinho" (little cripple) filled a large part of the state of Minas Gerais with strikingly beautiful baroque church buildings. His works exhibit such originality and new approaches to the architect's and sculptor's art as to make him stand conspicuously above all Brazilian artists. Pedro Calmon, in his *História da Civilização Brasileira*, says of him: " 'Aleijadinho' gave architecture in imitation of the Italian an unmistakable imprint in the association of sculpture and construction. He worked admirably in the soapstone of the state of Minas Gerais. No colonial architect surpasses him in creative imagination; no one can so well express the possibilities of an animated and personal style in this tropical region—a style which gave added value to human impulses and feelings, purifying and discovering spiritual forces, the artistic ideal suggested by the freedom of lines, by the ornamental opulence and by the independence of the Baroque conception."

In 1943 the Museum of Modern Art in New York City sponsored for seven weeks an exhibition of Brazilian architecture. Both the noteworthy monuments of the past and the excellent contemporary achievements were shown in a series of large photographs. It was the opinion of those responsible for the collection that modern Brazilian architecture was the finest not only in this hemisphere but in the entire world.

The "modernist" movement in Brazilian art begins with a São Paulo exhibition held in 1922 which vigorously dominated all serious art efforts until 1945. That year marks the early death of Mário de Andrade, who had constituted himself the chief architect of the modernist aesthetics. The effects of this movement were noticeable in the fields of music, literature, choreography, and architecture, as well as in painting and sculpture. An excellent exhibit of "modern" plastic and graphic art was sent by Brazil to the Seattle World's Fair in 1962.

It would of course be impossible to make a unified characterization of the art works produced by the younger generation of Brazilian artists. Like their fellow artists in the United States, they show such a variety of techniques and styles as to give the impression that they lack assurance, at times even find themselves confused. In spite of this general impression, they never fail to give evidence of strength and freshness.

The largest one-man show in the 1948 New York season was held by Lasar Segall, an ardent expressionist from Brazil. The collection was later shown in the Pan American Union in Washington. Segall was born in Vilna, Poland; was educated in Germany; and in 1923 moved to Brazil to make his permanent home there. The influences of Poland, Germany, and Brazil are all easily seen in his works, whose principal burden seems to be the melancholy portrayal of human ills. While the artist's sympathy for mankind's suffering is unmistakable, his detachment and beauty of execution are often praised.

Cândido Portinari.—Cândido Portinari was born in Brodowski, state of São Paulo, in 1903, of Italian parents. That Brazil considers him its best painter is evidenced by the fact that, when the government received an invitation to send some paintings to the United States for a Latin American exhibition, it sent a one-man show of Portinari. His government appointments to teaching positions and to commissions for the execution of murals were frequent. His works have been popular in the United States also, since, in 1935, the Carnegie international jury awarded him an honorable mention for his large, now famous piece "Coffee." The mural Portinari prepared in 1939 for the Brazilian pavilion at the New York World's Fair attracted unusual attention.

Portinari moved to Rio de Janeiro when he was thirteen years of age. At the age of twenty-five he was enabled, by means of a traveling scholarship, to visit Spain, Italy, France, and England for study purposes. The French modernists, especially Picasso, Modigliani, and Rouault, exercised the strongest influence upon him in the development of his creative processes. However, every work to come from the brush of Portinari has been definitely stamped with his individuality. He became a most prolific producer of full-bodied portraits, sparkling frescoes, and patternistic murals and also found time to interest himself in art education for the younger Brazilian generation. His draftsmanship was exceptionally facile;

he showed a fine decorative sense and a rugged feeling for form. This has had a little to do with making and keeping critical opinion about Portinari's artistry sharply divided.

The inspiration for Portinari's works of art comes principally from his native land and from his fellow countrymen. What he depicts in them runs the entire gamut of life's experiences there, from the gayest of carnival scenes to the most dismal of peasant burials. His versatility seems unbounded, which makes it extremely difficult to classify his work. He is at once a classicist, a primitive, an expressionist, and a surrealist. He changes from mood to mood, from style to style, with great facility, always selecting and adapting the style of his expression to the problem at hand. A marked personal curiosity keeps him constantly experimenting. The stylistic devices he used some time ago in his abstract studies often resulted in a weird dissociation of line, form, and color.

In 1940 Robert C. Smith, then of the Library of Congress, said of him: "Portinari is one of the most gifted of living artists. . . . He has proved that Brazilian painting, in spite of its exotic past and constant borrowings from foreign sources, can be monumental and original." In many respects, Portinari is among Brazilian painters what Villa Lobos is among Brazilian musicians. His ready use of many distinct styles; the constancy of his easily recognized individualism; his frequent roughness; his sources of inspiration; the stupendous volume of work he turned out—all these combine to emphasize the resemblance. In 1962 Portinari died in Rio de Janeiro.

Architecture

How did it happen that Brazil shows an architectural standard so high that the wonder of it is spreading throughout the world like a tropical plant? At least two events were involved in its development. The Modern Art Week, held in the Municipal Theater of São Paulo (1922), included exhibitions of works by avant-garde painters and a sculptor; recitals of modern dance and music; and lectures on literature, architecture, and the fine arts generally.[1] This spiritual revolt against the Parnassian and restricting academic atmosphere struck like a bombshell. Artists and critics attacked the prevailing preconceptions and eclecticism and tried to establish relationships with the highest values in life, the land, and its people. The spontaneity of aboriginal culture, refined by Portuguese and other European civilizing influences, was held up as an ideal.

The other influential event was the Revolution of 1930, led by Getúlio Vargas, which enforced a new regime that deeply affected all levels of

1. Anita Malfati, Di Cavalcanti, Oswaldo Goeldi, Regina Graz, J. F. de Almeida Prado, painters; Vitor Bricheret, sculptor; Guiomar Novaes, pianist; A. Moya, J. Przyrembel, architects; Graça Aranha, Mário de Andrade, and others, lecturers on music and literature.

people. It produced an upheaval and a clamor for fresh starts not only in politics, but also in the social and economic life of the country as well.

Lúcio Costa.—Lúcio Costa was the first Brazilian architect to succeed in calling to the attention of the entire civilized world what was happening in South American architecture. He became the leader among a highly individualistic group of architects who created an artistic system of building suited to tropical and semi-tropical conditions. Practical and decorative were the *brise-soleils*, shell vault constructions, and the airy way of setting even tall buildings on *pilotis* that left the ground floor completely open.[2] The more elegant constructions replaced the customary paint on stucco with the native blue and white tiles. Such *azulêjos* were used later in a great variety of colors.

Lúcio Costa, appointed head of the National School of Fine Arts in Rio de Janeiro (1930), intended to overhaul and modernize its whole curriculum. However, in less than one year Lúcio Costa was dismissed by a misunderstanding administration, and the student body, who had had a taste of Costa's modern ideas, went on strike against the school. Gradually these students became ever more interested in the period's new artistic ideas. After six months the students won a victory for anti-academicism and progress in all the arts. In spite of the fact that the Constitutional Revolution of 1932 slowed down a promised national building program, Lúcio Costa succeeded in initiating the "Cariocan" school of architecture.

Le Corbusier.—Charles Edouard Jeanneret Le Corbusier, born in Switzerland, but generally considered a French architect, had a revolutionary effect on the international development of modern architecture. He was a pioneer in the architectural use of re-enforced concrete. In 1929 he visited Costa and his group of modernists and made them acquainted with his new and radical approach to the technical and aesthetic problems of building. Later, Le Corbusier made a month-long visit to Costa and his young architects. When Lúcio Costa was commissioned to design the university city for Rio de Janeiro, he invited Carlos Leão, Jorge Moreira, Affonso Eduardo Reidy, and, a bit later, Oscar Niemeyer and Ernani Vasconcellos to work with him on this large project. Le Corbusier actively helped them plan and execute this important undertaking. Such contacts with the world-famous French architect were of lasting benefit to the aspiring Brazilians.

Oscar Niemeyer.—Oscar Niemeyer, born in 1907, the most brilliant and best-known modern Brazilian architect, was noted for his daring conceptions and purity of line. He opined that modern architecture should tear

2. A *brise-soleil* (literally a sunbreak) is a panel or wall of wood, bricks, tiles, or concrete to serve as a sunshade that allows ventilation. A *piloti* (from French *piloti* or *pilotis*) is a column of iron, steel, or re-enforced concrete supporting a building above an open ground level.

itself loose from its prevailing rigidity and find such simple functional forms as evoke feeling and surprise, through which a people's new way of life can be reflected.

Niemeyer was one of the chief collaborators in the design of the famed Ministry of Education and Public Health Building in Rio de Janeiro (1937–1943). He designed several large structures, including the Boavista Bank Building of Rio de Janeiro (1946) and many beautiful residences, especially the House Tremaine in Santa Barbara, California (1947), and his own home in Rio de Janeiro. In 1939, together with Lúcio Costa and P. L. Wiener, Niemeyer designed the Brazilian pavilion for the New York World's Fair. For Pampulha, a new, planned district in Belo Horizonte, he designed several buildings, among which the church is internationally admired. Niemeyer's most notable architectural achievement was Brasília, the new capital of Brazil, located 600 miles northwest of the old, for whose creation he directed a group of domestic architects.

Brasília.—The creation of Brasília is in many respects a remarkable accomplishment, a dream come true after having persisted since the last part of the preceding century. It is remarkable, not just because some different and strikingly beautiful government buildings were erected there,[3] but because the entire city and its surroundings were preplanned in every detail, largely the work of Lúcio Costa. The landscaping was done under the direction of one of the most efficient and artistic landscape architects the world has ever had, Roberto Burle Marx. Brasília is now the economic center of the vast west-central region of Brazil. As a cultural center, it boasts of 150 primary and 70 secondary schools and the most modern university in the country. Already 23 hospitals and special clinics are now operating there. It has viaducts without crossings, bus stations, a theater, a museum, a cathedral, and practically everything a modern, functional city would need. All government offices that have remained in the old federal capital (Rio de Janeiro) moved to Brasília in the fall of 1970.

Henrique E. Mindlin, himself a successful practicing architect, thoroughly committed to the highly appreciated modern architecture of his country, succinctly summed up its characteristics as (1) emotional spontaneity, (2) integration with circumstances of land and climate, and (3) constant re-assessment of all means of expression possible to the plastic language. All of this the modern Brazilian architect is striving to achieve under a constantly changing and growing intellectual discipline.

It seems perfectly appropriate, therefore, that the international awards for architectural excellence are now made at the São Paulo Biennial.

3. For instance, The Palace of the Dawn; O Itamarati; the Ministry of Foreign Affairs; The Parliament Buildings; the Cathedral; etc.

Biographical Sketches

Eric N. Baklanoff is now serving as the dean for international programs and professor of economics at the University of Alabama. He was formerly director of the Latin American Studies Institute and professor of economics at Louisiana State University and director of the Graduate Center for Latin American Studies and associate professor of economics at Vanderbilt University. He is past president of the Southeastern Conference on Latin American Studies (1963–1964) and was a fellow at the Center for Advanced Study in Behavioral Sciences, Palo Alto, California, and Fulbright Research Fellow in Chile. He is editor and contributor of *The Shaping of Modern Brazil*, Louisiana State University Press (1969); and of *New Perspectives of Brazil*, Vanderbilt University Press (1966); and has published articles in *Economic Development and Cultural Change*, *National Tax Journal*, *Revista Brasileira de Economia*, *Inter-American Economic Affairs*, *Journal of Inter-American Studies*, *Mining Engineering*, and other journals.

Donald R. Dyer is currently a geographic attaché for Latin America, United States Department of State. He was formerly associate professor of geography at the University of Florida, visiting professor at the University of Havana, and Fulbright Lecturer at the University of San Marcos, Lima. His publications include *Lesser Antilles*, Nelson Doubleday (1959); *The United States and Latin America: Problems in International Understanding*, National Council for Geographic Education (1962); "Population and Elevation in Peru," *Northwestern University Studies in Geography* (1962); "Growth of Brazil's Population," *Journal of Geography* (1966); "Research on Latin American Geography," *Latin American Research Review* (1967).

Sugiyama Iutaka is associate professor of sociology at the University of Florida on leave as visiting lecturer of sociology at the University of Reading, England. He was formerly research director of the Latin American Center for Research in the Social Sciences (Rio), professor at the University of Brazil, associate professor at the University of Texas, and research associate of its Institute of Latin American Studies. He has been project director of several research studies conducted in Brazil, including the Comparative Survey of Fertility and Family Planning in Seven Latin American Countries, supported by the Latin American Center for Research in the Social Sciences and the Latin American Center for Demography and the Population Council. He is the author of numerous papers, among which are "Intergenerational Mobility and Family Planning in Urban Brazil," *Proceedings of the World Population Conference, Belgrade*, United Nations (1965); "Social Stratification Research in Latin America," *Latin American Research Review* (1965); "Social Mobility and

341

Differential Occupational Opportunity in Urban Brazil," *Human Organization* (1966); "Comments on the National Mobility Survey of Colombia," *Milbank Memorial Fund Quarterly* (1968); and "Critique on the Relationships between the Quantitative and Qualitative Analysis of Warnesian and Millsian Social Class" in Anthony Leeds, ed., *Stratification and Social Mobility with Special Reference to Latin America*, Pan American Union (1968).

GERRIT DE JONG, JR., professor of Portuguese and dean emeritus of the College of Fine Arts at Brigham Young University, is also a distinguished composer of symphonic, choral, and chamber music. A native of Amsterdam, he did undergraduate work at the University of Utah and did graduate work there, at the Kaiser Maximilian Universität in Munich, and at the Universidad Nacional in Mexico (A.B., M.A., Utah; Ph.D., Stanford University). He served as executive director of the Centro Cultural Brasil-Estados Unidos in Santos, São Paulo, Brazil. In 1969 the Brigham Young University Press published his *Four Hundred Years of Brazilian Literature*.

ANYDA MARCHANT is an attorney for the legal department of the International Bank for Reconstruction and Development, Washington, D.C. She was formerly chief of the Anglo-American law section and assistant chief of the Latin American law section in the Law Library of Congress; associate of Covington and Burling, Washington, D.C.; legal assistant to the president's office of the Brazilian Traction Company, Rio de Janeiro; and legal analyst for the Bureau of Foreign and Domestic Commerce, United States Department of Commerce, Washington, D.C. Her major publications include *Viscount Mauá and the Empire of Brazil*, University of California Press (1965); and numerous articles in such publications as *The Hispanic American Historical Review*, *The Americas, Frontiers, Michigan Law Review*, and others.

J. V. FREITAS MARCONDES is presently chairman of the department of Sociology and Philosophy of the Faculdades Metropolitanas Unidas of São Paulo and professor of sociology and labor law in the post-graduate social science course of the Escola de Sociologia e Política, a "complementary" institute of the University of São Paulo. He was formerly lawyer-in-charge of the Legal Consultation Bureau (Consultoria Jurídica) of the state of São Paulo. He founded the Cultural Labor Institute of São Paulo and was its first superintendent. He has been visiting professor at Mississippi State University and at the University of Florida and has lectured at various institutions in Mexico, Colombia, Brazil, and Argentina and at the Free University of Berlin and at Heidelberg. Among his published works are *First Brazilian Legislation Relating to Rural Labor Unions*, University of Florida Press (1962); *Revisão e Reforma Agrária*, São Paulo (1962); *Radiografia da Liderança Sindical Paulista* (1964); and *São Paulo, Espírito, Povo e Instituições* (editor and contributor), São Paulo (1968); and numerous studies published in Brazilian and American journals including *Rural Sociology, Social Forces, Journal of Inter American Studies*.

WILLIAM H. NICHOLLS is a professor of economics and director of the Graduate Center for Latin American Studies at Vanderbilt University. He has served as a consultant on Brazil for the Ford Foundation and as a research agricultural economist for the Getúlio Vargas Foundation, Rio de Janeiro. His publications include *Ninety-Nine Fazendas: The Structure and Productivity of Brazilian Agriculture* (with Ruy Miller Paiva) and numerous articles and chapters in books, including *Perspectiva Estatística da Estructura Agrária do Brasil, The Transformation of Agriculture in a Semi-Industrialized Country: The Case of Brazil, The Changing Structure of Farm Product and Input Markets in Brazil, The Brazilian Food Supply: Problems and Prospects*, and *The Agricultural Frontier in Modern Brazilian History: The State of Paraná, 1920-65*.

JOSÉ ARTHUR ALVES DA CRUZ RIOS is a sociologist at the Center of Social Sciences at Catholic University, Rio de Janeiro. He was formerly coordinator of the Campaign for Rural Education; the secretary for social welfare of the city of Rio de Janeiro; visiting professor at Vanderbilt University and at the University of Florida; director of a private research and planning bureau (SPLAN), and consultant for urban renewal plans and social welfare projects to the state governments of Espírito Santo and Bahia. His major publications include *A Educação dos Grupos* (with others), 2d ed., Rio de Janeiro (1958); *Aspectos Humanos da Favela Carioca*, São Paulo (1956); *Recomendações sobre Reforma Agrária*, Rio de Janeiro (1961); and *A Reforma Agrária—Problemas, Bases, Solução* (co-author), Rio de Janeiro (1964).

JOHN SAUNDERS is professor of sociology at the University of Florida. He was formerly Ford Foundation Advisor in Lima, Peru; director of the Latin American Language and Area Center at the University of Florida; and associate professor of sociology and chairman of the Graduate program in Latin American Studies at Louisiana State University; Fulbright Lecturer in Ecuador; has been on lecturing assignments for the Organization of American States in Mexico and elsewhere; and has been a visiting professor at Catholic University, Lima. He received a grant from the United States Office of Education for research in Brazil and more recently from the Population Council for a Peruvian population study. He is the author of *Differential Fertility in Brazil*, University of Florida Press (1950); *The Population of Ecuador, A Demographic Analysis*, University of Florida Press (1960); "Education and Modernization in Brazil," a chapter in *The Shaping of Brazil*, E. N. Baklanoff, ed., Louisiana State University Press (1969); and translator with Alfred Hower of *Marcoré*, a novel by Antônio Olavo Pereira, University of Texas Press (1970). He has published articles in Latin American and United States journals.

T. LYNN SMITH, graduate research professor of sociology at the University of Florida, has served as professor and head of the departments of sociology and rural sociology at Louisiana State University; as professor and head of the department of sociology and anthropology, as well as the director at the Institute of Brazilian Studies, at Vanderbilt University; and as senior agricultural analyst for the United States Department of State. His publications include: *Brazil: People and Institutions*, Louisiana State University Press (1946, 1954, 1963); *The Sociology of Rural Life*, Harper and Brothers (1940, 1947, 1953); *Colombia: Social Structure and the Process of Development*, University of Florida Press (1967); *Studies of Latin American Societies*, Doubleday and Company (1970); and *Fundamentals of Population Study*, Lippincott (1959).

ANISIO S. TEIXEIRA has been professor of school administration and comparative education and a member of the National Faculty of Philosophy at the University of Rio de Janeiro (formerly the University of Brazil) and an educational consultant at the Fundação Getúlio Vargas and at the Companhia Editôra Nacional, São Paulo. He has served in many official positions, some of which are: director general of public education of the state of Bahia; director of the Department of Education and Culture of the Federal District; professor of philosophy of education at the teachers' training school of the University of the Federal District; advisor on higher education for UNESCO; director of the National Institute of Pedagogical Studies, Ministry of Education; professor of philosophy of education at the Institute of Education, state of Guanabara; and professor of school administration and comparative education at the National Faculty of Philosophy, University of Brazil. He has been president and rector of the University of Brasília; a member of the Federal Council of Education; visiting professor at Columbia University; visiting professor at the University of California, Los Angeles; and educational consultant at the Fundação Getúlio Vargas. He has written *Education for Democracy*, Rio de Janeiro (1936); *The University and Human Liberty*, edited by the Service of Documentation of the Ministry of Education and Culture (1954); *Education and the Brazilian Crisis*, Rio de Janeiro (1956); *Education and the Modern World* (1968); *Education in Brazil* (1969); and numerous other treatises. He was the victim of a fatal accident in March 1971.

EARL W. THOMAS is a professor of Portuguese and Spanish at Vanderbilt University. His major publications include *The Syntax of Spoken Brazilian Portuguese*, Vanderbilt University Press (1969); "Emerging Patterns of the Brazilian Language," a chapter in *New Perspectives of Brazil*, E. N. Baklanoff, ed., Vanderbilt University Press (1966); and "Folklore in Brazilian Literature," in *Three Papers*, Vanderbilt University Press. He has been the recipient of Social Science Research Council and other grants for research on Brazilian language and literature.

DORIVAL TEIXEIRA VIEIRA holds the positions of professor of economics of the Institute of Economic Research and professor of economic analysis in the School of Economics and Business Administration at the University of São Paulo. He formerly served at the University of São Paulo as director of the economics department and as director of the Deliberative Committee of the Institute of Economic Research. He is the Brazilian representative before the International Economic Association, consultant to the Commercial Association of the state of São Paulo, and was representative of the School of Economics and Business Administration (University of São Paulo) at the Sixth Plenary Assembly of the Interamerican Council on Commerce and Production, Lima (1952). Among his published works are: *Monopólio Bilateral e Seus Principais Problemas Teóricos*, São Paulo (1952); *Economia e Sociedade-Panorama das Ciencas Econômicas Contemporâneas*, São Paulo (1960); *O Desenvolvimento Econômico do Brasil e a Inflação*, São Paulo (1962); *A Evolução do Sistema Monetário Brasileiro*, São Paulo (1962); and *Formação de Preços para Administradores de Empresas*, São Paulo (1968).

Index